Approaches to Teaching the Works of Christine de Pizan

Approaches to Teaching the Works of Christine de Pizan

Edited by

Andrea Tarnowski

The Modern Language Association of America
New York 2018

85 Broad Street, New York, New York 10004
www.mla.org

To order MLA publications, visit www.mla.org/books. For wholesale and international orders, see www.mla.org/bookstore-orders.

The MLA office is located on the island known as Mannahatta (Manhattan) in Lenapehoking, the homeland of the Lenape people. The MLA pays respect to the original stewards of this land and to the diverse and vibrant Native communities that continue to thrive in New York City.

Cover illustration of the paperback and electronic editions:
"Allégorie de la tempérance." *L'Epistre Othea la deesse, que elle envoya à Hector de Troye, quant il estoit en l'aage de quinze ans*, by Christine de Pizan. Source: Bibliothèque Nationale de France, Français 606, fol. 2v cadré.

Approaches to Teaching World Literature 148
ISSN 1059-1133

POD 2023 (first printing)

Library of Congress Cataloging-in-Publication Data

Names: Tarnowski, Andrea, editor.
Title: Approaches to teaching the works of Christine de Pizan / edited by Andrea Tarnowski.
Description: New York: The Modern Language Association of America, 2018. |
Series: Approaches to teaching world literature,
ISSN 1059-1133; 148 | Includes bibliographical references and index.
Identifiers: LCCN 2018021528 (print) | LCCN 2018021543 (e-book) |
ISBN 9781603293280 (EPUB) | ISBN 9781603293297 (Kindle) |
ISBN 9781603293266 (cloth: alk. paper) | ISBN 9781603293273 (pbk.)
Subjects: LCSH: Christine, de Pisan, approximately 1364-
approximately 1431—Study and teaching.
Classification: LCC PQ1575.Z5 (ebook) | LCC PQ1575.Z5 A48 2018 (print) | DDC 841/.2—dc23
LC record available at https://lccn.loc.gov/2018021528

CONTENTS

PREFACE

Christine de Pizan has now fully entered the canon of Western literature, her place secured over the last several decades by intense and ever-greater critical engagement with her work. Her renown in her own day was both great and hard-won; she read assiduously, wrote prolifically, and maintained loyal relations with patrons. Through the fifteenth century and into the sixteenth, her work was known not just in France but in England and elsewhere on the Continent.

Although Christine's name reappeared on occasion in literary histories of later periods, and enthusiasm resurfaced at certain junctures—for example, among pre-Raphaelites, who had a taste for the Middle Ages, and during the women's suffrage movement—it was only in the last quarter of the twentieth century that the depth and breadth of her work were progressively revealed to an audience beyond a small circle of scholars.[1] Her modern-day reputation set its roots in her adroit and vigorous defense of her sex, which readers found both astonishing and compelling at a distance of six hundred years. Her *Book of the City of Ladies*—which imagines a community of women, united in talent, skill, and virtue, protected from the misogyny of received societal beliefs—was the impetus for her critical rebirth. But Christine composed more than forty works, in a broad range of genres: short lyric poems, allegorical tales in verse, political portraits in prose, treatises on the conduct of war and the prosecution of peace, and conduct manuals for young princes and every class of women. Thus, as more and more of her texts were edited and translated, whether into modern French or English, the great range of her concerns came to the fore. She lamented the pain of widowhood in ballades and warned against inconstant love; she pledged her faith in learning over the course of extraordinary travel narratives. A staunch partisan of her adopted homeland, France, she sought to advise the king, queen, and royal princes by means of historical and legendary examples of great feats. In the isolation of her study she wrote prayers and devotional meditations. Throughout her work, there run twin threads of practicality and aspiration, negotiation with circumstances and the vision of ideals. Always, there is probity.

Christine de Pizan was the first professional woman author in France; she made a living from her writing. While we can identify a small group of other women writers from the Middle Ages, she was unique in building what can be called a career. This observation has been another spur to contemporary readers' interest, and that interest has in turn shaped specialists' focus and instructors' choices when teaching her work. It remains a highly rewarding exercise to teach a single lyric poem by Christine on the merits of language alone; yet the classroom is also an excellent forum for tracing her development over time as a producer of books. She composed her texts, often acted as her own copyist, hired artists to illustrate her manuscripts, and presented dedicated bound volumes to patrons she wanted to please and praise—or whose conduct she aimed to reform. Digital surrogates of her manuscripts online allow access to the material evidence of her trajectory as author, editor, and publisher and thus make history immediate. Students can add layers of visual information to their work with Christine's words to give context to their reading. Through the (virtual) materiality of these manuscripts, they gain appreciation for her politics, both in the sense of her communication and rapport with figures of the royal court and in the exposition of her views on the French nation, on the qualities needed to govern wisely, and on the supreme need for concord among those in power.

Part 1, "Materials," presents the bibliographic means to make choices concerning the teaching of Christine's work. The section on editions and translations discusses all her compositions that have been edited in Middle French, modern French, and English, a selection that is great and still growing. There is also a review of the early translations of her texts into English; these works of the fifteenth and early sixteenth centuries are fascinating comparison points to her French oeuvre, proof of her early and far-reaching fame, and exciting teaching tools. This section is followed by a table of her works that visually categorizes information on available texts.

At the beginning of this project, a survey was conducted involving instructors teaching Christine's work. Their resulting recommendations have been used to guide the content of the "Instructor's Library," which suggests specific items from the vast critical bibliography on the author, grouped under rubrics that, according to survey participants, target the most important and helpful resources.

The "Materials" section concludes with Mark Aussems's essay, "Aids to Teaching Christine de Pizan Online," a survey of key Web sites focused on Christine, her work, and fifteenth-century France. These resources are meant to animate and enhance classroom experiences.

Part 2, "Approaches," offers an introduction to Christine with a focus on her profound dedication to books: those whose contents she absorbed, those she composed, and those whose production she oversaw. The essays are gathered under three headings: "Gender and Self-Representations: Cultural Contexts," "Christine across the Disciplines," and "Classroom Contexts." These essays provide hands-on accounts of treating Christine in the syllabi of various courses, as well as perceptive commentary on the rhetorical, sociological, and philosophical richness of her texts. It is hoped that they will prompt instructors to explore the array of poetry and prose that constitute Christine de Pizan's legacy and inspire us today.

NOTE

[1] By convention, Christine de Pizan is referred to by her first name rather than her last. This is not a function of her status as a woman but instead reflects standard practice for authors of the Middle Ages (Dante Alighieri is a prime example).

Part One

MATERIALS

Editions and Translations

Christine de Pizan was a prolific author who lived in the early 1400s and thus composed in Middle French, a language closer to modern French than, say, the English of Chaucer is to modern English but abounding in difficulties nevertheless. The volume of her production, the labor necessary to transcribe her manuscripts, and the desire to make her work accessible to a broad audience—scholars, students, and lay readers—have meant that publishing Christine has unfolded in stages, over several dozen years, a process that has not yet reached an end.

The comprehensive list of Christine's texts, given in table form below, is divided into categories for easy consultation: those works that exist in Middle French editions, those that have been translated into modern French, and those that are available in modern English. There is of course overlap among these; some of Christine's texts exist in all three forms. A fourth category, late medieval and early Tudor English versions of her work, can be profitably exploited in the classroom, and thus these editions are listed briefly before the comprehensive list.

Middle French Editions

Though Christine de Pizan wrote more than forty works, and though thirty years ago few existed in readily accessible modern editions, the great rise in her popularity in the late twentieth and early twenty-first centuries has meant a steady increase in the availability of her writing, to the point where only one or two texts remain unavailable in manuscript or online transcription.[1] Scholars, for their own research or for exploration with graduate students, now have easy access to the original Middle French texts of *Le livre de l'advision Cristine*, *Le livre du chemin de lonc estude*, *Le débat sur* Le roman de la rose (also edited as *Le livre des epistres du debat sus* Le rommant de la rose), *Le livre de paix*, *Le livre du corps de policie*, *Le livre du duc des vrais amans*, and *L'epistre Othea*, all of which have been published since the late 1990s; an edition of *Les sept psaumes allegorisés* is forthcoming. A Middle French edition of *Le livre des trois vertus*, also known as *Le trésor de la cité des dames*, dates to 1989.

Trois vertus / Trésor is a kind of sequel to Christine's most famous and popular work, *Le livre de la cité des dames*. For the first two decades of heightened modern interest in Christine de Pizan, the only available edition of *La cité des dames* was found in a 1975 PhD dissertation by Maureen Curnow, still useful today for its notes. But in 1997, a modern Italian translation of the book published as an affordable paperback included a facing-page edition of the Middle French text by Earl Jeffrey Richards. Because the book is listed in catalogs simply by its modern Italian title, *La città delle dame*, it is difficult to locate this indispensable Middle French edition unless one knows in advance what to look for. It should be noted that a new edition of *Le livre de la cité des dames* (accompanied by a new translation into modern French) is in the works: Anne Paupert, in collaboration with Claire LeNinan, serves as both its editor and translator.

Other works by Christine in mid-twentieth-century editions are readily available in libraries, including Suzanne Solente's two-volume *Livre des fais et bonnes meurs du sage roy Charles V* (1936–40) and her four-volume *Livre de la mutacion de Fortune* (1959–66).

Christine's lyric poetry, the initial source of her fame, was collected along with other pieces in three volumes in the late nineteenth century by Maurice Roy. Roy's work is still the reference point for her shortest verse compositions; the three volumes of his edition can be read online at www.gutenberg.org. While extracts and groupings of poems were published late in the twentieth century—Jacqueline Cerquiglini's *Cent ballades d'amant et de dame* (1982), now out of print, and Kenneth Varty's *Christine de Pisan's Ballades, Rondeaux, and Virelais* (1965)—there is no complete recent edition of Christine's poetry. However, some of her longer poems originally published in Roy have been brought out in modern editions: *L'epistre au dieu d'amours* and *Le dit de la rose*, edited by Thelma Fenster and Mary Erler, appeared in 1990, and both texts can also be found in Christine McWebb's *Debating the* Roman de la Rose*: A Critical Anthology* (2007). Three debate poems by Christine were also collected in an edition by Barbara K. Altmann in 1998: *The Love Debate Poems of Christine de Pizan:* Le livre du debat de deux amans, Le livre des trois jugemens, Le livre du dit de Poissy.

Christine's final text, *Le ditié de Jehanne d'Arc*, written in 1429 as Joan of Arc rode to liberate the French from their English occupiers, was edited in 1977 by Angus J. Kennedy and Kenneth Varty. This brief work is out of print but available in libraries or online at www.maidofheaven.com/joanofarc_song_pisan_contents.asp.

Modern French Translations

The foundation for classroom-friendly modern French versions of Christine's writings was laid in 1986 with Eric Hicks and Thérèse Moreau's *La cité des dames*, still widely used today. A new modern French translation of the text (along with a new edition) by Anne Paupert is forthcoming. Hicks and Moreau also produced *Le livre des faits et bonnes mœurs du roi Charles V le Sage* in 1997; in 2013, Joël Blanchard and Michel Quereuil returned to this text to provide readers with a new translation entitled *Livre des faits et bonnes moeurs du sage roi Charles V.*

In the last decade, a cluster of translations has enriched the Christine corpus in modern French. Danielle Régnier-Bohler's 2006 volume of writings by medieval French women, *Voix de femmes au Moyen Âge: Savoir, mystique, poésie, amour, sorcellerie, XII*[e]*–XV*[e] *siècle*, contains three key works by Christine: *Le* *livre des trois vertus* (translated by Liliane Dulac), *La vision de Christine* (Anne Paupert), and *Le ditié de Jehanne d'Arc* (Margaret Switten). The year 2006 also saw the publication of Virginie Greene's modern French translation of *Le débat sur* Le roman de la rose. In 2008, Hélène Basso brought out *L'épître d'Othéa*, part of a two-volume set that also includes a facsimile of a fifteenth-century illustrated *Othea* manuscript; this book would not be assigned for individual purchase by students but would work well as an aid for instructors who wish to present seminars with a physical example of the relation between text and image in medieval manuscripts.

At the other end of the spectrum in format and price are Dominique Demartini and Didier Lechat's *Le livre du duc des vrais amants*, and Andrea Tarnowski's *Le chemin de longue étude*; they are currently the only easily accessible texts by Christine that present both Middle French editions and modern French translations in facing-page layout. They are thus particularly appropriate for students and other readers of modern French who are curious to learn and explore Christine's original language.

Modern English Translations

Two anthologies constitute the reference bedrock for Christine in English. *The Writings of Christine de Pizan*, edited by Charity Cannon Willard, published in 1984, contains extracts of all major and many minor texts. In 1997, Renate Blumenfeld-Kosinski and Kevin Brownlee brought out an edition entitled *Selected Writings of Christine de Pizan*. The Willard volume and the Blumenfeld-Kosinski and Brownlee volume both contain selections from a broad range of Christine's work; and while each volume offers translations of about a tenth of the cycle of *One Hundred Ballads*, there is no overlap in the choice of poems. Excerpts vary greatly in length between the two volumes: Willard offers five pages from *The Book of the Long Road of Learning*, whereas the Blumenfeld-Kosinski and Brownlee text presents twenty-nine pages from the same work, there given the title *The Path of Long Study*. The Blumenfeld-Kosinski and Brownlee volume also includes a nearly full translation of Christine's final poem, *The Tale of Joan of Arc*, along with seven critical essays on the writer. Willard's selections are grouped thematically (e.g., "The Courtly Poet," "The Defense of Women," "The Fate of France"), while Blumenfeld-Kosinski and Brownlee's lineup is chronological.

Whereas the selections in these two anthologies range across Christine's oeuvre, other anthologies focus on a particular genre. Barbara Altmann and R. Barton Palmer's *An Anthology of Medieval Love Debate Poetry* contains one text by Christine, *The Debate of Two Lovers*, in addition to two judgment poems by Machaut (*King of Bohemia*, *King of Navarre*), Chaucer's *The Legend of Good Women*, and Alain Chartier's *The Book of the Four Ladies*. Fenster and Erler offer Middle French and English texts of two of Christine's works in a volume entitled *Poems of Cupid, God of Love: Christine de Pizan's* Epistre au dieu d'amours *and* Dit de la rose, *Thomas Hoccleve's* The Letter of Cupid, *with George Sewell's* The Proclamation of Cupid. Josette A. Wisman brought out a volume featuring three of Christine's texts, The Epistle of the Prison of Human Life *with* An Epistle to the Queen of France *and* Lament on the Evils of the Civil War, which contains both Middle French editions and English translations.

Two works in English present the multiple texts by Christine and a circle of clerics (Jean de Montreuil, Pierre d'Ailly, Pierre Col and Gontier Col, Jean Gerson) concerning *The Romance of the Rose*. McWebb's *Debating the* Roman de la Rose*: A Critical Anthology* provides chapters of contextualization ("Italian Humanism and French Clericalism in the Fourteenth Century," "The Defense of Courtly Discourse and Morals") before presenting the letters of the debate in both Middle French editions and English translations. David F. Hult's *Christine de Pizan: Debate of the* Romance of the Rose, published in 2010, is an all-English volume and thus has many more pages to devote to the primary texts; it also includes a rich introduction. Both McWebb and Hult provide copious notes and include sections on the works in which Christine spoke of *The Romance of the Rose* in the years following the debate.

In addition to anthologized works, English-language readers have a good number of full single-text volumes to choose from. Christine's verse romance *Book of the Duke of True Lovers* transposes figures and tropes from Jean de Meun's *Romance of the Rose* to critique courtly love. Christine's most autobiographical narrative, *The Vision of Christine de Pizan*, appeared in 2005 in a translation by Charity Cannon Willard and Glenda McLeod. *Christine de Pizan: Othea's Letter to Hector*, translated by Renate Blumenfeld-Kosinski and Earl Jeffrey Richards, seeks to instruct the prince by way of examples from classical mythology. A trio of compositions dedicated to Louis de Guyenne, the French dauphin between 1406 and 1414, illuminate Christine's political and moral views: *The Book of the Body Politic*, translated by Kate Langdon Forhan, appeared in 1994; *The Book of Deeds of Arms and of Chivalry*, by Sumner Willard and Charity Cannon Willard, came out in 1999; and *The Book of Peace*, Christine's last prose work, was published in a Middle French–modern English edition by Karen Green, Constant J. Mews, and Janice Pinder in 2008.

Finally, the two books Christine wrote specifically to defend women and define their roles in society both have two modern English translations. *The Book of the City of Ladies* was first translated into English by Earl Jeffrey Richards in 1982 and revised and reissued in 1998. In 1999, Rosalind Brown-Grant offered a new English translation. Richards produced an English text closer to the Middle French original, whereas Brown-Grant interpreted Christine's writing using a more liquid, modern idiom. The sequel to *The City of Ladies*, composed by Christine as *Le livre des .III. vertus a l'enseignement des dames* and later issued in print as *Le trésor de la cité des dames*, has two titles in English: Sarah Lawson's *The Treasure of the City of Ladies; or, The Book of the Three Virtues* was first published in 1985 and then revised in 2003; *A Medieval Woman's Mirror of Honor: The Treasury of the City of Ladies*, by Charity Cannon Williard and Madeleine Pelner Cosman, appeared in 1989.

As is evident from both this overview and the comprehensive list of Christine's texts, scholar-teachers have poured great energy in recent decades into making Christine's work available for use in the classroom at a variety of levels and in numerous disciplines. The effort continues: at this writing, English translations of *The Long Road of Learning* (Andrea Tarnowski) and of the *Book of the Deeds and Good Practices of the Wise King Charles V* (Nadia Margolis) are near completion.

Early English Editions and Translations

In 1402, Thomas Hoccleve translated Christine's *Epistre au dieu d'amours* into English as *The Letter of Cupid*. Stephen Scrope translated *L'epistre Othea* as *The Epistle of Othea* in the mid-fifteenth century, and the same French work was published in English as *The .C. Hystoryes of Troye* before 1549. Christine's *Proverbes moraulx* were translated by Anthony Woodville as *Morale Prouerbes* in 1478; in 1489, in *The Book of Fayttes of Armes and of Chyualrye* was translated by William Caxton. There was an anonymous translation in 1521 of *Le livre du corps de policie* as *The Booke [of] the Body of Polyce*, and Bryan Anslay's 1521 rendering of *Le livre de la cité des dames* bears the title *The Boke of the Cyte of Ladyes*; an edition of Anslay was published by Hope Johnston in 2014.

Comprehensive List of Christine de Pizan's Works

See the works-cited list for full bibliographical details of works listed below.

MIDDLE FR. EDS.	MODERN FR. TRANS.	ENGLISH TRANS.
***Advision.** Le livre de l'advision Cristine.* 1405.		
Le livre de l'advision Cristine. Edited by Christine Reno and Liliane Dulac, 2001.	*La vision de Christine.* Translated by Anne Paupert. Régnier-Bohler, pp. 407–542.	Excerpt in McWebb, *Debating*, pp. 404–12. *The Vision of Christine de Pizan.* Translated by Glenda McLeod and Charity Cannon Willard, 2005. *Christine's Vision* (excerpts). Blumenfeld-Kosinski, *Selected Writings*, pp. 173-201. Christine's *Autobiographical Vision* (excerpt). Translated by Christine M. Reno. Willard, *Writings*, pp. 3–26.
***Amant et dame.** Cent balades d'amant et de dame.* 1407–10.		
Cent ballades d'amant et de dame. Edited by Jacqueline Cerquiglini, 1982. *Amant et dame* (excerpts). Varty, *Christine de Pisan's Ballades*, pp. 2–124, 128–64 (notes). *Cent balades d'amant et de dame.* Roy, *Œuvres poétiques*, vol. 3, pp. 209–317.	Nos. L, and parts of C ("Lai de dame / Lai mortel"). Moulin, *Christine de Pisan*, pp. 113–14.	*One Hundred Ballads of a Lover and a Lady* (excerpts consist of dedication and poems 1, 2, 10, 24, 38, 39, 74, 90, 100). Blumenfeld-Kosinski, *Selected Writings*, pp. 216–24. *One Hundred Ballades of a Lover and His Lady* (excerpts consist of dedication and poems 1, 9, 10, 32, 39, 47, 99). Translated by Nadia Margolis and Sandra Sider. Willard, *Writings*, pp. 82–88.
***Autres balades.** Autres balades.* 1402–07.		
Autres balades (excerpts) in *Christine de Pisan's Ballades.* Varty, *Christine de Pisan's Ballades*, pp. 2–124, 128–64 (notes). "Autres balades." Roy, *Œuvres poétiques*, vol. 1, pp. 207–70.	*Autres ballades* (excerpts). Moulin, *Christine de Pisan*, pp. 41–68.	*One Hundred Ballads* and *Other Ballads* (excerpts). Blumenfeld-Kosinski, *Selected Writings*, pp. 5–15. *More Ballades* (excerpts consist of ballades 7, 14, 26, 35; rondeaux 1, 3, 46, 55, 66; a rondeau "My Good Lord"; and virelays 1 and 10). Translated by June McCash and James Wilhelm. Willard, *Writings*, pp. 49–56.
***Balades d'estrange façon.** Les balades d'estrange façon.* 1399–1402.		
Balades d'estrange façon. Roy, *Œuvres poétiques*, vol. 1, pp. 119–24.		
***Cent balades.** Cent balades.* 1399–1402.		
Excerpts in Varty, *Christine de Pisan's Ballades*, pp. 2–124, 128–64 (notes) Roy, *Œuvres poétiques*, vol. 1, pp. 1–100.	*Cent balades* (excerpts). Translated by Thérèse Moreau and Eric Hicks. Polet and Pichois, *Patrimoine littéraire européen*, vol. 6, pp. 139–41. Excerpts in Moulin, *Christine de Pisan*, pp. 41–68.	*One Hundred Ballads* and *Other Ballads* (excerpts consist of poems 14, 17, 18, 50, 53, 67, 69, 78, 79). Blumenfeld-Kosinski, *Selected Writings*, pp. 5–11. *One Hundred Ballades* (excerpts consist of 11, 12, 22, 24, 34, 42, 57, 70, 77, 88). Translated by Regina De Cormier. Willard, *Writings*, pp. 41–48.

MIDDLE FR. EDS.	MODERN FR. TRANS.	ENGLISH TRANS.
Chemin de lonc estude. *Le livre du chemin de lonc estude.* 1402–03.		
Le chemin de longue étude. Edited and translated by Andrea Tarnowski, 2000. *Le livre du chemin de long estude.* Edited by Robert Püschel, 1887.	*Le chemin de longue étude.* Edited and translated by Andrea Tarnowski, 2000.	*The Path of Long Study* (excerpt). Blumenfeld-Kosinski, *Selected Writings*, pp. 59–87. *The Book of the Long Road to Learning* (excerpt). Translated by Thelma S. Fenster. Willard, *Writings*, pp. 104–08. *Christine de Pizan: The Long Road of Learning.* Edited and translated by Andrea Tarnowski, forthcoming.
Cité des dames. *Le livre de la cité des dames.* 1404–05.		
La città delle dame. Edited by Earl Jeffrey Richards, translated by Patrizia Caraffi, 1997. "The *Livre de la cité des dames of Christine de Pisan:* A Critical Edition." Edited by Maureen Cheney Curnow, 1975. *Le livre de la cité des dames.* Edited and translated by Anne Paupert, forthcoming.	*Le livre de la cité des dames* (excerpt). Translated by Thérèse Moreau and Eric Hicks. Polet and Pichois, *Patrimoine littéraire européen*, vol. 6, pp. 139–41. *Le livre de la cité des dames.* Translated by Thérèse Moreau and Eric Hicks, 1986. *Le livre de la cité des dames.* Edited and translated by Anne Paupert, forthcoming.	Excerpt in McWebb, *Debating*, pp. 388–403. *The Book of the City of Ladies.* Translated by Rosalind Brown-Grant, 1999. *The Book of the City of Ladies.* Translated by Earl Jeffrey Richards, 1998. Excerpt in Blumenfeld-Kosinski, *Selected Writings*, pp. 116–55. Excerpt in Willard, *Writings*, pp. 171–212. Translated by Earl Jeffrey Richards.
Complainte amoureuse I. *Une complainte amoureuse.* 1407–10.		
Complaintes amoureuses: I. Roy, *Œuvres poétiques*, vol. 1, pp. 281–88.		Excerpt in Margolis, "Clerkliness and Courtliness," pp. 138–39.
Complainte amoureuse II. *Une autre complainte amoureuse.* 1399–1402.		
Complaintes amoureuses: II. Roy, *Œuvres poétiques*, vol. 1, pp. 289–95.		Excerpt in Margolis, "Clerkliness and Courtliness," pp. 138–39.
Corps de policie. *Le livre du corps de policie.* 1406–07.		
Le livre du corps de policie. Edited by Angus J. Kennedy, 1998. *Le livre du corps de policie.* Edited by Robert H. Lucas, 1967.		*The Book of the Body Politic* (excerpt). Blumenfeld-Kosinski, *Selected Writings*, pp. 201–16. *The Book of the Body Politic.* Translated by Kate Langdon Forhan, 1994. *The Book of the Body of Politic* (excerpt). Translated by Diane Bornstein. Willard, *Writings*, pp. 275–91.
Débat sur Le roman de la rose. *Le livre des epistres du debat sus le* Rommant de la rose. 1401–04.		
Le livre des epistres du debat sus le Rommant de la rose. Edited by Andrea Valentini, 2014. *The Debate Epistles (1401–02).* McWebb, *Debating*, pp. 107–97. *Le débat sur* Le roman de la rose. Edited by Eric Hicks, 1977.	*Le débat sur le* Roman de la rose. Translated by Virginie Greene, 2006. *Le débat sur* Le roman de la rose (excerpt). Translated by Thérèse Moreau and Eric Hicks. Polet and Pichois, *Patrimoine littéraire européen*, vol. 6, pp. 138–39.	*Debate of the* Romance of the Rose. Edited and translated by David F. Hult, 2010. McWebb, *Debating*, pp. 107–97. *Lesser Treatise on the Romance of the Rose, June-July, 1401.* Translated by Eric Hicks. Willard, *Writings*, pp. 151–61. *La querelle de la rose: Letters and Documents.* Translated by Joseph L. Baird and John R. Kane, 1978.

MIDDLE FR. EDS.	MODERN FR. TRANS.	ENGLISH TRANS.
Deux amans. *Le livre du debat de deux amans.* C. 1400.		
Roy, *Œuvres poétiques*, vol. 2, pp. 49–110. *Le livre du debat de deux amans.* Altmann, *Love Debate Poems*, pp. 81–152.		Excerpt in McWebb, *Debating*, pp. 94–105. *The Debate of Two Lovers. Anthology*, edited and translated by Barbara K. Altmann and R. Barton Palmer, pp. 257–306.
Dieu d'amours. *L'epistre au dieu d'amours.* 1399.		
Fenster and Erler, pp. 34–89. Roy, *Œuvres poétiques*, vol. 2, pp. 1–28.	Excerpt in Moulin, *Christine de Pisan*, pp. 87–88.	McWebb, *Debating*, pp. 50–91. *The God of Love's Letters.* Blumenfeld-Kosinski, *Selected Writings*, pp. 15–29. *Letter of the God of Love.* Fenster and Erler, pp. 34–89. *The Letter of the God of Love* (excerpt). Translated by Thelma S. Fenster. Willard, *Writings*, pp. 145–150.
Dit de Poissy. *Le livre du dit de Poissy.* 1400.		
Le livre du dit de Poissy. Roy, *Œuvres poétiques*, vol. 2, pp. 159–222. Altmann, *Love Debate Poems*, pp. 203–74.	Excerpts in Moulin, *Christine de Pisan*, pp. 89–90.	*The Tale of Poissy.* Translated by Barbara K. Altmann. Willard, *Writings*, pp. 61–69.
Dit de la rose. *Le dit de la rose.* 1402.		
Roy, *Œuvres poétiques*, vol. 2, pp. 29–48. Fenster and Erler, pp. 91–155.		McWebb, *Debating*, pp. 219–53. *Tale of the Rose.* Fenster and Erler, pp. 93–131. *The Tale of the Rose* (excerpt). Translated by Thelma S. Fenster. Willard, *Writings*, pp. 162–70.
Ditié. *Le ditié de Jehanne d'Arc.* 1429.		
Ditié de Jehanne d'Arc. Edited and translated by Angus J. Kennedy and Kenneth Varty, 1977.	*Le ditié de Jehanne d'Arc.* Translated by Margaret Switten. Régnier-Bohler, pp. 699–723.	*The Tale of Joan of Arc* (excerpt). Blumenfeld-Kosinski, *Selected Writings*, pp. 252–62. *The Poem of Joan of Arc* (excerpt). Translated by Thelma S. Fenster. Willard, *Writings*, pp. 352–63. Edited and translated by Angus J. Kennedy and Kenneth Varty, 1977.
Duc des vrais amans. *Le livre du duc des vrais amans.* 1404–05.		
Le livre du duc des vrais amants. Edited and translated by Dominique Demartini and Didier Lechat, 2013. *Le livre du duc des vrais amans.* Edited by Thelma S. Fenster, 1995. Roy, *Œuvres poétiques*, vol. 3, pp. 59–208.	*Le livre du duc des vrais amants.* Edited and translated by Dominique Demartini and Didier Lechat, 2013.	*The Book of the Duke of True Lovers* (excerpt). Translated by Thelma S. Fenster and Nadia Margolis. Willard, *Writings*, pp. 70–81. *The Book of the Duke of True Lovers.* Translated by Thelma S. Fenster and Nadia Margolis, 1991.

MIDDLE FR. EDS.	MODERN FR. TRANS.	ENGLISH TRANS.
Encore aultres balades. *Encore aultres balades.* 1407–10.		
Excerpts in Varty, *Christine de Pisan's Ballades*, pp. 2–124, 128–64 (notes). Roy, *Œuvres poétiques*, vol. 1, pp. 271–80.		
Enseignemens. *Enseignemens moraux.* 1401–02.		
Les enseignemens moraux. Roy, *Œuvres poétiques*, vol. 3, pp. 27–44.		Excerpt in McWebb, *Debating*, pp. 92–93. Translated by Earl Jeffrey Richards. *Christine's Teachings for Her Son, Jean de Castel* (excerpt). Translated by Charity Cannon Willard. Willard, *Writings*, pp. 59–60.
Epistre à la reine. *Epistre à la reine.* 1405.		
"Christine de Pizan's *Epistre à la reine* (1405)." Edited by Angus J. Kennedy. *Revue des langues romanes*, vol. 92, 1988, pp. 253–64. *An Epistle to the Queen of France.* Wisman, Epistle, pp. 70–83.	"*L'epistre à la reine* de Christine de Pizan (1405)." Translated by Thérèse Moreau and Eric Hicks. *Clio*, vol. 5, 1997, clio.revues.org/417.	*Letter to the Queen of France, Isabel of Bavaria.* Translated by Charity Cannon Willard. Willard, *Writings*, pp. 269–74. *An Epistle to the Queen of France.* Wisman, Epistle, pp. 70–83.
Epistre Othea. *L'epistre que Othea la deesse envoya a Hector de Troye quant il estoit en l'aage de .XV. ans.* 1400–01.		
Epistre Othea. Edited by Gabriella Parussa, 1999. *Épître d'Othéa* (manuscript facsimile). Translated by Hélène Basso, 2008.	*Épître d'Othéa.* Translated by Hélène Basso, 2008.	*Christine de Pizan: Othea's Letter to Hector.* Edited and translated by Renate Blumenfeld-Kosinski and Earl Jeffrey Richards, 2017. *The Letter from Othea* (excerpts). Blumenfeld-Kosinski, *Selected Writings*, pp. 29–41. Excerpts in Willard, *Writings*, 1994. Translated by Earl Jeffrey Richards. *Christine de Pizan's* Letter of Othea to Hector. Translated by Jane Chance, 1990. *The Epistle of Othea.* Edited by Curt F. Bühler, translated by Stephen Scrope, 1970.
Eustace Morel. *Une epistre a Eustace Morel.* 1404.		
*L'*Espistre a Eustace Morel *de Christien de Pisan.* Edited by Jean-François Kosta-Théfaine. *Le Moyen Français*, vol. 38, 1996, pp. 79–91. *Une espistre a Eustace Mourel.* Roy, *Œuvres poétiques*, vol. 2, pp. 295–302.		*A Letter to Eustache Morel (February 10, 1404).* Edited by Renate Blumenfeld-Kosinski, translated by Blumenfeld-Kosinski and Kevin Brownlee, 1997, in *Selected Writings*, pp. 109–11.

MIDDLE FR. EDS.	MODERN FR. TRANS.	ENGLISH TRANS.
Fais d'armes. *Le livre des fais d'armes et de chevallerie.* 1410.		
Le livre des fais d'armes et de chevallerie. Edited by Christine Moneera Laennec, 1988.		*The Book of Deeds of Arms and of Chivalry.* Edited by Charity Cannon Willard, translated by Sumner Willard, 1999. *The Book of the Deeds of Arms and of Chivalry.* Translated by Sumner Willard. Willard, *Writings*, pp. 292–303. *The Book of Fayttes of Armes and of Chyualrye Translated and Printed by William Caxton.* Edited by A. T. P. Byles, 1937.
Fais et bonnes meurs. *Le livre des fais et bonnes meurs du sage roy Charles V.* 1404.		
Le livre des fais et bonnes meurs du sage roy Charles V. Edited by Suzanne Solente, 1936–40.	*Livre des faits et bonnes moeurs du sage roi Charles V.* Translated by Joël Blanchard and Michel Quereuil, 2013. *Le livre des faits et bonnes mœurs du roi Charles V le Sage.* Translated by Eric Hicks and Thérèse Moreau, 1997.	*The Book of the Deeds and Good Conduct of the Wise King Charles V* (excerpt). Blumenfeld-Kosinski, *Selected Writings*, pp. 113–15. *The Book of the Deeds and Good Character of King Charles V the Wise* (excerpts). Translated by Eric Hicks and Glenda McLeod. Willard, *Writings*, pp. 233–48. *Christine de Pizan's* Book of the Deeds and Good Character of King Charles V, the Wise. Translated by Judith Laird, 1996. *Book of Deeds and Good Practices of the Wise King Charles V.* Translated by Nadia Margolis, forthcoming.
Heures de contemplacion. *Heures de contemplacion sur la passion de Nostre Seigneur.* Ca. 1420.		
Heures de contemplacion sur la passion de Nostre Seigneur Jhesucrist. Translated by Liliane Dulac and René Stuip, 2017.		*The Hours of Contemplation on the Passion of Our Lord* (excerpts). Translated by Charity Cannon Willard. Willard, *Writings*, pp. 346–47.
Jeux à vendre. *Jeux a vendre.* 1399–1402.		
Roy, *Œuvres poétiques*, vol. 1, pp. 187–206.		*Songs for Sale* (excerpts). Translated by Charity Cannon Willard. Willard, *Writings*, pp. 57–58.
Lamentacion. *La lamentacion sur les maux de la France.* 1410.		
Lament on the Evils of the Civil War. Wisman, Epistle, pp. 84–95. "*La lamentacion sur les maux de la France* de Christine de Pisan." *Mélanges*, edited by Angus J. Kennedy, pp. 177–81.	*La lamentation sur les maux de la guerre civile* (excerpt). Translated by Thérèse Moreau and Eric Hicks. Polet and Pichois, *Patrimoine littéraire européen*, vol. 6, pp. 142–43.	*The Lamentation on the Evils That Have Befallen France.* Blumenfeld-Kosinski, *Selected Writings*, pp. 224–29. *Lamentation on the Woes of France.* Translated by Charity Cannon Willard. Willard, *Writings*, pp. 304–09. *Lament on the Evils of the Civil War.* Wisman, Epistle, pp. 84–95.
"Lay de dame," or "Lay mortel." "Lay de dame." 1414.		
	"Lai Mortel." Moulin, *Christine de Pisan*, pp. 111–14.	Brief paraphrase under the title "Mortal Lay of the Lady." Blumenfeld-Kosinski, *Selected Writings*, p. 224.

MIDDLE FR. EDS.	MODERN FR. TRANS.	ENGLISH TRANS.
Lays. *Lays*. 1390–1402.		
Lai leonine. Edited and translated by Liliane Dulac et al. *Desir n'a repos*, edited by Florence Bouchet and Danièle James-Raoul, pp. 28–36. Excerpts in Laidlaw, "Christine's Lays—Does Practice Make Perfect?" Roy, *Œuvres poétiques*, vol. 1, pp. 125–48.	*Lai leonine*. Edited and translated by Liliane Dulac et al. *Desir n'a repos*, edited by Florence Bouchet and Danièle James-Raoul, pp. 36–42.	
Livre de paix. *Le livre de paix*. 1412–13.		
The Book of Peace *by Christine de Pizan*. Edited and translated by Karen Green et al., 2008. *The* Livre de la paix *of Christine de Pisan*. Edited by Charity Cannon Willard, 1958.		The Book of Peace *by Christine de Pizan*. Edited and translated by Karen Green et al., 2008. Excerpts in Blumenfeld-Kosinski, *Selected Writings*, pp. 229–48. Excerpts in Willard, *Writings*, pp. 310–17.
Mutacion. *Le livre de la mutacion de Fortune*. 1403.		
Le livre de la mutacion de Fortune. Edited by Suzanne Solente, 1959–66.	Excerpt translated by Thérèse Moreau and Eric Hicks. Polet and Pichois, *Patrimoine littéraire européen*, vol. 6, pp. 135–37.	*The Book of the Mutability of Fortune*. Edited and translated by Geri L. Smith, 2017. Excerpt in McWebb, *Debating*, pp. 381–87. *The Book of Fortune's Transformation* (excerpts). Blumenfeld-Kosinski, *Selected Writings*, pp. 88–109. *The Book of the Mutation of Fortune* (excerpts). Translated by Nadia Margolis. Willard, *Writings*, pp. 109–36.
Oroison de Nostre Dame. *Une oroison de Nostre Dame*. 1402–03.		
L'oroyson Nostre Dame. Roy, *Œuvres poétiques*, vol. 3, pp. 1–10.	*Oraison Nostre Dame* (excerpt). Moulin, *Christine de Pisan*, pp. 117–23.	*Prayers to Our Lady* (excerpts). Translated by Regina De Cormier. Willard, *Writings*, pp. 323–24.
Oroison de Nostre Seigneur. *Une oroison de la vie et passion de Nostre Seigneur.* 1402–03.		
Une oroyson de Nostre Seigneur. Roy, *Œuvres poétiques*, vol. 3, pp. 15–26.		
Pastoure. *Le dit de la pastoure*. 1403.		
Roy, *Œuvres poétiques*, vol. 2, pp. 223–94. "A Critical Edition of Christine de Pizan's *Dit de la pastoure*." Edited by Mary Virginia Reese, 1992.	Excerpts in Moulin, *Christine de Pisan*, pp. 94–96.	*The Tale of the Shepherdess* (excerpts). Blumenfeld-Kosinski, *Selected Writings*, pp. 45–59.

Prison de vie humaine. *L'epistre de la prison de vie humaine.* 1414–18.

MIDDLE FR. EDS.	MODERN FR. TRANS.	ENGLISH TRANS.
The Epistle of the Prison of Human Life. Wisman, Epistle, pp. 2–69. *Epistre de la prison de vie humaine.* Edited by Angus J. Kennedy, 1984. "Un traité inédit de Christine de Pisan: *L'epistre de la prison de vie humaine.*" Edited by Suzanne Solente. *Bibliothèque*, vol. 85, 1924, pp. 263–301.		*The Letter on the Prison of Human Life* (excerpts). Blumenfeld-Kosinski, *Selected Writings*, pp. 248–52. *A Letter Concerning the Prison of Human Life* (excerpts). Translated by Charity Cannon Willard. Willard, *Writings*, pp. 338–45. *The Epistle of the Prison of Human Life.* Wisman, Epistle, pp. 2–69.

Prod'ommie (see also **Prudence,** another version of the same work). *La descripcion et diffinicion de la Prod'ommie de l'omme selon l'opinion de Monseigneur le duc d'Orléans.* 1407–08.

MIDDLE FR. EDS.	MODERN FR. TRANS.	ENGLISH TRANS.
Excerpts. Solente, *Christine de Pisan*, pp. 411–14.		*Book of Man's Integrity* (excerpts). Translated by Charity Cannon Willard. Willard, *Writings*, pp. 261–68.

Proverbes moraulx. *Proverbes moraulx.* 1400–01.

MIDDLE FR. EDS.	MODERN FR. TRANS.	ENGLISH TRANS.
"Les *Proverbes moraux* de Christine de Pizan." Edited by Gilbert Ouy and Christine M. Reno. *Pour acquerir honneur*, 2004, pp. 557–72. "Les *Proverbes moraulx* de Christine de Pizan." Edited by Jean François Kosta-Théfaine. *Le Moyen Français*, vol. 38, 1996, pp. 61–77. Roy, *Œuvres poétiques*, vol. 3, pp. 45–58.		

Prudence (see also **Prod'hommie,** another version of the same work). *Le livre de Prudence a l'enseignement de bien vivre.* 1407–08.

MIDDLE FR. EDS.	MODERN FR. TRANS.	ENGLISH TRANS.
		Book of Man's Integrity (excerpts). Translated by Charity Cannon Willard. Willard, *Writings*, pp. 261–68.

Quinze joyes Nostre Dame. *Les .XV. joyes Nostre Dame.* 1402–03.

MIDDLE FR. EDS.	MODERN FR. TRANS.	ENGLISH TRANS.
Les .XV. joyes Nostre Dame rimees. Edited by Jean-François Kosta-Théfaine. *Cahiers de recherches médiévales*, vol. 16, 2008, pp. 255–77. *Les XV joyes Nostre Dame.* Roy, *Œuvres poétiques*, vol. 3, pp. 11–14.		"Christine de Pizan: *The XV Joys of Our Lady.*" Translated by Glenda Wall, 1985.

MIDDLE FR. EDS.	MODERN FR. TRANS.	ENGLISH TRANS.
Rondeaux. *Rondeaux*. 1399–1402.		
Excerpts in Varty, *Christine de Pisan's Ballades*, pp. 2–124, 128–64 (notes). Roy, *Œuvres poétiques*, vol. 1, pp. 147–86.	Excerpts in Moulin, *Christine de Pisan*, pp. 69–86.	*Rondeaux* (excerpts consist of poems 1, 3, 46, 55, 66, 70). Translated by James Wilhelm. Willard, *Writings*, pp. 52–55.
Sept psaumes. *Sept psaumes allegorisés*. 1409.		
Sept psaumes allegorisés. Edited by Christine Reno and Bernard Ribémont, 2017. *Les sept psaumes allégorisés*. Edited by Ruth Ringland Rains, 1965.		*The Seven Allegorized Psalms* (excerpts). Translated by Charity Cannon Willard. Willard, *Writings*, pp. 325–37.
Trois jugemens. *Le livre des trois jugemens qui s'adrece au Seneschal de Haynault*. 1405.		
Le livre des trois jugemens. Altmann, *Love Debate Poems*, pp. 153–202. Roy, *Œuvres poétiques*, vol. 2, pp. 111–58.	*Le livre des trois jugements* (excerpt). Moulin, *Christine de Pisan*, pp. 98–100.	
Trois vertus. *Le livre des .III. vertus a l'enseignement des dames* [*Trésor de la cité des dames*]. 1405.		
Le livre des trois vertus. Edited by Charity Cannon Willard and Eric Hicks, 1989.	*Le livre des trois vertus*. Translated by Liliane Dulac. Régnier-Bohler, pp. 543–698.	*The Treasure of the City of Ladies; or, The Book of the Three Virtues*. Translated by Sarah Lawson, 2003. *A Medieval Woman's Mirror: The Treasury of the City of Ladies*. Translated by Charity Cannon Willard, 1989. *The Book of the Three Virtues* (excerpts). Blumenfeld-Kosinski, *Selected Writings*, pp. 155–173. *The Treasury of the City of Ladies* (excerpts). Translated by Charity Cannon Willard. Willard, *Writings*, pp. 213–28.
Virelays. *Virelays*. 1399–1402.		
Excerpts in Varty, *Christine de Pisan's Ballades*, pp. 2–124, 128–64 (notes). Roy, *Œuvres poétiques*, vol. 1, pp. 101–18.	Virelais (excerpts). Moulin, *Christine de Pisan*, pp. 103–10.	Virelays (excerpts). Translated by Charity Cannon Willard. Willard, *Writings*, pp. 55–56.

The Instructor's Library

Basics

For instructors, four titles suggest themselves as places to begin reading or to extend existing knowledge about Christine and her work. The first is *The Selected Writings of Christine de Pizan*, edited by Renate Blumenfeld-Kosinski and translated by Blumenfeld-Kosinski and Kevin Brownlee. Apart from offering substantial excerpts in English of nearly all Christine's works, the volume contains a valuable introduction and a series of key critical essays by well-known scholars. It gathers multiple means with which to understand Christine's literary production.

The second work recommended is *Christine de Pizan: A Casebook*, edited by Barbara K. Altmann and Deborah L. McGrady. Its fifteen essays cover the genres Christine explored, her political self-positioning and defense of women, and her manuscripts and their reception.

The third work, *An Introduction to Christine de Pizan*, by Nadia Margolis, provides chapters on the politico-historical situation in France during Christine's lifetime, the sources exploited in her work, and the literary and philosophical stakes of the works themselves. This book could engage undergraduates as well as their instructors.

Instructors who read French and wish to know more about medieval manuscript production and the artistic, political, and economic factors that influenced it will want to consult the fourth work, *Album Christine de Pizan*, by Gilbert Ouy, Christine Reno, and Inès Villela-Petit. This work explores how and by whom Christine's works were transcribed, what ink and parchment were used, who decorated their borders, what painters illuminated them, and which collectors acquired them.

Reference

Angus J. Kennedy marshals annotated bibliography pertaining to the full spectrum of Christine's production in his *Christine de Pizan: A Bibliographical Guide* and its two supplements, and Liliane Dulac provides a meticulous bibliographical essay in *Trente ans de recherches en langues et littératures médiévales*. Tracy Adams follows in Dulac's footsteps with her own bibliographical overview in *French Studies* ("Christine de Pizan"). *Dictionnaire des lettres françaises*, in its revised edition by Geneviève Hasenohr and Michel Zink, is an invaluable source of articles and biblography on individual authors, documents, and literary forms; Sylvie Lefèvre composed the dictionary's excellent entry on Christine de Pizan.

Among more narrative general works, Zink's *Introduction à la littérature du Moyen Âge*, also available in English translation, serves as an overview for anyone wanting to refresh or contextualize knowledge of the period. Denis Hollier's *A New History of French Literature*, while spanning a broad chronology from literature's beginnings through the twentieth century, is notable for a score of fine essays concerning the Middle Ages; see especially the article by the distinguished *pizaniste* Jacqueline Cerquiglini-Toulet pegged to the year 1401, when Christine's literary career was gathering momentum. In *The Cambridge Companion to Medieval French Literature*, edited by Simon Gaunt and Sarah Kay, an essay by Marilynn Desmond is devoted specifically to Christine de Pizan, though other chapters of this volume, such as Jane H. M. Taylor's on the lyric poetry of the late Middle Ages, are also germane to students of Christine's work. The anthology of medieval texts *Woman Defamed and Woman Defended*, by Alcuin Blamires (with Karen Pratt and C. W. Marx), has multiple connections to Christine's work but is particularly useful for a passage from Jehan Le Fèvre's *Lamentations of Matheolus*, the text that the Christine figure reads dispiritedly at the beginning of *The City of Ladies* and that catalyzes her fight against misogyny.

Biography and History

Charity Cannon Willard's *Christine de Pizan: Her Life and Works* has long been the principal book-length biography in English. More recent biographies are Simone Roux's *Christine de Pizan: Femme de tête, dame de cœur* and Françoise Autrand's *Christine de Pizan: Une femme en politque.*

Familiarity with the history of late-fourteenth- and early-fifteenth-century France, and particularly with life in Parisian court and humanist circles, will help illuminate the context in which Christine wrote, explain the choice of some of her themes, and define the figures who were her patrons and audience. Among broad-based histories, Johan Huizinga's century-old *The Autumn of the Middle Ages* sheds light on the world-in-decline motif in Christine's work. Charles F. Briggs's *The Body Broken: Medieval Europe, 1300–1520* offers a panoramic examination of the unity and fragmentation of a Christian ideal in the late Middle Ages—an ideal that permeates Christine's writing. Claude Gauvard's *Le Moyen Âge* and *La France au Moyen Âge du Ve au XVe siècle* both reward consultation; in the latter, chapters 13 and 14, "La dynastie des Valois s'impose (1364–1392)" and "France du roi, France des princes (1392–1440)," are most relevant. On the subject of dangerous princely rivalries at the start of the fifteenth century, see Bernard Guenée's *Un meurtre, une société: L'assassinat du duc d'Orléans, 23 novembre 1407.* Françoise Autrand's *Charles V le Sage* and *Charles VI: La folie du roi* examines the French kings whose reigns imprinted themselves on Christine's work, and Autrand's *Jean de Berry* tells the story of France's best-known patron-prince.

The literary scholar Tracy Adams has published two books that reexamine Christine's historical context: in *The Life and Afterlife of Isabeau of Bavaria*, Adams retools the negative reputation of the queen of France, the dedicatee of the most lavish copy of Christine's collected works; in *Christine de Pizan and the Fight for France*, she makes the argument that Christine was a loyal Orleanist-Armagnac throughout her career. Blumenfeld-Kosinski's "Enemies Within / Enemies Without: Threats to the Body Politic in Christine de Pizan" is a convincing account of Christine's position in the face of civil strife and the English threat to France. On the subject of the English menace and France's response, the historical and biographical guide offered by Deborah A. Fraioli in *Joan of Arc and the Hundred Years War* can help both instructors and students gain a sense of Joan's importance; Christine took Joan's triumph in battle against the English as the subject of her final composition, *The Tale of Joan of Arc.*

Also useful is volume 2 of *Histoire de la vie privée: De l'Europe féodale à la Renaissance*, translated into English as *A History of Private Life: Revelations of the Medieval World* (Ariès and Duby); the chapters by Danielle Régnier-Bohler, "Imagining the Self," and by Georges Duby and Philippe Braunstein, "The Emergence of the Individual," are particularly relevant.

To parse the papal schism that anguished Christine and her contemporaries, readers can refer to Walter Ullmann's *A Short History of the Papacy in the Middle Ages*; to understand the writing produced in the context of the split in the Church, they can consult Blumenfeld-Kosinski's *Poets, Saints, and Visionaries of the Great Schism, 1378–1417.* Information on the significance of material culture in the religious thought and practice of this period can be found in Caroline Walker Bynum's *Christian Materiality: An Essay on Religion in Late Medieval Europe.*

On the particular form of history that is myth, and on Christine's use of the legends of antiquity in her work, see Blumenfeld-Kosinski's *Reading Myth: Classical Mythology and Its Interpretations in Medieval French Literature*, and volume 3 of Jane Chance's *Medieval Mythography*, which contains two chapters dedicated to Christine. Lori Walters writes on both memory and projected history in the form of future authorial renown in her essay "Constructing Reputations: *Fama* and Memory in Christine de Pizan's *Charles V* and *L'advision Cristine.*"

Women, Widows, Mothers

Numerous resources can be used to understand the strong thematization in Christine's work of a woman's place and women's roles and her status as France's first professional woman writer. *Women in the Middle Ages: An Encyclopedia*, edited by Katharina M. Wilson and Nadia Margolis, is a solid reference tool. Volume 2 of *Histoire des femmes en Occident* or, in English, *A History of Women in the West* (edited by Christiane Klapisch Zuber) is the sweeping, broad-brush counterpart to an encyclopedia's fine-stroke entries; the introductory essay to this volume, entitled "Including Women," begins with and focuses on Christine. *The Cambridge Companion to Medieval Women's Writing* contains Jennifer Summit's essay "Women and Authorship" and Barbara Hanawalt's "Widows"; other essay categories (virginities, marriage), as well as a piece by David F. Hult on *The Romance of the Rose* and the *querelle des femmes,* highlight Christinian themes. Angela Jane Weisl considers women on either side of marriage in "The Widow as Virgin: Desexualized Narrative in Christine de Pizan's *Livre de la cité des dames,*" in *Constructions of Widowhood and Virginity*, edited by Cindy L. Carson and Weisl.

For a better understanding of the metaphor of motherhood that Christine often uses, see *Medieval Mothering*, whose essays span texts and practices from across Europe, and which has a useful introductory essay by its editors, John Carmi Parsons and Bonnie Wheeler. Clarissa W. Atkinson's *The Oldest Vocation: Christian Motherhood in the Middle Ages* includes discussion of gender roles and the historical development of the maternal.

Caroline Walker Bynum's *Holy Feast and Holy Fast: The Religious Significance of Food to Medieval Women* remains a touchstone for conceiving of the medieval female body. Roberta Gilchrist's "Medieval Bodies in the Material World: Gender Stigma and the Body," in Sarah Kay and Miri Rubin's *Framing Medieval Bodies*, likewise centers on the notion of corporeality. Also germane to this theme is Jane Tibbetts Schulenberg's "Heroics of Virginity: Brides of Christ and Sacrificial Mutilation," in Mary Beth Rose's *Women in the Middle Ages and the Renaissance: Literary and Historical Perspectives.*

Feminism and Christine

Some critics have based their interpretations of Christine's work on claims and counter-claims concerning her feminism or protofeminism. Joan Kelly's classic essay "Did Women Have a Renaissance?" is found in *Becoming Visible: Women in European History*, edited by Renate Bridenthal, Susan Stuart, and Merry E. Wiesner-Hanks. Sheila Delany penned a provocative article entitled "Mothers to Think Back Through: Who Are They? The Ambiguous Example of Christine de Pizan" (*Medieval Texts and Contemporary Readers*, edited by Laurie A. Finke and Martin B. Shichtman). Christine Reno responded to Delany in "Christine de Pizan: At Best a Contradictory Figure?" (in Margaret Brabant's *Politics, Gender and Genre: The Political Thought of Christine de Pizan*). Maureen Quilligan addresses early feminism in her influential work *The Allegory of Female Authority: Christine de Pizan's* Cité des dames; other excellent resources are Helen Solterer's *The Master and Minerva: Disputing Women in French Medieval Culture*, Rosalind Brown-Grant's *Christine de Pizan and the Moral Defence of Women*, and Alcuin Blamires's *The Case for Women in Medieval Culture.* Finally, Margaret W. Ferguson devotes a chapter entitled "An

Empire of Her Own" to Christine's *Book of the City of Ladies* in *Dido's Daughters: Literacy, Gender, and Empire in Early Modern England and France.*

Responses to Christine: Collective Works

While Christine's oeuvre attracts scholars from many disciplines, most are specialists in literature, whether they teach courses on lyric poetry or on the "mirror of princes" tradition. Since the early 1990s, a series of international colloquia associated with the Christine de Pizan Society has produced collections of essays; these include Margarete Zimmermann and Dina De Rentiis's *The City of Scholars: New Approaches to Christine de Pizan*, Liliane Dulac and Bernard Ribémont's *Une femme de lettres au Moyen Âge: Études autour de Christine de Pizan*, Eric Hicks's *Au champ des escriptures: 3e colloque international sur Christine de Pizan*, Angus J. Kennedy's *Contexts and Continuities: Proceedings of the Fourth International Colloquium on Christine de Pizan*, Liliane Dulac et al.'s *"Desireuse de plus avant enquerre . . .": Actes du VIe colloque international sur Christine de Pizan*; Patrizia Caraffi's *Christine de Pizan: La scrittrice e la città*; Anna Loba's *Ton nom sera reluisant apres toy par longue memoire*; and Olivier Delsaux and Tania van Hemlryck's collection of essays across two issues of the journal *Le moyen français* (vol. 75 [2014]; vols. 78–79 [2016]). Each publication contains contributions in English and French.

In addition to this succession of works, other symposia and collaborative projects focused on Christine and her work have been published: Margaret Brabant's *Politics, Gender, and Genre: The Political Thought of Christine de Pizan*, Marilynn Desmond's *Christine de Pizan and the Categories of Difference*, Earl Jeffrey Richards's *Reinterpreting Christine de Pizan* and *Christine de Pizan and Medieval French Lyric*, and Juliette Dor and Marie-Élisabeth Henneau's *Christine de Pizan: Une femme de science, une femme de lettres.*

Finally, a host of edited volumes that do not take Christine as their principal object nevertheless contribute to the critical context; these include Kevin Brownlee and Sylvia Huot's *Rethinking the* Romance of the Rose: *Text, Image, Reception*; Chance's *Gender and Text in the Later Middle Ages*; Rebecca Dixon and Finn Sinclair's *Poetry, Knowledge and Community in Late Medieval France*; Thelma S. Fenster and Claire A. Lees's *Gender and Debate from the Early Middle Ages to the Renaissance*; Henrik Syse and Gregory M. Reichberg's *Ethics, Nationalism, and Just War: Medieval and Contemporary Perspectives*; and Bonnie Wheeler and Charles T. Wood's *Fresh Verdicts on Joan of Arc.*

Poetry, Art, Politics, Theory

Daniel Poirion's *Le poète et le prince: L'évolution du lyrisme courtois*, published in 1965, was a catalyst for sparking interest in Christine as a poet and has achieved the status of a landmark study. Another important examination of poetry and poetics is Jane Taylor's *The Making of Poetry: Late-Medieval French Poetic Anthologies*. Jacqueline Cerquiglini-Toulet addresses the central role of books in the late medieval imagination, with Christine's work as a prime example, in her evocative *La couleur de la mélancolie: La fréquentation des livres au XIVe siècle, 1300 1415*, also available in English translation. Sandra Hindman's *Christine de Pizan's* Epistre Othéa*: Painting and Politics at the Court of Charles VI* examines the messages of Christine's manuscripts. Joël Blanchard and Jean-Claude Mühlethaler explore the political power of the pen in *Écriture et pouvoir à l'aube des temps modernes*. Jacques Krynen treats writing for the benefit of those who reign in *Idéal du prince et pouvoir royal en France à la fin du Moyen Âge, 1380–1440: Étude de la littérature politique du temps*, and Daisy Delogu continues in this vein in *Theorizing the Ideal Sovereign: The Rise of the French Vernacular Royal Biography*, which contains a chapter on Christine's portrait of, and paean to, King Charles V. In *Allegorical Bodies: Power and Gender in Late Medieval France*, Delogu highlights the fact that while France prohibited women from acceding to the throne, its discourse of state depended on the elaboration of female allegories. Sarah Kay focuses on place images as markers of posited truth and consensus in *The Place of Thought: The Complexity of One in Late Medieval French Didactic Poetry*, which includes a chapter entitled "Melancholia, Allegory, and the Metaphysical Fountain in Christine de Pizan's *Le livre du chemin de long estude*." Douglas Kelly likewise makes the status of truth and subjectivity his topic in *Christine de Pizan's Changing Opinion: A Quest for Certainty in the Midst of Chaos*.

A Contemporary of Note: Jean Gerson

Gerson scholarship has greatly increased since the turn of the century and merits note for the depth it adds to our picture of the political and religious controversies of France in the reign of Charles VI. See especially Brian Patrick McGuire's *Jean Gerson and the Last Medieval Reformation* and Daniel Hobbins's *Authorship and Publicity before Print: Jean Gerson and the Transformation of Late Medieval Learning*. McGuire's *A Companion to Jean Gerson* contains an essay by Blumenfeld-Kosinski on Gerson's role in France's first great literary quarrel, "Jean Gerson and the Debate on the *Romance of the Rose*." Two essays in Dixon and Sinclair's *Poetry, Knowledge and Community in Late Medieval France* engage with Gerson: Lori J. Walters's "Gerson and Christine, Poets" and Mishtooni Bose's "Jean Gerson, Poet." Another essay by Walters homes in on Gerson's connection to what is no doubt Christine's most famous self-description: "The Figure of the *Seulette* in the Works of Christine de Pizan and Jean Gerson." Nathalie Nabert examines Gerson and Christine as moral reformers in "Christine de Pizan, Jean Gerson et le gouvernement des âmes," in *Au champ des escriptures*, edited by Hicks. Finally, Earl Jeffrey Richards defines the connection between Christine and the University of Paris cleric in "Christine de Pizan and Jean Gerson: An Intellectual Friendship," in *Christine de Pizan*, edited by John Campbell and Nadia Margolis.

NOTE

[1]These are *Le livre de prudence* and *Le livre de la prod'hommie*, two versions of the same work. An edition of *Le livre de prudence* is in preparation by Barbara Falleiros.

Aids to Teaching Christine de Pizan Online

Mark Aussems

For *études christiniennes*, the study of the life and works of Christine de Pizan, the Internet contains a profusion of information. It is reassuring to see that Christine, on her "long road of learning," has firm footing on the Web and that the information available is diverse and ever-expanding.[1] This essay provides an overview of some of the most interesting and inspiring Web sites dedicated to Christine de Pizan and her oeuvre, as well as to fifteenth-century Paris and its literary circles. The goal here is not to list academic research tools but rather to provide instructors with a set of reliable Web resources that they can use to enrich their classes and lectures. These resources are divided into three categories: digital innovations concerning the manuscripts of Christine's works, Web resources pertaining to Christine's life in fifteenth-century Paris, and tools for studying the medieval French language in which Christine wrote.

Manuscripts and Illuminations

Christine de Pizan's works were published in manuscript form, copied by scribes and embellished by skilled illuminators. Of the many manuscripts of Christine's texts that have survived, no fewer than fifty were produced under Christine's own supervision. Besides being invaluable testaments to fifteenth-century bookmaking, these original manuscripts provide the largest corpus of supervised manuscripts of any medieval French author. As these manuscripts paint a unique picture of a medieval author's involvement in their production process, the study of Christine's original manuscripts plays an important role in *études christiniennes*.

In recent years, new developments in data analysis and digitization processes have brought about major innovations in this field. The Christine de Pizan Research Project at the University of Edinburgh carried out pioneering research into the manuscript called London, British Library, Harley 4431 (or MS Harley 4431). Known as the Queen's Manuscript, this is often described as the most important collection of Christine's works. The project Web site contains digital editions of all the texts in this manuscript, as well as a detailed codicological description. It also offers high-resolution images of the manuscript (www.pizan.lib.ed.ac.uk/gallery).

The Bibliothèque Nationale de France (BNF) has made available 109 manuscript documents concerning Christine de Pizan (among them the fabulous codices f.fr. 603, 605, 607, and 12779) through their image repository *Gallica* (gallica.bnf.fr).[2] Taken together, these London and Paris manuscripts provide a fascinating look into the principles behind the production of manuscripts and the extent to which these principles gradually change from the early days of Christine's career (MS 12779, produced around 1399–1405) to the production of MS Harley 4431 in 1412–1413, which represents the apogee of her fame.

As for the production of medieval manuscripts in general, the Getty Museum's Web site features a section entitled "The Making of a Medieval Book," where short videos explain the different stages in the laborious process of producing a manuscript from parchment to binding (www.getty.edu/art/exhibitions/making). The Web site of the Fitzwilliam Museum in Cambridge, England, has a section "Making Art: Medieval Manuscripts" that illustrates similar processes (www.fitzmuseum.cam.ac.uk/pharos/sections/making_art/index_manuscript.html).

Christine and Fifteenth-Century Paris

Among notable biographical descriptions available online are Brian Pavlac's *Women's History Resource Site* (departments.kings.edu/womens_history) and Doré Ripley's detailed online essay "Christine de Pizan: An Illuminated Voice" (www.ripleyonline.com/Under%20Discussion/Christine/Christine.htm). As for Christine's works, there is no better online bibliography than the section devoted to her on the *Archives de littérature du Moyen Âge* (ARLIMA; www.arlima.net/ad/christine_de_pizan.html). For each of Christine's works, ARLIMA offers basic information, such as the date of composition, the dedicatee, and the incipit and explicit, followed by an overview of surviving manuscripts, existing editions and translations, and studies of the text in question. Another noteworthy repository is Robert Peckham's Web site *Textual Sources of Christine de Pizan* (www.utm.edu/staff/bobp/vlibrary/christine.shtml).

Less widely used in the classroom, but certainly worth knowing, are digital versions of older editions of Christine's works. The *Internet Archive* contains, among others, Maurice Roy's 1886–96 edition of Christine's *Œuvres poétiques*, as well as Mathilde Laigle's 1912 edition of *Le livre des trois vertus*. The *Internet Archive* also houses several other notoriously difficult-to-find essays and studies of aspects of Christine's life and works; most prominent among them is Raymond Thomassy's *Essai sur les écrits politiques de Christine de Pisan*, dating from 1838 (www.archive.org/details/texts; search for "Pizan" as well as "Pisan").

Christine de Pizan lived through a turbulent period in the history of France. The untimely death of King Charles V in 1380 shook the French nation to the core, and the attacks of madness that plagued his son and successor, King Charles VI, caused despair and anxiety in the government. Good background information about the reign of Charles V is available in the "Classes" section of the BNF Web site. Similarly interesting is the BNF's digital exhibition featuring the famous fifteenth-century painter and illuminator Jean Fouquet (classes.bnf.fr/dossitsm/b-charlv.htm; expositions.bnf.fr/fouquet). In addition, an online article "Assassinat dans la rue Vieille de Temple" describes how the assassination of Charles VI's brother, Louis, duke of Orléans, by his cousin, Jean, duke of Burgundy, in November 1407 sparked a twenty-eight-year civil war between the two most important houses of France (www.herodote.net/23_novembre_1407-evenement-14071123.php).

The spirit of Christine's fifteenth-century Paris is slightly more difficult to evoke on the Web. Despite the large number of search results for queries such as "medieval Paris" or "Paris médiéval," few Web sites offer reliable, compelling information about the French capital in the Middle Ages. The online *Musée nationale du Moyen Âge*—in particular its section "Le Moyen Âge au quotidien"—is probably the most useful resource on this subject (www.musee-moyenage.fr; under the Collection tab, see "Parcours Découverte"). Also noteworthy is the online guide to a medieval Paris walking tour; among its many fortes are its ability to connect the medieval past of Parisian locations to other historical and modern events that took place at the same sites (dimeliandco.net/paris-medieval) and its large collection of images.

A different approach to recreating medieval Paris has been taken by McMaster University of Hamilton, Ontario; their *Medieval Women* Web site includes a 3-D virtual tour of (a remodeled) Paris. The end result successfully calls up the atmosphere of a medieval city (mw.mcmaster.ca/home.html).

Language Tools

With the advent of programming and languages such as XML, Javascript, and PHP, the Internet has become not just a database of images and texts but also a place where these can be analyzed and interpreted. The *Dictionnaire du moyen français*, for instance, is available online in an updated version (www.atilf.fr/dmf). This site includes as a separate section the *Lexique de Christine de Pizan*, the most important resource for understanding Christine's language, choice of words, grammar, and spelling (www.atilf.fr/dmf/Pizan [*Pizan* is case-sensitive]).

A Web site of similar importance is James Laidlaw's *Christine de Pizan Database*; of the forty-plus works in Christine's oeuvre, an impressive thirty-three are included in this database, which consists of lists of words and rhyme words (both lists also in reverse form) and proper names, as well as a full A-to-Z concordance of every word encountered in these texts (www.ed.ac.uk/literatures-languages-cultures/delc/french/research-projects/christine-de-pizan-database).

Loci, a tool developed by Charles Mansfield for the aforementioned Christine de Pizan Research Project in Edinburgh, provides insight into the frequency and distribution of words in Christine's Harley 4431 manuscript. *Loci* can search up to three different words at a time in the manuscript and displays them in different colors; as such, it is ideal for showing the fluid nature of the French language in the early fifteenth century (eserve.org.uk/loceme/loci.htm).[3]

No selection of Web sites can do justice to the diversity and variety of online resources connected to Christine de Pizan and her era. While a great many of the almost 350,000 *Google* hits are superfluous, many other Web sites could have made it onto these pages in addition to the ones mentioned. A *desideratum*, therefore, is a complete, up-to-date, and digital overview of Web resources on Christine.

NOTES

[1]While a *Google* search for "Christine de Pizan" yielded about 120,000 results in April 2011, it had close to 350,000 results in November 2017.

[2]In the dropdown menu next to the search bar, click on the collection "Manuscrits" and search for "Pisan."

[3]As an example, try searching for *doulz*, *doulx*, and the modern equivalent *douce*; or try *alieurs*, *aillieurs*, and *ailleurs*.

Part Two

APPROACHES

Introduction: Christine de Pizan, Building with Books

Andrea Tarnowski

Christine de Pizan fascinates because, unlike many authors of the Middle Ages, she has a name and a relatively detailed biographical identity. Her compositions are not disembodied or fragmented; they very much belong together. And so instructors can draw an individualized portrait of a young widow who turned to writing to earn a living, producing first court poetry, then narratives of fantastic discovery, then works of political science, then works of consolation and prayer. Whether the tales are personal, familial, or historical, they exist alongside available biographical details that feed readers' desire to know the author behind the work. One might think critical study of Christine's work would suffer because of her status as France's first professional woman writer. The temptation to privilege her life over her work has given pause to more than one instructor theoretically committed to separating literary analysis from biographical anecdote but caught up in the pull of a unique story—the image of a fifteenth-century laywoman who achieved a literary reputation of the highest order, who on the strength of her own merits and shrewdness gained favor with royal princes, who produced numerous volumes in a great variety of genres and then extended her control by copying her own texts, overseeing their illustration, and presenting them to patrons as magnificent as the queen of France.

For this particular medieval author, however, cordoning off life stories from literary texts is neither necessary nor, perhaps, desirable. Christine's writing again and again catalyzes personal circumstances or contemporary events. A consistent and recognizable self-image is a key element of her writing. The protagonists of her works tend to be called Christine. In manuscript miniatures, it is as easy to identify the woman in the simple robe and white headdress as it would be to tag a familiar photograph. Christine's self-narration contributes to her authorial self-creation. The point is not to collapse distinctions between author and character, literature and history but to maintain them and to explore the material connecting them.

Sometimes Christine characterizes her eponymous stand-in as an apprentice; this is the case, for example, in *Le livre du chemin de lonc estude* (*The Path of Long Study*). The narrative poem depicts a voyage of discovery in which the Cumaean sibyl arrives at Christine's bedside to guide her first around the world and then into the heavens to witness a debate in the court of Queen Reason. Overwhelmed at the honor of being selected but eager to set out, Christine enjoins the sibyl, "Go first, and I will come behind" (Chemin [Tarnowski], line 698; my trans.). The pair remain in this hierarchical configuration throughout their journey. The mentor-mentee rapport is calculated to recall that of Virgil and Dante in the *Commedia*, but unlike in Dante's text, in *The Path of Long Study*, Christine does not leave the company of her leader as she gains knowledge and understanding; she remains under the sibyl's protection. It is also worth noting that despite the singularity of Christine's trip, she does not experience anything that is foreclosed to others. She visits distant lands and contemplates celestial spheres, but what makes these acts possible is study, learning, and reflection; she is elected by the sibyl because of her penchant for these things rather than because of an essential talent or superiority. The lessons she learns on the order immanent in nature and on the too-frequent human choice of strife will unfold for anyone who devotes energy to thought. In addition, the celestial debate, whose subject is the qualities most important in a ruler, illustrates an analogy between society and the individual: the humility, generosity, and fairness necessary to successful governance is also necessary in good self-governance.

Christine portrays herself as both an apprentice and a teacher in *The Book of the City of Ladies* and its sequel, *The Book of the Three Virtues*. In *The City of Ladies*, three authorities, Reason, Rectitude, and Justice, appear to a persona of Christine who is bewildered and discouraged by the misogyny she finds rife in books. They reassure her and aid her in the construction of a walled fortress that will shield good women from detractors. But once the city is finished, Christine turns outward toward a putative female audience to exhort it to deserve the city's security with irreproachable behavior. Here, she acts as author and activist, speaking commandingly. She is not a fictional figure, an allegory such as Lady Justice, but rather the human link between the tales of the city and their application to a listening, reading public. The narrative arc of *The City of Ladies* transforms a despondent and fearful pupil into an authoritative teacher.

The Book of the Three Virtues begins by drawing on the credit Christine established in *The City of Ladies*: the first line refers to the earlier work, noting the labor it required. However, Christine does not strike out on her own entirely; she remains under the aegis of Reason, Rectitude, and Justice, who urge her to gather her energy and continue writing—under their direction. She is their scribe, the vehicle of their teachings into the world. More emphasis is placed on the present and future inhabitants of the City of Ladies, which is now referred to not only by that name but also as the College of Women, the University of Women, and the College of Wisdom. While the city remains a place of protection, these names emphasize communal learning and cast the city structure as an institution for the recognition and inculcation of virtue. Christine eventually takes even more responsibility for guiding this community than she did in *The City of Ladies*; at the end of the text, Reason and her companions vanish once and for all, and Christine summarizes, reviews, and revises the written work, making it her own. *The Three Virtues* concerns itself with how to convey a message of virtue throughout the world and across generations (see Krueger's essay in this volume). In other words, Christine focuses on the enduring nature of writing and books. Teaching what is right and true becomes closely linked with enhancing her authorial renown.

Christine took practical steps to influence posterity and further her authorial career by overseeing the material production of her works. She often acted as her own scribe or copyist; she decided what passages in her texts would be highlighted by color-rich illustrations; she bestowed her volumes on powerful patrons to ensure her financial security and augment her reputation. Visible and tangible traces of her historical existence lend her manuscripts particular interest and can be extremely engaging for students as artifacts of another age (for digital reproduction of the pages of Christine's longest and most important collected manuscript, see the Web site *Christine de Pizan: The Making of the Queen's Manuscript* (www.pizan.lib.ed.ac.uk/). But in addition to providing evidence of her skill at making sure she would be read, the physical existence of these manuscripts bespeaks her belief in what we might call moral materiality. That is, books are the site of virtue and a source of goodness (see Walters's essay in this volume). Christine closely associates herself with books; the painted miniatures that accompany her texts—*Les proverbes moraulx* (*Moral Proverbs*), *Othea's Letter to Hector*, *The Book of the Three Virtues*—show her consulting, holding, or proffering bound volumes. In the dedication of her collected works to Queen Isabeau of France, she speaks of books as being a garden of delight; they should be cherished because they improve the reader, making her or him more learned and worthy.

By the time Christine's reputation reached its height circa 1405, the author did not hesitate to use her status to intervene in situations of political conflict. Her brief but passionate *Epistle to the Queen of France* urges Queen Isabeau to intercede for peace among warring members of the royal household; one senses that Christine, despite her many expressions of humility, is close to upbraiding the queen for failing to do more and do it more quickly. Five years later, another epistle, this time addressed to Christine's generous patron Duke John of Berry, again decries the catastrophe of civil war and designates John as the man to bring his relatives back from the brink of a clash. Christine moves boldly to instruct those whose position and influence might be expected to have kept her in a subdued state of deference.

But even before her stature allowed her to address her dedicatees with relative freedom, we see in Christine's work the desire to mediate that marks the true teacher. The 1402 *Oroyson Nostre Dame* (*Prayers to Our Lady*) synthesizes in compact but simple form several defining features of her style and self-presentation. The Virgin Mary is the addressee of every strophe (just as she is the crowning figure of *The City of Ladies*); traditionally appreciated as an intercessor, the Virgin is a model for connecting the terrestrial to the celestial world, the human to the divine. Christine, too, is a go-between from human beings to the heavens in the sense that she favors action motivated by ideals. In her prayer, then, she expresses her reverence for the Virgin's grandeur—she is the greatest female guide of all, surpassing the sybil of *The Path of Long Study* or the allegorical Reason, Rectitude, and Justice—but at the same time suggests an analogy between the work the Virgin does and the way Christine herself proceeds in her writing. The value of that writing is additionally reinforced by her references to the texts of her predecessors—among them, as models, the works of Augustine, Cicero, and Boethius, and, as countermodels, those of Jean de Meun and Boccaccio. In the *Oroyson Nostre Dame*, this point is made with authorial guarantees immediately after every invocation of the Virgin. Christine says to Mary: "[You] . . . are the root of all goodness, as Saint Jerome tells us," or "[You] are a fountain full of pity . . . as Saint Bernard says in his sermon" (L'oroyson [Roy], lines 38–39, 133–35). As each segment of the poem unfolds, she asks the Virgin to protect another person or group: the French king, the queen, the royal children, the realm of France, the nobility, merchants, laborers. And finally, the "devout feminine sex" (line 199). It is striking to the reader, and typical of Christine, that women should be portrayed as a cohesively virtuous assembly and that they should be highlighted in some way—here, by their placement as the strong endpoint of Christine's list.

Part 2 of this volume comprises essays that analyze and share techniques for teaching Christine's work situated in the context of her life. It is divided into three sections. The first, "Gender and Self-Representations: Cultural Contexts," presents essays that illuminate the connections among gender, writing, patronage, Christine's self-representation, and her participation in the intellectual issues of her day. Jeff Rider details Christine's biography and her authorial personae. Deborah McGrady discusses Christine and her audience. Renate Blumenfeld-Kosinski treats Christine's use of ancient and contemporary history in her writing, while Christine's insistence on the value of memory forms the basis for Julia Simms Holderness's essay. The means and methods of art history are brought to bear on Christine's work by Mary Gibbons Landor, who analyzes the way in which Christine's hands are depicted in manuscript illustrations, revealing her as, by turns, an author, a scholar, a student, and a narrator. The essay on the *Debate on* The Romance of the Rose, by David F. Hult, reviews Christine's role as the instigator of France's first documented literary quarrel. Daisy Delogu studies the tripartite structure of Christine's homage to a revered king in *The Deeds and Good Practices of the Wise King Charles V*. Andrea Tarnowski's essay on *The Book of the City of Ladies* examines the architectural metaphor that the work deploys over its own three-part structure.

The second section, "Christine across the Disciplines," begins with an essay by Benjamin M. Semple that treats the simultaneously theological and personal cast of Christine's idea of virtue. Cary J. Nederman then discusses Christine's entry into the role of political counsel by way of both study and experience. Patricia E. Black, who writes on teaching Christine's poetry from a musical perspective, considers the genealogical line between Guillaume de Machaut and Christine and examines the growing divide in the late fourteenth century between music and lyric. Susan J. Dudash describes the organization of a class around a single ballade that features one of Christine's alter egos, the goddess of wisdom and arms, Pallas Athena. Barbara K. Altmann's essay on intertextuality examines how Christine inserted herself into the existing tradition and developed a personal style. The last essay in this section, by David Joseph Wrisley, takes the data of place-names mentioned in Christine's oeuvre and renders it interpretable through digital mapping.

The last section, "Classroom Contexts," begins with Ellen M. Thorington's description of Christine's place in a three-semester, chronologically organized honors humanities course. Karen Robertson and Christine Reno provide a narrative of reading the author with a group of women's and gender studies students. Two essays on Christine in England and in English follow: Theresa Coletti examines Christine's status in late medieval and early Tudor England. A. E. B. Coldiron looks at the English reception of Christine and the five main early printed translations of her works (1478–1549). The essay by Roberta L. Krueger on *The Book of the Three Virtues* primes students to read this work of advice for women by reflecting on the range of topics represented in the self-help aisles of modern-day bookstores. The essay by Lori J. Walters on the prologue of the Queen's Manuscript, the sumptuous volume Christine gave in gift to the queen of France, discusses the pedagogical opportunities provided by examining various aspects of the work. Finally, Nadia Margolis highlights the teaching potential of *The Tale of Joan of Arc*, the only non-anonymous literary witness to the warrior-saint.

GENDER AND
SELF-REPRESENTATIONS: CULTURAL CONTEXTS

Becoming a Man: Christine de Pizan, 1390 to 1400

Jeff Rider

In fact, a woman also possesses this difference in respect to a man which the body has in respect to the soul in the literal sense inasmuch as a woman is devoted to birth and children. If, however, she should wish to be devoted to God more than to the world, she will cease to be a woman and be said to be a man, because we all desire to attain to the perfect man (Eph. 4.13).

—Jerome, commentary on Ephesians

Eugenia put on men's clothing and went to a monastery. Helenus, a man of God, was the head of this monastery, and Helenus would not allow a woman to come near him. . . . When Eugenia approached Helenus and said she was a man, he replied: "Rightly do you call yourself a man, because you act like a man though you are a woman." . . . Eugenia therefore . . . received the monastic habit from Helenus, and thenceforth was called Brother Eugene. . . . and when Helenus died, Brother Eugene was elected to replace him.

—Jacobus de Voragine, *The Golden Legend*

Then my body and face changed
Into those of a perfect, natural man.

—Christine, *Le livre de la mutacion de Fortune*

The reign of King Jean II (1350–64) was one of the low points for France during the Hundred Years War, and the reign of his son, Charles V (1364–80), must have felt in contrast like something of a golden age for the inhabitants of France, especially those of Paris. Toward the beginning of his reign, around 1366, Charles invited Thomas de Pizan, a minor noble and former professor at the University of Bologna, who was then a counselor of the Republic of Venice, to come to his court in Paris to serve as a royal doctor, astrologer, and counselor. Charles seems to have appreciated Thomas and was generous with him. Simone Roux has estimated that Thomas's income toward the end of Charles's reign was around 1,920 livres parisis per year, at a time when an income of 500 livres placed one in the middle nobility; the royal treasurer and the presidents (magistrates) of the Parlement of Paris (the highest appellate court) received 500 livres a year, and the first president of the Parlement received 1,000 (79–80; Autrand, *Christine de Pizan* 37–38). Thomas had left his wife and children in Italy when he went to Paris to test the waters but arranged for them to join him in 1368, when his daughter Christine was probably four.

Charles V's death in 1380 at the relatively young age of forty-two was undoubtedly a blow to the aging Thomas and his family, but his daughter had married Étienne de Castel in 1379—when Étienne was twenty-five, and she was fifteen—and her father probably thought that he had secured her against at least the most violent winds of fortune through this marriage. Étienne may have been the son of an Étienne de Castel who appears in written records as an armorer, *valet de chambre*, and embroiderer to Charles V.[1] It is a sign of the older Étienne's rank and connections in royal circles that Gilles Malet, Charles V's librarian, served as one of the executors of his will when he died in 1371, since Malet likewise served as an executor of Charles V's will in 1380 and continued to serve as the royal librarian until his death in 1411.[2]

The younger Étienne was, like Christine, of noble origin—their daughter became a nun at the Dominican priory of Poissy, where Christine herself eventually retired around 1418 and which received only women of the best classes[3]—and he became a royal notary and secretary the year that he and Christine married. The royal secretaries, who composed and sealed the king's correspondence and whose name came from their access to his *scel secré* ("privy seal"), formed a small, influential, well-to-do, elite, close-knit group, often allied by marriage: Étienne and Christine's son, Jean de Castel, became a royal secretary like his father and married the daughter of another royal secretary (Samaran 399). Roux estimates that notary secretaries earned between one hundred and two hundred livres parisis per year (80), while Françoise Autrand estimates that they earned around 379 livres parisis a year (*Christine de Pizan* 39). Étienne thus earned considerably less than Christine's father but still enjoyed a substantial income.

Christine speaks highly of her father in her works and his death in 1387 was surely a great personal loss to her, as was her two brothers' subsequent return to Italy. One supposes that she and her husband suffered financially as a result of Thomas's death, since the family lost Thomas's significantly greater income.

Christine's life seems to have continued relatively happily, however, until her husband's sudden death from illness while in Beauvais with Charles VI in 1390.

Christine was twenty-five when her husband died and she became the head of a household that included three children, born between 1381 and 1385 (Laidlaw, "Christine de Pizan, the Earl of Salisbury" 131; Willard, *Christine de Pizan: Her Life* 202), her mother, and a niece. When the thirty-five-to-forty-year-old and increasingly successful Christine looked back over the decade between 1390 and 1400 in 1400–1405, she wrote famously that her husband's death had forced her "to become a man" (*Le livre de la mutacion*, lines 139–56, 1025–32, 1159–64, 1356–61, 1391–1408; cf. *Le livre de l'advision*, 3.21.27–28). Scholars have often interpreted statements Christine made about her life, above all in her *Livre de l'advision Cristine*, to mean that she experienced serious financial difficulties after her husband's death; it has even been suggested that she had to work as a copyist in order to make ends meet. However, her seemingly carefree childhood, her relative youth at the time of her marriage, her husband's background, and her domestic preoccupations during her marriage all suggest that she grew up in an extraordinarily wealthy, highly privileged social group and that what seemed like adversity to her may not have seemed like adversity to most people of the time. Thanks to her father's position at court and her husband's position in the king's administration, she was well connected in the royal administrative circle, and several members of this circle came to her aid after Étienne's death (Willard, *Christine de Pizan: Her Life* 42–43). She knew the king's librarian, Gilles Malet. She likewise knew at least two of the *marmousets* (the name given to a group of Charles VI's ministers) relatively well (42). She knew, first, Jean de Montaigu, the son of a royal secretary, who eventually became Charles VI's superintendent of finances and grew so rich that he provoked the envy of the king's uncles and cousins; he was arrested and executed by John the Fearless, duke of Burgundy, in 1409 (Christine, *Le livre des fais et bonnes meurs* 1: lxxvii; cf. Rouse and Rouse 1: 217–25). Second, Christine knew Bureau de la Rivière, chamberlain and friend to Charles V and in whose arms the king died. Bureau was another of Charles V's executors (Christine, *Le livre des fais et bonnes meurs* [Solente] 1: lxxiv–lxxvi, 1: 192 [part 3, chap. 71]). She was also well acquainted with Philippe de Mézières, another counselor to Charles V, who had known her father since before she was born and who purchased from her a dwelling in Miremont, near Perthes, in 1392 (Willard, *Christine de Pizan: Her Life* 19, 40). These influential connections made possible the marriage of Christine and Étienne's son, Jean, to the daughter of a royal secretary and his appointment as a royal secretary himself.

When we read about Christine's trials after the death of her husband in her *Livre de l'advision*, we should not confuse Christine the author and Christine the character. The character's complaint to Philosophy at the beginning of the third book sounds at times like the whining of a spoiled child—she describes herself as having been "brought up in pleasures and coddled" and "too coddled" (3.6.33–34, 3.9.9)—and we need to remember that the character is presented as someone in need of correction, someone who has chosen an unproductive attitude toward the events in her life and must change it. In *Le livre du dit de Poissy*, in contrast, the character Christine is comfortable. This later work refers, to be sure, to circumstances in 1400 rather than 1390, but it seems unlikely that the real Christine was ever destitute or forced to earn a living through labor like most women of the lower classes.[4] Roux estimates that Christine's revenues after the death of Étienne were one hundred to one hundred and fifty livres parisis a year, and both Roux and Autrand note that Christine was able to maintain her aristocratic lifestyle during the 1390s (Roux 80–84; Autrand, *Christine de Pizan* 55–57). Had she ever experienced real financial hardship, she could, like most upper-class medieval widows, have remarried. That she did not indicates that she had sufficient resources, and thus the liberty, not to do so.

Étienne's death required Christine to assume responsibilities and roles for which she was not prepared and that she found difficult. It would have been normal in such circumstances for her to feel resentment toward her husband and her father, toward indeed an entire social system that had not prepared her for the tasks she now had to undertake, as well as a sense that what had happened to her was profoundly unjust. Faced with such challenges, many people would have succumbed and either remarried as quickly as possible or fallen out of the social class in which she managed to maintain herself and her family. We should not make little of the emotional, social, and financial challenges she faced or her achievement in overcoming them, but it is also true that she had access to social and financial resources that were not available to most people, men or women, of her time.

When Christine looked back in 1400–05 and wrote that Étienne's death had forced her to become a man, it seems she was thinking not primarily of the difficulties his death had caused but more of the ways in which his death had given her a chance to change the course of her life. She recognized that his death had offered her opportunities she would not have had if he had lived. In the *Livre de l'advision*, she has Philosophy remind the character Christine that she would not have been able to become a writer and an intellectual if her husband had not died (3.18.16–32). The status of widow, at least of aristocratic widow, was the estate in which medieval women enjoyed the greatest freedom, and this freedom may have had much to do with her decision not to remarry. As the extracts at the beginning of this essay suggest, moreover, being a man or a woman was already recognized in the patristic period and the Middle Ages as a gendered role that was not determined by biological sex. It had long been recognized and accepted that a female might become a man if she devoted herself to manly pursuits like philosophy, politics, and literature. This is, I believe, what Christine meant above all when she said that she had become a man over the preceding years.

Christine dates her first poetic efforts to "the youth of my widowhood" (*Livre de l'advision* 3.7.1–2), by which she probably means c. 1390–95 (see 3.6.224–28). Her earliest datable work is a ballade from 1395–96, and the earl of Salisbury had already seen some of her work when he met her while on a diplomatic mission to Paris in 1398 (Laidlaw, "Christine de Pizan, the Earl of Salisbury" and "Christine and the Manuscript Tradition" 233; Willard, *Christine de Pizan: Her Life* 42). It thus seems reasonable to assume that she decided to begin circulating her work publicly somewhere around 1395. It is unlikely that the poems she published at that time were her first efforts, so she probably began writing poetry well before the mid-1390s.

One source of her decision to write, as Jacqueline Cerquiglini has noted, was "loss, death—the death of King Charles V, the death of a father, the death of a husband" ("Christine de Pizan et le scandale" 46). Writing poetry was probably an emotional outlet ("[I]t is most grievous to keep suffering closed up without complaint" [*Livre de l'advision* 3.7.131–14]) and gave her something to do other than care for her family, worry about her finances, and argue with officials, lawyers, and judges ("And likewise to pass the time and bring some cheer to my sad heart, I started to write amorous and happy poems about feelings other than my own" [21–22]). Perhaps these poems were likewise a way of remembering her childhood and her marriage (the "poets' little muses . . . made me rime weepy laments, aching for my dead friend and past good times" [16, 18–20]). These are all, however, private reasons for writing poetry, which do not require the publication of the poems. The decision to publish her poems was perhaps motivated in part by a desire to further secure her financial position through gifts from wealthy patrons—although no one, not even Eustache Deschamps, could earn his or her living solely by writing at the time (Willard, *Christine de Pizan: Her Life* 44)—but it seems principally a social decision to reposition herself in her world in a specific way, a *mutacion* that would add poet to her status as daughter, mother, and widow.

Her decision to write and publish poetry rather than another genre may have been spontaneous, but it was also shrewd. Following Michel Zink we can divide the complex and well-developed field of French literature at the end of the fourteenth century into three major categories (Zink, *Littérature française* 269–352). The first, "forms of reflection: witnessing, judging, knowledge," included historical works, didactic or political works, religious works, and translations of scientific and philosophical literature in Latin. This field of literature was more or less closed to Christine, at the beginning of her career at least, by her lack of formal education. A second category, "forms of representation," included romances and a wide range of theatrical representations. Christine might have been able to write romances, and the public that appreciated them was largely the same as that for which she began to write, but this field too required a substantial, if less formal, education, which she appears to have lacked. Her work also suggests that she was not naturally inclined to writing fiction.

Christine chose instead to enter the literary field in the third category: poetry. This field, and above all fixed-form poetry like ballades, rondeaux, virelais, lais, and so on, was the most accessible to a woman writer in the last decade of the fourteenth century and the one that gave her the best chance to succeed. These light forms—short, courtly, and sentimental, sometimes bordering on precious—were much appreciated in courtly milieus at the time, and this was likewise the moment when "the association—natural for us but new then—between writing verse and writing about oneself came into being" (Zink, "Poètes courtois" 44). Poetry no longer required a display of learning, and a poet could, as Christine did, draw on her experiences for the subjects of her poems. Her descriptions of her losses and her woes were also a way, as Daniel Poirion wrote, "to win the pity of important people" whose goodwill was important to her (*Littérature française* 242). Given that writing poetry was an acceptable trade for a woman, that she had inherited or had access to the necessary tools—a good informal education, experience of the court, and books—and that she had connections in circles in which her product would be appreciated, poet was probably the easiest profession for Christine to take up, the easiest way for her to reinsert herself in court life, in the mid-1390s.

Writing poetry was not Christine's only solace and pastime during the 1390s, however. She also appears to have undertaken a long-term project of reading and self-education that would ultimately be of tremendous importance to her future as a writer. Cerquiglini asks, "Where does the book spring from" for Christine? And she answers, "From books" ("Christine de Pizan and the Book" 118; Christine, *Livre de l'advision* 3.10.32–34). Cerquiglini suggests elsewhere that there was in general for Christine "an eroticization of the desire for learning, a transformation of sexual desire into a desire for knowledge" ("Le goût" 599). Indeed, in *Le livre de la mutacion de la Fortune*, Christine writes, "I am like lovers who burn hotly for and desire passionately to enjoy what they cannot see or hear; I resemble them in this way, for I desire what I do not have, which is to say the treasure of great knowledge given to those who love to have it" (lines 439–46). This eroticization of knowledge is perhaps not unrelated to the deaths in a relatively short time of the most important men in her life—Charles V, her father, and her husband—all associated with learning in Christine's mind. Cerquiglini suggests that these losses, or this single great loss, was the source of her decision to educate herself.[5]

By the end of the 1390s, Christine was ready for another *mutacion*. Her daughter Marie had entered the royal Dominican priory at Poissy in 1397; Christine had found a place for her son in the household of the earl of Salisbury in 1398 (Laidlaw, "Christine de Pizan, the Earl of Salisbury"); and her third child, a daughter, seems to have died at about the same time (Willard, *Christine de Pizan: Her Life* 42–43). She had acquired a respectable reputation as a poet in court circles and educated herself extensively in "serious" literature. The first manifestation of this new change were three works written around 1398–1400: her *Enseignemens moraux* (*Moral Teachings*), a book of instruction written ostensibly for her adolescent son on his departure for England; the *Epistre Othea* (*Othea's Letter to Hector*), a "mirror for princes" written for Louis of Orléans in the form of a letter from the goddess Othea to the fifteen-year-old Hector; and *L'epistre au dieu d'amours* (*Letter of the God of Love*), a treatise against those who speak ill of women, presented in the form of a letter from Cupid. Although these works manifest a significant shift in the tone and focus of Christine's writing, they grew out of her experience and past work. In the first two works, she plays a motherly role that was familiar to her personally and had established literary precedents, while the third, despite its new ideas, still belonged to the genre of love poetry and was based on her personal experience.[6]

Christine's *mutacion* during these years is marked most prominently by her participation in *Le débat sur* Le roman de la rose (1401–02), a public argument over the value of Jean de Meun's portion of the work and, more generally, the misogynous treatment of women in literature, of which it was held to be an example. Christine was disturbed by the portrayal of women she found in many of the works she had read over the preceding ten years and wanted to do what she could to change a cultural discourse that continued to belittle their abilities and achievements. She was also aware, however, that some part of her success and fame was due to the fact that she was a woman.[7] There is moreover something vaguely patricidal in Christine's criticism of Jean de Meun. As Zink points out, the poetic tradition through which Christine had established a place for herself at the court and in her world "was the daughter of the *Romance of the Rose* and owed almost everything to it" ("Poètes courtois" 42). Her critique of this ur-poem was probably heartfelt, but it also represented a break with the literary fathers in whose shadow she had matured and offered a rare opportunity for an established woman poet to enter a new, more "serious" part of the literary field.

Christine saw the years between 1399 and 1402 as a time of careful transition. She knew that she was writing a new kind of literature that required the authority that comes with learning and reflection and that had been relatively closed to women up until then. As Andrea Tarnowski writes, Christine's dedication of *Le chemin de lonc estude* (*The Path of Long Study*) to Charles VI in 1402 conveys

> not only conventional humility, the modesty required of an author addressing a powerful patron, but also genuine timidity on Christine's part. She begs the king not to fault her for being presumptuous; she is well aware that her womanhood is an 'indignité' (line 28) . . . her status is precarious . . . . The *Chemin de long estude* . . . is thus at once a *mise en scène* of the uncertainty Christine feels about her ability, or her right, to write like the erudite men of her day, and the remedy for the same uncertainty.
> ("Lessons" 182; see Christine, *Chemin*, lines 23–34, 51–56 and *Le livre de la mutacion*, lines 1–50)

In her *Livre de l'advision* a few years later, Christine herself divides her production into two periods, the work before 1399 and the work afterward: "Then I began to forge pretty things, more superficial when I began, and like the artisan whose work becomes more subtle the more he works, my understanding was increasingly imbued with uncommon things as I continued to study various matters, from 1399, when I began, until this year of 1405, and I have not yet stopped" (3.10.45–51).

Christine developed her manliness, in the sense meant by Jerome and by Jacobus de Voragine, over a period of roughly ten years (1390–1400) punctuated by two major *mutacions*: her decision to become a poet and undertake a substantial self-education around 1392 and her decision to become an author of serious literature rather than simply a poet around 1399. She may at one point in her life have complained facetiously that she had not been born a man (*Città delle dame* 44, 46; 1.1) or even felt that she in fact had been born one (*Livre de la mutacion*, lines 171–72), but as the trajectory of her career shows, to paraphrase a more recent author, one is not born a man, one becomes one.[8]

NOTES

Translations from Middle and modern French are my own unless otherwise noted.

[1]Christine, *Le livre des fais et bonnes meurs du sage roy Charles V* 1: ix; Willard, *Christine de Pizan: Her Life* 34. It is intriguing, however, that a Pierre du Chastel is listed among the royal notaries in a royal ordinance concerning the royal notaries and secretaries from 1359 (Morel 516).

[2]Delisle 1: 10–20; Christine, *Livre des fais et bonnes meurs* 1: ix (note 3), lxxvi–lxxvii; Willard, *Christine de Pizan: Her Life* 28, 30, 42.

[3]*Le livre de l'advision* 3.4.29; Christine, *Livre du dit de Poissy*; Altmann, *Love Debate Poems* 20–21; Willard, "Dominican Abbey."

[4]It is interesting to compare Christine's situation with that of Agnès d'Orléans, the wife of a Parisian *libraire* who died in 1349 or 1350, leaving her with three young children to support (Rouse and Rouse 1: 273–74, 2: 12).

[5]See *Le livre de l'advision* 3.5.1–3.6.17, 3.8.2–9, 3.9.2–21; Cerquiglini, "L'étrangère" 243, "Le goût" 597–600, "Christine de Pizan and the Book" 112, and "Christine de Pizan et le scandale" 46.

[6]On her artistic and intellectual caution and her tendency to base her authority on experience rather than on learning as she evolved during this crucial period, see Dulac, "Thèmes"; Christine, *Le livre de l'advision* xvii, xx–xi and *Chemin* 22–28; Roux 224–25.

[7]"I gave gifts [to princes] of new things . . . my volumes on various subjects, which they welcomed and received joyously out of their grace as kind and most humane princes—more, I believe, because it is unusual for a woman to write, and had not occurred for a long while, than for the distinction of the things they contained" (*Le livre de l'advision* 3.11.10–16; cf. 3.12.2–6).

[8]Beauvoir 497.

Christine and Her Audience

Deborah McGrady

Christine de Pizan can easily take on monumental proportions in the classroom because of her extraordinary position as a woman author, a protofeminist, and a prolific poet. Whether I am teaching her alone or as one of many writers—either in a medieval context, a survey course, or a women writers seminar—graduate and undergraduate students alike never cease to express astonishment at her daring pronouncements against contemporaries, her haughty didacticism, and her unrelenting condemnation of unacceptable behaviors, whether about the treatment of women or the failures of princes to rule appropriately. As a student once exclaimed after reading *Le livre de la cité des dames*, "This lady is unplugged!" For that student and many others, Christine's writing seems to test the limits of social acceptability. And yet, key to understanding Christine is the realization that she was speaking to an attentive and, by all appearances, enthralled audience. Regardless of course context, I always reserve time to consider this audience. The student's reference to her being "unplugged," a term used generally to refer to acoustic music and colloquially to refer to unguarded speech, is rich with significance. The success of Christine as a writer was not exclusively based on what she dared to say but also on the ways she manipulated conventional author-audience dynamics to ensure a more favorable venue for her texts and her message.

To appreciate Christine's savvy manipulation of the medieval literary economy, we must first consider her known and implied readers as well as the audience dynamics, both real and imagined, that shaped her works. Shifting attention to her audience exposes the limitations of the traditional approach to medieval literary dynamics, which prioritizes the patronage paradigm. Christine's corpus challenges this paradigm through the sheer quantity of dedicatees named in her works as well as through the varied accounts of literary circulation that define her writings. In this essay, I present the vibrant account of medieval literary economics revealed in her corpus, then discuss how this material can be integrated into a single lesson focused on the author's audience.

Christine's Privileged Readers

Conventional scholarly wisdom claims that medieval authors, whether wandering minstrels or court-appointed writers, depended on an intimate and personalized relationship with a generous lord or lady for financial and social survival. Typically this relationship is viewed as an intimate, exclusive, and mutually beneficial bond between two individuals. As Paul Zumthor puts it, the medieval poet served as mouthpiece or entertainer for the patron and lived by the maxim "À toi ma prose ou mes vers, avec ta permission ou sur ton ordre; à moi, de quoi manger" ("To you my prose or my verses, either with your permission or by your command; to me, the means to eat"; 45; my trans.). Medieval textual and visual depictions of patronage appear to justify this reading. Manuscripts are populated by dedicatees who are portrayed receiving gift books, identified as having requested works, and on occasion presented as creative collaborators. Dedications draw on the mutually dependent tropes of gift exchange and feudalism to create a hieratic relationship in which the dedicatee is cast as patron. In presentation scenes, the author is depicted on bended knee to reinforce the power and esteem conferred on the chosen recipient. But these accounts narrate events that have not yet occurred when the book is completed; they are best understood as scripts that imagine what might transpire between author and dedicatee. An intimate scene of transmission often disguises a more complex calculus of exchange.

Christine regularly revealed the dissonance between scripted scenes and actual literary circulation practices. In *The Vision of Christine de Pizan*, also translated as *Christine's Vision* (*Le livre de l'advision Cristine*), for example, she explains how her literary fame developed:

> It is true that as word of the order and manner of my life, that is its studiousness, had already spread and even among the princes—for even though I would have preferred it hidden, it was revealed to them—I presented them as novelties, small and feeble though they were, from my books on various subjects, which by their grace, as kind and gentle princes, they willingly saw and joyfully received them and more, I think, for the novelty of a woman who could write (since that had not occurred for quite some time) than for any worth there might be therein. In this way my said books were in a short time discussed and carried into several places and various countries. (*Vision* [McLeod and Willard] 106)

The author's savvy use of the humility topos should not distract us from the unusual account of literary circulation detailed here. Where tradition suggests that the poet must seek out a potential patron, Christine reveals that her works quickly became commodities in high demand. This shift in the status of her books is at first disguised by her scripted language —"I presented" and "they . . . received"—but even here the shift from a single recipient to many recipients troubles the narrative. She acknowledges that her works thereafter circulated throughout Europe and beyond her control, shattering the myth of literary intimacy. In *Christine's Vision*, this unconventional account of the author's fame is supported by examples of how her success took shape: she recalls the ensuing invitations she received for her son to represent her at the court of England (106) and for her to reside both at the royal English court and at the court of the duke of Milan (106–08).

Additional references to her readers in her corpus reveal a veritable who's who of fifteenth-century France. Among her dedicatees are the queen of France,

Isabeau of Bavaria; the king of France, Charles VI; two of the king's uncles, Philip the Bold, duke of Burgundy, and John, duke of Berry; Mary of Berry, the youngest daughter of the duke of Berry; Duke Philip's successor, John the Fearless; the king's brother, Duke Louis of Orléans; Charles d'Albret, cousin to the king; the seneschal of Hainaut, royal officer and fellow poet; and the dauphin and dauphine, Louis and Margaret of Guyenne.

Always attentive to the political climate, Christine introduced a number of strategies to accommodate her ever-growing audience and the political conflicts in which its members were embroiled. She sometimes played off of these conflicts to position her writings. For instance, at the head of *Le débat sur* Le roman de la rose (*The Debate on* The Romance of the Rose), she invites Isabeau of Bavaria to adjudicate the quarrel, thereby reiterating the queen's official role since 1401 as arbiter between the rival dukes of Orléans and Burgundy (see McGrady, "De 'l'onneur'"; see, more generally, Adams, *Life*). The dispute between these dukes may also explain her decision to preface the *Epistre Othea* (*Othea's Letter to Hector*) originally dedicated to Louis of Orléans with a revised dedication addressed to the new recipient, the duke of Burgundy.[1] A different strategy marks the dedication to *Le livre du chemin de lonc estude* (*The Book of the Path of Long Study*), where King Charles VI was declared its first recipient, while a generalized address to other "princes tres haulz" ("most worthy princes," lines 10–23) opened the door for a second wave of dissemination. In fact, Christine supervised the production of multiple copies of the work that were then distributed to the Valois dukes. Her next work, *Le livre de la mutacion de Fortune* (*The Book of the Mutation of Fortune*) omitted entirely the dedication and thus named no privileged recipient, a strategy that facilitated multipronged dissemination of the work to the dukes of Berry and Burgundy in 1404, with a third copy likely undertaken for the duke of Orléans (Ouy et al. 413–76). Christine later identified the last of these gift books as having inspired the duke of Burgundy to assume the official role of patron and to commission *Le livre des fais et bonnes meurs du sage roy Charles V* (*The Book of Deeds and Good Practices of the Wise King Charles V*)(2: ii, 43). When the duke suddenly died before the work was completed, Christine cultivated a new audience by embedding in the biography praise for several living Valois princes who could be expected to take an interest in the work. Finally, between 1406 and 1411, she undertook large-scale projects for several members of the dynasty. The new duke of Burgundy rewarded her first in 1406 and then in 1411 for books received; the duke of Berry paid her for a collection of her works in 1408; and Christine answered a royal request in 1410–1411 when presenting the queen of France with an anthology of her writings. The Queen's Codex, British Library, Harley 4431, opens with a dedicatory prologue in which the poet recalls the queen's commission and details the work it required (lines 49–60). The accompanying frontispiece conjures an intimate donation scene that places Christine in the queen's private chambers surrounded by the queen and her ladies-in-waiting. This staged exchange trumped all the other presentation scenes included in the codex, where the poet was depicted offering the enclosed works to different dedicatees (McGrady, "What Is"). Christine's success as France's "first author" (Poirion, *Littérature française* 206) or "first professional writer" (Willard, *Christine de Pizan: Her Life and Works*, 2) is due in large part to these shrewd manipulations. She chose to curry favor from many rather than limit herself to intimate exchange with a single individual.

Christine on Literary Exchange Economies

Christine's dealings with multiple potential patrons were at the time unparalleled, and they document an array of economic networks that are frequently glossed over in discussions of her patronage activity. Note that she describes her works in three ways: those that circulated as unsolicited offerings, those that were commissioned or solicited, and those that were created to meet a demand.

Christine characterized several of her early literary forays as unsolicited gifts freely offered. The prologues of her three judgment poems, *Le livre du debat de deux amans* (*The Book of the Debate of Two Lovers*), *Le livre des trois jugemens* ("The Book of the Three Judgments"), and *Le livre du dit de Poissy* (*The Tale of Poissy*), express the hope that their designated recipients will enjoy and benefit from her offerings. Sometimes she presented unsolicited gifts within the formalized structure of New Year's gifting. In these cases, gift poems repackaged a work as an *étrenne* or gift, as is the case in ballades 26 and 21 of *Autres balades* ("Other Ballades"), where copies of works are presented to the queen and to Charles d'Albret, respectively. The *Epistre Othea* was packaged as a New Year's gift for Louis of Orléans (line 33), and Christine states that she offered the duke of Burgundy a copy of the *Mutacion* as a New Year's gift in 1404 (*Livre des fais et bonnes meurs* [Solente] 1: 1, 43). These unsolicited offerings, however, went with an expectation of reciprocation, a condition that Marcel Mauss associates with all gifts. Christine regularly intimated that future requests for her works would be a worthy response to her gift. For example, tailored addresses to the dukes of Berry and Burgundy heading their personalized copies of *Othea* suggest that they might "develop an appetite" ("prendre appetit"; appendix 1: 504, line 28, and 508, line 28) for her other works that treated worthy subjects. It appears that the dukes took Christine up on her offer, since, as we have seen, Duke Philip commissioned his brother's biography thereafter and Duke John of Berry acquired a copy of her complete works around 1408.

Christine's unsolicited gifts, under the best circumstances, resulted in commissions. A commission, whether for a new work or a copy of an earlier work, established a clientelistic relationship between the recipient, now officially the patron, and the author, who would answer the needs and demands of the patron. A commission entailed a request for work in advance, thereby introducing an implicit agreement from the outset that the poet would be rewarded for the final product. Even when a work did not reflect her interests, Christine found value in acknowledging its commissioned status. *Le livre du duc des vrais amans* (*The Book of the Duke of True Lovers*) and the *Cent balades d'amant et de dame* (*One Hundred Ballades of a Lover and Lady*) open with an account of the recipient-author arrangement: the poet expresses her noninterest in the imposed topic and describes the resulting work not as a gift but as a debt (*amende*) owed to her superior (McGrady, "Authorship" 31).

That Christine could play so boldly with a system that obviously ensured her survival speaks to the steady growth of her fame and the eventual introduction of her works into a demand-driven economy. She made clear the demand for her books when recounting the development of her fame in *Christine's Vision*. Her awareness of public demand for her writings might explain why she increasingly addressed a diverse public in her later works. We have already seen how she expanded her audience of noble readers, but she also increasingly acknowledged a more humble audience beyond the princes and princesses whose requests occupied so much of her professional life. In *Le livre de la cité des dames* (*The Book of the City of Ladies*), *Le livre de l'advision Cristine*, *Le livre des fais d'armes et de chevallerie* (*The Book of the Deeds of Arms and Chivalry*), *Les heures de contemplacion sur la passion de Nostre Seigneur* (*The Hours of Contemplation on the Passion of our Lord*), and *Le ditié de Jehanne d'Arc* (*The Tale of Joan of Arc*), she eschews dedications to list numerous individuals or groups as part of her anticipated audience. Even works that do identify a privileged recipient, such as *La lamentacion sur les maux de la France* (*The Lamentation on the Woes of France*), offered to the duke of Berry; *Le livre de paix* (*The Book of Peace*), presented to the dauphin; and *L'epistre de la prison de vie humaine* (*A Letter Concerning the Prison of Human Life*), addressed to Marie de Berry, acknowledge an audience beyond the immediate recipient. The *Lamentation* reminds all princes of their obligations, and the *Prison* speaks of the work having been commissioned to comfort all ladies who have lost loved ones during the war. Finally, when producing luxury copies of her collected works, Christine and collaborating artists emphasized her vast community of readers. In Harley 4431, the illuminators responsible for the 132-miniature cycle included numerous depictions of an anticipated readership that went beyond the nobility to include Christine's son, clerics, members of the bourgeoisie, courtiers, and women of all classes.

Audience in the Classroom

Despite her protestations, Christine was not a curiosity but a savvy exploiter of the contemporary demand for books. She cultivated a diverse audience and actively oversaw the expansion of her fame. To bring students to this realization, I use a discovery mode of teaching, having them confront their own stereotypes about author-audience relations as they reenact Christine's description in *Christine's Vision* of the progressive transformation of her writings from small individual gift offerings to medieval best sellers bought and collected across Europe.

My lesson dedicated to Christine's audience always comes after one to several days of discussion about Christine. In preparation for class, students read a selection of prologues and key passages from Christine's writings dealing with audience. The following texts have proved the most successful, because they introduce students to a diversity of exchange situations: the prologues to *The Debate of Two Lovers* and *The Path of Long Study* invite discussion of the conventions of patronage rhetoric; the prologue to *The Book of the Duke of True Lovers* presents students with a countermodel of literary relations; the prologue to Charles V's biography, *Le livre des fais et bonnes meurs*, speaks to commissions; the closing address in *The City of Ladies*, the prologue to *The Tale of Poissy*, and the dedications preceding the *Debate on* The Romance of the Rose lead to a consideration of audience that includes members beyond the nobility; and the dedication to the queen of France in Harley 4431 or the various prologues to *Othea* introduce the logic of redistributing earlier works to new readers.

Given the radical alterity of medieval literature in terms of language, culture, and structure, students rarely stop to consider the context in which these works were produced or their intended public. I therefore begin our study of medieval patronage by posing a series of general questions concerning the role of the public in contemporary culture: Today, to what extent do music and movie producers, publishing houses, news presses, radio and television, art galleries, and finally the target audience dictate what art is? To what extent do writers, musicians, and artists take into account their intended audience when creating works of art? Who are today's patrons? Students' answers to these questions often lead to a lively conversation about the importance of audience to artistic production, the role of those who dictate what is filtered to the public, and issues of propaganda, censorship, and elitism. By beginning with questions about students' own culture, I am able to set the terms for a more complex consideration of medieval audience.

I then ask some basic questions about Christine: Who was her audience? How would the audience access a work by her? How did the work circulate? Answers vary with each class, but responses always generate a list of named patrons from assigned readings as well as more generalized audiences (e.g., the court, women). Students' answers, written on the board, are visual evidence that Christine was widely read. I present a map that indicates the territorial divisions of the period, and I locate the different courts on that map. I add to the list of audience members the names of patrons not mentioned in students' readings. For instance, I recount the stories of Henry IV and of the duke of Milan, who both took special interest in Christine. I then introduce the types of literary exchange networks, discussed above, that defined a given text as an unsolicited gift, a commission, or a commodity and ask the students to provide examples of these types from their readings.

I place students into small groups and ask each group to examine closely one of three prologues from the previous evening's reading assignment. I provide them with a corresponding miniature decorating a copy of the work in question. I typically choose images from the Harley manuscript (www.pizan.lib.ed.ac.uk/output.html) or from the complete works collections purchased by the duke of Berry and now housed at the Bibliothèque Nationale de France (gallica.bnf.fr). I restrict discussion to these two collections so that after comparing text-image relations, we can consider the dialogue between miniatures in a given manuscript cycle as well as the potentially different messages communicated by each codex.

From Christine's remarks in her prologues and from the students' answers to questions, we have gathered information about Christine's audience. We then compare the prologues with the illuminations: What supplementary information about the literary exchange dynamics can be culled from the visual depiction of a scene? What aspects of the text does the illustration privilege?

Each group shares its observations with the class. I use their comments as an impetus to cover additional information. I introduce students to the codicological scholarship of James Laidlaw, Christine Reno, and Gilbert Ouy that argues for Christine's role as supervisor of the production of many of her manuscripts, as well as Tracy Adams's recent reassessment in *Christine de Pizan and the Fight for France* of Christine's efforts to support Louis of Orléans's political agenda in her writings. With this scholarship in mind, we consider how the artists who created the miniatures portrayed Christine in both dress and posture as occupying a predominantly subservient role. I draw their attention, however, to visual assertions of authorial ownership as suggested by the firm grasp Christine always keeps on her books, the near-constant costume she dons (which facilitates identification of the author), and the use of rubrics to identify the poet in the image. When considering the opening illuminations to *The Path of Long Study* or the *Othea*, I direct students' attention to the important role clothing, accoutrements, and location play in identifying the recipient as a formidable figure and worthy reader of Christine's work. Scenes from *Othea* also imply a larger audience by depicting an entourage observing the donation. The hand gestures of these witnesses often direct our gaze to the gift and help visually signal the value placed on the book. In the Queen's Manuscript, we analyze the aggressive interpersonal dynamics displayed in the opening miniature to *The Book of the Duke of True Lovers*, in which the poet appears trapped by the duke and his men, who block the door, as well as the significance of locating the patron in the poet's study. This invasion of the poet's work space contrasts sharply with previous scenes of the poet's bringing the bound book to the patron. We compare this image of poet and patron in the poet's study with the unique donation scene heading MS Harley 4431, which transpires in the queen's private chambers. Students are by this point attuned to the alternative message of collaboration between poet and patron and the notion of a community of like-minded readers expressed in this frontispiece.

I present several other evocative illustrations, especially those depicting a nonnoble audience, such as the frontispieces to *Enseignemens moraux* (*Moral Teachings*), *Proverbes moraulx* (*Moral Proverbs*), and various scenes from the *Othea* where large audiences read from books. I invite students to consider the possible response of the queen to the codex she was offered: What would she think, turning the folios, about seeing images that so many other readers were seeing? I lead students to consider how the illustrations suggest the notion of Christine's corpus as a coveted object desired and read by many. We also discuss the hidden message recorded in the many images decorating the queen's book. Isabeau was clearly not Christine's exclusive patron but rather the owner of this specific copy of her works. Returning to *Othea* illustrations and the groups of readers they depict, I inform students that this work in particular represents the most widely disseminated text by Christine and that given the quality of a number of copies, we suspect it was purchased and owned by many nonnoble readers. Clearly, her audience reached beyond the elite readers spotlighted in these texts.

I close the lesson by handing out the quotation from *Christine's Vision* cited above and invite students to consider the fossilized accounts of literary exchange and the restrictive views on the success of women writers, stereotypes that Christine reshaped when positioning herself in the literary economy. I conclude by pointing out that, both in her texts and in conjunction with the miniaturists responsible for decorating these collections, she deliberately influenced these viewpoints to cultivate a unique and memorable authorial identity. By the end of class, I hope that students realize that far from being "unplugged," Christine was highly attuned to contemporary literary systems and that she manipulated them with great skill in order to promote her works.

NOTE

[1] In total, three known new dedications were composed for later dissemination of the *Othea*. For treatment of these prologues, see *Epistre Othea* [Parussa] 81–87; all extant versions of the prologue are provided in appendix 1 (501–09).

Visions of History in the Works of Christine de Pizan

Renate Blumenfeld-Kosinski

"Je suis comme toi femme italienne" ("I am, like you, an Italian woman"), Christine de Pizan says to Minerva in the prologue to her *Livre des fais d'armes et de chevallerie* (13; *Book of Deeds of Arms and of Chivalry*), but every element in her political writings and her approach to history tells us that she loved the French nation and that its well-being and unity were close to her heart. This emotional investment in her adopted country frequently led Christine to interweave her own story with ancient and contemporary French history, a technique that represents a thoroughly original approach to writing history.[1]

I teach Christine's works in a variety of settings: a graduate seminar devoted exclusively to her works; a graduate course called Literature and Politics in the Late Middle Ages; and an undergraduate course taught in French or English, Women's Voices in French Literature from the Middle Ages to the Twenty-First Century. I place different emphases on her historical writings, depending on the course. In a seminar focused primarily on Christine's texts, students can chart the progression from her early lyric production to her more serious works (often in prose) that provide insights into medieval history and use ancient history in a moral and exemplary mode. A good passage for analyzing this evolution is chapter 10 in the third book of *Le livre de l'advision Cristine* (*Christine's Vision*), in which Christine describes her early "choses jolies" ("pretty things") giving way to the "plus grant soubtillité et plus haulte matiere" (111; "great subtlety and more serious subject matter") of her later works.

In a course on late medieval literature and politics, students can compare Christine's works with those of her contemporaries, such as Philippe de Mézières (1327–1405) and Alain Chartier (1385/95–1430). Philippe de Mézières's *Songe du viel pelerin* (*Dream of the Old Pilgrim*), for example, in many ways prefigures Christine's *Le livre du chemin de lonc estude* (*The Book of the Path of Long Study*), showing a traveler accompanied by allegorical figures bearing witness to the political crises of his times. In Alain Chartier's *Quadrilogue invectif* (*An Invective of Four Voices*), students can trace many of the themes of Christine's *Advision*, in particular the allegorical figure of France complaining to her children, and the use of ancient Roman history to provide behavioral models for contemporary rulers and knights.

Finally, in my course Women's Voices, which is focused on how women writers create authority, I stress the emergence in Christine's works of the unprecedented voice of a female historian. Good starting points for a discussion on her authority as a historian include the opening sections of the *Chemin* and the *Advision*, as well as the sections in *Le livre de la mutacion de Fortune* (*The Book of the Mutability of Fortune*) in which Christine's authorial persona transcribes the historical events depicted on the walls of Fortune's castle.

Throughout her career Christine inscribed historical events into her works, often in ways that depart, sometimes radically, from the conventions of contemporary chronicles and historiography. The historical for her was always firmly embedded in the literary and even the autobiographical. Her texts are anchored in past and present events but also point to the future, a positive future that she hopes to shape through her literary interventions.

The Main Crises of Christine's Time

Christine responded in both poetry and prose to the many crises of her time. For any class on her it is a good idea to highlight those events and analyze how she wrote about them: the Hundred Years War as it progressed from the time of Charles V to the arrival of Joan of Arc; Charles VI's madness, which began in 1392, resulted in the ascendancy and conflicts of his uncles and cousins, and culminated in the civil war triggered by the assassination of Louis, duke of Orléans in 1407; and the Great Schism of the Western Church (1378–1417).[2] For every one of these crises Christine's major concern was that of unity: the integrity of France was being destroyed from without by the English and from within by warring factions; the Church was torn apart by two and eventually three popes, and this division undermined the unity of Christendom. Christine saw herself as a witness to the history of her time as well as a participant who sought to intervene.

In the *Advision*, the Hundred Years War is singled out by the allegorical figure of France as the moment when true disaster struck. Christine dramatizes France's complaint by having France lay out the details of recent French history, beginning in book 1, chapter 10. Here students, analyzing the vocabulary of rape and mutilation, can understand how Christine emphasizes the vulnerability of her adopted country by representing that country as a suffering female figure. After the composition of the *Advision* in 1405, the Hundred Years War recedes from Christine's historical writings, only to reemerge in 1418 as the motivation for her composition of *L'epistre de la prison de la vie humaine* (*A Letter Concerning the Prison of Human Life*). The battle of Agincourt, which in 1415 killed or imprisoned the flower of French chivalry, is the impetus for this spiritual letter addressed to Marie de Berry. Christine advocates a turning away from this world, exhorting her readers to embrace the next world as the only consolation left to them. She thus depicts the situation in France as hopeless—and it was, for in 1420 the English King Henry V (1387–1422) was recognized as the heir to the French throne in the Treaty of Troyes, and the dauphin Charles, after his father's death in 1422, was forced to wander France without having been crowned. The hopelessness reflected in the *Epistre* is finally dispelled in Christine's *Ditié de Jehanne d'Arc* (*Tale of Joan of Arc*) of 1429. The divine mission of the young peasant girl from Lorraine, in eastern France, was to chase the English from French territory, and at the moment Christine writes the poem, it looks as if Joan might succeed. Joan did crown King Charles VII in 1429 but was betrayed and executed shortly afterward. The *Ditié* is a wonderful text to teach as marking the endpoint of Christine's career and as temporarily fulfilling her dream of French unity and the end of the war between the French and the English.

The second great crisis of Christine's time, the French civil war, surfaces vividly in the *Advision* as the figure of France blames revolts and civil strife for her wounds. Chapter 14 of book 1, in which France contends that her maternal body has been lacerated and torn apart by her own children, contains excellent passages for student analysis (*Le livre de l'advision* 25–27). This chapter also provides an opportunity for students to explore Christine's comparison of the body politic and a suffering female body.

The most important text for understanding Christine's grief and outrage in the face of the growing civil war is *La lamentacion sur les maux de la France* (*The Lamentation on the Evils That Have Befallen France*). Students can hear her tearful voice and analyze the striking imagery she uses to exhort the warring dukes to peace. Metaphors of the body and of illness, appeals to family relations, and predictions of France's ruin all contribute to her dramatic portrayal (Blumenfeld-Kosinski, "Enemies"). This heartrending work will bring home to students how Christine viewed the effects of this conflict.

Finally, teachers can ask students to trace the chronology of *Le livre de paix* (*The Book of Peace*) in order to demonstrate that the very composition of this tripartite work dramatizes Christine's awareness of and close involvement with the contemporary developments of the civil war. As Christine states in her preface, she began to write on 1 September 1412, when a peace treaty was concluded between the ducal parties. She stopped writing when the treaty was broken, and she restarted the book in September 1413, when peace again seemed at hand (Book of Peace [Green] 58, 200). *Le livre de paix* also provides good examples of her view of historical continuity when it comes to discord: she shows that societal self-destruction through internal division can be traced from Troy and Rome all the way to France: "par discord perirent" ("through discord they perished"; 231 [1.3]; 94). This trajectory from Troy via Rome to France reflects the medieval topos of *translatio imperii*, or the movement of empires. Usually employed to highlight the transmission of the glory of empires, the topos here serves as a warning of the dangers posed by perpetual civil strife.

Students will probably not be as familiar with the Great Schism of the Western Church as they are with the Hundred Years War. It is therefore important to stress that this long-lasting division of the Church—opposing two and at times even three popes in often violent conflict—caused much anxiety among medieval Christians (see Blumenfeld-Kosinski, *Poets*, esp. ch. 5). Unlike the Hundred Years War and the plague, the schism did not become part of the popular *imaginaire* of the calamitous fourteenth century, but Christine paid much attention to it. In the wake of her contemporaries Philippe de Mézières and Honorat Bovet (Bovet wrote a dream vision of the schism in 1389), Christine addressed this problem in a number of her works. In the *Chemin*, for example, she bemoans the desolation of God's Church, abandoned by its pastors (lines 371–75). In her 1403 prayer to the Virgin, *L'oroyson Nostre Dame* (*Prayers to Our Lady*), she prays for the Church's salvation. But it is in the *Mutacion* that she speaks most forcefully about the schism: she indicts the two popes, neither of whom wants to yield his power (*Le livre de la mutacion* [Solente] 2: 145 [esp. lines 4315–34]). She also blames the secular rulers, who through their adherence to one or the other pope divide all Europe.

A year later we find Christine astutely analyzing the origins of the schism in mostly muted terms in ten chapters of her biography of Charles V, but at the end she cannot restrain her emotions and exclaims, "Ce doloreux sisme, et envenimée plante contagieuse, fichée par instigacion de l'Anemi ou giron sainte Eglise. O quell flayel!" (2: 155–56 [Solente]; part 3, ch. 61; "This painful schism and poisonous, contagious plant that was thrust into the bosom of the Holy Church at the instigation of the devil. Oh, what a scourge!"). The following year she returns to the schism in the *Advision*, where in the preface she refers to the ruin of the Church (10) and expands on this crisis in a veiled, allegorical manner (bk. 1, ch. 12). In the *Sept psaumes allégorisés* ("Seven Allegorized Psalms"), she responds to recent developments of the Council of Pisa that resulted in three popes' vying for power. Analyzing her concern with the schism can show students that her engagement with contemporary history extended beyond the immediate concerns of France and included the pan-European problem of the divided Church.

The Voices and Forms of Christine's Historical Writings

Christine found herself at the intersection of multiple political and ecclesiastical crises that took on ever greater importance in her works, and over the years her involvement in politics became more and more direct. Her voice is not, however, that of an objective chronicler of her time; it is shaped by a passionate participation in the mostly troubled history of the late fourteenth and the first half of the fifteenth centuries. This emotional involvement and the many voices Christine creates to convey historical events and her feelings about them sets her apart from her male contemporaries.

The *Chemin*, an allegorical dream journey, can be considered Christine's first overtly political text. Close readings of crucial passages demonstrate how Christine creates a persona that will authorize her to intervene in the politics of her time. Pivotal scenes include her meditations on Boethius, which lead her to an exposition of her society's problems; her encounter with the sibyl who will be her guide; the discussions at the heavenly court that define responsibilities for all parts of society; and her designation as secretary and messenger, authorized by heavenly beings to intervene in contemporary history (lines 453–786, 2599–6278, 6279–398).

In her works, Christine participates in various ways in the historical events she describes. In the *Chemin* she is a traveler who witnesses the problems of her contemporary environment, while in the *Mutacion* she provides an allegorical version of her life story in the opening section. This biography includes her famous transformation into a man, signifying her assumption of a new social position but also the creation of a new, masculine voice, that of a historian. But the manuscript illuminations that show her contemplating the walls in Fortune's castle depict her as a woman; thus, a new species is created: the female historian (see Margolis, "Poetess"). Given this new female authoritative voice, it is striking that in the *Mutacion* women's roles are not the crucial element of the world's history they will become in *Le livre de la cité des dames* (*The Book of the City of Ladies*) a few years later. In part 3 of the *Mutacion*, Christine justifies her exclusion of women from her universal history: "Ci dit la cause pour quoy femmes n'ont esté ci ramenteues" (lines 6617–74; "she explains why women are not remembered here"). Even vicious women (and there are some, though not many) have little impact on the state of the world, since they play no role in government affairs (lines 6624–30). This passage provides a good springboard for a discussion comparing Christine's stances in the *Mutacion* and the *Cité des dames*. Has Christine changed her mind about women's roles? Is her exclusion of vicious women from the city the key to women's history? How is the *Cité des dames* a response to the exclusionary stance she adopted in the *Mutacion*, and what does the text say about her ideas concerning female rulership (see Adams, "Christine de Pizan")?

Christine's technique of recounting history in the *Mutacion* relies on the rhetorical figure of ekphrasis; that is, the paintings on the castle's walls and what they depict are described: segments of her society, the seven liberal arts, and the history of the world from creation to her time (though there is a huge gap between Julius Caesar and the late fourteenth century). Her voice here is that of a learned observer, a transmitter of historical facts, and a moralizing commentator.

Eventually Christine becomes a historian of France. In the *Advision*, book 1, chapters 5–6, she describes how she attained her greatest desire: to make the acquaintance of the "dame renommee," the famed lady that is France. The lady bestows the greatest honor on her by naming Christine her "antygraphe" ("scribe"). Christine's vocation as a historian is confirmed as a "divine and natural" mission, and French history takes on a confessional cast when France tells her:

> Amie, a qui Dieux et Nature ont concedé oultre le commun ordre des femmes le don d'amour d'estude, apreste parchemin, ancre et plume et escrips les parolles yssans de ma poitrine, car a toy me vueil je du tout manifester et me plaist qu'a tes saiges bien vueillans faces d'ores en avant present des memoires escriptes de ma dignité. (16)

> Dear friend, to whom God and Nature have granted the gift of the love of learning beyond the common order of women, prepare parchment, ink and quill and write down the words issuing from my breast, for I want to reveal everything to you, and I am pleased that through your wise good-will you will from now on present written memories of my worthiness.

No passage from Christine's work can better help students analyze her methods of self-authorization as a serious writer of history.

As the text continues, Christine assumes the voice of a privileged listener while the allegorical figure of France recites her own painful history. At the end of the first book of the *Advision*, France once again defines Christine's task, but now the mission is polemical: Christine must urge France's children to have pity on their tender mother and not suck her sweet breasts down to the blood (50). Christine has transformed herself from a chronicler into a writer who exhorts the population of France to restore internal peace.

Her voice changes as events in France become more and more dire and as she chooses nonallegorical genres for her texts. In her biography of Charles V, she acts as a witness to the reign of this wise king, deriving her own authority in many ways from that of the monarch (see Dulac, "Authority"). In *Le livre du corps de policie* (*The Book of the Body Politic*), she adopts the didactic voice of the mirror-of-princes genre, instructing the rulers of her time in the virtuous princely conduct required in order to maintain a just body politic. She argues that women have a more passionate nature than men as a means to introduce her polemical goal of counseling the dauphin to become the perfect ruler: "Se il est possible que de vice puist naistre vertu, bien me plaist en ceste partie estre passionnee comme femme" ([Kennedy] 1; "If it is possible that virtue can be born from vice, it pleases me in this part to be as passionate as a woman"). This passion, a possible vice, informs her voice in this work dedicated to the dauphin, Louis of Guienne (1397–1415). In this period, the rivalries between the dukes of Orléans and Burgundy turned deadly: the duke of Orléans was murdered on the order of his cousin, the duke of Burgundy, in November 1407. Christine clearly sees her book as a means to intervene in this historical crisis.[3]

Her voice becomes even more passionate in *La lamentacion sur les maux de la France*, written in 1410, a critical moment when the warring dukes formed more coherent parties and set armies against each other. On one side was the party of the Armagnacs (also known as the League of Gien), formed with Charles d'Orléans (whose father-in-law was Bernard of Armagnac) and the dukes of Berry, Brittany, and Bourbon. On the other side was the powerful Burgundian party led by John the Fearless. Armagnac forces are moving on Paris when Christine cries out to the duke of Berry in her *Lamentacion*:

> Seulette à part, et estraignant à grant paine les lermes qui ma veue troublent et comme fontaine affluent sur mon visage, tant que avoir puisse

> espace de escripre ceste lasse complainte, dont la pitié de l'eminent mischief me fait d'ameres goutes effacier l'escripture, je m'esbahiz et en complaignant dis. ([Kennedy] 180)

> Alone and apart I hold back with great difficulty the tears that obscure my vision and run like a fountain over my face, so that I will have room to write this sad complaint; the pity for the great misfortunes causes me to erase my writing with bitter drops. I am stunned and cry out plaintively.

This exhortation at the eleventh hour to stop the growing civil war is one of Christine's most powerful texts, a forceful attempt to intervene in the course of French history.

Finally, Christine's voice changes to one of triumph and celebration when, in her last work, the *Ditié de Jehanne d'Arc* (*Tale of Joan of Arc*), she paints the victorious campaigns of the Maid, who crowned King Charles VII and seemed on the brink of chasing the English from French territory.

Christine's personal history often serves as a foil and reference point for historical events. Students might explore this technique by juxtaposing the *Mutacion* and the *Advision*. In the former, Christine's allegorical autobiography establishes her persona and culminates in the creation of a female historian. In the latter, her confession to Lady Philosophy (who eventually transforms herself into Lady Theology) comes after an exposition of French history and intellectual life, perhaps confirming Christine's startling claims in the preface to the *Advision* that her own life can be read as a parallel to sacred history: her family's arrival in France, for instance, can signify how faith was brought to France or even stand for the people of Israel arriving in the Promised Land (*Le livre de l'advision* 6). Teachers might dramatize this point by comparing passages from Jean Froissart or from Michel Pintoin (the chronicler of Saint-Denis) with some of Christine's historical works. Although both these chroniclers have well-defined personas and present themselves as witnesses, their life stories do not appear in their chronicles—nor do they suggest, as Christine does, that their biographies help us understand history.

The lessons Christine draws from ancient historians, such as Valerius Maximus, inform many of her works. In a manner that is more in line with the male chroniclers of her time, she uses stories from ancient history as both positive and negative examples of political and moral conduct. She integrates them in a variety of ways into her own texts: in *Le livre du corps de policie*, for instance, ancient examples are piled one on top of another to illustrate the necessary virtues of the prince, and in other texts ancient history is woven into various allegorical constructs. For the most part, Christine's sources for these ancient stories were French, not Latin, texts. She drew from compilations such as *Histoire ancienne jusqu'à César* (*Ancient History up to Julius Caesar*), a French prose text from the early thirteenth century that was the major source for her *Mutacion*, or from French translations of ancient historians, several of them commissioned by Charles V. Especially important was the translation of Valerius Maximus, made in 1375 by Simon de Hesdin. Students can derive Christine's motivations for quoting him abundantly from a passage in the *Corps de policie*: "Pour ce que le notable livre que fist Valere le grant des fais des Rommains me donne matere de prouver par exemple l'entencion pure a quoy je tens, laquelle est . . . de donner cause d'esmouvoir le couraige a vertu et bien vivre . . ." ([Kennedy] 22); "Because the important book that Valerius wrote about the deeds of the Romans gives me the subject matter to prove by example the pure intention I hold dear, which is to motivate people to live virtuously and well . . ."). This moral function of ancient examples is of course also the prime inspiration for *Le livre de la cité des dames*, in which the stories of women in ancient myth and history provide the building blocks for a new history based on feminine achievements.

Christine believed that ancient history was not as well known as contemporary history. This is why in her *Mutacion* she feels she has to justify the fact that she has spent over 20,000 lines on that subject:

> Les ancïenes racontees
> Plus prolixement et contees
> Ay que n'ay fait les plus nouvelles,
> Pour cause que l'en ot pas d'elles
> Tant parler comme des derraines,
> Qui plus sont communes et pleines (lines 283–88)

> I treated ancient history more at length than recent history because one does not hear as much about it as about more recent history, which is more commonly known and more complete.

She goes on to describe recent events, such as the life of Pierre de Lusignan, king of Cyprus (assassinated in 1369); the civil wars in Italy; the deeds of Jean le Bon, father of Charles V; and the death of the English king Richard II in 1400. By the impressive length of the sections on ancient history in the *Mutacion* students can see the importance Christine attributed to a solid foundation of historical knowledge. In addition, this prolix display of the deeds of the ancients allowed her to strengthen her new historian's voice, thereby establishing herself as a learned woman author.

The examples of her historical writings briefly laid out here demonstrate that she not only was aware of the historical events unfolding around her but also saw herself as a *poète engagée*, a writer engaged with history, be it ancient history marshaled for its vital lessons, or contemporary history, in whose disastrous course she attempted to intervene.

NOTES

All translations are my own. Translations are based on the following editions of Christine's works: *Le livre des fais d'armes et de chevallerie* (Laennec); *Le livre de la mutacion de Fortune* (Solente); *Le chemin de longue étude* (Tarnowski).

[1] For detailed analyses of how Christine constructed the historical and political voices of *clergesse* ("female clerk") and prophet, as well as of her uses of allegory and exemplary stories in her political writings, see Le Ninan.

[2] I provide concise information on the most important historical facts in the first section of "Christine de Pizan and the Political Life in Late Medieval France." For a more expansive treatment see Tracy Adams, *Christine de Pizan and the Fight for France.*

[3] Although a number of earlier scholars argued that Christine's loyalties were divided between the Burgundian and Armagnac factions, Tracy Adams makes a strong case for Christine's consistent support of the Armagnac faction and especially of Queen Isabeau of Bavaria, the wife of King Charles VI and the mother of the future Charles VII and a series of dauphins who died early deaths (*Christine de Pizan*).

Christine's Consoling Memory

Julia Simms Holderness

The confessional nature of Christine de Pizan's early writings has long fascinated scholars, and her moving story is an ideal path of entry for students into her work. But the nature of Christine's self-memorializing deserves reexamination. Undergraduates often first read her story as a tale of pluck and heroism: a remarkable woman overcomes bereavement, poverty, and sexual discrimination through courage and creative thinking. This interpretation has merit, but, with a little prodding, students can recognize her personal narrative as a rhetorical construction. Scholars have read that narrative as a conscious self-fashioning of Christine as woman-author or woman-scholar, and, indeed, she was nothing if not a savvy self-promoter (Brownlee, "Le projet 'autobiographique'"; Quilligan). But this interpretation does not address the disappearance of Christine's personal story from her later works; we must ask why Christine, the late medieval queen of confession, stopped writing about herself after 1405. Given that she was an engaged writer, we must also ask what motivations beyond self-interest might have dictated her self-memorializing and subsequent silence.

Christine's performance of memory is informed by a broad tradition, and inquiring into this tradition can help provide students with a nuanced understanding of her rhetoric.[1] By the same token, studying Christine is a wonderful way to introduce students to the art of memory itself, which formed a vital part of premodern culture (Yates; Carruthers). People in ancient and medieval Europe cultivated prodigious powers of recall. Memory made the oral tradition possible and, with it, a host of popular songs, tales, and epics in vernacular languages. It was key to religious devotion and prayers for the dead (Geary). Memory was also essential to scholars for whom scarce books constituted an aide-mémoire (Clanchy, *From Memory*). The widespread and multivalent practice of memory translated into an equally multifaceted theory of memory. In both Latin and vernacular sources, memory held a place of honor in discussions of rhetoric, artistic creation, intellectual training, and spiritual ascent. This last idea is evident in Augustine's autobiographical *Confessions* (397 AD), a key source for Christine. In the *Confessions*, Augustine finds spiritual conversion in his "memory, which is like a great field or spacious palace" (214 [bk. 10, sec. 8]), and his readers are meant to find conversion through his example. Christine does follow his example, associating the practice of memory with intellectual and spiritual development.

Christine also portrays the practice of memory as a consolation. The medieval idea of consolation is largely unfamiliar today, but it was at the heart of much philosophical and literary reflection (Courcelle). Consolation usually meant renouncing worldly pleasures in favor of the pleasures of the mind. Like conversion, consolation involved a regimen of meditation designed to improve human understanding; in theory, this new understanding would bring peace of mind (Hadot 22–23). Jean Gerson, an influential preacher and theologian (as well as a friend of Christine), wrote the Latin treatise called the *De consolatione theologiae* (*Consolation of Theology*). In the vernacular, the terms *confort*, *reconfort*, and *soulas* signified both "consolation" and "delight." The foundational source for all these reflections was the *Consolation of Philosophy*, a dream vision composed by the Roman statesman and intellectual Boethius in 524 AD. The *Consolation* inspired many learned commentaries and even more translations, sometimes by great authors in their own right, such as Chaucer and Jean de Meun. Medieval commentaries on the *Consolation* predicated philosophical consolation on the practice of memory. Clearly, Christine knew them well.[2]

A voracious and creative reader, Christine melded Augustine's and Boethius's ideas into a coherent and compelling notion of her own, the consolation of memory. She understands memory (*memoire*) in two ways: as an intellectual faculty—that is, a way of perceiving experience—and as the perception of that experience. She sees a close relation between these two forms of memory, both of which can trigger consolation. This theory gives her works their distinctive autobiographical shape. In the *Cent balades* (*One Hundred Ballades*), *Livre du chemin de lonc estude* (*The Path of Long Study*), *Livre de la mutacion de Fortune* (*Book of the Mutability of Fortune*), *Livre de l'advision Cristine* (*Christine's Vision*), and *Livre de la cité des dames* (*Book of the City of Ladies*), her literary alter ego seeks consolation by refining her power of memory. Like Boethius and especially Augustine, she personalizes the pursuit of enlightened happiness.

Christine's notion of transformative, consoling personal memory finds its corollary in the divinely inspired memory underlying universal history in Augustine's *City of God*, a work Christine knew well and on which she drew extensively. Absent this kind of consolation, the *Mutability of Fortune*'s narrator fails to see any transcendent meaning underlying his ambitious narrative. A man himself (the narrator Christine's *mutacion* ["transformation"] is a sex change), he is most certainly a denizen of Augustine's city of man, portrayed here as Fortune's floating castle in the air. Only when the narrator is consoled (and refeminized) is she able to build an Augustinian city of ladies, a stand-in for the city of God (Holderness, "Christine, Boèce").[3]

Christine's theory of consoling memory is at the core of her projects for political reform, because her first readers, the French royal family and its circle, needed a balanced perspective in order to govern well. The king, Charles VI, himself experienced episodes of mental illness that contemporaries diagnosed as a kind of memory loss. Christine's political engagement is inseparable from the king's illness and the social upheavals it provoked (Adams, *Christine de Pizan*). And so why is her personal story largely absent from those works that postdate the *City of Ladies*? This essay concludes with a consideration of her later self-imposed oblivion.

Teaching Christine's Intellectual Background

Teaching Christine's idea of consoling memory creates space for discussion of both Augustine and Boethius. In my experience at both state and private universities, in an advanced undergraduate literature course one or two students will have previously read parts of the *Confessions* or *City of God*; nobody will have heard of the *Consolation of Philosophy*. And yet these seminal works of the Western tradition can be made accessible to undergraduates, and they can help pave the way for further study of Christine.

One may view the *Confessions* as a mnemonic triptych. At the center, book 10 establishes memory's role in the soul's ascent toward God. Book 10's abstract meditations offer a key to understanding the rest of the work, and although I usually teach the work through excerpts, I emphasize its overall structure. The lengthy personal narrative of books 1–9 performs memory; after invoking God's mercy, the author discusses infantile amnesia and associates his earliest memories with the ability to speak and reason. Next comes a flood of remembrance and confession detailing Augustine's pursuit of rhetoric and philosophy, as well as his manifold sins, and culminating in his conversion to God and renunciation of the worldly life. This narrative, framed as a confession to both man and God, is the first step in his performance of memory. Books 11–13 perform a more transcendent kind of memory: the author meditates on the origins of human history and time itself, as they appear in the first three lines of the Book of Genesis. Christine seldom invokes the *Confessions* directly, but Augustine's movement through and beyond personal memory is clearly present in her *One Hundred Ballades*, *Path of Long Study*, *Mutability of Fortune*, *Christine's Vision*, and *City of Ladies*.

Christine replaces Augustine's personal narrative with her own; she also introduces Boethius's life story, even though it is largely absent from his own work. By grafting an Augustinian-style personal narrative onto Boethius's abstract philosophical dialogue, she highlights memory's role in the process of consolation. Although Boethius alludes to a Platonic ideal of anamnesis, nowhere does he explain it as clearly as does Augustine in book 10 of the *Confessions*, or as does Boethius's own commentator (Boethius [Stewart et al.] 138–39 [bk. 1, prose 2]; Cropp, *Le livre de Boèce* 91 [bk. 1, prose 1, gloss]). Christine draws her version of Boethius's life from the *accessus*, or introduction, that accompanied the *Consolation*, along with learned commentaries, in medieval manuscripts. Wrongly accused of treason by the emperor Theodoric, Boethius was condemned to death; while in prison awaiting punishment, he composed the *Consolation*.

Boethius alludes only fleetingly to his situation, but Christine enlarges on his story. According to Christine, Boethius made enemies by offering consistently honest advice; in the murky world of sixth century imperial politics, his altruism was not considered a virtue, and it eventually led to his downfall. In the *Path of Long Study*, she writes, "He was wrongly exiled / For having given good counsel / And serving the common good" (lines 219–21).[4] In the *Mutability of*

Fortune, she writes, "The valiant / Boethius lost all his wealth / And was exiled / By the ill-counseled Romans" (6863–66). Boethius's story helps us understand Christine's; her works are full of advice, and she portrays herself as an adviser. In the *Path of Long Study* she makes it clear that she sees herself as a modern Boethius: "When I looked again in Boethius's book / At the wrongs done [to him], I saw myself there" (215–16). She evokes Boethius's lesson of consolation throughout her works, weaving it into her own Augustinian-style narrative. When teaching the *Consolation*, I tend to focus on book 1, meter 1, through book 1, prose 4, the opening scene that recurs in various forms throughout Christine's works; I also include the discussion of Fortune in book 2.

Teaching Christine's Idea of Consoling Memory

Christine's early works illustrate the power of memory by returning over and again to key moments from her life: the narrator is born into a distinguished intellectual family, receives an education in the classics from her father, and then marries her father's charming young colleague. Her husband's premature death throws her into a state of emotional and financial disarray; she seeks his back pay in the courts but to no avail; to gain mental relief, she composes poetic laments and then picks up the books that she had set aside at her marriage. These books, especially the *Consolation of Philosophy*, prompt her to rethink her personal story, and gradually she finds peace of mind. Elements of this story, such as the identity of her father, Thomas de Pizan, and the complications following the death of her husband, are based on events in the life of the historical Christine de Pizan. It is nonetheless a rhetorical construction, as the presence of allegories like her mother, Nature, and her mistress, Fortune, suggests. The author crafts a remarkably compelling story of the consolation of memory; the early phase of this memory regime is painful, but with practice it brings happiness. Like Augustine's autobiography of spiritual wandering and eventual conversion, Christine's story ends shortly after her consolation is complete. And like Augustine's story, Christine's story is exemplary, a model for her readers to consider and imitate. Her detailed portrait of the interplay between intimate recollection and public memorializing and her observations on their philosophical implications are fascinating in their own right and offer a pedagogical entry point into the works of other late medieval writers, such as Guillaume de Machaut, Charles d'Orléans, and René d'Anjou. In an undergraduate course, one is most likely to teach only one or two of Christine's works at a time, but because her narrative runs so consistently throughout her early works, I discuss them as a unified group.

Memory and Melancholy

Like Boethius's *Consolation*, Christine's autobiographical works typically open with a scene of painful memory and the arrival of an otherworldly consoler.

These are memories within memories; the narrator recalls how she was once overwhelmed by the memory of loss. The unreasoning despair that such memories provoke is much like the condition that Christine's contemporaries knew as melancholy. In an earlier time melancholy was classified as one of the four basic human temperaments, but by Christine's day it was seen as a transitory condition (Klibansky et al. 31–197). Poets such as Guillaume de Machaut, Eustache Deschamps, Christine herself, and Charles d'Orléans all sang of melancholy (Cerquiglini-Toulet, *Couleur* esp. 11–12).

Christine's literary alter ego first gives way to melancholy in the *One Hundred Ballades*, a loosely organized lyric cycle which stages multiple perspectives, both male and female, on the vagaries of love, as well as gender-neutral reflections on moral issues. The most famous, ballade 11, expresses the speaker's alienation in its opening line: "Alone am I, and alone I wish to remain" (line 1; "Seulete suy, et seulete vueil estre"). The speaker's despair gradually intensifies until she declares, "Alone am I more than any earthly creature" (17; "Seulete suy plus qu'autre riens terrestre"). Her self-absorption prevents her from analyzing her situation. In the *Path of Long Study*, the narrator Christine echoes this early poetry, declaring that since her bereavement,

> I am often alone [seulete] and melancholy,
> Grieving for happier times
> Which are past
> And now utterly lost because of Fortune and death,
> The memory of which gnaws on me,
> As I ceaselessly recall
> The one and only man
> With whom I once lived in joy. (lines 68–75)

A little later she states that her great love "does not let / . . . / me forget, / However much . . . / . . . I may pretend, / That I do not remember / The pain" (135–44). Her description of memory's power over her state of mind is mimetic; as she describes the faculty of memory, she gives way to a host of specific recollections of her marriage and widowhood. Her awareness of social constraints only increases her bitterness and confusion. In the *Mutability of Fortune* the narrator declares that her cries rent the fabric of heaven, but that "[t]his yielded no consolation, / For my loss grieved me too much" (1289–94). In *Christine's Vision* even recollections of the narrator Christine's "good fortune" (bk. 3, ch. 4) come under the heading of "Christine's Complaint to Philosophy" (bk. 3, ch. 3). The narrative is a tour de force, but it is just as much a rhetorical construction as the *Mutability of Fortune*'s allegories or indeed as Augustine's *Confessions* and yet with time and practice the narrator's meditation on the past will become therapeutic.

Memory and Consolation

In all but one of her autobiographical works, the narrator Christine eventually finds consolation through memory. Even the pessimistic *Mutability of Fortune* points to memory's critical capacity.

Ballade 97 of the *One Hundred Ballades* presents memory in the context of a Boethian discussion of Fortune and Nature. The speaker cites the *Consolation* to extol the worth of Nature's gifts over those of Fortune: men may prefer the worldly honors and material wealth that Fortune can bestow, but they are fleeting in comparison with Nature's riches, which depend only on the mind. Citing Aristotle, she adds that the chief of these intellectual gifts is memory. The discussion of Fortune and Nature originates in *Consolation,* book 1, prose 5, but the specific gifts attributed here to Nature derive from a medieval gloss on book 1, prose 1, according to which the chief faculty over which Philosophy holds sway is memory (Cropp, *Le livre de Boèce* 91 [bk. 1, prose 1, gloss]). Memory's association with Nature derives from Aquinas's commentary on Aristotle's treatise *On Memory and Recollection*; like her contemporaries, Christine did not distinguish overly much between the *auctores* and their commentators. Aquinas places the faculty of memory very high within the natural order of being, and he links it particularly to the capacity for reason (156, 185–86). By invoking Aristotle, Christine also suggests a distinction between two different kinds of memory: Aristotle distinguishes between the ability to retain information and the ability to recall it once it has been forgotten. He also says that "generally speaking, the slow-witted have better memories, but the quick-witted and those who learn easily are better at recollecting" (449b). For Aristotle, memory-as-recollection relies on inference and deliberation (453a). Drawing on a web of learned allusions, ballade 97 argues that rational, deliberative memory can make sense of Fortune's twists and bring peace of mind. This ballade, so close to the end of the collection of one hundred, puts the preceding ballades into perspective. The *One Hundred Ballades* begins with regrets for a lost past but ends with a philosophical meditation on memory's power to console.

The intellectual faculties invoked in ballade 97 receive a more detailed discussion in the *Mutability of Fortune,* where they are described allegorically as four jewels in a diadem given to the narrator Christine by her mother, Nature. Chief among them are *Retentive* (memory as retention) and *Memoire* (memory as recollection). According to the narrator, "If a clever person / Had these two jewels, I really think / That, if he did his duty well, / He would gain both renown and intelligence" (634–37). She adds that they are really parts of the soul and, as such, gifts from God, and that Nature's primary role is to join them to the physical body (662–88).

The *Mutability of Fortune* is nothing if not an exercise in memory, moving from the narrator's personal recollections to his recollection of the history of the world. Fortune's great hall, whose murals remind him of world history, is a mnemonic device that classical orators knew as a memory palace. It is also a failed exercise, for, despite his natural gifts and despite the *Mutability of Fortune*'s great length, he remains a discontented follower of Fortune to the work's final lines: "Serving my mistress Fortune, / But still out of favor" (23, 601–02). In a discussion of medieval reworkings of the Hercules story, Liliane Dulac has noted that in the *Mutability of Fortune* the moralizing commentaries that were so central to one of its key sources, the *Ovide moralisé*, disappear. Dismissing the *Mutability of Fortune*'s reminders of Fortune's influence as a "leitmotiv," Dulac explains what she terms the poem's "perfect neutrality" as a way to suppress the commentaries' misogyny and make way for a more striking portrait of the hero's virtues ("Le chevalier Hercule" 17–20). But although the author's commitment to combatting misogyny is undeniable and her portrait of virtue is real, the *Mutability of Fortune*'s foray into universal history is no more neutral than its regendered narrator. The narrator's recurring statement that Fortune is unpredictable is unproblematic, but his inability to point to a more positive lesson *is* a problem. Christine knew the *City of God* very well, primarily from a contemporary glossed translation by Raoul de Presles. According to Augustine, Fortune is far less powerful than divine providence. The notion appears even more clearly in Raoul's glosses, which remind readers to reread Boethius on the same subject (Holderness, "Christine, Boèce" 281–85).

The *Mutability of Fortune*'s narrator has not found the consolation sketched out in the *One Hundred Ballades,* and despite the divinity that he has recognized in memory, he seems nowhere near the sort of conversion that Augustine imagined in the *Confessions*. Nonetheless, the *Mutability of Fortune* helps pave the way for the personal transformations found in the *Path of Long Study, Christine's Vision,* and the *City of Ladies*. Christine does after all point to memory's divine origin and its influence on individual well-being. And by shifting from a personal to a quasi-universal narrative, she mimics the same shift to be found in the *Confessions*. Augustine's extended personal confession (books 1–9) is what makes his analysis of Genesis (books 11–13) possible. His meditation on memory in book 10 makes this clear; through memory, he eventually transcends the personal in favor of the divine.

Consoling memory is key to the *Path of Long Study*. The narrator's sorrow over personal misfortunes diminishes as she recalls the trials undergone by Boethius as well as his consoling conversation with Dame Philosophy. She casts his words as a confession and those of Philosophy as an absolution:

> A priest absolves
> The sinner who makes his confession,
> And in this way, Boethius confesses
> At the end of his work, for he well sees that
> [Philosophy] is telling him what is right and true. (lines 276–80)

This is the most direct association between consolation and memory in Christine's oeuvre. But her transformation is incomplete; almost as soon as she sets

Boethius's book down, she reverts into a lament about the misfortunes of the world. Her *contemptus mundi* presents only half of Philosophy's lesson; missing is the complementary idea that one should take comfort through the exercise of one's intellectual faculties. But as Aristotle notes, memory's path can be circuitous, passing from one cue to the next until it reaches its goal. In this way, Christine passes from a partial recollection of Philosophy's teachings to a memory of Philosophy herself. The worry-worn heroine receives an unexpected visit from the Cumaean sibyl, who materializes at the head of her bed. The appearance of a wise female teacher is a recollection of the *Consolation*'s opening passage, and indeed the sibyl presents herself as a comforter. The sibyl is usually associated with prophecy, but in the *Path of Long Study* she is also a figure of memory. Unlike Philosophy, an atemporal abstraction, the Cumaean sibyl is ostensibly a historical figure. She tells Christine how she foretold the birth of Jesus and about her encounters with Aeneas, Tarquin, and the god Apollo. The last encounter left her with the dubious gift of an unnaturally long life—a thousand years. But even this lifespan cannot explain how the pre-Christian sibyl could be still be active on 5 October 1402, which is Christine's date for the start of the *Path of Long Study* (185–88). This temporal incongruity is mirrored by the sibyl's self-description in the past tense—"I want you to know who I am: / . . . I was called Almethea" (506–11)—and the even stranger "I lived a thousand years" (581). Christine responds in kind, addressing her teacher in the past tense as "Lady, you who were so learned" (863). The sibyl's consolation hinges on the exercise of the faculty of memory, as she tells Christine: "And for the good of your memory / Which I see ready to conceive, / I like you, and I want to teach you / Some of my secrets" (498–501). Christine's subsequent journey with the sibyl leads her into encounters with personifications of Imagination and Reason, both key aspects of memory. She listens attentively to a debate held under Reason's auspices, and at the end she produces a complete transcription: "I drew from my breast / A transcription of the debate" (6363–64). This is the emblematic gesture of memory, which is traditionally identified with the heart (in Latin, *recordatio*; in French, *mettre par cœur*; in English, to learn by heart).

Christine's Vision takes the exercise of memory still further, providing a passionate confessional backdrop for the subsequent philosophical consolation of its narrator. The work opens with a seriocomic Boethian pastiche featuring a "creature" called Chaos. Like Boethius's Philosophy, his head pierces the heavens, as his feet plumb the abyss. Like Philosophy's pupil, he weeps and moans. Christine's gloss on this passage sets the scene for the work's conclusion. She states, "[Th]is image may be understood as an individual human being. . . . The stars which decorate his brow are the virtues of the soul, including understanding, knowledge, memory, and the rest. . . . His feet tread on the abyss, that is hell, where he will fall if he is not careful" (Gloss, p. 4). The *Mutability of Fortune*'s thinking cap is back, a remedy for the melancholy into which one may sink if one is not careful.

In her *Vision*'s final section, Christine draws explicitly on the *Consolation of Philosophy*, describing a conversation between her literary alter ego and Dame

Philosophy. But her unacknowledged source is the *Confessions*; drawing on Augustine's storytelling power, she breathes life into Boethius's abstract dialogue. Her memories of tribulation and transformation come to a head in the chapter entitled "Christine Tells How She Changed Her Manner of Living" (3.8), followed by another entitled "Christine Tells How She Began to Study" (3.10), and another entitled "The Pleasure That Christine Took in Study" (3.11). This intellectual conversion is what makes her subsequent dialogue with Philosophy possible. But her conversion is not yet complete at the time of her confession. Unlike Augustine, who confesses to manifold faults, Christine casts herself as a victim of circumstance, and in this she resembles the still unreformed Boethius of *Consolation,* book 1, meter 1. But her performance of memory brings her to a second conversion, as she realizes that the Philosophy with whom she has been speaking is actually Theology, who is herself a face of God: "You have shown yourself to me in the form of Holy Theology, for which I thank God who is you and you who are in Him" (3.27).[5] This joyful epiphany accomplishes the anamnesis that Philosophy proposed to Boethius at the beginning of the *Consolation* (bk., 1, prose 2).

The City of Ladies picks up where *Christine's Vision* leaves off; Christine's personal question ("Why did God make me a woman?") is quickly superseded by a more global one ("Why did God make women?"). Her initial distress, once again couched in Boethian terms, finds its consolation in the construction of an Augustinian memory palace, the city of ladies, a stand-in for the City of God (3.18). Her distress summons up a trio of Philosophy figures—Reason, Rectitude, and Justice—who pile story on consoling story to illustrate women's worth. As in the *Confessions,* individual memory becomes collective and brings the rememberer closer to God; it also brings her consolation (3.19).

Beyond Memory?

The City of Ladies marks a turning point in Christine's oeuvre. After 1405, she retains her identity as a woman writer, but her personal memories are ancient history. She turns her attention to impersonal arts of war and peace and devotional texts. When she does adopt a Boethian tone, it is from the perspective of Philosophy herself, as in the *Epistre de la prison de vie humaine* (*Letter Concerning the Prison of Human Life*). Given the tumult of early fifteenth-century politics, we may question whether Christine ever truly found consolation through memory: in her final work, the *Ditié de Jehanne d'Arc* (*Tale of Joan of Arc*) (1429), she confesses that she has wept for the whole eleven years of the dauphin's exile (1–7); but until that moment her works steer clear of personal recollections: she maintains the appearance at least of a consoled woman.

Memory's path is seldom straight, so it seems fitting to close with a second look at *Christine's Vision,* in which Christine relates to Philosophy what her mother, Nature, once told her: "Now I want new books to be born from you, which will in the future perpetually present your memory to all the princes and to the whole universe, and you will give birth to these books in joy and delight from your memory [*memoire*]" (3.10). Is Nature calling for Christine to gain artistic renown? If so, one would have to read the word *memoire* in two different ways: first as renown, second as an intellectual faculty. And if so, Christine's path would be toward self-interest, not away from it. But as we may recall, in the *Mutability of Fortune* Nature endowed Christine with a set of intellectual faculties, including memory; it seems likely that she is using the word *memoire* in the same way throughout her exhortation. Christine's joyful, consoling memory is still on display for princes and students alike.

NOTES

[1]For analysis of the role that memory plays in Christine's advocacy for women, see Zimmerman, "Mémoire" and "Christine de Pizan: Memory's Architect"; Enders. While acknowledging their important contribution to scholarship, this essay focuses on the more personal side of Christine's memory.

[2]Christine read a verse-prose translation of Boethius whose author is anonymous, although it was commonly attributed to Jean de Meun in the manuscript tradition. This translation was often accompanied by the Latin glosses of William of Conches (died 1154), an abridged French translation of these glosses, or a combination of the two. On Christine's knowledge of this translation, see Glynnis Cropp's magisterial edition of this work (10); on her knowledge of the glosses, see my "Christine et ses 'bévues': Sens et portée de quelques assimilations abusives" (150–51n2).

[3]For further discussions of Christine's take on universal history, see Margolis, "Poetess"; Richards, "Christine de Pizan and Sacred History"; Dulac, "Le chevalier Hercule." This rich topic lies beyond the scope of this essay, but I have found that it meets with great interest from students, especially when they are presented with corresponding images from key manuscripts. For key images of the interplay between memory and history in Christine's memory palaces, see the online versions of Bibliothèque Nationale de France, Fond français 603, folio 127v and British Library, Harley 4431, folios 290r and 323r.

[4]All translations from the Middle French are mine. Translations are based on the following editions of Christine's works: *Le chemin de longue étude* (Tarnowski); *Le livre de la mutacion de Fortune* (Solente); *Cent balades* (Roy, *Œuvres poétiques*, vol. 1); *La città delle dame* (Richards); *Ditié de Jehanne d'Arc* (Kennedy and Varty); *Le livre de l'advision Cristine* (Reno and Dulac).

[5]This realization is like Augustine's in the *Confessions:* the young Augustine picks up Cicero's *Hortensius* because of its elegant style, but he falls in love with it because of its wisdom: "In Greek the word 'philosophy' means 'love of wisdom,' and it was with this love that the *Hortensius* inflamed me" (3.4). And so begins the spiritual quest that will end in his religious conversion. This etymology informs much of Christine's work, and indeed Philosophy greets her in the *Advision* by acknowledging "the love that you bear me" (3.1). Moreover, Christine cites Augustine as the source of her realization of Philosophy's true identity (3.27).

On Hands: Visual Narrative in Christine de Pizan's Manuscripts

Mary Gibbons Landor

Christine's self-proclaimed involvement in the production of her manuscripts, and her expressed interest in the choice and placement of the illuminations, prompt us to consider with students the part images play in her narratives and how they interact with the text. Apropos of her participation in the making of the collection she presented to Queen Isabeau she says:

> Si l'ay fait, ma dame, ordener
> Depuis que je sceus qu'assener
> Le devoye a vous, si qu'ay sceu
> Tout au mieulx et le parfiner
> D'escripre et bien enluminer. . . .
> (Roy, *Œuvres poétiques*, 1: xv [dedication, lines 49–53])

> I had it compiled, my lady, since I knew that I was to address it to you, just as I did my best to finish it, to write it and to illuminate it well.
> (McGrady, "What Is a Patron?" 195)

The belief she professed in the *Le livre de l'advision Cristine* (*The Vision of Christine de Pizan*) and the *Epistre Othea* (*Othea's Letter to Hector*) about the validity of multiple layers of meaning and interpretation further emphasizes the importance of integrating the visual narrative into a study of Christine's works. That narrative, understood as another language, sometimes parallels the text and sometimes intersects with it. The visual may complement or supplement and enrich what is written or may differ markedly from a relevant passage. Introducing students to the interplay of text and image will sharpen their appreciation of both formats and afford them additional critical tools.

This essay homes in on one aspect of visual narrative that directly conveys a communicative act: gestural behavior, especially of hands. Although focusing on hands alone might limit or even skew our interpretation, it can nonetheless expand our knowledge of the part hands play in the construction of visual narrative. If we look at Christine's hands as they grasp her book, *Le livre du chemin de lonc estude* (*The Path of Long Study*), when she presents it to Charles VI (fig. 1), we immediately realize the import such a gesture has in the story: it mimics the live experience of the observer.

Hands and facial expressions are universally recognized as a language in themselves. Their code is the most prominent among those embedded in visual images and perhaps the most expressive. Since antiquity they have been

Figure 1. British Library, MS Harley 4431, fol. 178r. Christine presents her book to Charles VI. © British Library Board MS Harley 4431.

considered primary bearers of meaning. Taking his cue from Aristotle's words, "The soul is like the hand: for the hand is the instrument of instruments" (*On the Soul*, book 3, 432a), Quintilian writes, "As for the hands, without which all actions would be crippled and enfeebled, it is scarcely possible to describe the variety of their motions, since they are almost as expressive as words. For other portions of the body merely help the speaker, whereas the hands may almost be said to speak" (289 [line 85]).

Modern scholars, with the exception of Liliane Dulac ("*La gestuelle*" 609–26), have paid little attention to the function of hands in Christine's works, even though Christine herself was very aware of body movements, as she states in *Le livre du corps de policie* (*The Book of the Body Politic*). She says of Valerius Maximus's thoughts on eloquence, "[Q]uant grand eloquence est conduite par sage ordre avec le deu mouvement du corps, elle envaist les oyans par trois manieres. Car elle prent les couraiges des uns et les oreilles des autres, aux autres elle adoulcist et atendrist les yeulx" (*Le livre du corps de policie* [Kennedy] 44); "When eloquence is combined with gentle movement of the body, it affects the listeners in three ways: it affects the spirit of some and the ears of others, and it seduces and sweetens the eyes of others" (Forhan, *Political Theory* 46).

Analyzing hand gestures and comparing the actions they signify with the corresponding texts by Christine can markedly increase our understanding of an entire text, particularly with respect to her self-presentation. What, then, can we learn about her in her role as an intellectual by observing patterns of hand gestures? It is in presentation scenes that we begin to find answers to this question. A study of hands as part of gesture must initially rely heavily on François Garnier's useful book *Le langage de l'image au Moyen Âge*, which is based on his examination of thousands of miniatures in medieval manuscripts.

Christine the Author

Christine follows the presentation scene tradition by having herself depicted as author in her own work. An early instance of this topos—dating earlier than 1285, more than a century before her work appeared—shows Primat presenting the *Grandes chroniques de France* to Philip the Bold (MS782, fol.326 v, Bibliothèque Ste. Geneviève). The illuminator of this work, in which the participants are silhouetted against a simple checkered background, has given the hands the leading role in the ceremony.

In three presentation miniatures of Harley 4431, those of the *Chemin*, the *Epistre Othea*, and in the prologue dedicating the whole collection to Queen Isabeau, the central position of the participants' hands and the glances of their eyes emphasize their exchange. These three examples illustrate how only slightly differing hand positions alter the meaning of the narrative.

In the *Chemin* presentation scene (fig. 1), there is a notable divergence between image and text. Charles VI and Christine face each other, he in black and gold, seated, she in a simple dull gray dress, kneeling. Close behind the king in the boxlike space where the scene takes place, four of Charles's courtiers, clothed in blue, orange, pale-green, and rose robes, direct their gazes to the hands of Charles and Christine, where the exchange of the book occurs. Overhead to the left, a striking canopy of gold fleurs-de-lis on a blue background directs the viewer's eye to the foreground action. As she offers her book to Charles, Christine grasps the underside of it with her right hand in such a way that only the fingers are visible; thus her tome appears to be heavy. Her left hand, palm down, rests on top of the book. Simultaneously, Charles reaches out to grasp the book with his left hand, the thumb extension clearly indicating how thick it is. His right hand, palm turned in, third and index fingers separated from the fourth and little fingers, fixes the viewer's attention on their interaction. No other hands are visible in this miniature. Although Charles looks into the distance as if detached from his bodily movements, he eagerly grasps the book, signifying that he is taking possession of the manuscript and suggesting that he both commissioned the work and acknowledges Christine as its author. In the text, however, she not only expresses conventional humility toward a powerful patron but also reveals her profound uncertainty about the task that she, as a woman writer, has undertaken. She says:

> Princes tres haulx, a vous tant humblement
> Comme je puis de cuer me recommand,
> Pryant mercis par grant affection
> Que repputé ne soit presomcion
> D'escripre a vous de tele dignieté,
> A moy, femme, pour mon indignieté,
> Ainçois vous plaise acepter le desir
> Qu'ay de servir ou faire aucun plaisir
> A vostre tres digne et haulte noblece . . . (*Chemin*, lines 23–31)[1]

> Most high princes, I present myself to you with extreme and heartfelt humility, in order to implore you very sincerely not to take as presumptuous the fact that I, an unworthy woman, write to such worthies as you. May it please you, rather, to accept my desire to serve you or to give you some pleasure, you whose nobility is so exalted and so well merited.
> ("*The Path of Long Study*" 61)

Although similar in compositional layout to that of the *Chemin*, the comparable scene of the *Othea* (Harley 4431, fol. 95r), in which Christine presents her book to Louis, duke of Orléans, carries a very different message. Louis, like Charles, is seated; Christine kneels while three of the duke's attendants stand close behind them and focus their attention on the book and the hands of Louis and Christine. Again the event takes place in the customary boxlike space. Here, however, the brilliant oranges, blues, greens, and golds suggest a more flamboyant occasion. The proliferation of hands is spread out rather than clustered in one small area of the picture. Louis's gaze is fixed on the book as Christine directs her attention to his face. Her hands—the left grasping the book by its spine, the right steadying the book on the opposite (opening) side—are more tentative in their position than in the previous image. Louis's hands are occupied with other activities, positioned far from the book, almost belying his intense concentration on it, while Christine focuses her attention on his face. The duke's left hand holds his staff, his right grasping the folds of his robe. The most expressive hands in the miniature, however, belong to Louis's attendant, who is dressed in a sumptuous orange robe trimmed in gold and who wears a magnificent tall black hat with orange and white feathers. His hands, read in relation to each other, announce that the negotiation is taking place. The left index finger of the attendant rivets our attention as he points conspicuously to Christine's book, while his right thumb and index finger form a U to hold the pendant in the shape of a porcupine, Louis's emblem (Hindman, *Christine de Pizan's* Epistre Othéa 44–51, 187–88). Christine, in contrast to Louis's attendant, is dressed in black. She seeks Louis's patronage in offering her manuscript to him, while his aide urges Louis to accept it. The connection between the author and her dedicatee is less direct here than in the *Chemin* image; the multiplication of hands, as well as the black-hatted attendant's indication of both Christine's book and his Orléans-emblem necklace, may suggest the *Othea*'s value as a work that promotes chivalric virtues to a broad courtly audience.

Of the many precedents for prologue scenes with which Christine was likely familiar, one—Nicole Oresme's presentation of his translation of Aristotle's *Ethics* to Christine's mentor, Charles V, of circa 1372 (Sherman, *Imaging Aristotle* 45–48)—shows us how such a potentially formal confrontation can be turned into an intimate conversation by the activity of the hands and their arrangement. In that scene, the intimacy of the relationship between Charles and his friend emerges from the movement of the hands. In concert, Charles and Nicole actively engage with the book, the very medium of their interaction.

What now should we make of the Harley illumination (fol. 3r) showing Christine presenting her collected works of thirty manuscripts to Queen Isabeau (fig. 2)? It represents a remarkable departure from the norm of this genre. Although the illumination is the grand introduction to Christine's entire oeuvre, it takes place in the intimate setting of the queen's bedchamber rather than in the throne room; it also occurs in the company of an exclusively female audience. Isabeau and Christine face each other, Christine in vibrant blue and kneeling in the center foreground, Isabeau seated off to the left in a gold-figured red gown trimmed in ermine. Six ladies-in-waiting sit behind Christine in the elegant and spacious room occupied at right by the queen's resplendent red canopy. The whole is surrounded by a curtained wall of gold fleurs-de-lis on a blue ground. At first glance the exchange between author and patron seems to follow the usual pattern, but close inspection reveals otherwise. Christine holds the book in the usual way, with both hands, the right gripping the book from underneath, with only her fingers visible; the left hand grasps it on the short side, its thumb extended as far as possible from the index finger. These gestures emphasize the thickness of the volume. Isabeau sits back, her right hand grasping her left wrist. Her left hand rests on her lap, the index and third fingers extended, the other fingers flexed. According to Garnier's classification, one hand grasping the wrist

Figure 2. British Library, MS Harley 4431, fol. 3r. Christine presents her collected works to Queen Isabeau. © British Library Board MS Harley 4431.

commonly denotes a state of powerlessness, a gesture we would not expect from either a noble patron or a queen (198–202). But Deborah McGrady, analyzing the text of the Isabeau prologue, argues that in this instance Christine usurps the patron's authority over the book and substitutes the author as the controlling power ("What Is a Patron?"). Isabeau's hand gesture, however subtle, is significant and a visual demonstration of McGrady's thesis. The queen's female attendants merely observe and converse, their inert hands signifying their passive role as spectators. Conforming to tradition, Christine kneels in deference to the queen, but her placement of herself in the center foreground bestows on her the most authoritative and powerful position in the transaction, and her hand gestures, as we have seen, highlight the heft of the volume, a heft that confirms the importance of her work. Although Isabeau occupies the superior physical position, as befits royalty, her hand gesture here denotes her receptive response to the author, Christine. Because the text of this prologue gives no hint of the message conveyed in the illumination by the body language and hand gestures, Christine has asserted her control by visual means.

Although the two Harley 4431 presentation scenes representing Charles VI and Louis in some respects display the conventional depiction of the relationship between author and patron, Christine often conceived ingenious strategies for establishing her authority. The extent to which her departures from traditional topoi were a consequence of her gender is a subject that invites speculation.

The Scholar in Her Study

When we turn to the ancient theme of the scholar in his study, we see that Christine has appropriated for herself what was traditionally a male role, familiar to her visually from images such as that of Charles V in his study reading John of Salisbury's *Policraticus* (Sherman, *Imaging Aristotle* 6–11). In MS 10982 of the *Chemin* (Royal Library of Belgium, Collection of the Dukes of Burgundy), Christine sits reading in her airy study with its open slender archways and muted pastel colors, focusing intently on the open book before her. Other books are spread out on the desk. Her hand and arm gestures direct our attention to her activity. Her left arm bent at the elbow at a ninety-degree angle, her hand raised and open, her right arm and hand bent at a forty-five-degree angle, her right index finger pointing to the palm of the left hand, denoting the ancient practice of *disputatio*, in which the right fingers enumerate the points of an argument on the left palm. It seems likely that Christine is committing portions of the text to memory for later use in oral or written argument. Even before Guido d'Arezzo, the legendary eleventh-century music theorist and pedagogue, described this gesture as a teaching method, the left hand was used as a device for teaching and memorizing various subjects, both musical (the tetrachord) and nonmusical (calendar, computation). The hand used in this way in music came to be known as the Guidonian hand.

At the beginning of the *Cent balades* in Harley 4431 (fig. 3), we find another variation on Christine the scholar. Dressed in deep blue and with her small dog at her side, she sits in her little Gothic-style study, engaged in writing what presumably is the *Cent balades* itself. Her hands expressively display her inner concentration. She marks her place in the text with her right index finger while writing with her left hand. This way of writing suggests that she was left-handed, but there is no other indication that she was. More probably, in this instance of learning, she is depicted as writing with her left hand because her right index finger is needed as the didactic instrument and therefore takes precedence. The distinctive manner in which the fingers are curved seems anachronistic, recalling much earlier representations, such as the twelfth-century figure in *Les lettres de Saint Gregoire* (MS180, fol.1, Dijon, bibl. mun; Garnier 28). In the portrayal of Christine, the visual image clearly conveys how she would like to be judged, and the hands serve to support her self-presentation. This depiction of the intellectual in her study, one that confidently positions itself in the long tradition of such scenes, gives no inkling of the doubts and tensions she expresses in the text; nor does it allude to the text's conflicting discourses as described by McGrady ("Authorship"). Like the first image in the Harley manuscript after

Figure 3. British Library, MS Harley 4431, fol. 4r. Christine in her study. © British Library Board MS Harley 4431.

the presentation scene with Queen Isabeau, the miniature reinforces for readers Christine's dedication to her work and her status as an author. Students moving through the manuscript on the *Christine de Pizan:* The *Making of the Queen's Manuscript* Web site (www.pizan.lib.ed.ac.uk/) can take in these visual emphases.

Christine the Student

Christine is engagingly represented as a student or apprentice in eight miniatures that accompany the allegory of her intellectual pilgrimage, *Le chemin de lonc estude*. She is guided on her travels by the wise Cumaean sibyl. Although not so conspicuous here as in the presentation scenes, hands nevertheless prominently and eloquently define both Christine's role as student and the sibyl's role as teacher. Two of the miniatures in Harley 4431 give us an opportunity to see Christine succeeding in her assigned tasks. The first stop on the journey of learning, corresponding to the second miniature in the work, is the bath of the Muses (Gibbons). She is astounded by the scene before her. In a verdant landscape, the nine Muses, nude except for the contemporary headdresses known as *bourrelets*, are bathing in the Fountain of Knowledge. The winged horse Pegasus, whose hooves brought forth the fountain, hovers overhead. The sibyl literally takes her charge in hand, grasping Christine's left hand with her right; with her nearly vertical left index finger, thumb extended and other fingers closed, she explains to Christine what she sees:

> La montaigne que vois lassus
> Est appellee Pernasus,
> Ou mons Helicon est de moult
> Appellé ce tres beau hault mont.
> Et la fontaine que sus vois
> Est celle qui a si grant voix
> De noblece et de renommee,
> Qui de Sapience est nommee
> Fontaine, dont les beaulx ruisseaulx
> Vont arrosant les vers rinsseaulx
> Qui le monde tient en verdour
> Et dont le fruit rent grant odour.
> Et le nom te vueil enseigner
> Des dames que tu vois baigner,
> A quoy ententivement muses.
> On les appelle les .ix. muses. (*Chemin*, lines 977–92)

The mountain that you see above is called Parnassaus, or Mount Helicon, as many call this very beautiful high mountain. The fountain you see upon

> it is that which has such a reputation of nobility and fame; it is called the Fountain of Wisdom (Knowledge), whose beautiful streams water the verdant boughs from which the world benefits and whose fruit gives off an intense perfume. And I want to teach you the name of the ladies whom you see bathing, and upon whom you are attentively musing: they are called the nine Muses. (my trans., with Leslie Callahan)

More than two hundred lines of text elaborate extensively on the import and implications of the encounter, which is distilled in one memorable visual image. The teaching gesture of *declamatio* here employed by the sibyl also appears in countless medieval illuminations, of which the Ascension scene from *La vie et miracles de St. Denis* (BNF 1098, fol. 29v; Martin, fig. 2, pl. 2.8) is a typical example. The sibyl's hands accentuate her active role as she leads Christine, whose hands and posture, in contrast, express her diffident demeanor.

The third miniature depicts the moment when Christine and the sibyl have ascended a ladder to arrive in the heavens. We see a glorious blue sphere with a scalloped edge, punctuated by concentric circles of gold stars, a sun, and a moon (*Chemin*, lines 1785–880, Harley 4431, fol.189v). Christine and the sibyl stand in the center, Christine assuming a more active stance than she did on Parnassus. At this point the sibyl, no longer holding Christine's hand, continues to instruct Christine further, her right arm and hand elevated. Christine's left hand, silhouetted against the blue sky, now signs her acceptance, affirming what she has learned. An image from the thirteenth-century *Bible moralisée,* illustrating Jesus and two apostles (MS 2554, f.40v, Vienna; Garnier 153, 172c) shows this type of gestured exchange between an authority figure and a subordinate. Jesus assigns their mission to his followers, and they in turn respond in acceptance or agreement with the same gesture of acceptance.

Christine herself appears in the role of teacher at the opening of *Les enseignemens moraux* (*Moral Teachings*, Harley 4431, fol. 261v), where she instructs her son, Jean de Castel. She sits in an imposing, high-backed, cathedra-type chair, with the book from which she is teaching open on the table in front of her. Jean, framed against a low wooden wall pierced by cubbyholes, stands on the other side of the table and looks directly at his mother. Christine's hands—the left raised and open or predicative, the right with the index finger pointing to a passage in the open book (again, the teaching gesture of *declamatio*)—convey the energy with which Christine undertakes this task. Jean's crossed arms, with the gesture of hands in armpits (apparently rare), indicates his inactive or receptive state (Garnier, *Langage* 216–17, fig. 169). It is hoped that he is listening to his mother's advice! This is one instance where the symbolism of medieval gesture may differ from our modern understanding; whereas students might assume that the body language of crossed arms indicates that Jean rejects Christine's teachings, the message here is of passivity rather than ill humor.

Although similar in setting to the scene in which she teaches her son, the scene in which she teaches a group of male clerks in the *Proverbes moraulx*

(*Moral Proverbs*, Harley 4431, fol.259v), is more animated. It is not so different from Sappho's reading to a male audience in Boccaccio's *Famous Women* (Buettner, *Des cleres*, fig. 45; BNF 12420, fol. 71v, ca. 1402). From her massive seat, the back and canopy of which envelop her, Christine reads to the men about moral conduct. The men, dressed in green and scarlet, huddle together in front of a rust-colored background lavishly decorated with gold arabesques. She rests her left hand on the book, the basis for her authority, and raises her right hand, its thumb extended, toward her audience. In response to her directives, two of her listeners, as indicated by the positions of their hands, are actively discussing the material presented, while a third stands, hands and arms folded in his sleeves, and a fourth looks on from behind. The two men who flank the passive man in the center are engaged in an argument (*disputatio*). Their gestures, which represent that activity, follow the tradition illustrated in a fourteenth-century manuscript of the *Roman de la rose*, by Guillaume de Lorris (MS665, fol. 60v., Chantilly, Musée Condé; Garnier 210B), which portrays Abelard and Heloise in *disputatio*.

To conclude this examination of Christine in the role of the intellectual, we study the *incipit* miniature of the Harley *Livre de la cité des dames* (*Book of the City of Ladies*) at fol. 290r (fig. 4). It comprises two episodes that present Christine as author-creator-builder. The scene is divided into two parts. On the left, in a light-blue, box-like room resembling a study, she stands and reads to Reason, Rectitude, and Justice from a specific passage in her book, to which she points with the index finger of her right hand, her left resting underneath and on

Figure 4. British Library, MS Harley 4431, fol. 290r. Incipit, *The Book of the City of Ladies*. © British Library Board MS Harley 4431.

her body. Reason holds a mirror in her right hand, Rectitude a ruler, and Justice grasps a jar with both hands; standing on the far side of Christine's desk, they listen attentively to her *declamatio.* On the right, Reason, who is helping Christine build her city, hefts a large stone recalling the shape of a book, while Christine, holding a trowel in her right hand, applies the mortar. The obvious crossing of her forearms in both these views prompts the viewer to question its possible psychological meaning and reminds us of the extent to which the meaning of a gesture is dependent on its context. Crossed arms and hands are often a sign of impotence or submission to a higher authority, as was noted with respect to Isabeau's gesture when she received Christine's collected works. An eloquent earlier example of this gesture is the image of the Tower of Babel builder in the thirteenth-century *Histoire universelle* (MS 562, fol. 9, Dijon, bibl. Mun.; Garnier, *Langage* 72, 214, 217, fig. 145). Unlike the submissive Tower of Babel builder, Christine in the *Cité des dames* miniature vigorously participates in the building of the city. How are we to read this behavior? Is she demonstrating her ability to construct the city while at the same time acknowledging the superior societal and political power of Reason? Christine herself refers to the coexistence of multiple layers of meaning in the *Advision* and the *Othea.*

In contrast to the right side of the illumination, on the left side the two layers of meaning are given unequal weight. Christine is shown in the visual narrative in the commanding role of teacher; she explains her important points to the three ladies. They in turn stand with their attributes in hand behind her book-laden desk, attentive to her words. Yet the text in its opening section gives the instructor's role to Reason, Rectitude, and Justice, who have come to educate Christine in the mission she has been chosen to carry out; in recognition of both their exalted status and her humble one, she prostrates herself at their feet. The depiction on the right side of the illumination, where she stands in a lower position than Reason with her crossed arms clearly visible, seems more in agreement with what the manuscript expresses. In our visual analysis of the gestures in this illumination, we have discerned multivalent meanings not found in the corresponding text. Students should be encouraged to make their own detailed visual readings, whether they study Christine's words in French or in English.

The tension and conflict Christine experiences as both a woman and an author in assuming an authoritative role emerges in the *Cité des dames* text, as in many of her other works. The visual image expresses these conflicts and tensions in its own language, parallel to but distinct from that of the text. It speaks to us in a register apart and remains imprinted in our visual memory.

Christine the Narrator

One of Christine's love debate poems, the *Le livre du debat de deux amans*, provides an opportunity to consider Christine in still another one of her self-defining roles, in this case that of narrator-interlocutor. Like her two other debate poems, the *Le livre des trois jugemens* and the *Le livre du dit de Poissy*, the *Deux amans* has only one introductory miniature. Although a debate between squire and knight constitutes the substance of the poem and occupies 1933 lines of a total of 2023, the one scene represented visually takes place at the very end of the work (Harley 4431, fol. 58v). Christine occupies center stage as an intermediary who introduces the duke to the squire and the knight as the judge of the debate between them. Hand gestures play a crucial role in this exchange. The duke displays rich trappings that denote his noble status. He is seated in the highest position on his chair under the royal canopy decorated with fleurs-de-lis as he holds his baton of office in his right hand and raises his left. Yet Christine commands the viewer's attention, both by virtue of her position in the foreground and, more important, through the pointing gesture of her right hand. This gesture, together with the eye contact between her and the duke, clearly relates the textual moment when she brings the debate to its conclusion. This single miniature of the *Debat de deux amans* distills the poem into one memorable image that bestows on the poet the most important role in the work.

Through the juxtaposition of visual and verbal images, we have seen Christine's presentation of herself in several intellectual roles: as author, as scholar, as student, and as narrator. A creative woman who lived more than six hundred years ago in a male-dominated society, Christine nevertheless was able to make a success of a most difficult undertaking and to leave a legacy of inspiration that continues today.

NOTES

Mary Gibbons Landor died in November 2017 as this volume was being prepared for publication. We remember her with admiration and affection; she was a fine art historian and an engaging companion.

[1]This essay cites Tarnowski's edition, *Le chemin de longue étude*.

France's First Literary Quarrel: *Le débat sur* Le roman de la rose

David F. Hult

At the opening of the fifteenth century, literary composition in the vernacular in France was not in its infancy, but there is little or no evidence of a self-conscious literary critical tradition—that is, the existence of works, be they in French or in Latin, that discussed the contents of previous works with the goal of providing some kind of interpretation. This is not to deny the existence of what goes today by the word *intertextuality*, comprising poets' or authors' literary rewriting or imitation of previous works—itself quite self-conscious—but rather to suggest that a nonfictional discourse aimed at appreciating or critiquing the ideas or effects (social, cultural, political, devotional) of literature had scarcely arisen in the domain of vernacular letters. Therefore the debate that occurred in 1401–02 over the merits of the notorious and extremely popular *Roman de la rose* (*Romance of the Rose*) occupies a special place in French literary history. And while the *Roman de la rose* was widely imitated, quoted, and occasionally criticized in the fourteenth century (as Badel has extensively documented), it had never been scrutinized as it was in this debate.

The principal reason for the debate's current renown and for the voluminous scholarship on it is the participation of Christine de Pizan, widely known as one of the first self-consciously female writers in the French tradition, if not the first. She was certainly the first woman to make her living as a writer and producer of manuscripts and was an early spokesperson for what is now known as feminism. Accordingly, readers often view the debate from the angle of Christine's unquestionably woman-centered position, and it is undoubtedly from this protofeminist perspective that the debate is usually presented to students. Yet anyone who has taught the debate in classes of advanced undergraduates or graduate students soon finds that the feminism represented by Christine is not appealing or interesting to modern sensibilities, however intriguing she is as a literary figure and however important her writings are as cultural landmarks (Brown-Grant, "Christine de Pizan as Defender" 95). As scholars such as Beatrice Gottlieb have suggested in recent years, Christine's defense of women is founded on traditional values. These values are anchored in the beliefs and moral standards of medieval Catholicism. In particular, they are rooted in an understanding of women's role as subservient wives, as mothers, as keepers of the household—a role that is most fully developed in Christine's *Livre des trois vertus* (1405; *Book of the Three Virtues*). As my students have said over the years, the lady depicted in Alain Chartier's *La belle dame sans mercy* (1424; *The Beautiful Lady without Mercy*) is much more interesting as a protofeminist icon than, say, the lady in Christine's *Cent balades d'amant et de dame* (1409; *One Hundred Ballads of a Lover and Lady*). Even a 2002 attempt (Nowacka) to address occasionally severe criticisms of Christine's feminism (Delany, "Mothers") seems only able to make that feminism palatable by emphasizing that it is embedded in her remarkable commitment to a humanist ethics. Other readings of Christine's ethical stance in the debate focus on her struggle with the prevailing misogyny in French society of the time. They posit an "ethics of reading" that views misogynous speech (such as that represented in the *Rose*) as leading to physical violence in the form of "wife abuse" (Desmond, *Querelle* 176, 177) or, alternatively, a more politically situated ethics of "verbal injury," understood as defamation and, ultimately, as a "civic threat" and "the gravest crime" (Solterer, *Master* 162).

Such studies of the social and personal effects of misogyny on women in the fifteenth century are obviously of crucial importance. In this essay I discuss teaching the debate as a wide-ranging phenomenon that took place in 1401–02. This helps students understand, first, the debate's context but does not privilege a priori any of the participants or the text that inspired it and, second, the stakes of debates in a more general sense that pertains to our contemporary modes of inquiry.

The *Roman de la rose* dates to the thirteenth century, some 150 years before the time of the debate. The poem is partly a love allegory encased in a dream (the dream lover seeks to attain the titular rose, object of his desire, but does not wake up or accomplish his quest), attributed to an author named Guillaume de Lorris. Some forty years later (probably around 1270) a second author named Jean de Meun grafted a continuation onto Guillaume's unfinished narrative that is about four times as long as his predecessor's text. In so doing, Jean completed the central thread of the narrative (the author–dream lover attains the rose with the help of an army of personifications, headed by the God of Love). The length of the continuation is, however, a result of Jean's inclusion of excerpts from a wide variety of texts, including ancient philosophy and rhetoric; the tremendously popular *Consolation of Philosophy*, by Boethius (which had not yet been integrally translated into French—Jean would do that some years later); the erotic writings of Ovid; contemporary thirteenth-century tracts reflecting religious controversy in university circles in Paris; and works belonging to a long-standing misogynous tradition—all translated from the original Latin into French verse. Largely because of the access that Jean provided to works that both lay and clerical readers alike had difficulty reading in the original Latin, the work became a "best seller," the most widely circulated French work of any genre in the fourteenth and fifteenth centuries. As a result, Jean de Meun, as author-figure, was lionized by readers and considered a great writer and thinker, as well as a cunningly manipulative one—an attribute that arises frequently in the course of the debate.

Christine de Pizan was at an early stage of her career at the time the debate opened, in the spring of 1401. She had started her career writing lyric poetry and in 1399 published a collection of those poems in a volume entitled *Cent balades*. That same year, as James Laidlaw has shown ("Publisher's Progress";

"Manuscript Tradition"), she undertook writing the first of what would be several manuscripts in which she compiled her collected works. Her "publication" career (Ouy et al.; Delsaux) would find its crowning achievement in her last such production, the justly famous, lavishly illustrated manuscript she presented to the queen of France (British Library Harley 4431), which has been most recently dated by Laidlaw to early 1414 (Laidlaw, "Date"). It is clear from statements Christine makes in her semi-autobiographical *Livre de l'advision Cristine* (1405; *Christine's Vision*), however, that before that time she circulated her poetry, undoubtedly in presentation copies of individual works, to important members of the nobility, extending from the earl of Salisbury and King Henry IV of England to the most important French nobles at the time, the dukes of Berry, of Burgundy, and of Orléans. Their support was crucial for her precarious financial position, but it also satisfied what was certainly her increasing desire for fame. Christine's activities during and immediately following the period of the debate seem to be especially tireless. The production of manuscripts was accelerating: the first manuscript of her collected works, mentioned above, was completed in June 1402; Andrea Tarnowski (*Chemin* 63–64) posits that five of the extant manuscripts of the *Livre du chemin de lonc estude* (*Path of Long Study*), a work completed in February 1403, were transcribed by late spring of that year, all presentation copies prepared under her supervision (Laidlaw, "Manuscript Tradition" 243–44). As far as her writing was concerned, between October 1402 and November 1403 Christine composed the *Chemin* and brought to completion her *Livre de la mutacion de Fortune* (*The Book of the Mutability of Fortune*), both destined for noble patrons. Taken together, these two works total an astonishing thirty thousand lines of verse. It was thus within two years following the completion of her first major work and only months before the production of her first manuscript collection, at a moment of remarkable productivity as a writer and a publisher, that the *Rose* affair was launched. As Christine says with great pride in the *Advision*, "From the year 1399, when I began, up to the present year, 1405, in the course of which I have not yet stopped, fifteen major works were compiled in this space of time, without counting the other separate small poems, which together are contained in seventy large-size quires" (Reno and Dulac 111 [part 3, section 10, lines 50–54]).[1]

Christine seems by all accounts to have been the instigator of the debate. In April 1401 (Hicks and Ornato 62–64), Jean de Montreuil, provost of Lille and secretary to King Charles VI, had been pushed, indeed compelled, by his colleague Gontier Col, another of the king's secretaries, to read the *Roman de la rose*, as he tells us in one of his letters written in Latin to an unnamed colleague, undoubtedly Pierre d'Ailly, noted theologian and bishop of Cambrai (*Débat* [Hicks] 28–29; Hicks and Ornato 47–49; Hult 49–50). After he read the text, Jean wrote a treatise in French in which he sang the praises of it and its author. As we find out from Christine herself, Jean sent her a copy of this treatise following a verbal disagreement between them. In response, she redacted a letter that countered point by point Jean's praise of Jean de Meun and the

Rose. Gontier Col requested a copy of the letter, which he had heard about. After receiving it, he chastised Christine for her position and, in a letter dated 15 September of the same year, ordered her to recant. Christine refused and reiterated the righteousness of her position.

Although these documents are interesting in themselves, the next step in this brief debate is more noteworthy: Christine took it upon herself to gather together the documents and to present them with two dedicatory epistles, one to the queen of France, Isabeau of Bavaria, dated 1 February 1402, and one to an important noble and ally of the king, Guillaume de Tignonville, provost of Paris—both potential supporters and patrons. If the exchange of letters had previously circulated among a small number of individuals associated with the royal chancery, Christine's confecting of the dossier, quite certainly in the form of a pamphlet, made it henceforth a public affair destined for the court. Moreover, in the affair she is portrayed as both the victim of her assailants and a heroine, managing to trump their arguments despite being "of feeble intelligence" (Hult 100; cf. *Débat* [Hicks] 7).

Now, the manner in which the documents were assembled and the brief history of the debate not only suggest an alternative to the interpretation of Christine as precocious and earnest defender of women that has been handed down to us by literary history but also demystify the way she wanted to present herself. Far from being the weak or inadequate woman ganged up on by the learned male clerks surrounding her, she shows herself to have been very much in control from the beginning. She speaks frequently in her debate letters, as in other works, of her intellectual inadequacy, yet she proves through writing that she is at least equal to her opponents. Her enterprising outreach to patrons suggests likewise that she was a shrewd businesswoman. One notes, for instance, that she includes the "woman" question in her dedicatory epistle to the queen: "the honor and praise of women, which many clerics and others have endeavored to belittle through their writings—something one is not allowed to tolerate or endure" (Hult 99; cf. *Débat* [Hicks] 6). But in her letter to Guillaume de Tignonville she says virtually nothing about the content of the debate. Instead, she accentuates her intellectual disadvantage, what she calls "female ignorance," in the "war" she was waging against her powerful attackers (Hult 100; cf. *Débat* [Hicks] 7). She asks for Tignonville's aid and support, as would a defenseless woman ask of a knight whose mission it was to protect her. In other words, she uses the general issue of the defense of all women as a way of forging a gender bond with the queen, whereas she accentuates her personal role as a victim in order to motivate the chivalrous support of her male protector. In addressing both her patrons and her opponents, she minimizes her assets, rhetorically speaking, as a strategy for maximizing her impact. She downplays her awareness that her intellect serves as significant capital not only to best her rivals, to argue the case for women, and to earn a living but also to establish herself as an important authorial figure. Her awareness of the path to glory is made very clear, however, when she recounts in the *Advision* the fictional words that the goddess Nature "spoke" to her at the outset of her career: "Now I want you to give birth to new volumes, which will manifest your memory to the world, in the ages to come and perpetually, before princes and everywhere throughout the universe" (Reno and Dulac 110 [3.10.38–41]).

Our perception of Christine's purely ideological opposition to the *Rose* is further belied by her remarks about the text spread over her entire career. Alongside her most adamant statements against the allegorical work and its author, such as the one placed in the mouth of the God of Love in her early *Epistre au dieu d'amours* (1399; *Letter of the God of Love*), are found others that attenuate her seeming condemnation. For example, Lady Opinion reveals in the *Advision* that she motivated the debate to cultivate knowledge through productive dialogue. And in the *Cité des dames* (1405; *City of Ladies*), Christine is self-reproachful: Reason chides the narrator-persona for a critical naïveté in interpreting misogynous texts.

At the same time, Christine's adherence to feminism is too often stressed at the expense of her moral and religious stances, which are predominant in her first volley in the debate, the letter to Jean de Montreuil (Hult 12–13). This is not to say that the question of women is not important but that a considerable amount of its thrust is related to Christine's professional packaging of herself. After answering Jean de Meun's condemnation of all women by providing, in her letter for Jean de Montreuil in the debate, a brief list of virtuous women of the past and present (foreshadowing the *Cité des dames*), Christine turns to self-justification:

> But do not believe, dear sir (and may no other person be of this opinion), that I have stated or enumerated the aforementioned justifications, inflecting them with biased excuses, because I am a woman; for in truth my motivation stems from nothing other than simply advocating pure truth, since by proven knowledge I know this truth to be contrary to the statements refuted by me. And insofar as I am in fact a woman, I am better suited to attest to these matters than he who, not having had this experience, speaks instead through conjecture and in a haphazard manner. (Hult 60; cf. *Débat* [Hicks] 19)

Just as she had opened the letter by proclaiming her status as a woman ("from me, Christine de Pizan, a woman of untrained intellect and uncomplicated sensibility" [Hult 50; *Débat* [Hicks] 12]), she also closes it thus: "Finally, may it not be attributed to folly, arrogance or presumptuousness that I, a woman, dare to reprimand and refute so subtle an author and to divest his work of its renown, when he, just one man, dared undertake to defame and condemn without exception an entire sex" (Hult 63; cf. *Débat* [Hicks] 22). Christine shows an awareness of her feminine identification as a way of acquiring fame and later, in her reply to Pierre Col, refers to the "novelty" of her undertaking that attracted her first patrons (Hult 191; cf. *Débat* [Hicks] 148). The term could seem ambiguous were it not glossed in her later *Advision*. There, she asserts that interest in her modest works arises from their having been composed by a woman: "the unaccustomed fact that a woman might write" (Reno and Dulac 111 [3.11.14–15]). She also speaks with her familiar trope of modesty:

> [I]nasmuch as my aforementioned volumes had already brought me renown, due to the gifts of them that had been made to many princes of foreign countries, not sent by me but by others, as novel products of a woman's intellect—for, as the proverb says, new things bring pleasure (I say it not at all to boast, for that would not be appropriate). . . .
> (Reno and Dulac 113 [3.12.2–7])

Christine responds to Gontier Col's insulting reaction to his reading of her letter, her last word in this first dossier that she assembled for the queen of France, by bluntly summarizing her reasons why the *Rose* is to be condemned. Yet she does not specifically single out Jean de Meun's attack on women or marriage:

> I declare . . . that . . . it can be the source of a wicked and perverse instigation to very abominable behavior encouraging the dissolute life: a doctrine full of deceit, a path to damnation, a public defamer, a cause of suspicion and distrust and shame to many people, and perhaps of heresy, and, in many parts, a most indecent reading experience.
> (Hult 98; cf. *Débat* [Hicks] 26)

The only portion of this enumeration that could be considered related to misogynous speech is "a public defamer, a cause of suspicion and distrust and shame," but these are issues that could likewise apply to Jean de Meun's criticisms of religious hypocrites. Earlier in this letter, she mentions the cause of women, but only as it relates directly to her own undertaking and as a defensive response to Gontier Col's deprecating comment about her limited capacities as a woman ("reproaching my feminine sex" [Hult 97; cf. *Débat* [Hicks] 25).

Critics often do not make enough of the oddities and inconsistencies lurking behind the debate participants' critical stances. Christine's professional motivations in bringing the debate to a public forum are evident in her presentation letter to Guillaume de Tignonville, which is curiously friendly: "the amiable, and not spiteful, debate motivated by contrary opinions among worthy people" (Hult 100; cf. *Débat* [Hicks] 7). Her assessment lies some distance from the not infrequent vituperative passages in the letters. Even as she writes the conclusion of what will be her last word on the subject, after justifying herself and her personal motives to her later opponent, Pierre Col, she will refer to the affair as a "debate, devoid of acrimony, that was begun, elaborated, and ended in a spirit of cheerful entertainment, disrespectful to no one" (Hult 193; cf. *Débat* [Hicks] 150). Instead of dismissing these comments as a kind of window dressing, it is important to consider the social and professional context in which the debate arose.

We do not know the day-to-day relationships of the main participants, but the participants do belong to a rather rarefied group of functionaries-clerks occupying positions in the royal chancery, which, as Badel has shown with utmost clarity, was a hotbed of the new pursuit of humanism (462–82). Christine, herself a widow of one of the king's secretaries, seems to know Jean de Montreuil personally. On the other hand, she states that she is unacquainted with Pierre Col, and the tone of Gontier Col's request for a copy of her letter likewise suggests that Gontier Col does not know her. Jean Gerson (chancellor of Notre Dame), Jean de Montreuil, and the Col brothers, like the other foremost intellectuals of the day, several of whom participated in the *Rose* debate, were accustomed to debate for debate's sake.[2] Such debate was undertaken both to exercise polemical skills in discussing literary and cultural issues of the day (Hill 163) and to hone their Latin style, frequently descending to the ad hominem aspect of the genre (Badel 462–63).

What modern readers typically accept as a serious discussion that is based on ideas and moral convictions would perhaps better be seen, as Badel has argued, as a circumstance reflecting a moment of play among the kings' secretaries and their extended intellectual milieu (both lay and ecclesiastical), a way for France's earliest humanists to throw around ideas about reading and interpretation in a ludic context. Christine's transformation of sincere and deeply felt ideas about men's ungracious if not insulting treatment of women, including verbal assaults and defamation in writing, into a public cause célèbre suggests another type of interest beyond, or adjacent to, the disinterested ideas Christine champions. For even as she insists that the debate came about as a matter of pure chance ("For the beginning of it happened by accident and not by a preconceived intention" [Hult 191; cf. *Débat* [Hicks] 149]), she knew how to exploit this chance event to the fullest, as Badel cannily suggests by calling her initial publication of the debate a "disingenuous gesture" (431).

To insist on Christine's seriousness in support of the feminist, or woman, cause is to paradoxically discount her cleverness and her control of the issues and the strategies of rhetorical argumentation. It is to buy into her claims that she is simple, has a straightforward style, is lacking in sophistication, and must defend herself. Ultimately, it is to place her in the position of helpless female that she constructs for herself, instead of in the role of a "strong or mannish woman" (*virilis illa femina*) or even "Amazon" (*virago*) that Gerson attributes to her, given her debating skills (Hult 226; cf. *Débat* [Hicks] 168). After all, Christine famously characterizes her independent life following the death of her husband as a physical transformation from woman to man (*Mutacion* [Solente] 1: 1321–408). Her repeated claims to mediocrity are a rhetorical strategy, as Pierre Col remarks in the final words of his fragmentary second letter (Hult 194; cf. Débat [Hicks] 154). They are meant to glorify her image, but they likewise mask the many agendas she was balancing in her work and life—which may amount to the same thing, as she made her life the center of her work, at least in this formative period. Furthermore, her sense of irony is obvious at certain moments, such as when she trades miracle stories with Pierre Col regarding how reading the *Romance of the Rose* induced readers to various actions: Pierre Col states that a friend of his had borrowed a copy of the *Rose* from him and was cured of his foolish passions after having read it, to which Christine retorts that, since the discussion had come to the "miracles of *the Romance of the Rose*" (Hult 182; cf. *Débat* [Hicks] 139), she had heard talk of a jealous husband who, when he became fiercely irritated with his wife, would read out passages from the *Rose* to her and accompany his words with kicks and slaps.

Another issue of importance is self-expression and personal style—including ambiguity or the failure to express a clear judgment regarding what is good and what is evil. On this, Gerson and Christine are in complete agreement. For writing to be useful—a category that Christine evokes with some frequency—it must clearly state what is good or virtuous and unambiguously condemn what is evil or sinful. This tenet was not emphasized by Christine in her first letter, but Pierre Col's defense elicits from her a considerable expansion on this topic, displaying what is perhaps her principal misgiving about Jean de Meun and one of her major targets in the debate: her disdain for deceit and trickery, especially in speech.[3] Jean de Meun seems to represent, for her, trickery incarnate: "The nature of the deceiver is to be a liar, perjurer, a hypocrite, a flatterer, a traitor; he is misleading, malicious, spying, underhanded, and an infinite number of other evil things" (Hult 173; cf. *Débat* [Hicks] 130). In fact, as Rosalind Brown-Grant (*Christine*) has argued, what ties together Christine's varied work in the period 1399–1405 is not a narrow defense of women but, more broadly, a commitment to ethics and morality. I would be more precise and suggest that what is pitting these two sides in the debate against each other is a broad ethics of speech (*speech* here taken as the defining component of the activity of debate itself), which is called into play by the two dispositions I have already mentioned, the serious and the ludic. Whereas both Gerson and Christine are adamant about the need to state clearly the moral entailments of one's writing, Pierre Col appreciates the twists and turns that Jean de Meun engages in through the manipulations of his fictional characters. Likewise, Jean de Montreuil portrays this failure to agree as a fundamental difference in perspective, indicating that most people simply don't tolerate ambiguity, "chiefly because human nature is accustomed to find ambiguities (*ambigua*) perverse rather than to take them in the most positive way" (Hult 65; cf. *Débat* [Hicks] 32). Some critics have rightly defended Gerson and Christine against charges that they were unfamiliar with the literary and rhetorical theories lying behind Jean de Meun's play of voices through personification (Hill; Minnis). And, as Lionel J. Friedman suggested years ago, Christine predicated her career on knowingly voicing opinions and sentiments of others while distancing herself from them in such a way that she "confronts us with the irreducible fact that no man can know what another thinks" (443).

We would seem to be at an impasse in our attempt to gauge the participants' stake in the debate, especially Christine's, unless we accept the possibility that the debate, while being a seriously felt and reasoned exchange of opinions on both sides, took place on a plane of mock-seriousness in which each of the participants constructed a quasi-fictional role: some showed their argumentative virtuosity; others allowed the ironies of the situation to flow freely. For Christine, the affair provided an opportunity to establish dialogue with a learned group she undoubtedly admired and envied while publicizing her talents and garnering patronage. By looking at it this way, one can understand why it was precisely Jean de Meun (and not, say, Ovid or Jehan Le Fèvre, the French translator of the notoriously misogynous *Lamentations de Matheolus*) who became the center of debate: he was at once an author who exercised exceptional influence on her and one whose numerous obscene and misogynous gestures were anathema to her—and whose ambiguous and provocative style was far from her ideal of straightforward, moralizing instruction. The progression of her statements about Jean and the *Rose* over the first ten years of her professional career would indeed seem to indicate that she had come to terms with this important author and that the debate was an important step in her development, not just one that she had got past but one that, in her increasing subtlety, she learned to appreciate as worthwhile and productive. One tends too often to forget that she is beholden to Jean de Meun for more than the *Rose* and what it taught about the writing of didactic allegorical fictions. He was also the renowned author of a translation of Boethius's *Consolation of Philosophy*, a text that was an important influence on her moral and personal vision. As Glynnis Cropp has shown ("Boèce"), Christine used a well-known version falsely attributed to Jean de Meun (see also *Livre de l'advision* [Reno and Dulac] xxviii–xxxi), as Christine herself indicates when she refers knowingly to Jean's prologue to the Boethius translation in her letter to Pierre Col (*Débat* [Hicks] 121; Hult 165).

In short, the *Rose* debate does not need to stand for students as simply a quaint affair in which Christine de Pizan nobly stood up for the cause of women and for what is frequently considered an outdated Christian morality. The debate not only reveals the terms used in debates over obscene speech and censorship, which retain their currency in our own twenty-first-century debates (Henninger), but also more profoundly suggests that debating is not totally based on substance, ideas, or moral convictions. The question of positionality and contradiction in such debates, extending from the adamant moralist obsessed by the dangerous attractions of obscenity to the ironic satirist celebrating verbal or visual license regardless of its potentially personal or public repercussions, can easily be mapped by students onto behavior in our society that is all too current. But, lest we forget, at the root of the debate was the figure of Jean de Meun, as a provocateur and satirist of the first order whose attacks on hypocrites, specifically of the religious stripe, are even more devastating than his misogynous gibes. At one crucial moment in his narrative, he anticipates criticism of these attacks in the following way:

> [I]t was never my intention to speak against any man alive following holy religion who spends his life in good works. . . . I let my arrow fly collectively in order to wound. To wound? Rather to recognize those cursed men that Jesus calls hypocrites. . . . And if, to receive the blow, it happens that someone willingly places himself in front of the arrow, who in his pride so deceives himself as to get himself shot and then complains that I have injured him, I have no guilt on that account and never will, even if he were to die because of it. (Strubel 802–05)

As Eric Hicks pithily remarked, "[I]f the *Roman* fit so easily into the debate, it is because the debate was already in the romance" (*Débat* [Hicks] xix).

NOTES

[1] Unless otherwise indicated, all translations are my own.

[2] Although the other participants in the debate remain unnamed, Jean de Montreuil refers to these detractors of the *Rose* as "many learned men of no little authority" (Hult 65; cf. *Débat* [Hicks] 32).

[3] This issue goes back to the *Epistre au dieu d'amours*.

Christine's Kingly Ideal: *Le livre des fais et bonnes meurs du sage roy Charles V*

Daisy Delogu

Christine de Pizan's *Livre des fais et bonnes meurs du sage roy Charles V* (*Book of Deeds and Good Practices of the Wise King Charles V*) was completed in 1404, approximately a decade into her career as an author. It may be considered her first political treatise (see Dulac, "Authority"), ushering in a new phase of her literary production, one marked by more overtly political and didactic works composed for the most part in prose. Christine's biography of Charles was instrumental in shaping late medieval notions of kingship, retooling the model of the fourteenth-century king for use in the dawning fifteenth century and beyond.

The *Fais et bonnes meurs* constitutes an excellent point of entry into the study of Christine's works, for it deals with issues and themes that are raised by her other texts, including her self-representation and claims to literary authority, her didacticism, and her use of compilation as a compositional technique. Nonspecialists tend to turn first to the *Livre de la cité des dames* (*The Book of the City of Ladies*), perhaps the best known of her works, when constructing their syllabi. However, the *Fais et bonnes meurs*, which is available in modern French (translated by Blanchard and Quereuil, and Hicks and Moreau) and English (translated by Laird), would provide much to talk about in courses such as French or world literature, women's studies, history, or political science.

Like many of Christine's works, the *Fais et bonnes meurs* is tripartite. Christine explains the organization of her text explicitly at the outset and frequently returns to her proposed plan to demonstrate her adherence to it, justify digressions from it, or further refine it. The *Fais et bonnes meurs* may be considered in the light of the Suetonian biographical tradition, which favors a thematic rather than a chronological organization (Willard, *Christine* 118–33). As Christine states in her prologue, book 1, composed of thirty-six chapters, addresses nobility of heart. Book 2 (39 chapters) discusses chivalry and how it is exemplified by Charles. Book 3 considers the nature of wisdom and its manifestation in the wise king. At seventy-two chapters, book 3 is by far the longest of the three, thereby reflecting the primacy of this virtue. In each book, Christine further parses the quality that is her main focus, separating it into its constitutive parts, each of which she examines in turn. Her thematic approach allows her to memorialize Charles and to provide a model of ideal kingship and also to display her own erudition, demonstrating herself to be a fifteenth-century Ciceronian orator figure capable of guiding the powerful on the path of virtue for the greater good of France.

Christine as Author

Sensitive to her status as a female author, even one with an increasingly impressive body of works to her credit, Christine constantly asserts her literary authority (Dulac, "Authority"). In the prologue of the *Fais et bonnes meurs* she describes the text's commissioning by Philip of Burgundy, brother of Charles V and uncle of the reigning king, noting the time and manner in which she was summoned and recounting the conversation that unfolded between her and the duke. This opening allows her to present herself as an established author, for she affirms that Philippe's commission was a direct result of his appreciation for her *Livre de la mutacion de Fortune* (*Book of the Mutability of Fortune*), which she had presented to him as a New Year's gift. The *Fais et bonnes meurs* also marks a shift in her political allegiances or a reconsideration of her hopes for the future of France, which she pins here on Philip of Burgundy rather than her former patrons and dedicatees: the dauphin, Louis of Guyenne, and the king's brother, Louis of Orléans (Gauvard; Mombello 100–10). Moreover, this personal scene illustrates from the outset how, as in her other works, Christine's vision of history is always inflected by her situated perspective.

That presence is keenly felt throughout the *Fais et bonnes meurs*. In addition to describing her meeting with Philip of Burgundy, at the start of book 2, Christine mourns his death as a loss to her personally, thereby linking her welfare to that of the kingdom (Walters, "Christine de Pizan as Translator" and "Christine de Pizan, France's Memorialist"). She evokes her interactions with other princes, including Louis II of Bourbon and Louis of Orléans, and explains how her family came to reside in France as a result of her father's invitation to the court of Charles V (bk. 1, ch. 15).[1] Her physical description of Charles V and his outings on horseback is based on her own recollections of the king (ch. 17), while her father is given as the source for several of the events she recounts, principally the death of the king (bk. 3, ch. 71; Solente, Introduction lvi–lx). Her name-dropping shows that she is a person of importance and establishes her as one of the sources for the material she includes in her text, yet her anecdotes create a certain intimacy between author and subject that suggests that she is uniquely well suited to writing the late king's life (Dulac, "Authority"). Her privileging of personal experience may be remarked in a number of her other works as well and provides an alternative source for her authorial credentials, given her lack of conventional, clerkly authority (Blanchard, "Christine de Pizan").

Christine further reinforces her literary authority by citing her prior works in a way that presumes her public's familiarity with them and that places her literary production on the same level as the other authoritative texts that she incorporates into her own, including those of Aristotle, Vegetius, and Giles of Rome. Her use of other texts exposes her to one of the most serious accusations leveled against her literary authority—by some modern critics as well as by her contemporaries—namely, that she is incapable of original thought and does no more than reassemble excerpts from other sources, adding nothing to them. In a preemptive response to her imagined detractors, she provides what is perhaps her most famous defense of compilation as a compositional technique (Blanchard, "Compilation"). In chapter 21 of book 2, she constructs an extended metaphor based on the figures of the embroiderer and the architect, who do not fabricate the threads or the stones with which they work but who are responsible for arranging them into a beautiful and significant order that transforms and endows them with new meaning:

> [T]out ainsi vrayement n'ay je mie fait toutes les matieres, de quoy le traittié de ma compilacion est composé; il me souffist seulement que les sache appliquer à propos, si que bien puissent servir à la fin de l'ymaginacion, à laquelle je tends à perfaire. (2: 191)

> In such a manner, truly I have not made all of the materials from which the substance of my compilation is composed. It suffices that I know how to apply them appropriately, so that they might well serve the idea which I endeavor to accomplish.

In order to further highlight the expertise and effort required by compilation, Christine comments frequently on her writing process, discussing her movement from one subject to the next and portraying herself hard at work selecting and assembling her materials (Dulac, "Authority").

The Fais et bonnes meurs*: Biography? History? Mirror for Princes?*

Although Christine insists on rigorous organization, her text is characterized by numerous digressions: historical anecdotes, technical descriptions, especially of military matters, and philosophical speculations dominate each of the three books of the *Fais et bonnes meurs*, respectively (Dulac, "De l'art"). She employs an array of sources, including oral accounts, florilegium-type books, and chronicles (Hicks, "Excerpts"; Solente, Introduction xxxii–lxx). Her propensity for digression and her reliance on a variety of sources point to a certain tension produced by her multiple, and sometimes conflicting, textual goals. She intends to focus on Charles—indeed she is careful to explain how her digressions relate to her biographical subject—but also wants to provide a taxonomy of royal virtue. She tends to idealize the late king—there is not a quality that he cannot be seen to illustrate—yet she also wishes to commemorate the real life of a historical figure (Blanchard, "Christine de Pizan" 214; Zimmermann, "Mémoire"). Her wide-ranging ambitions for her text allow her work to be considered not simply as a biography but also in relation to a number of other discursive traditions.

Even though her text constitutes one of the principal historical sources on the reign of Charles V, Christine in no way purports to provide a history of the life or the reign of the king. Indeed, she very clearly distinguishes her text from historical accounts, sometimes referring her public elsewhere—to the *Grandes chroniques de France*, for instance, or Cuvelier's life of Du Guesclin—if they wish to learn the details of historical events. Yet she espouses certain historical methods. Like the chronicler Froissart, who relied on witness accounts in the composition of his text, she declares that "me suis informée, tant par croniques, comme par pluseurs gens notables encore vivans jadis ses serviteurs, de sa vie, condicions, meurs et ordre de vivre, et de ses fais particuliers" (1: 9; "I informed myself—as much by chronicles as by several illustrious people still alive who formerly were his servants—about his life, his disposition, his morals and manner of living, and about his personal actions"). As with her recollections of the king, this method privileges personal experience, raising it to the level of written sources. At the same time, it bolsters her authority, showing her to be a person with access to those who were intimate with the king. Christine's text certainly does not eschew history altogether. In chapter 5 of book 1 she provides a history and genealogy of the kings of France, beginning with France's Trojan origins and insisting particularly on the continuity of French royal succession, a pointed reminder of Valois legitimacy at a time when it had long been contested by the English.

Christine seeks to provide not a historical account of Charles's reign but an edifying moral portrait of the wise king. In this respect the *Fais et bonnes meurs* reflects the didacticism that is present in all her works. While in many of her earlier texts she discussed courtly love, advising women how to preserve their honor and reputations, later she reflected on proper political and social conduct and addressed a wide range of publics. The *Epistre Othea* (*Othea's Letter to Hector*) is a guide to virtuous living written for Christine's son, Jean; the *Livre des trois vertus* (*Treasure of the City of Ladies*) provides moral and social guidance for women of all ranks; and the *Livre des fais d'armes et de chevallerie* (*The Book of Deeds of Arms and of Chivalry*) offers instruction to knights. Here, Charles V's life functions as an exemplum, providing a model of kingship for the dauphin and other princes.

Christine has almost nothing to say about the king's childhood or adolescence, beginning her narrative instead with what she describes as a kind of epiphany that took place in Charles at the time of his coronation, when he awoke to and embraced his kingly duties (bk. 1, ch. 8). Her silence concerning the king's youth has opened her text to the charge made by some modern readers that it offers little more than panegyric, that she is interested in furnishing not an objective depiction of Charles but an idealized and unrealistic portrait that reflects her own notion of kingly virtue rather than the reality offered by his life. Her representation of Charles does in fact reflect the strong medieval belief in the power of exempla to shape conduct. Charles's actions are explicitly held up as models for Christine's contemporaries: at the time of his coronation Charles dismissed his bad counselors

> [l]equel exemple noter seroit expedient aux princes et nobles, tant en leur fait, comme en gouvernement de leurs meneurs, lesquelz sont par

> mauvaiz losengeurs plus admonnestés es folies peut-estre, que meismes nature ou jeunece ne les admonneste ou semont. (1: 37)

> an example which it would be advisable for princes and nobles to observe, as much in regard to their own conduct, as with respect to the government of their wards, who are perhaps incited more by evil flatterers to perform foolish acts than even nature or youth induce or lead them to do.

Likewise his mercy and generosity are "digne de estre nottée et receue en forme de exemple" (1: 64 [bk. 1, ch. 24]; "worthy of being noted and received as examples").

If Christine fails to discuss Charles's faults, it is not because she is blind to them, as has sometimes been alleged, but because of the conscious choice that she made in relation to the various miniportraits of notable figures that are painted in the course of book 2. She explains—in response to another imagined reproach, that she flatters those whom she describes—that it would be inappropriate for her to discuss the failings of the princes and nobles she depicts, if indeed they possess any. These failings should be corrected by their friends in private; the public airing of them would serve no purpose. Because flattery consists of "faintement par mençonge louer aultrui par controuvées blandices" ("falsely praising another with lies or with invented adulation"), a truthful description of a person's good character and actions is not flattery. Indeed, failing to provide the good examples of people to her reading public would be a crime against virtue: "taire vertu et bienfait, où qu'il soit veu et aperceu, devroit estre reputé comme raim de envie ou reprimacion de salutaire exemple" (1: 183; "to be silent about virtue and good conduct, there where it is seen and perceived, should be considered an offshoot of envy or the repression of a salutary example"). This explanation is equally applicable to her biographical project. Praising Charles is not—or not the only—aim of her book, which is oriented also "à l'augmentacion de vertu et destruisement de vice" (1: 102; "toward the increase of virtue and the destruction of vice").

Christine's Ideal Sovereign

If Charles's character and deeds constitute a moral example for Christine's readers, her more general reflections on the nature of various virtues allow Christine to consider the very institution of kingship and the ideal sovereign (Delogu, *Theorizing*). Her portrait of the king, as it emerges from the *Fais et bonnes meurs*, possesses elements that are both conventional and distinctive, and her unique vision not only reflects but also helped shape late medieval notions of kingship.

Medieval authors had a great many virtues—biblical, classical, and chivalric—from which to choose in their construction of an ideal of kingship, and it is important to look closely at the particular qualities that a given author chooses to privilege (Forhan, *Political Theory* 82–84). The virtues around which Christine structures her work—nobility of heart, chivalry, and wisdom—indicate what qualities she believes to be the most important.

Charles's nobility of heart is manifested principally by the order that Charles maintains and imposes in all areas of life. Order is one of the three Augustinian requisites for kingship, along with peace and justice, and is fundamental to Christine's representation of his kingship. In book 1, chapter 16, Christine describes an assortment of well-ordered or orderly rulers, while chapter 17 examines in detail the nature and significance of Charles's order. Following Giles of Rome, whose extremely influential *De Regimine Principum* (translated into French by Henri de Gauchy in the early fourteenth century) was divided into three books—governance of self, of one's family, and of the state—she affirms that "la science de politiques, suppellative entre les ars, enseigne homme à gouverner soy-meismes, sa maisgné et subgiez et toutes choses selon ordre juste et limité" (1: 52; "the understanding of politics, supreme among the arts, teaches man to govern himself, his household and subjects, and all things according to a just and fixed order"). The word *order* and its cognates are repeated almost obsessively in her description of Charles's typical day, his outings, his household. Order is the basis for his subjects' fear of him, which derived not from his rigor but

> [p]ar pure amour de laquelle vient crainte bien ordennée, qui les faisoit doubter offenser sa digne majesté, car toutes choses tant par ordre estoient menées en tous ses fais, que riens n'y eust fait où il n'eust gardé raison, ordre, temps et mesure. (1: 81)

> from pure love, from which comes well-ordered fear, which made them dread to offend his worthy majesty, for in all his actions all things were conducted according to order, such that he would have done nothing in which he did not preserve reason, order, time, and measure.

Order also provides the foundation for other qualities. In book 2 Christine states that "il n'est chose plus neccessaire à avoir ordre qu'il est en l'excercite et fait d'armes" (1: 119; "there is no area in which it is more necessary to have order than in the exercise and undertaking of arms"), and disorder is the undoing of many military enterprises, an observation that surely would have resounded with Christine's public, who had witnessed the recent military disaster of Nicopolis and who still felt the effects of the earlier losses of the Hundred Years War, such as those at Poitiers (1356) and Crécy (1346). Her admiration for Charles's order leads naturally to her discussion of his administration of justice, since justice itself may be defined as "ordre, mesure et balance de toutes choses rendre à chascun selon son droit" (1: 63; "order, measure, and equilibrium in rendering all things to each one according to his rights"). Justice is another Augustinian—and Aristotelian—virtue, and it is perhaps the most fundamental quality of kingship. For most medieval thinkers, the administration of justice constitutes the origin and the justification for the very institution of kingship, and the failure to maintain justice is the most serious lapse of a king's obligations toward his subjects and indeed toward God. Christine's description of Charles's justice (bk. 1, ch. 23) recalls the celebrated justice of Saint Louis. Like his saintly forefather, Charles sought justice for all, not only for the rich, important, and powerful, and he was personally involved in and committed to the administration of justice.

As for peace, Christine is obliged to put a new spin on this quality, the third Augustinian kingly virtue. Here Charles departs from the example of Saint Louis, who was renowned as the king of peace, since Charles's reign was marked by warfare, specifically the reconquest of those lands that were lost to the English after his father's defeat at Poitiers. Christine needs to show how warfare, not peace, was in the best interest of the French. To this end she depicts Charles as the good shepherd (bk. 2, ch. 5), one who resumed hostilities only after careful consideration and with the support of his counselors in order to safeguard the kingdom, his people, and his rights. She articulates an important principle, that of the inalienability of the French territory, which Charles and his counselors had themselves endeavored to promote during his reign. According to this idea, the kingdom was not the personal property of the king, to do with as he pleased, but transcended the authority of any individual king, whose duty it was to preserve it intact for his successors. From this perspective the Treaty of Brétigny, signed by Jean II, which gave the English king approximately one third of the kingdom, was not binding, for "convenance ou promesse faitte ou prejudice de l'utilité publique et meismement par contrainte ne doit estre tenue" (1: 127; "an agreement or promise made to the detriment of the public good and likewise under duress should not be upheld"). Christine's perception that care of *l'utilité publique* can trump the word of a king reflects the influence of Aristotle's *Politics* on late medieval thought and marks an important development in perceptions of the duties and authority of the king.

Christine similarly reinterprets other qualities of kingship in order to better demonstrate how they are exemplified by Charles V. Generosity, for instance, traditionally a chivalric virtue, is redefined in the *Fais et bonnes meurs* to include benevolence toward one's household and followers rather than material largesse (bk. 1, ch. 27). She redefines even more radically the notion of chivalry, which she depicts as an intellectual, not a physical, enterprise. To support this position she cites the military historian and theoretician Vegetius, who "dit . . . que plus doit estre louée chevalerie menée à cause de sens que celle, qui est conduitte par effett d'armes" (1: 132–33; "says . . . that chivalry conducted by means of intelligence is more to be praised than that driven by the action of arms"). Christine goes on to compare Charles's successes with those of the Romans, models of military achievement (1: 133), and in so doing she vastly expands the idea of chivalry, which embraces all successful and effective government.

Charles's chivalry is illustrated by his ability to raise and pay great armies and to conquer or reconquer lands, but equally by his ability to construct public works, maintain an impressive household, and avoid burdening his people with taxes (Forhan, *Political Theory* 143). Charles V is further presented as the fourteenth-century incarnation of his namesake, Charlemagne, the warrior-king par excellence. By foregrounding the intellectual aspects of chivalry, Christine creates a new vision of the warrior-king, illustrated by both Charles V and Charlemagne, in which "the brave knight cedes his place to the tactician" (Krynen, *L'empire du roi* 213; translation mine).

It is no coincidence that Christine's defense of compilation appears in the same book as her reformulation of chivalry, for as Christine would have it, she and Charles V are engaged in parallel enterprises. Just as Christine seeks to highlight the originality and the importance of her own literary undertaking in spite of her reliance on a range of written and oral sources, so too Charles is presented as a true warrior-king, even though he did not physically engage in the reconquest, but depended upon the military expertise of his constable, Bertrand Du Guesclin, and others. In this manner Christine associates her own literary authority with Charles's kingly virtue.

Christine's reformulation of chivalry as an intellectual endeavor derives from her belief that wisdom constitutes the principal quality of kingship and the one best exemplified by Charles V, to whom she gave his sobriquet, the Wise. As elsewhere, her aims in book 3 are multiple. Christine wishes to consider the nature of wisdom, which she divides into its constitutive parts and examines systematically, and also to show how Charles was a "vrai philosophe" ("true philosopher"), a true "ameur de sapience" (2: 13; "lover of wisdom"). The king had long been enjoined to surround himself with wise counselors, but the notion that the king himself should possess wisdom was more recent, traceable in large part to John of Salisbury's observation, in his *Policraticus*, that "rex illiteratus quasi asinus coronatus" (1: 254; "an illiterate king is no better than a crowned ass"). Accordingly, Christine shows over the course of book 3 that Charles was versed in the seven liberal arts, read Latin, respected clerics, and was a skilled orator as well as a true artist. In chapter 13, Charlemagne and Charles are again placed in parallel, this time as two great patrons of learning, the first of whom founded the University of Paris that the other so loved and supported. In chapter 12, Christine celebrates the foremost intellectual achievement of Charles V's reign: his project to have translated into French a considerable number of Latin works—both medieval and classical, such as Augustine's *City of God*; Aristotle's *Politics*, *Ethics*, and *Economics*; and the *Policraticus*—which were then made available in the royal library, housed in the Louvre. As with the reconquest, the success of which was credited to Charles's exemplary oversight rather than to the military figures who carried out the operations, Christine makes Charles responsible for the translations, failing to name any of the scholars who labored under his patronage (Lefèvre). She thereby again reinforces her literary authority by instituting an implicit parallel between herself and the wise king, both of whom marshal the labor and intellect of others, in the process demonstrating the superiority of their endeavors.

The most important component of wisdom is prudence, which Christine depicts as a kind of applied wisdom (Green, "On Translating"; Richarz). It is prudence, defined as "memoire, intelligence et pourveance" (2: 21; "memory, intelligence, and foresight"), that allows Charles to clarify the laws of succession, disagreements concerning which had led to the Hundred Years War, to plan public works projects, and to ensure the love and loyalty of his subjects by means of carefully staged consultations. His prudence engages him in a practical and results-oriented approach to kingship. He chooses counselors based on their expertise, not their rank; selects works of science, mathematics, and political philosophy as objects for translation; and, perhaps more problematically, understands that values can be relative: "[L]es circonstances font les choses bonnes ou mauvaises, car en tel maniere peut estre dissimulé, que c'est vertu, et en tel maniere, vice" (2: 74; "Circumstances make things good or bad, for in one way something can be dissimulated and it is a virtue, and in another way, a vice").

Charles was a pivotal figure in the development of ideas about kingship. His alliance of political power and intelligence make him a forerunner of humanism (Zimmermann, "Mémoire"), while the sensitivity to circumstances, focus on results, and flexibility regarding means when pursuing a desired end, which characterize much of his approach to kingship, prefigure Machiavelli's prince. Christine's *Fais et bonnes meurs*, though not extensively disseminated in manuscript form, was widely influential, and was the most frequently edited of her works (Zimmermann, "Mémoire" 160). Throughout the long centuries when Christine's considerable literary production was largely neglected, her reputation hinged on her biography of Charles, which even today provides much of what we know about Charles V and his reign and continues to shape our impressions of the wise king.

NOTE

[1]The text of *Fais et bonnes meurs* cited in this essay is taken from Suzanne Solente's edition. Text citations give the volume and page numbers, while more general ideas or arguments give Christine's book and chapter numbers. The English translations are mine.

Ethical Architecture in the *Cité des dames*

Andrea Tarnowski

People who focus too closely on one aspect of an issue and thus fail to grasp the whole are told they can't see the forest for the trees. When students read *The Book of the City of Ladies* they may miss the city for the bricks.[1] This text cites or recounts scores of stories of virtuous women, each of which counts as a stone in an edifice that Christine has been chosen to build (pt. 1, story 14.4). The names of the virtuous women—from antiquity, mythology, French history, and hagiography—will almost all be unfamiliar to undergraduates. *The City of Ladies* participates in the medieval genre of the compendium or compilation; thus, readers do not acquire a detailed sense of a few characters who run through the narrative but instead are presented with an accumulation of examples, or instances, of various virtues. The profusion of names and capsule tales can overwhelm, and instructors may be asked why Christine found it necessary or desirable to illustrate a point with ten stories, when one or two might have sufficed. One approach to this question is to concentrate attention on the larger project of *The City of Ladies* as a work of ethical architecture. *Ethical architecture* describes both action and design, both practice and theory; in the text, Christine builds as she goes along, yet construction proceeds according to an encompassing, predetermined plan. The guiding principle of the city building is justice; its result is a community. The women whose stories constitute by far the greatest part of the text are not important for what or who they are but rather for what they do and what they represent. The conjunction of deed and meaning is the lesson of every story and of *The City of Ladies* as a whole.

Architecture and building are evoked at the structural junctures of the text; the metaphor returns each time a new section of the city is begun or completed. *The City of Ladies* is divided into three books that correspond to parts of the city: foundations and walls in book 1; palaces, inns, and mansions in book 2; and roofs in book 3. Medieval reliance on moral and religious hierarchy thus informs the notion of building from the ground up; stories from book 1 concern pagan women and goddesses; those in book 2 portray a range of figures from mythology, history, and the Old Testament; and book 3 consists entirely of tales of saints and holy women. The author connects the stories and makes a whole of them through references to the city's construction. Had she not allowed readers these landmarks or resting places—moments when one building stage is summarized and the next undertaken—the text would appear more a series of things than an organization of them and present more units than unity. Yet in emphasizing to students how the metaphor of edifice governs the work, the instructor should also note how few passages of text are involved. Christine lays out narrative markers sparingly, just as the character Christine is only occasionally described as having mixed mortar or placed a stone. Most of the stories of virtuous women are recounted as such, without return to the thematics of building. If we compare the city Christine erects with other allegories of place among her sources, it is clear that she could have stressed either the physicality of the locus or its static, transcendent nature more than she did (see Mann). When Dante makes his tripartite voyage through hell, purgatory, and heaven, the tangible, material aspect of each landscape is pursued in an abundance of detail, so that environments of mud and marble impose themselves on the senses. When the orchard wall is figured in *The Romance of the Rose*, all its portraits—Avarice, Sadness, Poverty—convey unchanging qualities or states rather than human beings. Christine pursues neither of these effects, instead finding a middle way that focuses on individual stories to prove virtue's enduring nature.

The simultaneous concern for both action and idea, or example and principle, is evident in her development of the architectural metaphor and the way she depicts herself in relation to the project. The simple but strenuous gestures of the builder stand in contradistinction to the conceptual effort of the architect. Which figure is more accurately associated with Christine? The author's work partakes of each function; she necessarily stands outside the text and holds purchase over all, but also executes the narrative and brings it progressively into being. Christine's discussion of both design and building in other works, notably *Les fais et bonnes meurs du sage roy Charles V* (*The Book of Deeds and Good Practices of the Wise King Charles V*), has led scholars to emphasize the wide-ranging mastery that an architect brings to his or her enterprise, affirming that "The genius of the construction . . . lies in having the global vision of the end product" (Delogu, "Christine de Pizan" 150). But the builder's on-site contribution should not be diminished; in *Fais et bonnes meurs* (1: 191), Christine draws an analogy between herself and "l'ovrier de architecture ou maçonnage" ("a laborer in architecture or masonry"). She never loses sight of the value of doing. It could be argued that in conjoining the ideas of manual labor and architecture, or for that matter of architecture and masonry, she offers up a uniquely medieval notion of the designer as builder; her age did not insist on a separation of these roles. As the author of *The City of Ladies*, she exploits the tools of both trades.

This duality of function also plays itself out explicitly in the tale, where the character Christine appears as protagonist. As the first book opens, Christine is in her study reading. When she comes upon a work of misogynist calumny, she falls into despair at having been born a woman. In the midst of her shame and sorrow, she is visited by three ladies, Reason, Rectitude, and Justice, who announce that she should take heart; a great task lies before her. She will build a city to protect all virtuous ladies. But the figure actually responsible for planning and constructing the city remains ambiguous throughout the text—this point can be examined with students in order to see what authority Christine claims. In the beginning of the ladies' visit, Reason affirms that Christine will "establish and build" the city, from stone and mortar that the allegorical trio will provide (1.4.1, 4.3). This suggests that the ladies will merely supply materials—sources and stories of virtue—that Christine will use, arrange, organize, and oversee. In every way, she will create the city. But in the same speech, Reason tells her that she must follow the ladies' plan to set the city's foundations and must follow Reason's commands so that her work will be without error (1.4.3). The implication is that the three ladies have fully conceived the city's design and address Christine as a helpmeet. Being allegories, they have a superior status and are not subject to the doubt, fear, and error that beset Christine. They have descended to earth to correct her misperceptions. When Reason explains, "[W]e have come to vanquish from the world the same error into which you [fell]" and says that the city "has been predestined and established by our aid and counsel for you to build" (1.3.3), the reader perceives the allegories as both initiating and directing the project.

The degree of power and control that Christine accords herself in the narrative remains unclear. On the one hand, at the end of each stage of building, one of the allegories asserts that Christine has completed the work of the allegory; on the other, the allegories sometimes describe themselves as Christine's assistants (1.5.1). At the close of book 1, Reason speaks of "the walls I have built for you to enclose the City" (1.48.1); in book 2, Rectitude says, "I have built [the city] up with beautiful palaces . . . I have populated it for your sake" (2.68.11); in book 3, Justice concludes, "I have acquitted myself well . . . in completing the high roofs of your City" (3.18.9). But in the rubric that introduces the building project, the role of Christine is highlighted: she is to "construct a city with the help of these . . . three ladies" (1.3.1). Tracing her claims to and retreats from authority for the city's construction can engage students to think about the status of ideas and principles in the text. Can a human being act as a reliable purveyor of truth, or is this function better shifted to a suprahuman character? If the flaws and faults inherent in humanity become part of a discussion of virtue, will the goal of attaining virtue necessarily be diminished?

In addition to the text of *The City of Ladies* and such half-textual, half-visual elements as rubrics, the miniatures that illustrate the work are invaluable subjects for analysis. Three beautifully colored and detailed illuminations, one before each book, accompany *The City of Ladies* in the most lavish manuscript of Christine's collected works; they are easily found online in the gallery of *The Making of the Queen's Manuscript* Web site (www.pizan.lib.ed.ac.uk/gallery/; folios 290r, 323r, 361r), but are also reproduced in black and white in Earl Jeffrey Richards's English translation.[2]

This translation places the illuminations, as the fifteenth-century manuscript does, at the beginning of each of the three books, so that readers can gain some small sense of what it was like to read the work in its original format and can consider the textual interpretations inherent in illustration. For the question of Christine's role in the building of the city, the first miniature in the Queen's Manuscript is particularly relevant. Divided in two, it gives viewers a dual vision of Christine; in the left-hand image, she stands at a desk in a walled room, several books at her side and one open before her; the three allegorical ladies stand opposite, each holding her identifying attribute (a mirror for Reason, a ruler for Rectitude, and a measuring vessel for Justice). In the right-hand image, the circular wall of the city begins to take shape. Christine, in the same outfit she wears in the left-hand image, stands outside the wall and leans over to use a trowel to spread mortar; on the inside of the wall, facing her, an allegorical lady bends, carrying a neatly cut rectangular stone to lay on the spot that Christine is preparing. The most striking feature of this illustration is that it depicts Christine as both a thinker and a builder, someone familiar with books and deeds. That the two images are presented to be read like a text, from left to right, shows that reflection must beget action. The placement of the three ladies across from Christine in the left-hand image provides information as to how to read their roles in the text. Reason, who will be the first to speak and whose discourse governs book 1, stands farthest from the viewer and has no direct contact with Christine; their gazes do not intersect. The mirror that Reason holds up to encourage orderly introspection—she subscribes to the dictum "know thyself"—would, in a real physical setting, reflect Christine's profile, while it would reflect the reader-onlooker in full face. Its position at the center of the left-hand image signals the importance of the reader's engagement in the City of Ladies project. The reader may be a potential candidate for entry into the city—as was the historical dedicatee of this manuscript, the queen of France, whom Christine enjoined on various occasions to be morally worthy of her exalted position.

Access to the city is gained through moral conduct, and so it is Rectitude who stands in the middle of the miniature's allegorical threesome. Fittingly, she occupies the threshold that leads out of the walled room into the space where the city is under construction. Indeed, one line of sight in the miniature moves from a window behind Christine, to Christine's head, to Rectitude's ruler, and then to the doorway behind Rectitude. Behavior, comportment, the ways one chooses to act are morally and visually central to the existence of the city. In the text, Rectitude speaks throughout book 2, the middle section of the work. It is the longest part of the three and contains the most examples of virtuous women. It also contains the most dialogue; Christine questions Rectitude extensively, intervening and commenting on the stories recounted, affirming the excellence of women's virtues and deploring misogynist criticism. In book 1, Christine has a more discreet presence; in book 3, the transcendent voice of Justice takes over entirely. Thus, when Christine the author describes the attitudes and actions over which any individual can have the most control, the role of Christine the character expands. Rectitude's book explores the best of human qualities—devotion, loyalty, courage—and Christine participates in examining what lies in human scope.

The third lady in the work's opening miniature is Justice. She stands in the foreground of the image, visually linked to Christine in two ways. First, it is to

Justice that Christine turns her body, her gaze, and the instructional pointing gesture of her fingers, which are positioned to indicate in the same movement the open book on the desk and the allegorical figure. Second, a series of closed books with colored bindings lies between Christine and Justice, making something of a visual stepladder from one figure to the other. The portrayal of this special bond is in keeping with Justice's status as the first among equals in *The City of Ladies*. Though the three allegorical ladies are distinguished by their clothing and the attributes they hold in the work's opening miniature, the distinctions are more nuanced in the text. When the character Christine describes her wonder at the beauty of the first lady (subsequently introduced as Reason), she expresses equal admiration for the others: "I did not know which one to look at, for the three ladies resembled each other so much that they could be told apart only with difficulty, except for the last one" (1.3.1). Justice later confirms both the similarities between her and her sisters—"we are as one and the same"—and her own superior status: "I have a special place among the Virtues, for they are all based on me" (1.6.1). Justice, who oversees the third book, completes the roofs of the city, tells the stories of holy women, and invites the Virgin Mary to reign over the city as its queen, thus marking the pinnacle of the allegorical hierarchy. Hell, Earth, and Heaven all submit to Justice's jurisdiction; every domain is subject to her principle (1.6.1). Focusing on her role in *The City of Ladies* will help students grasp the purpose of the city, for indeed the whole edifice is founded on justice. Christine initially despairs because she thinks the authors who denigrate women must be right; she cannot question their criticisms. As she listens to the ladies' stories and reflects on her own experience, she comes to realize the truth. But understanding is not enough; she must publicize this truth, save those who live exemplary lives, and claim redress for past and even future wrongs by erecting the protective, preserving city. The pursuit of justice motivates her building.

I draw students' attention to the section of narrative that begins after the three ladies' arrival and comes to a close as Reason lays the first stone of the city (the tale of Semiramis, queen of the Amazons [1.14.4–15.1]; the Amazons' kingdom will be compared unfavorably with Christine's city in 2.12.1). Before building, Christine and Reason must excavate the earth and remove "black, dirty and uneven stones" (1.8.3), the misogynist stories told by men. This is also the place to refute persistent calumnies, such as the saying that women are good for nothing but weeping, speaking, and sewing (1.10.3–8). The pages that follow the introduction of the three ladies are thus devoted to undoing injustice; they remove all that would be inimical to the construction of the City of Ladies. Next, Reason presents a group of stories; though similar in format to the dozens of stories that will be part of the city, these precede the beginning of construction. The tales in the pre-city group concern women who govern those who, we might say, represent justice on earth. Between the two textual actions of clearing the ground and starting to build the wall, justice is at issue. A series of examples of women who ruled well is headed by the Empress Nicaula, singled out as "the first to begin to live according to laws and coordinated policies. . . . She herself instituted laws of far-reaching justice for governing her people" (1.12.1). I would submit to students that the early part of the *City of Ladies* seeks to detail and expose injustice, and the rest of the text enacts its opposite: it gives or applies justice, commemorating and sheltering virtuous women. The early pages of the text that advocate just rule also indicate the work's larger project: its moral architecture.

Although justice is the goal of the City of Ladies and the actions of Lady Justice may be examined with particular attention, no single lady or quality should be studied to the exclusion of the others; indeed, the text insists on the solidarity of the three virtuous allegories and the indissolubility of their bond. It can be a fruitful classroom assignment to ask students to develop the point of view of Reason, Rectitude, or Justice or to place any individual story of an inhabitant of the city in the context of one of these virtues, but there is always the need to return to the structure of the text as a whole; its constituent parts, once detailed, should be resynthesized. This point is valuably illustrated in the miniatures that accompany *The City of Ladies* in the Queen's Manuscript. For while the Christine character is recognizable from image to image, wearing a blue dress and white headgear throughout, the portrayal of the allegorical virtues shows a different kind of consistency.

In the first half of the first image, the three ladies are dressed in varying colors and styles, and each carries her own attribute. Their unifying traits are their fair, similarly styled hair and their golden crowns. But in the second half of this image, where Christine and Lady Reason begin building the city, the appearance of Reason has changed: her dress is still red, as in the left-hand side of the miniature, but its style has been altered. This would not in itself mark a shift in character, as the continued red color of the dress creates a visual link between the two images, and the viewer easily assumes, from prompts in the text, that it is indeed Lady Reason, the main allegory in book 1, who is here depicted laboring with Christine. But in the other two miniatures to the text, which precede books 2 and 3 and show the later stages of city building, the image of the allegorical lady in restyled garb remains the same. That is, although the text apportions one part of the construction work to each of the three ladies, the miniatures show the same allegorical virtue working throughout. After laying stones with Christine in the initial illustration, this virtue leads a group of ladies into the city in the miniature that introduces book 2 and welcomes the Virgin Mary and holy ladies into the city in the image that opens book 3. Thus it is clear from looking at the miniatures as a group that the appearance, and hence the identity, of the personified virtue depicted with Christine has intentionally been kept uniform. The crowned lady in red and white in each of the three miniatures is not presented as either Reason, Rectitude, or Justice but as virtue per se. The effect of this equating is both to highlight Christine's importance—Christine is always identifiable as herself—and to mark the help that she receives as stemming from a single, transcendent source. The ladies say they are as one. Visually individualizing the personifications who preside over each of the three books might humanize them too much; Christine must be the only human character involved in the development of the city. It is equally significant that she works in conjunction with all virtue and yet remains distinct from it.

Perfect virtue must be humanity's ideal but cannot be called its reality. For all the beauty and permanence of the City of Ladies, neither its architectural design nor the stone-and-mortar structure of the edifice is its most essential feature. Rather, this building erected for the sake of justice creates a community of women: a set of examples from the past and the possibility of access for all in the future. When the Christine character breaks with her listening-and-dialogue mode at the end of the second and third books, her voice fusing with the author's and addressing all women, she speaks each time of "our city" (2.69.1, 3.19.1) and includes real readers as well as the city inhabitants represented by stories. Much has been made of the importance of memory in this text, and there can be no argument that Christine de Pizan plumbs cultural memory to build a monument to women's virtue (see Zimmermann, "Mémoire"; McCormick; Tarnowski, "Lessons"). But the insistence on both the possibility and the necessity for ethical practice in the moment makes the city not a walled fortress of exclusion but a sanctuary that will always embrace newcomers. Protecting women from evil, the city does in fact exclude those who prove themselves unworthy, but its purpose is more to gather increasing numbers of women together than to set a group apart.

In the illustrations to the Queen's Manuscript, progressive visual emphasis falls on the city's residents rather than on the building itself. On the right-hand side of the first miniature, Christine and the allegorical lady work alone, and there is a larger degree of distance between the onlooker and the two figures erecting the city wall (it is relevant that the stones they use are depicted as stones instead of women; the miniaturist overseen by Christine chose to represent the women as building blocks). In the second miniature, eight female figures stand front and center before the nearly completed structure. The abstract, checkered background and large patches of grass and rubble of the first miniature have given way to an image that is nearly all women and buildings; only a bit of grass and a few flowers remain for the group to tread on. The miniaturist seems to be cropping out the extraneous, homing in on the essential. Finally, the third miniature uses a lens even more closely focused: the viewer is nearer to the women of the city, whose number has increased and who now occupy more than half the miniature's height and almost all its width. The group of holy women on their way into the city extends past the left-hand limit of the frame. The massing of women inside the city is likewise rendered as a multitude; fragments of veils, individual reaching hands, and partial views of faces all contribute to the sense of a crowd extending back beyond the city's open doorway. Because more space is accorded the women, a smaller part of the city is visible than in the preceding miniature; the city towers evoke less depth and constitute more of a backdrop for the advancing women than an architectural vision.

The increasing emphasis on the women of the city reflects the accumulation of women's stories in the text, but it also subtly diminishes the importance of architecture as such. Or, we might say, it puts the architecture in its place. The character-author proclaims in her final speech that the substance of the city is wholly virtue; she disengages herself from her material metaphor to concentrate on its meaning. She tells women that this virtue is "so resplendent that you may see yourselves mirrored in it" (3.19.1); the heft and solidity of stone is transformed and transcended. Indeed, the city inhabitants who can see themselves in this city are like the Christine character and the reader; all can and should see themselves in the mirror Lady Reason holds aloft in the work's first image. Ethical practice, close adherence to the principles presented and discussed throughout *The City of Ladies*, will ensure a welcome for all.

Engaging the architectural metaphor of the text offers a way to guide students through the entirety of the work, linking component parts that might initially appear unrelated. Other angles of approach could be just as useful in the classroom—for example, students could look at the startling ways Christine reworks her main source text, Boccaccio's *De claris mulieribus*. Or they could study the series of qualities *The City of Ladies* attributes to women to see the stakes of the debate on women's worth. The reason for suggesting that the architectural metaphor be explored and its ethical component highlighted is that this way leads from one end of the text to the other and beyond; it keeps the stories channeled to a purpose and privileges the worth of that purpose.

NOTES

[1]This essay cites Earl Jeffrey Richards's 1998 translation of *The Book of the City of Ladies*.

[2]For a detailed and nuanced discussion of the miniatures in the Harley 4431 version of *La cité des dames*, see Hindman, "'With Ink and Mortar,'" especially pp. 465–70.

Teaching the Concept of Virtue in *The Book of the City of Ladies*

Benjamin M. Semple

Even as more and more of Christine de Pizan's texts are appearing in English or modern French translations, I continue to find that her signature work, *The Book of the City of Ladies*, is her most accessible text for the level of students I teach, college undergraduates. Over the course of this work, Christine systematically refutes the unsubstantiated assertions of medieval misogyny, using an engaging allegory. Casting herself as an apprentice to three divine ladies—Reason, Rectitude, and Justice—she builds a city in which each woman's story provides material for the foundations, walls, and houses. She then introduces the city's inhabitants one by one, relating the story of each woman as the woman takes her place in the city. My students, like many modern readers, enjoy becoming acquainted with Christine as the stonemason in training and staunch defender of women in *The City of Ladies*.

In spite of its accessibility to the modern reader, however, I would not characterize *The City of Ladies* as an easy text to teach. The subtleties of its narrative patterns can elude students. In addition, perhaps because its message of validation of women seems so familiar to a modern audience, students can easily read the work as if a contemporary woman had written it, without fully appreciating the medieval intellectual, moral, and artistic context from which it sprang.

One of the most effective ways to enable students to see this work in its medieval context is through a rigorous examination of Christine's explicitly stated purpose: to demonstrate the virtue of women. Through examination of what Christine means by virtue, they become closer and more historically informed readers of this work, while also acquiring a richer knowledge of the medieval civilization that produced it. During the four to six class periods that I devote to *The City of Ladies*, I organize both prereading activities designed to give students necessary historical background about virtue in the Middle Ages and discussions focused on narrative features related to the theme of virtue.

The City of Ladies develops the metaphor of a city constructed by a woman for women. Although the stories of women selected to furnish the building materials and inhabitants of the city occupy the forefront of the reader's attention, Christine also indicates (without belaboring the point) that the city is not a home for all women. Before the construction of the city begins, the character Reason announces that "the walls of the city will be closed to those women who lack virtue" (*Book of the City of Ladies* [translated by Richards] 11; "*Livre de la cité*" [edited by Curnow] 630).[1] As construction proceeds, both the narrator and the speech characters remark approvingly on the virtue of the women they place in the city, thus continually reminding the reader why each woman deserves to be there. At the end of the work, in an address to her readers, the narrator presents the finished city and, looking back on the now completed structure, confirms that the city is made "entirely of virtue" (254; 1032). In short, it does not suffice to be a woman to live in the city: each inhabitant must possess virtue.

In basing her ethical system on virtue, Christine places her work in a moral universe that already permeated the cultural environment of her readers. Before describing some ways to introduce students to that cultural environment, I first review its origins and three of its underlying principles.

Both Greco-Roman antiquity and the early Christian fathers bequeathed to the Middle Ages a conception of moral psychology that stressed the need to develop virtue in oneself. Throughout the medieval period, a variety of artistic and intellectual channels, in both learned and popular culture, transmitted knowledge of the virtues. Hagiography, allegorical literature, theology, religious rituals (for instance, confession and penance), sermons, books of hours, biblical exegesis, manuscript illumination, cathedral sculpture, and stained-glass work all elaborated on the importance of virtue. The concept of virtue thus circulated through a variety of media: written texts, oral discourse, visual arts, and social practices.

Three tendencies recur throughout this protean tradition. The first was to analyze virtue as a whole into its component parts. Virtue in the Middle Ages rarely appears as a monolithic entity; rather, it appears as a series of separate moral qualities. Traditional lists—the seven cardinal virtues, the seven deadly sins, the seven contrary virtues—aided the laity in identifying and memorizing those qualities.[2] In more elevated intellectual circles, medieval thinkers created systems of moral classification that expanded on the principal virtues. For example, Thomas Aquinas related a number of subsidiary virtues to the overarching virtue of temperance: mildness, modesty, chastity, abstinence, sobriety, and humility (*Summa Theologiae* 13: 28–30). His taxonomy reflects the medieval preoccupation with isolating and enumerating individual virtues and determining their relation to one another.

The second tendency was to conceptualize virtue in juxtaposition or conflict with vice (Vincent-Cassy 1511–12). Each virtue opposed a contrary vice. Traditional pairs of virtues and vices were humility and pride, envy and charity, avarice and generosity, sloth and diligence, faith and idolatry, patience and wrath, abstinence and gluttony, hope and despair, fortitude and fear, prudence and folly, chastity and lust. The constant portrayal of virtue as the opponent of vice sent an important moral and psychological message: the acquisition of virtue also wards off vice; when virtue is left uncultivated, vice creeps back into the human soul and fills the vacuum permitted by this lack of moral effort. In medieval moral thought, satisfaction with the current state of one's virtue is interpreted as a sign of pride—the worst sin of all. The concern with virtue's leading to self-congratulation explains why *The City of Ladies* closes with a warning against pride: Christine enjoins her female readers not to succumb to pride at the spectacle of so much female virtue but rather to redouble their efforts to attain it (*Book* 254–55; *"Livre"* 1032).

The third tendency was to use imagery and symbols (either visual or linguistic) to dramatize the virtues and encourage their practice. For instance, one pictorial symbol of the virtues portrayed them as rungs on a ladder ascending toward heaven (Katzenellenbogen 22–26). Medieval allegorical narrative depicted personified virtues as combatants against vices (Vincent-Cassy 1512; Mâle 100–05; Katzenellenbogen 1–13). In addition to being a subject of personification, virtues and vices were often associated with an attribute, such as an emblematic object or an animal symbol, which revealed their identity to the reader or viewer.

The prereading activity I organize to introduce students to the medieval understanding of virtue and vice takes the iconographic tradition as a point of departure. I have two goals. The first is to familiarize students with the vocabulary they will need to discuss virtue. Because they may not know the terms designating the virtues in French, a preliminary discussion of virtues and vices acquaints them with these words and integrates vocabulary acquisition with the task of literary analysis. The second goal is to give students the opportunity to arrive by induction at their own understanding of the principles informing medieval thinking about virtue and vice.

In the first stage of this activity, I focus on each virtue or vice separately. The illustrations I use come primarily from two excellent resources, Émile Mâle's classic study *L'art religieux du XIIIe siècle* (especially book 3, "Le miroir moral") and Adolf Katzenellenbogen's *Allegories of the Virtues and Vices in Medieval Art*. The study of individual virtues and vices familiarizes students with the iconographic conventions used by medieval artists. Conducting this part of the exercise as a whole-class activity allows me to provide vocabulary and to help with interpretation of the iconography as needed.

In the second stage of the prereading activity, students examine the meaning conveyed by the spatial arrangement of the virtues and vices. For homework, they have read Katzenellenbogen (75–81) and studied plates 73a–73b. In this text, the author discusses the layout of the virtues and vices on the façade of the cathedral of Notre-Dame de Paris; these bas-reliefs are found at ground level on either side of the central entrance (Katzellenbogen 75; Mâle 99). The virtues and vices occupy parallel horizontal registers, with the twelve virtues (humility, prudence, chastity, charity, hope, faith, courage, patience, kindness, concord, obedience, and perseverance) in the upper register and the twelve contrary vices (pride, foolishness, lust, avarice, despair, idolatry, fear, wrath, malice, discord, willful disobedience, and inconstancy) in the lower one (Katzenellenbogen 75–76). As preparation for the class exercise, I make a set of photocopies of each individual virtue and vice from Katzenellenbogen's plates (there are twelve virtues and twelve vices). I divide the class into groups, provide each group with a set of the twenty-four virtues and vices, and ask them to reconstruct the layout of the façade, referring to Katzenellenbogen's text as necessary. As they perform this activity, I ask them to discuss the subject matter and iconography of each virtue and vice. To conclude the exercise, I ask them to discuss the implicit principles of aesthetic representation and moral psychology underlying the façade sculptures. In follow-up discussion with the entire class, I verify that students have reached the outcomes of the prereading—namely, the ability to identify, name, and define the virtues and vices and to understand the principle of opposition between virtue and vice, a key concept in our later examination of *The City of Ladies*.

The class is now ready to proceed to direct analysis of *The City of Ladies*, which I organize into two stages. First I conduct an examination of the overall structure of the work as a whole-class discussion. We isolate and analyze the two principal organizational features: the metaphor of the city, with its component parts (foundations, walls, houses, inhabitants, gateways) and dialogue structure (which divides the work into question-and-response segments). These features create a highly structured and, on first impression, compartmentalized narrative. This compartmentalization lends itself to analysis of the capacities (or virtues) of women as discrete behavioral elements. Often the parts of the city or specific groups of its inhabitants correspond to specific virtues. Courage, for example, is the exclusive building material of the city's foundations, prudence provides much of the substance for its walls, and faith characterizes its aristocracy, the saints. The vertical rise of the city introduces a notion of hierarchy, as does the reference to an aristocratic class. However, the division of the city into higher and lower dwelling places or into social strata is balanced by the interdependency among the parts of the city. I ask students, Could the city survive without its foundations, which are composed of the lowliest members of the city? Without them, the city would have no walls and would stand defenseless. Christine's metaphor imparts to the reader the understanding that the city's parts are hierarchically ordered but also interdependent. The highest members of the city rely on its lowest members.

The class concludes this first stage of the discussion by pointing out the limits of such analysis. Discussion has established that divisions in the work can be associated with specific virtues, but I qualify this conclusion by emphasizing that virtues are not neatly confined to separate narrative units but rather spill over the boundaries assigned to them by the narrative. Christine often adds details concerning the courage or chastity of her heroines in instances where these virtues are unrelated to the stated reason for including the protagonist in the city. In addition, virtues of the highest importance (for instance, humility) have no designated place in the city's structure, yet they permeate the entire edifice. To gain a fuller understanding of virtue, we must delve beyond the work's overt structure.

The overarching question that guides the second phase of class discussion is, How does Christine narrate (*raconte*) virtue? What recurring narrative features does she use to make virtue tangible for her audience? I provide three narrative features to focus discussion: the virtuous choice (or choices) made by the protagonist, in relation to choices she could have made or in contrast with those that others would make; the trials (in the dual sense of "tests" and "tribulations") she must endure because of her choice; and the psychological dimension of her virtue, as revealed principally through references to feelings or, to use the term current in medieval psychology, passions. Classroom discussion is a dynamic process, and no template can account for its contingencies, but here are some key texts to analyze and some conclusions that could emerge when the discussion is organized around these three narrative features.

One of the most consistent features of Christine's stories of virtuous women is that her protagonists actively choose their destiny and the difficulties associated with it. The choice to pursue virtue is generally the obvious choice to maintain the moral principle at stake in the narrative, such as fidelity to a spouse, protection of the community, or devotion to a family member. Christine's protagonists do not usually find themselves in morally ambiguous situations, where they have to weigh equally compelling moral imperatives: they are placed in situations where the virtuous action is clear and where the reasons why they might shirk virtue are equally clear. At the moment when she makes the virtuous choice, the protagonist knowingly sacrifices an obvious temporal advantage, such as the privileges of social rank, the inertia (and psychological comfort) of habitual behaviors, material comforts, wealth and the advantages derived from it, preservation of her physical appearance, or psychological security. Frequently, the virtuous choice jeopardizes even her ultimate temporal possession, her life. If she acted instead to maintain these temporal advantages, she would display a vice, such as fear, pride, or laziness. In accordance with the principle that virtue and vice exist in opposition to each other, Christine's protagonists do not choose between two virtues but between virtue and vice.

In her narrative technique, Christine makes the resistance to vice as explicit as possible by clear references in the text to the protagonist's sacrifices. For example, when she describes how Queen Hypsicratea accompanies her husband on his military campaigns and endures the rigors of army life, she includes a quotation from Boccaccio's version of this story,[3] which specifies that Hypsicratea had previously been "accustomed to living so delicately and to sleeping in soft beds and to having everything at her ease" (*Book* 121; *"Livre"* 822). In another story, when Christine relates how Argia, bereaved by the death of her husband, sets out to retrieve his unburied corpse from the battlefield, she once again inserts a quotation from Boccaccio's version, emphasizing how Argia "immediately laid aside her royal dress and adornment as well as the softness and easiness of her life in the sumptuously appointed chambers" (125; 828). In both of these examples, the determined opposition to vice is underscored by a description of the protagonist's unhesitating rejection of her worldly position and its easy comforts. To delve deeper into the textual specifics of these passages, it can be helpful to ask students why they think that Christine includes explicit references to her borrowings from Boccaccio in these two narratives, whereas in many others she borrows from him without attribution. Students could conclude that Christine, as a woman author writing about members of her sex and proclaiming the virtues of women, emphasizes Boccaccio's role when she thinks that her impartiality might be questioned. Because a male author has provided the original detail, readers (presumably male) cannot accuse Christine of embroidering on her narratives to exaggerate the virtue of women.

Christine also makes the exceptional character of her heroines more conspicuous for the reader by juxtaposing the protagonist's virtuous conduct with the moral deficiencies of other characters. In the story of Menalippe and Hippolyta, the courage of the two Amazon maidens contrasts with the timid caution of Hercules (*Book* 44–47; *"Livre"* 687–94). In the story of Hypsicratea, the demoralized dejection of her husband, Mithridates, renders her hopeful spirit more prominent and reminds the reader of how an individual of lesser virtue might behave (122; 823). (A medieval audience would have seen Mithridates's despondency not in psychological but in moral terms, as an incidence of the vice of *tristitia*—sorrow or melancholy.) In these stories, the vice or moral failing of one character throws the virtuous choice of the protagonist into bolder relief. Frequently, as in these examples, male vices supply the points of contrast with female virtues; thus, over the course of the narrative, Christine repeatedly redresses the moral imbalance evoked at the beginning of the work. From her readings, as she describes, she had internalized the belief that men represent moral perfection whereas women are "the vessel . . . of every evil and vice" (5; 620). The recurring comparison between male vice and female virtue corrects both these errors.

A second narrative feature on which I focus class discussion is the tests or trials resulting from the virtuous choice. In some instances, the protagonist faces a single test, as in the case of the vestal virgin Claudine, who abandons her habitual modesty and serene demeanor to become a fierce fighter when her father is threatened by assassination (*Book* 114–15; "*Livre*" 811–12). The virtue of Claudine originates in a sudden crisis; presumably, she returns to her former quiet conduct after this event. However, in other narratives, the protagonist faces a series of such trials—material, physical, and psychological—as the narrative develops. The ability to continue to make virtuous choices in the face of multiple deterrents and threats illustrates the constancy and perseverance of women. (I remind students that perseverance, contrasted with the vice of inconstancy, is one of the twelve virtues sculpted in stone on the façade of Notre-Dame de Paris.) Through these trials, Christine's narrative structure demonstrates the protagonist's willingness to accept the consequences of her initial virtuous action. Queen Hypsicratea, for example, sacrifices her comfort, her physical appearance, and the privileges of her social station to remain at the side of her husband during his long military campaigns and his exile. Students may not spontaneously connect her voluntary loss of beauty with virtue, so I explain to them that in medieval representations of women the vice of lust is revealed through excessive attachment to physical attractiveness. In support of this interpretation, students can study the stained-glass rose window of Notre-Dame de Paris, where lust is represented by a woman admiring her beauty in a mirror (Mâle 117). They can further reflect on how this particular vice was gendered, insofar as male lust is an inner desire, whereas the medieval preoccupation with lust as experienced by women focuses on a woman's attractiveness to the opposite sex.

The examination of the trials of the protagonist reveals the importance of suffering in Christine's view of virtue. Students may not always agree with the extent to which her moral system relies on such trials, especially when the trials result not from a stroke of fate but from the intentional cruelty, injustice, or selfishness of another. Tertia Aemilia, for example, undergoes the prolonged trial of her husband's infidelity, keeping her pain hidden and refraining from jealousy or resentment (*Book* 129; "*Livre*" 835–36). Griselda endures the series of psychologically cruel trials that her husband artificially manufactures to test her virtue (170–76; 900–10).

Does Christine intentionally or unintentionally legitimate injustice by representing it as a trial that women can and should endure in order to perfect their virtue? There is no short answer to this complex question. She accepted the idea that persecutors are instruments of God's will and that patient tolerance of persecution could be a virtuous practice (*Vision of Christine de Pizan* [McLeod and Willard] 119–21; *Livre de l'advision* [Reno and Dulac] 130–31). In the Bible, the words and deeds of Jesus also taught to "turn the other cheek" (Matthew 5.39). In the decision to submit to an injustice or rebel against it, Christine undoubtedly believed that many factors must be weighed, including the authority of those above us and the degree of the injustice. In some instances, tolerance of a slight or even significant injustice may be a means to preserve social harmony. (Students can be asked to recall that the virtues on the façade of Notre-Dame de Paris include Concordia and Oboedientia [Concord and Obedience]. Obedience is one means of preserving concord, though not one that always appeals to modern readers.) I do not try to gloss over this aspect of Christine's moral thought. I view it as an opportunity to study Christine in a truly historical spirit, not as a woman who reflects our views but who had moral beliefs that may significantly diverge from our own. I point out that not only she but all of medieval culture valued acceptance of hierarchy. It was typically construed as submission to traditional or institutionalized authority: of children to their parents, of wives to their husbands, of laypeople to the Church and its representatives, and of subjects to their lords. To balance Christine's apparent glorification of obedience, however, I do encourage students to consider narratives in *The City of Ladies* where Christine not only permits but also encourages rebellion against social hierarchies, especially when they adopt a tyrannical character or conflict with divine will. These acts of rebellion are particularly prevalent in the third part of the work, where women saints revolt against abuses of power in familial, legal, and political institutions. For example, the saints Eulalia, Barbara, and Christine rebel against parental authority (*Book* 229, 232, 234–37; *"Livre"* 994, 998, 1001–04). Theodosina and Christine find themselves in conflict with judges (231, 237–39; 996–98, 1005–08). And a host of saints, beginning with Catherine, must oppose political authority as embodied in the emperor (219–22; 978–82).

A third feature of narrative, the psychology of characters, provides one final focal point for examination of how Christine employed her literary craft to convey her concept of virtue. The presentation of her protagonists' feelings has many points in common with the scholastic psychology of the period, which examined not only the actions required by virtue but also the emotional states that should accompany virtuous actions. On an initial reading, students will often conclude that *The City of Ladies* promotes stoic restraint of feelings as the proper psychological state for a virtuous individual. This impression undoubtedly results from Christine's association of virtue with uncomplaining acceptance of adversity. Her protagonists appear to make their difficult decisions with ease and spontaneity, without regret, complaint, or resentment. Griselda, the supreme example of this absence of negative feelings in response to adversity, appears almost superhuman in her ability to refrain from sorrow or anger: repudiated by her noble husband and sent back to the miserable poverty from which marriage had allowed her to escape, she never shows "a single trace of sadness or regret" (*Book* 174; *"Livre"* 906). The cumulative effect of this absence of feelings in situations that would seem to provoke acute emotional responses can lead students to think that Christine's concept of virtue is affectless.

Christine does imply her approval of the suppression of certain passions. In marital relationships, her protagonists show no jealousy of other women with whom their husbands have been unfaithful and refrain from resentment either toward their husband or his mistress. Hypsicratea's devotion to her husband is unimpaired by his many "concubines" (120; 821). Griselda graciously receives the woman who (she believes) will replace her at her husband's side, without displaying any jealousy or anger (174–75; 907–08). Tertia Aemilia carefully disguises her pain at her husband's infidelity and, after his death, not only does not wreak revenge on the slave woman with whom her husband had an affair but also generously frees her (129; 835–36). Fear is another passion that Christine's protagonists frequently suppress. Either by strength of character or through a conscious effort, the protagonists purge themselves of fear to accomplish their acts of virtue. To protect her infant son and his kingdom, Queen Fredegund declares that she will "abandon all feminine fear and arm [her] heart with a man's boldness . . ." (59; 713). In defense of her father's life, the vestal virgin Claudine "lay[s] aside all fear and fright . . ." (114; 811). Believing that women have a natural tendency to be cautious rather than bold (37; 675), Christine stresses the need to transcend fear and the advantages of boldness in thought and action.

If Christine generally portrays jealousy and fear as emotions incompatible with virtue, however, the same cannot be said for her representation of other feelings. Grief, anger, and love often stimulate virtue in her protagonists. For example, Queen Berenice receives a sudden infusion of courage when her two sons are killed by their uncle (the queen's brother-in-law): "When . . . the uncle killed two of her sons, she was so grieved that her anger purged her of all feminine fear . . ." (61; 718). In another story, grief at her husband's assassination and her anger at the perpetrator, the emperor Tiberius, lead Agrippina to flout his authority publicly: "His good wife was so grieved at his death that she asked to be killed in a similar manner. She was, moreover, quite blatant indeed in expressing this intent, for she could not refrain from addressing great insults to Tiberius, for which he had her beaten and cruelly tortured and held in prison" (127; 831). In these examples, profound feeling catalyzes courageous action against the established authority of political hierarchy (Agrippina) or dissolves the internal constraints regarding appropriate behavior for one's gender (Berenice).

In this essay, I have omitted many of the details of the day-to-day organization of each class period, concentrating instead on the trajectory of the course as we read *The City of Ladies* over two to three weeks. By the time students reach the end of our sessions devoted to this work, my goal is for them to have moved beyond their initial perception of Christine de Pizan as a woman with social and moral views similar to those current today. I want them to begin to understand the different moral universe of this author and to read her work with a heightened sense of the historical perspective we must establish when reading a text written over six centuries ago. They will probably disagree with her moral thought on some points. But even when they do not entirely agree with her, they will have learned to respect and appreciate the narrative craft, psychological insight, and keen moral perception of *The City of Ladies*.

NOTES

[1]All English quotations are from the Earl Jeff Richards translation of *The Book of the City of Ladies*. Maureen Cheney Curnow's Middle French edition, "The *Livre de la cité des dames* of Christine de Pisan: A Critical Edition" is also cited for readers who wish to consult the original text.

[2]The seven cardinal virtues consist of the three "theological" virtues of faith, hope, charity, and the four "pagan" or "moral" virtues of justice, temperance, fortitude (i.e., courage), and prudence (Gueullette 1524). The seven deadly sins were pride, envy, sloth, wrath, avarice, gluttony, and lust. A list of the seven contrary virtues (so called because they were the opposites of the deadly sins) can be found in the writings of Christine's contemporary, the theologian Jean Gerson; it consists of "humility, love of one's neighbor, diligence, patience, generosity, abstinence, and chastity" (Gerson, *A.B.C des simples gens* 155; my trans.).

[3]Christine uses the *Des cleres et nobles femmes* (a French translation of Boccaccio's Latin treatise *De mulieribus claris*) as a source for many of her stories. She does not simply borrow from Boccaccio verbatim but often reworks his stories to alter their point of view and tone.

Governing the Body Politic: Christine's Political Advice

Cary J. Nederman

Christine de Pizan was the most prolific, and yet has been the most overlooked, author of princely mirror or advice books (*specula*) in medieval Europe. She is credited with no fewer than nine such treatises—a function, no doubt, of her presence at the court of the Valois kings in France—whereas her male counterparts usually wrote only a single *speculum* (Forhan, *Political Theory* 27). Yet the body of Christine's political writings has been systematically ignored or dismissed by mainstream scholars of medieval Western thought—the neglect a function more of her gender than of a careful reading of her texts, one suspects. Her name did not merit a mention in the classic surveys by L. K. Born ("The Perfect Prince") and Wilhelm Berges (*Die Fürstenspiegel des hohen und späten Mittelalters*) or in the more recent work of Bernard Guenée (*States and Rulers in Later Medieval Europe*). She is even left off Herbert Grabes's magisterial list of *specula* (*The Mutable Glass*), perhaps because none of her works contain mirror terminology in the title, even though she employs mirror imagery throughout her corpus in a manner entirely consonant with other texts of the genre.

Traditionally, scholars who have bothered to comment on the intellectual merits of Christine as a political theorist proffered largely negative evaluations. H. R. Dosher declines to count her as a "first-rate political thinker" on the grounds that she "not only repeated well-worn arguments found in French political literature of the Middle Ages but manifested a pedantic and pedagogical penchant for moralizing about the duties of kingship and the virtues of the ideal prince" (114; see Dosher 120–28). Sheila Delany proposed that Christine's political thought was sadly outmoded and signaled her essential conservatism: "In a time when even courtiers and clerics wanted change, Christine continues in her quiet neo-Platonic hierarchies and her feudal nostalgia" (Delany, "Mothers" 188). In a later reply to her critics, Delany is even more blunt:

> Christine's advice to rulers . . . is taken as evidence of a subtly subversive intent, as if it required some particular nerve to emit such flatulencies in public. But this is the sort of generic moralism an aristocrat could read in any collection of maxims or exempla in the voguish "mirror for princes" genre. . . . Christine's reiteration of moral commonplaces says little about her political allegiances, for we are talking parties and cliques here—quite murderous ones at that—not vapid abstractions. ("History" 198)

Delany has been challenged on a number of fronts, but her judgment still resonates with a certain school of Christine studies, as Susan Dudash documents (788–89nn3–4). The main issue in this debate largely revolves around whether Christine should be read as a courtly sycophant or an engaged and critical political author. At present, the tide of scholarship on her seems to have turned toward the latter view (see most recently Adams, *Christine de Pizan*; Delogu, *Theorizing* 153–83).

The large body of specialist literature on Christine that emerged during the past few decades has made little evident impact, however, on scholars in the field of medieval political thought, for whom she is nearly invisible. Major overviews of political ideas in the Middle Ages—for example, J. H. Burns's *Cambridge History of Medieval Political Thought*, Antony Black's *Political Thought in Europe*, Janet Coleman's *A History of Political Thought*, Joseph Canning's *A History of Medieval Political Thought* and *Ideas of Power in the Late Middle Ages*, Francis Oakley's *The Watershed of Modern Politics*—ignore her entirely or nearly so. The situation is worse still in the discipline of political theory generally. Three recent surveys of the field, for instance, do not mention her at all: Gerald Gaus and Fred D'Agostino's *Routledge Companion to Social and Political Philosophy*, Mark Bevir's *Encyclopedia of Political Theory*, and David Boucher and Paul Kelly's *Political Thinkers from Socrates to the Present*. This silence is in spite of the availability of most of her important political writings in English translation, as well as the inclusion of selections of her work in several lately published anthologies (Cohen and Fermon; Losco and Williams; Bailey et al.; Nederman and Forhan). In sum, Christine resides outside the canon of political theory—even medieval political theory—as defined by academic convention.

It should hardly be a surprise, then, that her name and writings seldom turn up in the college classroom, at least in departments of political science and history. A representative survey of syllabi available online for introductory courses on the history of political thought taught by political theorists and intellectual historians at a sampling of thirty major American universities (conducted by Thiago Talzzia, my doctoral student) found no classes that included her writings among their assigned readings. I am apparently the sole exception: as a specialist in the history of the field of political theory, I teach her work in an upper-division survey class on ancient and medieval political thought, a first-year seminar entitled Women and Politics from Antigone to Hillary, and an advanced course on political ideas from the late Middle Ages to the Reformation. In each case, students are surprised that a woman contributed substantially to the early development of political theory in Europe—or even that there were any professional female writers during Christine's time. The students in the first-year seminar, who are ordinarily women (the course enrolls very few men) right out of high school, were indignant to discover that they had never been exposed to her work. Moreover, students are intrigued to detect echoes of some of her remarks about the pragmatic conduct of rulers, especially queens, in later political texts, such as Machiavelli's *Prince*, in contrast to the standard forms of advice offered to rulers in more moralistic works, such as Giles of Rome's *De regimine principum* (*On the Rule of the Prince*), which was widely disseminated, both in Latin and in vernacular translations, during the later Middle Ages.

The dismissive attitude toward Christine among scholars and educators alike is unwarranted. Like some other later medieval advice writers, such as the authors of the *Speculum Justiciariorum* and the *Speculum Regis Edwardi III* (Nederman, "Mirror Crack'd"), she stretched the limits of the *speculum* genre in ways that demonstrate a far more original and innovative approach to the advice book tradition than has hitherto been recognized (Forhan, "Reflecting Heros"). In particular, her *specula* may be read as offering comprehensive social criticism, in response to her recognition that conventional mirrors overlooked the needs and interests of a large portion of the populace, among them women, city dwellers, and the poor. She thereby awakened her courtly audience to many of the new social and economic realities that were altering the landscape of late medieval institutions and creations. In this regard, Christine adopts a far more personal tone, rooted in her own experiences and observations, than is usual in conventional books of advice. In her three best-known *specula*—*Le livre de la cité des dames* (c. 1405; *The Book of the City of Ladies*), *Le livre des trois vertus* (c. 1406; *The Book of the Three Virtues* [translated under the title of *A Medieval Woman's Mirror of Honor: The Treasury of the City of Ladies*]), and *Le livre du corps de policie* (c. 1406; *The Book of the Body Politic*)—she identifies herself as writing from the perspective of a woman, an immigrant to France, and an individual of nonnoble birth (Willard, *Christine de Pizan*). She does not hesitate to deplore various mores and practices current in her time, basing her remarks on her knowledge of historical and geographic variations as well as on her familiarity with scholastic, scriptural, and patristic sources. Throughout her works, the advice she offers has a practical turn, suggestive of someone who has been on intimate terms with many stations of life and the travails they can cause. There are moments in her narrative—such as when she offers advice to widows about coping with their late husbands' creditors (*Medieval Woman's Mirror* 197–202)—that seem to stem directly from difficulties that she encountered in her own life.

Christine's most pronounced departure from the main contours of the mirror genre is the striking inclusiveness of the audience Christine addresses and the social complexity she acknowledges. In one of her two works directed explicitly to a female readership, the *City of Ladies*, she defends women as a group from various slanders against their intelligence and capacity to achieve moral and political virtue. The other of these writings, the *Three Virtues*, examines in minute detail the conduct appropriate to women of each and every social distinction, extending from princesses and the nobility to artisans, prostitutes, and the destitute. Likewise, Christine's *Body Politic* discusses in detail the humblest orders in the realm as well as the education and behavior of the king and his well-born companions.

Some might argue that her concentration on this social complexity excludes her writings from the *speculum principum* genre entirely, on the grounds that she moves beyond its confines and into other realms of political reflection. But her writings, especially the *Three Virtues* and the *Body Politic*, manifestly address a royal audience and remain firmly founded on such conventions of *speculum* literature as the primacy of the king in his country (*Body Politic*

48–49), the need for good councilors to be respected and evil advisers to be dismissed (*Medieval Woman's Mirror* 83, 87–88; *Body Politic* 35–36, 39–40), and the requirement that royal government be conducted in accordance with virtue and religion (*Body Politic* 14–15, 25–31).[1] While on some of these points her qualifications and pragmatic recommendations reveal her dissatisfaction with the standard advice contained in political mirrors, this dissatisfaction does not form an adequate reason to deny her a place in the genre. Rather, her departures from tradition suggest an attempt to draw on her own vast experience of the exigencies confronted by royal rulers.

Thus, for instance, she suggests that a princess who has definite knowledge of plots and machinations against her should dissemble with her enemies (*Medieval Woman's Mirror* 105–07). This advice is given as far more than a counsel of Christian charity; Christine regards it to be a practical guide to maintaining public order as well as personal reputation, so long as the deceit by the princess is not discovered (see Denery, *Devil*). She observes:

> The wise lady will use this prudent device of discreet dissimulation, which should not be considered vicious but rather a great virtue when employed for the common good, to maintain peace, or to avoid detriment or greater harm. Not only will she escape trouble but she will also achieve great benefit if she pretends not to notice conspiracy against her.
>
> (*Medieval Woman's Mirror* 106–07)

Similar mendacity is proposed for charitable works and benefactions. Christine counsels that the princess and her family must uphold their standing and reputation in the community by publicly endowing gifts to the poor and religious. Even if this giving amounts to hypocrisy, such conduct is wholly justified: "Justifiable hypocrisy is necessary for princes and princesses who must rule over others and thus be accorded more respect than others. Moreover, expedient hypocrisy is not unworthy for others desiring honor, as long as they practice it for worthy ends" (109). To say that the ends justify the means in Christine's view may be overstated. But she clearly believes that the maintenance of a decorous reputation matters a great deal to effective governance and that rulers ought to be seen as benefactors to their people. Time and again, she demonstrates as great a concern about the public image of the royal family and the order it engenders as about the existence of virtue in itself—although she obviously believes that the presence of virtue ensures the public image of it. This belief represents something of an inversion of the common position of advice books, according to which religion and virtue are seen to be their own rewards, quite apart from temporal consequences (Nederman and Lee Dow).

Perhaps as strikingly, Christine advocates the special competence of women to contribute to the tasks associated with the maintenance of peace and secular well-being. In *City of Ladies*, she proclaims that in case anyone says that women do not have a natural sense for politics and government,

> I will give you examples of several great women rulers who have lived in past times . . . [and] of some women of your own time who remained widows and whose skill governing—both past and present—in all their affairs following the deaths of their husbands provides obvious demonstration that a woman with a mind is fit for all tasks. ([Richards] 32)

Christine surely knew Aristotle's argument for the exclusion of women from a role in public life: it was a mainstay of medieval political literature (Mews, "Latin Learning" 71–72). She challenges this view directly, even to the point of asserting that a princess may help quell disturbances in her land that arise from her husband's acquiescence to evil councilors: "If the prince, because of poor advice or for any other reason, should be tempted to harm his subjects, they will know their lady to be full of kindness, pity and charity. They will come to her, humbly petitioning her to intercede for them before the prince" (*Medieval Woman's Mirror* 85). The princess is envisioned by Christine as a sort of ombudsperson, a conduit between hostile forces, whether within or without the realm, whose clashes might otherwise disturb the peace (84–87).

The peace of the kingdom and the threats that exist to it are themes in evidence throughout Christine's writings, such as her *Lamentation sur les maux de la France* (c. 1410; *Lament on the Evils of the Civil War*) and *Le livre de paix* (c. 1413; *The Book of Peace*). She views public tranquility as an immediate result of harmonious social organization and cooperation, on the model of the organic metaphor of the body politic that pervaded medieval political thought (Struve; Nederman, "Body Politics"). She declares that "everyone should come together as one body of the same polity, to live justly and in peace as they ought" (*Body Politic* 59). The organic analogy may appear designed to justify hierarchy, inequality, exclusion, and subordination, but for Christine the image of the body politic also suggested an inclusive, reciprocal, and interdependent conception of community:

> Just as the human body is not whole, but defective and deformed, when it lacks any of its members, so the body politic cannot be perfect, whole, or healthy if all the estates of which we speak are not well joined and united together. Thus, they can aid and help each other, each exercising its own office, which diverse offices ought to serve only for the conservation of the whole community, just as the members of the body aid to guide and nourish the whole body. (90)

Her very image of peace is when the health of the entire public unit is preserved through the mutual coordination of the tasks necessary for its existence (91). To despise any of the members, or reduce them to a state of servitude, is an attack on the well-being of the whole organism.

Christine's use of the organic metaphor extends medieval precedent in several vital ways (Nederman, "Living Body Politic" and "Christine de Pizan").

First, her thinking demonstrates a noticeably secular orientation. Unlike her source for the analogy, the *Policraticus* by the mid-twelfth-century churchman John of Salisbury (Forhan, "Polycracy"), she makes no reference to the soul of the body (i.e., the priesthood), nor does she draw on standard medieval depictions of the supremacy of the church to the temporal sphere. Of course, she expects that the king will honor God and care for the churches in his jurisdiction (*Body Politic* 12). But the *Body Politic* reverses the expectations of conventional mirrors by, for instance, asserting a corrective role for the good ruler, since no "prelate, priest, or cleric is so great that he will dare withstand or complain about the prince who reproves him for his manifest vice or sin" (14). This assertion is consistent with Christine's conception of the king as the ordainer and regulator of all the estates in the realm, including the priesthood, and her identification of the clergy in the body politic as one of the three branches of the common people (19, 95–99). No other late medieval thinker, with the exception of Marsilius (Marsiglio) of Padua in his *Defender of Peace* (completed in 1324), was so disposed to count the priestly function as essentially a civil office, contributing to an expansive and secularist idea of public welfare in which the salvation of the soul was not the only aim of political order.

Another significant departure Christine made was her detailed attention to the lives of merchants, artisans, and laborers. Although she again employed language reminiscent of the *Policraticus* (Forhan, "Polycracy" 43–44), she demonstrated far more appreciation for the contributions made by the humbler classes and sympathy for the plights arising from their varied tasks. She insists that burghers and men of commerce are not to be disdained if they are honest and knowledgeable in the conduct of their affairs (*Body Politic* 104):

> The merchant class is very necessary, and without it neither the estate of kings and princes nor even the polities of cities and countries could exist. For by the industry of their labor, all kinds of people are provided for without having to make everything themselves, because, if they have money, merchants bring from afar all things necessary and proper for their lives. (103; see also *Medieval Woman's Mirror* 196)

In similar terms, she praises craftsmen and peasants, since "if the republic excluded laborers and artisans, it could not sustain itself" (*Body Politic* 105). Indeed, she defends both groups against the ignominy that is heaped on them (see Dudash): "Although some think little of the office of the craftsman that the clerics call 'artisans,' yet it is good, noble, and necessary"; likewise, "the estate of the simple laborer or others of low rank should not be denigrated, as others would do. . . The estate of the poor which everyone despises has many good and worthy persons in purity of life" (105, 108, 109). Here Christine's devotion to the principle of social inclusion is much in evidence. Judgments may be made about how well individuals perform in their diverse offices, but no office in and of itself is to be demeaned or disdained if it contributes a vital function to the well-being of the organic community.

As a consequence of her insistence on cooperation among the various duties necessary to maintain the health of the body politic, Christine asserts that the king himself must be cognizant of the conditions of the lesser estates. Of course, the condescending precept that the greater should attend to the welfare of the lesser had long been a commonplace of medieval political thought. Giles Constable traces this doctrine back to Pope Gregory the Great (270). But Christine argues that the prince should familiarize himself with the daily conditions of the populace over whom he governs: "He ought to hear sometimes about the common people, laborers, and merchants, how they make their profit from the poor and the rich, and similarly all kinds of things, so that his understanding is not found ignorant of anything that can be virtuously known" (*Body Politic* 10).

In this way, the prince will appreciate fully the contributions that the lower orders make to the health of the realm and will not dismiss their importance to a peaceful reign. Moreover, he must be apprised of how his policies, as carried out by royal ministers, affect the living conditions of the people (40). Citing the deleterious effects of taxation on the impoverished, Christine reports, "There are some who come to pay this money imposed on them and then they and their poor household starve afterwards, and sell their beds and other poor possessions cheaply and for nothing. And it would please God if someone informed the king and noble princes" (20). As a consequence of the organic unity of the realm, the ruler must realize that his own actions may directly harm the material well-being of his subjects. Such injury will only redound to his own harm, since the people's despoilment means that the realm itself will become impoverished and generate less income in the future. Christine takes it as axiomatic that wise "princes would rather be poor in a rich country, than to be rich and have plenty in a poor country" (22). This is not merely a moral principle; it reflects an economic doctrine that naturally follows from an organic conception of communal interdependence.

The lessons about inclusion that Christine derives from the body metaphor she also transfers to her discussion of women's estates. The princess, as we have seen, is to further the process of intercommunication between the parts of the body by serving as a mediating force between the king and the people (*Medieval Woman's Mirror* 85). Nor does Christine deem it "unsuitable for a princess to lavish attention on her lowlier subjects" (110). Rather, the princess should meet on occasion with burghers, merchants, and artisans in order to facilitate "love and good will" among subjects and thereby strengthen public order and unity. Christine regards this function as crucial to the king's peaceful rule:

> The subjects create the lord, not vice versa. If people want to be troublesome, they will much more easily find someone to take them on as subject than a lord will find subjects to accept him as ruler. . . . Even if at a given time he had the military power to destroy them, he would also destroy himself. . . . Their respect for him will arise from his concern for them,

> rather than from force. Otherwise his power will be in question. A common proverb reinforces this point: "No one is lord in his country who is hated by his people." (110–11)

The princess thus plays a delicate role in maintaining the structure of reciprocity entailed by the organic order of the community. If she declines to perform this function, the health of the body itself is imperiled.

Christine also demonstrates sensitivity to the unique circumstances of humbler women's stations. She recognizes that to be a woman of the commercial or laboring classes imposes special burdens that may render it difficult for them to achieve the virtues espoused for royal or noble women. Not surprisingly, she evinces real compassion for the special predicament of poor women and is gentle in her admonitions toward them (219–23). By no means is her advice for the conduct of the female commoner any less practical than for the princess. For example, she warns the wives of merchants to "avoid ostentation" in dress not simply out of concern for moral rectitude but also because a conspicuous display of wealth "can cause new taxes for their husbands" (196). She is thus closely attuned to the complexities associated with the intersection of gender and social class and gives appropriate and useful counsel to women of various stations with the goal of sustaining a harmonious and cooperative body politic.

In the mirrors of Christine de Pizan, then, we encounter a theoretical framework designed to cope with a more diverse social order than that envisioned by the authors of conventional *specula*. Her attention to the needs and interests of women as well as of the disenfranchised and the poor in her vision of a properly regulated community stands in stark contrast to the narrow focus and condescension typical of traditional mirror literature. She does not dispense with instruction about the office of the prince, often couched in quite customary terms. But she alters the context for this conventional advice by setting it in a social order that is more intricate and requires of the ruler a greater measure of flexibility and a wider range of political skills than were envisaged by mainstream *specula*. Christine does not wish the prince to surrender the moral and religious precepts that earlier mirrors promoted. She believes, however, that these qualities are not sufficient for a prince to govern effectively in a diverse and complex society, especially one in which material well-being and economic profit compete with eternal salvation as goals worthy of recognition and pursuit. Hence her *specula* challenge the simplicity (and perhaps naïveté) of the worldview assumed by her predecessors. Kings will be able to maintain themselves on the throne, and their realm in peace, only to the extent that they prepare themselves to deal with the full range of subjects over whom they rule.

NOTE

[1]This essay quotes *The Book of the Body Politic* in Forhan's translation.

Christine de Pizan's *Ballades*: Lyrical Text and Its Musical Context

Patricia E. Black

Three works serve to crystalize for students the evolution of poetry and musical life of the fourteenth and fifteenth centuries and Christine's place in it. First chronologically, Eustache Deschamps (c. 1346–1406) wrote *L'art de dictier et de fere chancons, balades, virelais et rondeaulx* (1392). In this treatise he represents music as artificial and able to be mastered by study—unlike poetry, which is a natural music and a gift to those fortunate enough to receive it. This exposition of a divide in the art of lyric poetry begins to be manifested in contemporary fourteenth-century writers like Christine de Pizan, who, unlike her predecessors, did not set her own texts to music. Second in this chronology, Christine completed the *Cent balades* in 1402, in which the poem "Dueil engoisseux, rage demesurée" (ballade 6; "Anguished Mourning, Boundless Rage") appears. Third is Gilles Binchois (1400–60), who used this poem by her as text for a *chanson*. This composition was one of his most popular, quoted extensively in later musical works, sacred and secular (Kemp 520). These three works bookend not only musical practice of the late Middle Ages for students of music but also demonstrate for classes on literature how literary practice and the personal poetic voice develop.

As the disciple of Guillaume de Machaut (c. 1300–77), Deschamps stands at what we would consider the epicenter of poetic practice. In Guillaume's works, poetic practice still means musical composition; his music making reflects the performance practice of the time. Like other poet-musicians of the fourteenth century, such as Philippe de Vitry, he composes polyphonically. His works are the primary source of knowledge about the style called ars nova because of the lack of French musical sources between 1320 and his manuscripts. The term *ars nova* comes from a treatise ascribed to Philippe de Vitry and compiled between about 1316 and 1325 (Munrow 195). This polyphonic style of setting poetry consisted of the final development of a process, beginning in the thirteenth century, for determining a fixed length for every musical sound, so that the various voices could move in rhythm. Notwithstanding Machaut's artistry, voices and text go their separate ways, with text on one manuscript page and vocal parts on the other. Deschamps enters this divide to define poetry as an autonomous art, in opposition to music (Méchoulan 49). To give students a sense of Machaut's song style (song that is lyric poetry), I provide examples from the Ivrea Codex, as well as songs and virelays recorded by various artists (Guillaume de Machaut, *Motets*).

In the *Art de dictier* Deschamps gives to poetry and music separate roles as art forms; each can be enjoyed on its own merits. But music has limitations that poetry does not. The necessity of having more than one voice, the definition of polyphony, means that it is more difficult to render music, whereas poetry, which Deschamps separates from music, can go anywhere and be performed at any time because it depends only on the reciting voice (Page 485–87). This is the music Deschamps considers natural; it cannot be learned: "De ceste musique naturele, et comment home depuis qu'il se met naturelement a ce faire, ce que nul . . . ne lui sçauroit apprendre se de son propre et naturel mouvement ne se faisoit" ("Concerning this natural music, and how one, once he begins naturally, does that which no one . . . could possibly teach if not done from one's own and natural [rhythm, impulse] sense of motion"; "L'art de dictier" 272; my trans.).

The large corpus of poems by Deschamps, 1014 ballades and 138 *chansons royales*, shows that he rejects the topos of the sincere poet-lover as a lyric persona (Laurie 569). Thus, just as Philippe de Vitry appears to be the first to revolutionize musical practice by measuring notes and therefore leading to modern time signatures, Deschamps breaks the tradition of the traditional *trouvères*, by not composing music with his poetry and by abandoning the idea that the lady is the source of the poet's inspiration (570).

Christine therefore begins to write in a poetic milieu where poets no longer compose music to accompany their lyrics. She is part of the first generation that does not follow the *trouvère* model. Like Deschamps's subject choices, hers transcend the limitations of the poet persona inspired by love of a lady. In "Dueil engoisseux, rage desmesurée," she writes of her widowhood, a topic never before treated in any medieval French poem (Paden 39). Her poetic persona reprises the event, the death of her husband, that propelled her into professional writing. Many other women of the time had the same experience but did not write poetry as a result. Christine's contribution to poetry is therefore as significant as that of Deschamps or Philippe de Vitry with respect to music. She produced poems that were highly diverse on a technical level (Paden 35–36); even more, she brought a new sensibility and stance to the ballade, as this poem shows. Her collection of the *Cent balades* can even be considered a precursor to Baudelaire's *Fleurs du mal*. The formal beauty and innovations of the poetry of both convey a personal vision through readaptation of an existing poetic vocabulary but without the traditional hallmarks of lyric poetry.

In her life as in this essay, Christine was surrounded by men. She does not normally appear in literary history as a formal innovator, theorist, or creator of new directions for lyric poetry. Rather, it is Machaut, Deschamps, and Froissart who have the authorial reputation, status, and prestige that have guaranteed their place in literary history. For Christine, biography played a large role in how she is perceived. In the typical student edition of the Nouveaux Classiques Larousse of later medieval French lyric, Guillaume Picot wrote:

> Poète lyrique, elle a subi l'influence de Guillaume de Machaut et d'Eustache Deschamps . . . Plus intelligente que sensible, elle s'entend mieux à combiner les rythmes qu'à renouveler les thèmes habituels . . . elle ne par-

> vient guère à nous émouvoir que lorsqu'elle évoque avec *quelque* sincérité les tourments de son veuvage. (99; emphasis mine)

> As a lyric poet, she was influenced by Guillaume de Machaut and Eustache Deschamps. . . . More intelligent than sensitive, she is better able to combine rhythms than to make habitual themes new . . . she scarcely succeeds in moving us, except when she evokes, with *some* sincerity, the torments of her widowhood. (my trans.)

That Machaut and Deschamps had reputations as exemplary late medieval lyric poets counts against her; she began writing later. Because she was influenced by them, she was not original. Her intelligence is a negative attribute. The torments of her widowhood, reflected with "*some* sincerity" in her poetry, do no more than move her modern readers. Yet the way she subverts the poetic tradition she received in her creation of truly lyric work in the sense of Deschamps deserves more recognition (Richards, "Christine de Pizan and the Freedom" 7).

Binchois soon took up the task of setting to music the ballade "Dueil engoisseux, rage desmesurée." He may have chosen this particular ballade because of the originality of Christine's poetry. In musical style, he was one of the representatives of the Franco-Flemish school. Though little of his output now survives, his compositions were among the most copied in the 1420s and 1430s. Until recently, Guillaume Dufay held the attention of modern musicologists. However, the dissemination of Binchois's works during and after his life shows that his compositions were held in high esteem into the sixteenth century (Slavin, "Questions" 24) even though Binchois probably stopped composing in the 1440s. As was true of his musical predecessors (Machaut, Philippe de Vitry, Jean de le Mote) and contemporaries (Dufay, Dunstaple, Busnoys), he wrote music in many genres: movements for the Mass, psalm and canticle settings, and many forms of secular song. Like other composers of his era and beyond, he was also a practicing musician, a chapel singer at the Burgundian court. Music was his job, and he certainly did much of it in command performances. Today we think of composers as needing freedom and independence from constraints, but Binchois and others did their musical work at the behest of their patrons and for specific occasions.

Singers and composers like Binchois came from church milieus. Whether or not they were regular clergy (Binchois was not ordained a priest), they filled offices and derived their income from church sources. Binchois was paid for his work at the Burgundian court chapel, and he derived income from prebends.[1] As a practicing chapel musician, he had direct experience singing sacred texts, but his work at court would have given him experience singing secular song as well. The domain of secular music was also where stylistic innovation tended to appear in this era. In 1324–25, Pope John XXII denounced the use of ars nova in church composition (Munrow 196).

Binchois set to music primarily the texts of poems written in the fixed forms of rondeaux, virelays, and ballades. The strophic nature of these poems and their manuscript layout mean they do not demonstrate the kind of word painting found in Renaissance madrigals (Munrow 196). These pieces are more like hymn settings, where one stanza underlies the notes but all other stanzas must be fitted to the rhythm as much as possible. That during the Middle Ages professional singers performed most if not all songs in chapel or in court means that church congregations singing hymns had more difficulty fitting stanzas to melodic lines. Nevertheless, artists of the stature of Binchois would certainly have taken care that the song setting be appropriate for the poem overall, rather than for only the first stanza.

Ballade 6, "Dueil engoisseux, rage desmesurée," is one of a series of poems that begin a collection that Christine set out to write at the request of others, though she acknowledges that her subject matter will be neither joyful nor consoling (ballade 1). Ballade 2 takes up the theme of the good and valiant being overlooked; however, it also uses the phrase "grant dueil et grant rage" (line 25; "great grief-mourning and great rage"). Ballade 3 recounts the drowning of Lehander and uses the phrase "amoureuse rage" (line 23; "loving rage"). Ballade 4 concerns famous examples of betrayal and is part of the series of ballades that make references to antiquity (2–5). But ballades 5 and 6 abandon examples from well-known events and stories and suddenly apply the vocabulary that the narrator of Christine's autobiographical tale uses to discuss others objectively.

"Dueil" and "rage" are leitmotifs of ballades 5 and 6. The narrator speaks more personally in ballade 5, with many more first-person references than in 6. "Dueil engoisseux, rage desmesurée" is more removed from personal experience, even as it laments the torment caused by grief. Its applicability to anyone who has known grief could be one reason Binchois set this poem to music and why the song has been so often quoted by others.

A series of elements in ballades 5 and 6 show Christine's mastery in intertwining forms and themes. The rhyme schemes of these two ballades are similar. Their *ababbcbc* scheme provides both a break and continuity in the middle of the stanza. But the rhymes themselves are different: in ballade 5 they are all tense vowels, but in "Dueil engoisseux, rage desmesurée" there is greater contrast: the A rhyme in closed *e* (/e/) alternates with the B rhyme with nasal *a* (/ã/). The B rhyme then alternates with the /i/ of the rhyme syllable /rir/. In addition, the refrain line has an interior rhyme in the two antonymic words *garir, morir* ("to be cured," "to die"). Such poetic devices are musical in and of themselves. Moreover, they occur at strategic points for song setting, since they are both rhymes and refrain.

The first two stanzas of this ballade consist largely of lists of nouns modified by adjectives. This technique works well in the decasyllabic line, because the natural caesura occurs after a typical pairing of a noun of one syllable (like *dueil*, "grief" or "mourning") with a three-syllable adjective (like *engoisseux* [line 1; "anguished" or "anguishing"]) or a two-syllable adjective (like *triste* [10;

"sad") with a two-syllable noun (like *penser* ["thought"]). Many other combinations exist. The cumulative effect of such use of the resources of the poetic line conveys great emotion, as in the exclamation "O dure mort" (9; "O hard death"). The word pairings in ballade 6 also use the natural beats of the decasyllable to emphasize important words: beat 1 is *dueil*, beat 4 (*engoi*)-*sseux*, beat 5 *rage*, beat 10 (*desmesu*)-*rée* ("boundless, without measure").

Ignoring the beats of the lines, as in line 9, is another way to bring out word meanings and sounds: beats 1 and 2 are *fierté* ("pride"), beats 3 and 4 *durté* ("harshness"; two beats each because of the sense of the words, the alliteration of the /r/, and the interior rhyme /e/—the same as the A rhyme). But there is no real caesura after *durté*, because that noun is modified by the preposition *de* of the phrase *joye separée* ("separated from joy"). *Durté* is not definitively separated from *joye* and finally reaches its predicate in line 15, "Si sont en moy, sanz partir nullement" ("These are in me, never leaving"), where joy and harsh reality are both divided from their subject and brought together in the same person, no longer divided.

The third stanza changes the scheme set up in the first two. There begins to be more variety in noun modifiers. Two of the nouns are replaced by verbs (*veuillier, tressaillir*), which now occupy more ground than in the first two stanzas. Here, for the first time, Christine uses the resources of the stanza itself; she breaks it in half by the word *et*, which introduces a complex sentence with a relative clause. Each stanza leads to this point in some sense: line 7 has an infinitive, *cesser*; lines 14 and 15 contain a relative pronoun that embroiders on one of the nouns, summed up in "Si sont en moy;" lines 21–23 expand on what has been said before, as Christine's narrator puts it, *desmesuréement* (line 23).

The envoi cleverly uses the antonymic *briefment* in the prayer that death come soon. The reference to every ill with which Christine's narrator ended in stanza 3 returns, as does her harsh pain (line 27). Because of the refrain, the last word of this poem is *morir* ("to die"). Even to modern sensibilities, such an ending, as well as the rest of the sound and theme patterns of the poem, is lyrical. Christine's writing thus fits Deschamps's formulation of natural music even as it obeys all the dictates of the ballade form.

There are two sources for modern transcription of Binchois's song setting of "Dueil engoisseux, rage desmesurée": one is the edition of all his songs by W. Rehm (*Die Chansons von Gilles Binchois*); the other is W. Kemp's article "'Dueil Angoisseux' and 'Dulongesux.'" Because Kemp discovered other sources containing this song setting, he was able to compare them and arrive at a more complete reading than either gave alone. That other source was the *Buxheimer Orgelbuch* (c. 1470); as a piece for keyboard, it completely lacked text.

Binchois's song setting is in three or four parts and has two distinguishable sections that correspond to the two halves of the ballade stanza (*ababbcbc*), or the Aufgesang (*abab*) and Abgesang (*bcbc*), as they are known musicologically (Slavin, "Questions" 37). Despite the ornamentation rendered in the modern transcription, there is slower rhythm generally in all the voices for the first half of the stanza. There are various points of stasis created by voice leading. These conform to the rhythmic beat created by the series of nouns in Christine's poem. As was the practice in fourteenth- and fifteenth-century polyphony, Binchois approaches the first cadence with more rapid rhythms, especially in the upper voice. This kind of rhythmic treatment calls attention to a particular point of the text and musically prepares the cadence.

The second half of the stanza, where Christine begins to complicate syntax, is matched by Binchois's rhythmic and harmonic structure in the second half of his setting of the poem. As at the end of the first half of the song setting, the upper voice moves in rapid rhythms, a feature characteristic of Binchois (Trowbridge 150). Unlike the first half of the song setting, the two lower voices move scarcely at all. In fact, we could say that we have an early example of harmonic chords, although initially the two lower voices sing octaves, over which the melody in the highest voice moves. This model is the most familiar type of song setting for us, and there are moments in this work where the later evolution of song setting technique can be glimpsed. The ballade style, the setting of a song, allows ars nova composers to assign the greatest melodic importance to the highest voice (Van den Borren 53).

Kemp offers two possible alternatives for transcribing the end of the Abgesang. Though they share the same general musical material, they differ because of the variety of ways in which medieval mensural indications can be rendered in modern notation and because of the amount of embellishment an editor or musician chooses to include in a written version of the piece. Given the nature of medieval music manuscripts, particularly during the ars nova period but even with respect to *troubadour/trouvère* music, modern readers and performers of the music face many difficulties in realizing a version of the song. Pitch, phrasing, and ornamention are among the features of medieval songs that do not necessarily appear in the manuscripts (Munrow 196). The modern music devotee who makes the acquaintance of medieval music—as vast a field as that of medieval poetry—may be disconcerted to find that there is no medieval equivalent to our modern time signatures; indeed, there are many possible ways a modern transcriber can choose to render the medieval source (Kirkman and Weller 572). A medieval source therefore has much more flexibility than modern musical scores.

The musical setting that corresponds to the place where Christine's poem uses the C rhymes, and also increasingly insists on the ill that afflicts her narrator, has the most rhythmic and voice-leading movement of the entire song setting. Both Kemp's renderings reflect this tendency of the song manuscript. The second half of the stanza closes with the same type of cadence as the first—Binchois's attempt, perhaps, to reflect the cyclical nature of the ballade. Like the dance it imitates, it goes round and round.

Enough is known of the performance practice of the ars nova to write a typical conclusion. Let us imagine a congregation singing a hymn. There may be one stanza or ten. The same melody and harmony will be used for each. The performance practice of the organist, who learned this kind of improvisation through study, creates a sense of difference among the stanzas and leads the hymn to a conclusion that on paper it does not have. Kemp's transcription shows a typical closing coloration for this ballade (520). The rhythmic motion used in the second half of the ballade's stanza gradually slows, and one by one each voice reaches a final cadence. The manuscript containing Binchois's "Dueil engoisseus" would not have shown the performers what to do to bring the ballade to an end; their experience and study would have guided them.

As a representative of the Franco-Flemish school, Binchois shares characteristics of the Burgundian musical style that include motivic development and imitation, most familiar to us in the forms used by J. S. Bach. Two musical motifs stand out in the setting of "Dueil engoisseus." First is the dotted rhythm on the *do re mi* of the first full measure (of modern notation). This motif appears only in the first half of the poem, and the middle voice picks it up in imitation in the fifth measure. Second, the pitches *so la so mi* are repeated not only in the first half of the poem but also in the second, a kind of counterpoint to Christine's manipulation of rhymes and syntax. They too are imitated in the middle voice.

There are also features in Binchois that demonstrate the ars nova, metric subtleties, dissonance, and scarce attention to the text underlay (Olsson 37). Here the characteristic rhythm of dotted quarter followed by eighth note (modern notation) appears associated with certain pitches, but then Binchois also makes use of it as an organizational device that the upper and middle voices trade.

Dissonance in this song setting is limited to passing notes and preparation of the cadence at midpoint of the stanza. But there are also some instances that we might regard as a move toward another key signature—an anachronism when applied to Binchois—that represent the modern editor's resolution of cadential or ornamental issues called *musica ficta*, unnotated additions to the voice lines that we would regard as accidentals and that a modern composer would notate. From the twelfth century into the sixteenth, manuscripts did not notate departures from the modal system. These moves toward other step and half-step combinations occur in the second half of the song (measure 26). One could now say that the setting cannot decide whether it will be in what we perceive as major or minor tonality (Randel 85). This shift back and forth in the second half of the ballade stanza leads to tonal tension when the cadence finally arrives. The tension is another feature that helps the song setting orient itself linearly and escape the trap of unceasing circular repetition characteristic of ballade form. This feature distinguishes Binchois from his contemporaries Dufay and Busnoys.

The feature of the ars nova that has a composer devoting little attention to the text underlay explains why Binchois's song settings became so detached from their origins as musical interpretations of poetic text. "Dueil engoisseux" even became a keyboard piece, "Dulongesux," which no one recognized until the 1950s (Kemp 520). Other song settings by Binchois suffered the same fate.

How was this song sung? As a poem written by a woman and having autobiographical echoes that Christine's contemporaries would have recognized, we might expect that a woman sang Binchois's setting of this ballade. But despite the range, which is not excessively high but does correspond to the modern soprano, men sang all the parts. Musicologists have examined the chapel statutes of the court of Burgundy (though they do postdate Binchois's known lifetime) as well as the payment lists of the court choir of 1469. The lists make clear that not even boys sang the high parts; all the lines were sung by men, who used falsetto if necessary (Munrow 197). It is significant that in the second half of the fifteenth century there is documentary evidence that only men sang in public for both secular and sacred occasions.

Having broken with the traditions of the *trouvère* song, as Deschamps did, Christine also writes poems that do not repeat the commonplaces of love. Her lyric poetry remains "natural music" despite its subject matter (Laurie 570). Whether or not Deschamps wrote the *Art de dictier* to justify his inability to compose music with notes, Christine fell on the lyric poetry side of the equation and not on the musical side. Having broken the barrier to becoming a writer, she did not break the barrier that would have allowed her to become a composer. She may have also subscribed to the ideas her friend Deschamps expounded in his explanations of poetic practice (Paden 35). Because of the multitudinous unwritten conventions of performance practice as well as the complexities of ars nova compositional techniques, practitioners of music had to spend long years studying, which is how Deschamps characterizes "artificial music" (Slavin, "In Support" 189).

Binchois served as an organist as a young man and probably trained as a chorister from childhood. Thus his composing grew out of a lifetime of familiarity with performing and studying. Yet the impulse to make lyric poetry completely musical remains strong, as attested by the close dates between Christine's *Cent balades* (1402) and the one manuscript that both ascribes the songs to Binchois and contains almost half his secular music, copied c. 1428–36. Despite Deschamps's proclamation and the growing specialization of the two art forms, Christine's poetry, whose techniques now more embody the lyric tendency of the poetic forms, paradoxically became a more equal partner to ars nova polyphony, capable of creating a more harmonized musical form whose meaning thereby becomes audible (Beck 657).

NOTE

[1] Binchois received prebends established by the prince at St. Donatian, Bruges (7 Jan. 1430); Ste. Waudru, Mons (17 May 1437); St. Vincent, Soignies (from 1452); and St. Pierre, Cassel (21 May 1459).

Explicating Christine's Poetics: Pallas Athena and the Apple of Discord

Susan J. Dudash

Though Christine de Pizan would devote much of her life to writing advice books and prose texts aimed at achieving peace, it was her poetic works that put her name on the map. Verse not only launched her literary career but also continued to punctuate the subtler prose works that she would compose during the early 1400s, the most prolific period of her literary production. Verse also gave shape to the devotional texts that she penned near the end of her career and served as the vehicle of choice for her final flourish, a poetic composition in praise of the French national heroine, *Le ditié de Jehanne d'Arc* (*The Tale of Joan of Arc*).

My approach to teaching Christine's poetry capitalizes on the multivalent quality of her work and uses as its point of departure the close, critical reading characteristic of the French exercise of explication de texte. By providing the linguistic, historical, and theoretical tools necessary to explore the nuances of her original verse, this essay seeks to help students achieve greater insight into the techniques of textual analysis, Christine's authorial mission, and the concept of engaged literature. To this end, I offer suggestions for incorporating her poetics into the curriculum and recommend materials and pedagogical strategies to conduct a full-class explication de texte of one of her most multifaceted ballades, poem 7 of the *Autres balades* (*Other Ballads*; *More Ballades*), the first verse of which is "Se de Pallas me peüsse accointier" ("If Pallas I could only know").[1] The first section of this essay provides a framework for analyzing Christine's poetry, with particular emphasis on one of the central figures of ballade 7, Pallas Athena (Minerva). I then discuss my approach to the explication de texte, before moving to its application to ballade 7. The poem is reproduced in full in Appendix 1 below.

Christine in Context

For an introduction to French literature or textual analysis, as well as for more advanced courses on medieval France, I find that just a few poems can illustrate many of the principal themes of Christine's literary corpus. My selection typically includes examples of her innovative widowhood poetry, remarkably accessible in its treatment of universal sentiments such as love and grief, as in her celebrated ballade 11 of the *Cent balades*, "Seulete suy" ("Alone am I"),[2] and examples of her commentary on contemporary politics and the mythographical history of France, as in ballad 7 of the *Autres balades*. Ballades 11 and 7 exemplify some of what is best and most unique in Christine's verse while revealing several of her lifelong preoccupations: the amelioration of the status of women in society, a reexamination of the concept of amorous love, a devotion to learning, and the political rehabilitation of her adoptive France.

As a *mise en abîme* of Christine's thought on a variety of topics, poems such as ballades 11 and 7 serve as useful portals into several poetic contexts. First, they may be analyzed in tandem with other fixed forms found in her anthologies of individual ballades and rondeaux, the *Cent balades* (*One Hundred Ballads*; *One Hundred Ballades*) and *Autres balades*. Second, poems connected to her widowhood segue seamlessly into a discussion of her response to, and transformation of, courtly love poetry in the *Cent balades d'amant et de dame* (*One Hundred Ballads of a Lover and a Lady*; *One Hundred Ballades of a Lover and His Lady*). Ballades 11 and 7 could also serve as an introduction to Christine's other poetic compositions, such as the verse epistle response to the *Roman de la rose* called the *Epistre au dieu d'amours* (*Letter of the God of Love*); her historiographical and autobiographical *Le livre de la mutacion de Fortune* (*The Book of the Mutability of Fortune*); her contemporary celebration of the Maid of Orléans, the *Ditié de Jehanne d'Arc* (*Tale of Joan of Arc*); or even her *Epistre Othea* (*Othea's Letter to Hector*), a work that contains both verse and prose components. Finally, these ballades can be profitably integrated into a group of medieval French poetic works including selections of poetry by Rutebeuf (c. 1248–c. 1277); Guillaume de Machaut (1300–70); Guillaume's successor, Eustache Deschamps (c. 1340–1404); and Charles d'Orléans (1394–1465); in addition to the anonymous (and often illustrated) danses macabres.

Ballade 7, found in Christine's anthology of fifty-three poems composed before 1402 known as the *Autres balades*, covers thematic ground similar to that of the *Cent balades* (advice, social critique, mythological themes) and includes poetic requests for employment for her son. As in the rest of her literary corpus, mythology, politics, and the personal converge.

One of the most striking features of the poem is the appearance of Pallas (Minerva), a goddess who stars in Christine's oeuvre in a variety of contexts (Tarnowski, "Pallas"; Solterer, *Master* 151–75). For example, ballade 14 of the *Autres balades*, "Viegne Pallas, la deesse honnourable" ("Come Pallas, honorable goddess") addresses Pallas directly. The story of the Judgment of Paris, in which Pallas Athena occupies an important place, figures prominently in the *Epistre Othea* (chs. 13, 60, 68, and 73 are all relevant). Even Christine's *Livre des fais d'armes et de chevallerie* (*The Book of Deeds of Arms and of Chivalry*), a prose work on the art of warfare and just war, begins with the author's famous invocation of Minerva, the goddess of arms and letters, Pallas's Roman incarnation—and Christine's Italian compatriot. Minerva appears not only in the lines of Christine's text but also in the beautifully illuminated prologues of the *Fais d'armes*, which depict her and Christine in tandem, the former clad in her iconic armor, the latter equipped with the accoutrements of scholarship.[3] Such images could complement a full-class poetic analysis or help launch a discussion about genre.

Beyond Christine's oeuvre, the possibilities for further exploration of the Judgment of Paris in medieval French literature abound, as Jean-Charles Huchet and Margaret J. Ehrhart have shown. One striking analogue is Guillaume de Machaut's 1360 *Livre de la fonteinne amoureuse* (*The Book of the Fountain of Love*), a lyrical work that echoes and reinterprets earlier poetic dream visions, in particular the *Roman de la rose* (*Romance of the Rose*). Whether examined in conjunction with her other verse compositions or with those of her contemporaries, even one or two of Christine's poems can open a window onto her literary corpus as a whole and provide fertile ground for study.

The Explication de Texte

Although a classic explication de texte that examines each line and its unique characteristics in sequential order is a useful technique for poetic interpretation, I find that a broader approach, focused on the overarching themes and goals of the poem, can help students better analyze Christine's poetics in the larger frameworks of medieval French literature, culture, and politics. While the basic components of the two methods are the same—presentation of the poem's literary context, its main characters, and overall tone; dramatic reading, for oral presentations; explication, including synthesis of content and form; and conclusion—my approach focuses on major motifs to elucidate the poet's goals in composing the poem. In particular, I like to have my students focus on repeated words from given lexical fields groups (*isotopies*) and any ruptures or unexpected elements (*écarts*) in meter, rhyme, syntax, and signification to help flesh out the work's dominant themes and poetic mission. Since each composition typically exhibits its own distinctive constellation of features, students' explication should be tailored to suit. Appendix 2 below presents the guidelines I use for such an explication. The following section details my approach to illuminating some of these features in a full-class discussion of ballade 7.

New Sibyl, New Minerva: "Se de Pallas me peüsse accointier"

As Christine would write in her autobiographical works, she turned to study not only from a lifelong love of learning but also because as "captain of her own ship" (*Livre de la mutacion*, pt. 1, ch. 12) she had to negotiate the stormy waters of professional patronage, political intrigues and shifting allegiances, and unstable judicial practices in order to secure financial footing for herself and her family (*Livre de l'advision Cristine* [*The Vision of Christine*], pt. 3, ch. 11). Her devotion to learning and the betterment of France is evident in the structure of ballade 7, particularly in her plaintive refrain "Car de Juno n'ay je nul reconfort" ("For from Juno, I have no comfort").

To facilitate a full-class explication de texte of ballade 7, I ask my students to familiarize themselves with some essential background information. I provide handouts or digital slides on the cast of characters the poem invokes: Pallas, Juno, Venus, Paris, and Fortune (Brumble). I also offer a brief synopsis of the story of the Apple of Discord, such as this one, slightly modified from *Bullfinch's Mythology*:

> All the gods were invited to the wedding of Peleus and Thetis, except one: Eris, or Discord. Enraged by her exclusion, Discord threw a golden apple, inscribed "For the Fairest," among the guests. Juno, Venus, and Minerva each claimed the apple—and title—for her own. Jupiter, king of the gods, was unwilling to make such a potentially problematic decision, and thus committed the judgment to the attractive prince, Paris. Each of the goddesses attempted to bribe Paris by offering him a fabulous prize: Juno promised him power and riches; Minerva, glory and renown in war; and Venus, the most beautiful woman in the world, Helen. Paris gave the apple to Venus, making enemies of Juno and Minerva. With Venus's help, Paris sailed to Greece to try to convince Helen—the Spartan king's wife and the woman whom Venus had destined for Paris—to leave with him for Troy. Paris' subsequent abduction of Helen instigated the Trojan War, a subject commemorated in verse by Homer and Virgil and an important exemplum throughout the Middle Ages. (Bullfinch 192–93)

This information, which I typically provide a day or two in advance of our in-class exercise, put students in a better position to discern the significance of Christine's use of the goddesses in a courtly or political context.

On the day of discussion, I like to sketch a time line on the board to underscore the overlapping crises that beset France during Christine's lifetime, which include the Hundred Years War, civil war, the papal schism, popular uprisings, and plague. Added to these crises were the deaths of Charles V of France, of Christine's father, and of Christine's husband.[4] Above these historical events, I note her lifetime (c. 1364–c. 1431) and the start of her literary career (c. 1393). This visual schematic helps students keep in mind the multiple crises of the late fourteenth and early fifteenth centuries, which converged to leave their imprint on the politico-historical and literary landscape. Although this information could simply be presented on a digital slide, I find that eliciting students' input and constructing the diagram in class dramatizes the political and social turbulence that characterized Christine's life and heightens their awareness of her poetic distress. As she would write in the *Advision Cristine*, her fortunes and those of France were inextricably entwined (prologue; pt. 3, chs. 4–7). In fact, in the *Advision*, France is portrayed as a widow.

Once the contextual foundations are laid, an analysis of ballade 7 may comprise at least four different levels. On the mythological and historical level, the ballade reflects the transference of learning (*translatio studii*) and of power (*translatio imperii*) from ancient Greece, Rome, and Troy to the kingdom of

France. The political level, too, is connected to *translatio imperii* and what were believed to be the French monarchy's Trojan origins (*Epistre Othea* 195; Beaune 226–44). We explore how Christine might draw parallels between the decisions, actions, and battles of nobles in ancient times and in her own day; the ballade might thus serve as a vehicle for her commentary on the ethos of the French royal court. Moreover, for Christine, the political is personal. This leitmotif may be explored in ballade 7 by asking how the decisions and choices of an individual (Paris, Christine, the reader) may have consequences for a whole nation. Just as Paris's judgment brought catastrophe on his Trojan homeland, so could the individual decisions and acts of French nobles have far-reaching, and potentially disastrous, effects on France. The third stage of analysis involves literary themes such as ubi sunt, regret, and nostalgia for a golden age when learning was held in the highest regard and women were cherished and protected by valiant noblemen; this is a recurring thread in both Christine's corpus and that of close contemporaries such as François Villon. The explication's final level concerns Christine's own life experiences and her quest for solace following the traumatic deaths that determined the course of her personal and professional career. As Christine yearns to converse with Pallas—and in so doing rewrites the Judgment of Paris in a personal yet politicized way—the reader is implicitly invited to emulate the poet and consider Paris's choice anew. This part of the analysis is thus structurally and contextually bound to the others.

In order to bring these notions to the fore, we turn first to the ballade's overall structure. We determine the norm—decasyllabic verses (dizains) of ten verses per strophe—and any deviations that draw the reader's attention, such as the octosyllabic verses at lines 6, 16, and 26. This is also an opportunity to discuss the envoi, a stanza of two to four verses appended to the end of the ballade, which may function as a dedication, a conclusion, an explanation, or a summary. Although only eighteen of the hundred ballades in the *Cent balades* include an envoi, this final stanza provides additional interpretive possibilities: for example, underscoring the political foundation of Christine's works as well as her authorial mission. In ballade 7 the envoi appears as a summary or conclusion.

In terms of its rhyme scheme, ballade 7 is generally rich. Double rhymes ("soustenir" and "tenir" [lines 6–7]) and simple rhymes (the repetition of "fais" [4–5]) that occur on either side of the octosyllabic verses, thus accentuating their significance even further, deserve special emphasis. Similarly, I invite my students to comment on any poetic features they find striking or anomalous. These should include *rejet* and enjambment. A *rejet* occurs when a word or words syntactically necessary to complete the phrase continue past the normal metrical pause of a verse, either at the caesura or at the end of a verse, throwing the word or words into special relief (lines 3–4). Enjambment, however, a syntactical element that transcends the normal metrical limits at the end of a verse and would normally be preceded and followed by a pause, is not thrown into relief by punctuation and therefore does not result in particular emphasis on a given word or words but rather on the verse as a whole (line 26). In calling my students' attention to these poetic features, I remind them that such deviations often indicate crucial words, phrases, and concepts. In the *rejet* at line 4, for example, the word preceding the caesura, "reconfort," is repeated in the stressed position of the refrain and as the final word of the ballade. Moreover, elements like the enjambment at line 26 create a sense of instability around this octosyllabic line, further highlighting its significance. Students should be able to determine that the overall effect of these deviations is to express Christine's weakness and hence her need for help. She chooses Pallas, whose role it was to protect the vulnerable. I ask students why Christine prefers Pallas to Juno. Reviewing discordances in the structure of the poem thus helps elucidate some of its dominant themes.

In order to examine these motifs in greater detail, we next focus on the goddesses and their attributes. Christine's distinctive treatment of the Judgment of Paris may be brought to light by sketching a diagram of three columns, one for each of the goddesses. I ask my students to describe the goddesses' traditional symbols, adding the responses under the appropriate heading: love (and courtly love) for Venus; wealth, women, marriage, power, and aristocracy for Juno; and wisdom for Pallas.

When and how does each goddess appear in the poem? Venus, Paris's ultimate choice, is not mentioned until the second stanza. Juno, who is recalled repeatedly in the refrain, has turned a deaf ear to the poet's requests. But Pallas and all she symbolizes are foremost in Christine's thought: the goddess is prominently cited in both the first verse and the envoi. We also pay particular attention to Christine's choice of names: the goddess of wisdom is distinguished from the others by the use of her Greek name, Pallas, rather than the Roman appellations assigned to Juno and Venus. Juno and Venus produce the opposite of what they represent: the goddess of love gives birth not to joy but to death; Juno, who stands for wealth, marriage, and power, leads her followers only to indigence, widowhood, and weakness or vulnerability. But Pallas remains true: from wisdom comes wisdom, joy, and comfort. By all accounts, her election ensures a more propitious, desirable, and predictable outcome.

With these ideas in place, I ask my class to consider how these choices might be interpreted with respect to Christine's life. We reflect on her fate following the deaths of her husband, her father, and her protector, Charles V. Though a widow, vulnerable and impoverished (such are the effects of Juno), Christine nevertheless elected to forgo remarriage in favor of writing and the comfort of knowledge; she threw in her lot with Pallas. As further evidence for this interpretation, we consider how each goddess could evoke a type of existence, whether contemplative (Pallas), active (Juno), or sensual (Venus).[5] Moving from the personal, we ask how Christine's own choices might be interpreted vis-à-vis those of her aristocratic audience and contemporary France as a whole. If necessary, I jump-start the discussion by asking students to consider what outcomes her readers could expect if they were to imitate Christine or how personal choice might inform political virtue (a lesson no less germane today than in the fifteenth century).

Another, related level of interpretation may be explored through the primary contrasts of the ballade: past and future, weakness and power, love and death, abandonment and protection, belonging and exile. Here again I suggest that my students focus both on Christine's personal fortunes and the broader issue of France's political history and future. I encourage them to determine whether the poet's selection of the goddess of wisdom offers a solution, a means to effect the desired outcome. Then, I bring up the appearance of Fortune. Because Fortune evokes both past and present and her wheel symbolizes the vicissitudes of life (a fall from power to weakness, a rise from poverty to wealth), her presence in the poem strikes a note of warning for its aristocratic audience. Personal and political destinies are not fixed but mutable; they can change in an instant. Fortune thus becomes a kind of axis around which the fates of Paris, Christine, and France revolve. To highlight this message, I ask my students how Fortune relates to the deities in the ballad. Could Pallas provide a shield against Fortune, and if so, how? As Ehrhart notes, Pallas is the only goddess over which Fortune holds no sway (185); indeed, Pallas is invoked in direct opposition to Fortune in the ballade's first stanza.

From our consideration of the poem's characters and contrasts, we proceed to a closer study of its language. We attend to chains of thought and lexical groups (*isotopies*). To help students flesh out at least three major lexical categories, I guide them in creating clusters of expressions from the ballade. Vocabulary suggestive of the judicial milieu is one example: *chargier*, from stanza 1; *plaidier*, *tors*, *tenir à un jugement*, *jugia*, *detenir*, from stanza 2; and *meffais*, from stanza 3. Another category evokes burden, or duty, and the polysemous French *fais*—an obligation or responsibility and a difficult enterprise. This isotopic cluster is evinced by the many forms of *fais* and *faissel* in addition to words and expressions like *soustenir*, *poissant effort*, *aidier*, *maintenir*, and *aveir mestier de* (*avoir besoin de*), which may overlap with items from the first lexical group, like *chargier*. The third category concerns chivalry and nobility and points to the duties of this class. Words and expressions include *poissant effort*, *aidier*, *reconfort*, *grans pouoirs*, *fais* ("deeds"), *tenir sus* (*seigneurie*), *vaillant Pallas*, *biens*, *serve*, *maintenir le monde*, even *descort*. Determining the taxonomy is the first step.

Once the categories are in place, students should be encouraged to formulate their interpretations with a view to both the poet and France, paying particular attention to the poem's refrain. They can consider what a well-informed judgment should entail, Christine's legal difficulties and experience with judicial proceedings following the death of her husband, and the seriousness of making a decision about the proper course of action to follow, particularly one that looks on past evidence with an eye toward the future. To decode the second isotopic group, burden or duty, we target, on one hand, Christine's personal and professional existence, such as her responsibilities toward her family, and, on the other, the concept of noblesse oblige, the aristocracy's obligation to perform chivalrous deeds and acts—that is, to support and protect the weak and the French nation as a whole. Finally, the second and third isotopic groups are connected through the traditional duties of rulers, their *devoir.* What services should nobles render their subjects, according to Christine? To determine Christine's view of contemporary practices at court, students should focus on the ballade's plaintive refrain—especially stressed words such as *Juno* at the caesura and *reconfort* at the end of the line—on the choice of the present tense and on the use of strong negatives such as "n'ay je nul" ("I have none"). They should discern the poet's desire for concord, the wish that her noble readers will listen to wisdom and reason, and the hope that they will avoid following in the footsteps of their Trojan ancestors. Christine emphasizes that it is the responsibility of those with *grans pouoirs* ("great powers") to weigh their judgments carefully. For the powerful make the world go round, as the envoi suggests.

Christine proposes an alternative path, one that draws on the lessons of the past and looks to a more propitious future (line 29). I ask my class how the poem shows Paris's choice and its outcome as a negative historical exemplum. Expressions like "sovenir" ("memory") in verse 33 of the envoi, and "mors et deffais" ("dead and defeated") in verse 22, and the accumulation of past tenses in the second and third stanzas, bolster Christine's case for eschewing the mistakes of the past. At the same time, a possible future emerges through her use of subjunctive and conditional structures when she presents Pallas ("peüsse" ["could"]; "seroit . . . reffais" ["would be renewed"]; "Se Pallas" ["If Pallas"]; lines 1, 25). These are posed in contradistinction to life as it is, under Juno. Christine thus offers a different future, one founded in good judgment, which confers joy and all good things to those who choose the goddess of wisdom as their ally (29).

But what of justice, another of the lexical groups? Why might Christine have chosen to bring this vocabulary to the fore? Given her plaintive tone, particularly in the refrain, and her personal experience in court following her husband's death, what might be her goal? Christine the poet is pleading her case before her aristocratic audience, not merely in an attempt to obtain financial compensation or aid for herself as an individual, but to recall to her noble readers their chivalric duties. They should avoid the Trojans' mistakes by making wiser, more thoughtful judgments in weighty matters. She argues her case in a kind of judicial plea or court appeal; the poem itself becomes the evidence entered on behalf of the defense.

While Christine's literary career was launched out of necessity, it bore testament to her long love of learning and her enduring devotion to her family, monarch, and adoptive French homeland. Her poetic corpus in particular was born of loss, catharsis, and a compelling didactic drive—to guide her aristocratic readers and patrons to serve as models and to portray the personal as political. It is perhaps fitting, then, that her final composition, like her first literary works, was written in verse. Christine composed in celebration of an exemplary woman, the French national savior, Joan of Arc; her poem extolled the realization of myriad possibilities for women, king, and country.

NOTES

[1]Translations are my own unless otherwise noted. The Middle French poem appears on pp. 214–15 of Maurice Roy's edition of *Autres balades*. For published English translations, see the table in the "Materials" section of this volume.

[2]On this poem, see Barbara Altmann's essay in this volume.

[3]See, for example, the contemporaneous BNF ffr. 603, fol. 2r; and London, Harley MS 4605, fol. 3, which dates from 1434. The iconographical program of Christine's *Othea* is discussed by Hindman, *Christine de Pizan's* Epistre Othéa; as well as by Desmond and Sheingorn.

[4]For a fuller historical account, see the essays in this volume by Jeff Rider and by Renate Blumenfeld-Kosinski.

[5]On Christine's "oath of allegiance" to Pallas and the modes of life in ballade 7, see Blumenfeld-Kosinski, *Reading* 174–75; Ehrhart 184–85.

APPENDIX 1
Ballade 7, *Autres Balades*

Se de Pallas me peüsse accointier
Joye et tout bien ne me fauldroit jamais;
Car par elle je seroie ou sentier
De reconfort, et de porter le fais
Que Fortune a pour moy trop chargier fais;
Mais foible suis pour soustenir
Si grant faissel, s'elle ne vient tenir
De l'autre part, par son poissant effort
Pour moy aidier, Dieu m'i doint avenir,
Car de Juno n'ay je nul reconfort.

Pallas, Juno, Venus vouldrent plaidier
Devant Paris jadis de leurs tors fais,
Dont chascune disoit qu'a son cuidier
Plus belle estoit, et plus estoit parfais
Ses grans pouoirs que de l'autre en tous fais;
Sus Paris s'en vouldrent tenir,
Qui lors jugia que l'en devoit tenir
A plus belle Venus et a plus fort,
Si dist: "Dame, vous vueil je detenir,
Car de Juno n'ay je nul reconfort."

Pour la pomme d'or lui vint puis aidier
Vers Heleine Venus, mors et deffais
En fu après ; si n'ay d'elle mestier,
Mais de joye seroit mon cuer reffais,
Se la vaillant Pallas, par qui meffais
Sont delaissié et retenir
Fait tous les biens, me daignoit retenir
Pour sa serve : plus ne devroie au fort
Ja desirer pour a grant bien venir,
Car de Juno n'ay je nul reconfort.

Ces trois poissans deesses maintenir
Font le monde, non obstant leur descort ;
Mais de Pallas me doint Dieux sovenir,
Car de Juno n'ay je nul reconfort.

If I could befriend Pallas,
I would never lack joy and all good,
For through her, I would be on the path
To be consoled, and could bear the burden
That Fortune has laid heavy upon me.
But I am too weak to carry
Such a load, if she does not come to help
Hold up her side with strong efforts
To aid me. God grant that it come to pass,
For from Juno I have no comfort.

Pallas, Juno and Venus wanted to plead
Long ago before Paris about wrongs done them;
Each of them said she believed
She was the fairest, and that her powers
Were greater and more perfect than the others'.
They wanted to leave the matter to Paris,
Who judged that Venus should be held
Fairest and most compelling;
He said, "My lady, I would detain you,
For from Juno I have no comfort."

For the golden apple she received, Venus
Helped him to Helen; later,
He knew death and defeat. I have no need of her,
Then—but my heart would be renewed with joy
If valiant Pallas, who causes misdeeds
To be laid aside, and all good
To be retained, would deign retain
Me for her servant; then I would need
Desire no further good to come,
For from Juno I have no comfort.

These three mighty goddesses
Keep the world, despite their discord;
But may God recall Pallas to me,
For from Juno I have no comfort.

(Translation by Andrea Tarnowski)

APPENDIX 2
Elements of an Explication de Texte

Situation of the Poem

- presentation of aspects of the author's life that are directly related to the poem
- presentation of the poem in its relevant literary, cultural, and historical contexts
- dramatic reading (for oral explications)
- description of the poem: central theme(s) and poetic genre
- literal explication of primary characters
- explanation of difficult words, allusions, cultural references (for oral explications)

Versification

- organization of the poem (type, stanza structure)
- rhyme scheme (richness, masculine vs. feminine rhymes, associations)
- meter (norm, discordances and their effects)

Analysis of Signification

- oppositions (within each stanza and between stanzas; effects of oppositions)
- ruptures or discordances (syntactical, lexical, linguistic, cultural), parallels between metrical ruptures and ruptures in signification
- analogies, isotopic groups, repetitions and their effects, as well as any relations between these elements and the poet's use of sound and signifiers
- sonorous elements and their implications

Conclusion

- synthesis of form and content to define the poem's broader message, its mission, and its lessons for the reader

Christine de Pizan's Lyric Poetry and the Question of Intertextuality

Barbara K. Altmann

Christine de Pizan can be a challenge to teach because her work is in some aspects unique while in others highly conventional. What sets her apart first and foremost, of course, is that to our knowledge she was the only woman in France in her day who successfully crafted a persona as a female author and ensured the transmission of her work into the most elevated ranks of courtly society. Today her allegorical and political works, which are marked by an exceptional and sustained profeminist agenda, are largely what define her oeuvre. The disadvantage of focusing on the exceptional and uncommon, however, is that we tend to remove Christine from the mainstream of late medieval literature and teach her as an anomaly. We bring her into the canon, but often we do not place her in dialogue with her literary forebears and successors. In the classroom, for example, we infrequently teach her more conventional writings, including her lyric poetry, which draws heavily on the traditions established by Guillaume de Machaut and practiced by other authors from more or less the same time, such as Jean Froissart, Eustache Deschamps, and Alain Chartier.

Christine's contemporaries and Christine herself emphasized their debts to one another. One striking example is the circle of interlocutors she drew together from the epistolary debate over the *Roman de la rose* (*Romance of the Rose*), but the same kind of dialogic relation—wherein an author or a work speaks to and interacts with others—is constantly at play in the realm of her lyric poetry. Deschamps claims a close relationship with Guillaume de Machaut and writes of reading his work aloud. Deschamps also praises Christine. Christine in turn addresses poems to Deschamps and to Jean de Garencières, and Martin le Franc includes Christine among the worthy women praised in his *Champion des dames*. These relationships suggest that Christine's poetry should be read not in isolation but in a larger tradition, a tradition of which her generation of writers was acutely aware.

This essay concerns the question of Christine's work and the notion of intertextuality, by which I mean the precise borrowing from, as well as the imitation of, one particular piece of writing by another—that is, what one writer makes use of from another's work, often traced and analyzed in detail in the introductions of traditional editions. By *intertextuality* I also mean, however, the broad notion of shared literary conventions that loosely define a particular literary genre. Graham Allen describes the former aspect of intertextuality as "the transformative relationship between one text and another text" and the latter as "the relationship between a text"—or a group of texts—"and the literary system" (6). Placing Christine's work in a broader context puts us in the realm of what Gérard Genette calls "architextuality," the study of literature and its categories as a system from which an individual text or texts emerge (1).

The most important reason to take this approach is simply to understand Christine's work better by knowing how it relates to the writing of her contemporaries. In teaching medieval intertextuality, however, we also have to lay bare some of the differences between medieval and modern notions of literary poetics and aesthetics. For modern readers and critics, there is an ill-defined overlap between the notions of intertextuality and conventionality. In its broadest sense, the term *intertextuality* actually encompasses literary convention, as is clear in Allen's and Genette's definitions of it. In practice, however, critics tend to use the term *intertextual* for an aspect of the text they consider positive and worthy of notice, while *conventional* is often used with a negative valence: to describe a piece of writing as conventional or derivative usually means to dismiss it for lack of originality or uniqueness. In the Middle Ages, however, an author often imitated existing models to some degree in order to demonstrate his or her learning and knowledge of earlier writers and to share in the prestige of prior, successful examples. In such an aesthetic system, to say that a piece of literature is modeled on or reminiscent of another is not a pejorative assessment. Medieval writing placed a high value on convention. Along with referring or alluding to respected earlier writers (in Latin, "auctores"), writers worked in received forms as a tactic for ensuring acceptance of the text by its intended audience. Medieval writers inherited ideas about convention and working from models from the concept of *imitatio* ("imitation"), a strategy from Roman rhetoric. Imitation of a respected model—whether of its form, its content, or both—was the starting point for the production of a new work, and the author's job was to create something both recognizable and new. The importance of imitation as a source of inspiration extends beyond the Middle Ages and into the Renaissance, although sixteenth-century French authors chose models from Greco-Roman antiquity and Italian humanist writing while rejecting anything medieval (McKinley).

In Christine's day, treatises such as Eustache Deschamps's *L'art de dictier* (1392; "The Art of Composing Poetry") categorized existing models for poetry and laid out ground rules for their use. The popularity in the late Middle Ages of fixed-form poetry, including the ballade, the chant royal, the rondeau, and the virelay—all short verse forms for which Guillaume de Machaut established the basic template—demonstrates the importance placed on working in certain formal and thematic constraints. Along with the longer and more flexible *lai* and *complainte*, these poems account for the vast majority of lyric production by late medieval French poets, Christine among them. To appreciate the contribution of any given poet of the day it is necessary to recognize his or her reworking of familiar forms and themes, a subtle permutation of the usual elements, the introduction of new voices or perspectives into tried and true shapes. Daniel Poirion, in his comprehensive book on late medieval French lyric, says that to understand the history of fourteenth- and fifteenth-century lyric poetry, we need to discover the "substance vivante" ("living substance") of the poems behind the apparent rigidity of their formal properties and their seemingly unchanging themes (*Le poète et le prince* 313).

Lyric Inscribed in Tradition

How do we discover the "living substance" in Christine's lyric poems? Our task is first to determine the author's model and then to discover how she plays with its conventions, an exercise essential in the classroom for making meaning of any medieval poetry. The obvious place to start is with the poem "Seulete suy" ("Alone am I"), number 11 in Christine's collection *Cent balades* (*One Hundred Ballades*), assembled about 1402. This poem is often anthologized, no doubt for its spare, powerful semantics, its striking repetition, and a living substance more easily decipherable than in many of her other poems. While it is frequently reproduced or referred to, however, its boldness and distinctiveness are not often fully explicated. This particular poem is a productive case study in the inventive use of convention, and the following explication details the richness of its twenty-five lines. The poem's full text and an English translation are appended to this essay. To begin a close reading, however, the first strophe is enough:

> Seulete suy et seulete vueil estre,
> Seulete m'a mon doulx ami laissiée;
> Seulete suy, sanz compaignon ne maistre,
> Seulete suy, dolente et courrouciée;
> Seulete suy en languour mesaisiée;
> Seulete suy plus que nulle esgarée;
> Seulete suy sanz ami demourée. [refrain] (Roy, *Œuvres poétiques* 1: 12)

> Alone am I and alone I wish to be,
> Alone has my lover left me;
> Alone am I, without companion or master,
> Alone am I, sorrowful and filled with anger;
> Alone am I, miserable in languor;
> Alone am I, more lost than any other;
> Alone am I, left with no lover. (my trans.)

The ballade, a fixed-form type to which this poem belongs, was Christine's favorite lyric model, to judge by the large number of them in her collected works. It was the format par excellence for courtly lyric in the late Middle Ages. Guillaume de Machaut included 206 ballades in his *Louange des dames* ("Praise of Ladies"), for example; they are also an integral part of his *Prologue*, in which he lays out both a poetics and examples for the construction of verse. The format of the ballade dictates three identically structured strophes, each of which ends with a refrain. In the late medieval ballade, that is, once lyric poetry was no longer always accompanied by music, the poem often ended with another half strophe called an envoi. Line length, number of lines per strophe, and rhyme scheme could vary, and Christine played with the form. In "Seulete suy," she uses a ten-syllable line and a seven-line strophe, which rhymes *ababbcc*, and closes with an envoi that repeats the rhyme of the last four lines of the full strophes.

The first line of the poem discloses its subject: the speaker is alone and wants to stay that way. The second explains her aloneness: her lover, or "sweet friend," has left her "seulete," solitary. The refrain conflates those two bits of information into a third and similar line: "Alone am I, left with no lover." While the first strophe describes the nature and depth of her unhappiness, the second turns her solitude into seclusion. She is alone at a door or a window in a hidden corner, or locked in her room (lines 8, 9, 13). The third strophe then generalizes and broadens her pain: she is alone everywhere and in every place, wherever she goes or stays; she is more alone than any other being and abandoned by everyone (15–18). The short envoi then appeals to the outside world to witness her misery: "Prince," she says, in a direct address, "now has my sorrow begun." She is threatened by overwhelming grief and blackened by it (23, 24). The refrain closes the poem with the repeated image of her left alone, without a lover (25).

The most striking aspect of the content of the poem—apparent from just the first strophe quoted above—is the repetition of "Seulete" at the beginning of each line. This feature, immediately obvious to both the eye and ear, makes dramatic use of anaphora, a stylistic mechanism designed to draw attention to an element of particular significance. In this twenty-five-line poem (three strophes of seven lines plus a four-line envoi), all but one of the lines begin with this word, and twenty-three of those twenty-four extend the repetition to include the verb, thus beginning "Seulete suy." The inversion of descriptor and verb is significant; Christine could have used the more standard word order "Suy seulete," but the reversal privileges the adjective, literally moving it to the fore. For good measure, the first line, which states the topic of the poem, uses "seulete" twice. In French poetry, of course, the mute final *e* counts as a syllable except when followed by a word that begins with a vowel or at line end. Accordingly, these key words make up seven of the ten syllables in the opening line of the poem.

What makes this insistent recurrence so striking? On the purely phonetic level, all the sibilant sounds create an audible sigh in each line. That effect is further reinforced in the refrain (lines 7, 14, 21, and 24) by "sanz," a third word following the introductory phrase that begins in *s* and ends with it as well, once the liaison is made with the following *a* of "ami." Of course, most medieval poetry was intended to be read aloud. With a recitation of the poem, listeners can hear the unrelenting reprise of the sad exhalation, which becomes an incantation of sorts as each line brings it around again. Students might try a free translation or adaptation into English (a valid medieval practice), attempting to recreate a similar alliterative effect. The point to emphasize is that a common device of medieval lyric is the repetition of words or exclamations that convey heightened emotion. Elsewhere in the *Cent balades*, Christine plays with the adverb *tant* ("so much" [ballade 21]), in a reflection of the hyperbolic, excessive nature of love, and throughout the collection she begins many a poem with "Hé! Dieux," "Ha Dieux!" (ballades 5, 43, 58; "Oh, God!") or "Helas!" (ballades 15, 32, 38, 41, 73, 79; "Alas!"). "Seulete" itself recurs in other short lyrics by Christine from the same period (*Cent balades* 14; *Rondeau* 1, 3), building a leitmotif into her early work. But this particular poem pushes the technique of repetition to a level rarely matched by her fellow poets.

Given the stark effect of the repeated opening, the one line that differs jumps out at us. Why would Christine choose to start line 22, the beginning of the envoi, with "Prince"? On the one hand, one might legitimately argue that this abrupt exception to the poem's most conspicuous feature mars the effect and interrupts the flow. On the other, the interjection of the vocative "Prince" can be said to accentuate the uniformity of the rest, and heighten the return to "Seulete suy" in the following line. Christine herself hesitated. The version of ballade 11 that appears in her earliest collected manuscripts does not have the envoi, but the versions in the two later collections do (Laidlaw, "Christine de Pizan—An Author's Progress" 534–35). We know that she oversaw the production of her manuscripts, and so the choice was hers to make. In hesitating between the two variations, she was taking advantage of a feature of the ballade that was in flux. None of Guillaume de Machaut's ballades had an envoi. The appearance of this half strophe came later in the fourteenth century, when lyric poems were no longer necessarily set to music.[1]

In its origins, the structural intent of the envoi was to address and send (*envoyer*) the poem to a recipient. This gesture is what Poirion calls the "fonction sociale" ("social function") of the ballade. The recipient could be the judge of a poetry competition (usually referred to as "prince"), a patron, the subject of an appeal, or another poet invited to reply. In late-fourteenth- and fifteenth-century lyric, however, as the envoi became more widely used, it was often a rhetorical rather than a functional element, a gesture that allowed the ballade to serve as a sort of message or poetic letter (*Littérature française* 368). It appears infrequently in Christine's early *Cent balades*, but she used it in all the ballades in her later collections. A constructive exercise to encourage close reading is to ask students which version they prefer and why. Individually or in groups, they can use the text to build an argument that the poem is either stronger or weaker with the addition of the envoi.

This poem is, in fact, an illuminating example to demonstrate how form as well as word choice conveys meaning. As we delve deeper into the poem's mechanics, more and more constituent parts reveal their significance. Beyond the anaphora, the feminine presence in the poem is emphasized by the prevalence of the usually unaccented feminine final *e*. Because in French versification a word-ending *e* has full syllabic value unless it is followed by another vowel or it falls at the end of the line, every repetition of "seulete suy" counts as four syllables, and the second hemistich of the first line, "seulete vueil estre," again calls attention to the feminine *–ete* suffix. What is more, all three rhymes at line end throughout the poem are feminine (*–estre, –siée, –rée*). In that position, while the final *e* does not count as a syllable, it rounds out each line with an extra soft vowel that the medieval audience, alert to such nuance in oral delivery, would not fail to hear. It is hard to imagine a poem more steeped in the feminine.

Having looked at the structural components, the next task is to decipher the semantic content of the oft-repeated phrase. The adjective *seul*, meaning "alone," is a standard description of the despondent lover in medieval lyric and therefore part of the compendium of images available to Christine for love poetry. However, two variations set her "seulete" apart: First, she applies it to a feminine speaker (for which, anglophone students should be reminded, an additional *e* is required on the French adjective; a man is "seul," a woman "seule"). Second, she turns it into a diminutive by adding the suffix "et[t]e." This forlorn lament is not the only occurrence of a woman's lyric voice in such poetry—Christine's male contemporaries sometimes ventriloquized female voices—but it is enough to pique the reader's attention as a likely variation on a theme. The diminutive ending adds semantic content as well as an affective bias to the otherwise neutral adjective. In the figure of this woman alone, therefore, we also see a woman somehow diminished in stature or power by her grief, and we read that figure with sympathy and familiarity.

By the end of the poem, the accumulated force of the repeated word gives it substance, and we find that "seulete" has expanded its morphological range and taken on the freight of a noun as well as an adjective. This is another function of the suffix, which can nominalize an adjective, combined with the flexibility of Middle French syntax. In modern French, "seulet[te]" is preserved as an adjective only, but in Christine's fifteenth-century Middle French, in which a noun does not necessarily need to be accompanied by its article, the word functions equally well as a noun. "Seulete" can be read throughout the poem as an adjective (I have translated it as such below). We know, however, that Christine liked nominal constructions that use a diminutive. She used "la seulete" as an unambiguous noun form in the *Dit de la pastoure* (*Œuvres poétiques* 2: 237 [line 459]) and "lassette" ("unhappy one") in *Rondeau* 1 (1: 147 [line 2]) and in the *Cent balades d'amant et de dame* (3: 287 [ballade 78, line 2]). Of all her diminutive constructions, "femmelette" ("little woman") has received the most critical attention, for its connotations and strategic uses (Margolis, "Elegant Closures"). In this poem, nominalizing "seulete" concretizes the voice whose lament we are hearing: she is a "little lonely woman" or "little woman alone," a persona with which Christine identifies and on which she elaborates, in the *Cent balades* and elsewhere.[2]

It is a short leap from this sad, first-person lyric voice lamenting the loss of her lover to the well-known biography of Christine herself, who reveals elsewhere in her writing that she lost her beloved husband at a young age, was thrown into a sea of troubles by his death, and protested that she wanted nothing more to do with love. Many critics therefore see in this and in other poems in the *Cent balades* an accurate reflection of her own circumstances and take what are called the "poèmes de veuvage" ("widowhood poems") as autobiographical. The "ami" in the poem would then be Étienne du Castel, her husband, who died in 1390, and her determination to remain alone—"[s]eulette veuil estre" ("[a]lone I wish to be")—rings true to declarations elsewhere in her work that she embraced her widowhood and would not entertain the notion of loving again. If we understand the "seulete" as the young widow, the poem becomes as daring in its theme as in its format because it stages a portrait of conjugal rather than courtly love. This point bears repeating for students: happily married men, let alone women, are nowhere to be found in medieval lyric poetry, in which love can thrive only with a love object one chooses and only in secret, notions incongruent with the realities of marriage as strategic alliance. The women's voices typically found in medieval lyric are those of the "mal-mariées," unhappy wives married to unworthy men, and ladies pining over the loss of a lover who has left them unjustly and whom they can mourn only in private.

The overlap of the author's real life with what can also be read as a feminized version of the (usually male) bereft lover is perhaps the greatest innovation Christine brought to the late courtly lyric. To state the obvious, however, we cannot appreciate the singular quality of her work without some contextualization to help define it. One might point out that the author's voice and the lover's role had been conflated in courtly literature since Guillaume de Lorris's *Roman de la rose* in the romance genre and Guillaume de Machaut's poetry in the lyric. That is, the first-person voice in these works is both the teller of the tale and the protagonist of some kind of love experience. Guillaume de Machaut had pushed that fictional character to the limit of autobiography in his *Voir dit* (*The Book of the True Poem*), in which he purports to be recounting the love he shared with a lady known only as "Peronne," a relationship that plays out in and is coterminous with the poetry and letters they exchange. Christine would certainly have known the *Voir dit*, in many ways Guillaume de Machaut's masterpiece. She adopted and adapted the intriguing link between poetic and personal voice even further in her own lyric production: the "seulete" of the early *Cent balades* collection is echoed by a remarkably consistent authorial persona throughout the rest of her work. The lonely woman protagonist shares enough of the stock features of the downcast male lover to make her an acceptable variation of the expected lyric types. At the same time, her resemblance to the admirable and exceptional historical Christine moves this poetry beyond the sometimes stale tradition in which she was working. She succeeds in infusing the unexpected into the predictable, the remarkable into the standard. The autobiographical echo in her work is undeniably one of its most appealing characteristics today.

Christine's poem made its mark. Some years ago, scholarship uncovered the resemblance between her poem and a ballade written in English by Charles d'Orléans (1394–1465), a French nobleman heavily influenced by Christine's work (Charles d'Orléans 70 [ballade 59]). Despite some changes to the format (for example, eight-line strophes instead of Christine's seven), there is no mistaking the similarity. Charles's version begins "Alone am y and wille to be alone" ("Alone am I, and wish to be alone"; my trans.), a close rendering of Christine's opening, and his refrain, "Alone y lyue an ofcast creature" ("Alone I live, a cast-off creature"), is again quite faithful to his source. Curiously, Charles does use an envoi but does not address a prince his envoi instead maintains the unbroken anaphora of "Alone." Scholars debate whether Charles's version of the poem is an imitation or a translation of Christine's poem (Kosta-Théfaine). Whichever it is, Charles's version, cast in a male first-person voice, makes an excellent comparative study of shared elements. His is a good poem but not a great one. It lacks the striking feminization of the theme, semantics, and phonetics of Christine's, and its formal properties are less remarkable than its model. But we could hardly ask for a better pairing of poems to study the phenomenon of intertextuality in the lyric. Side by side these two ballades demonstrate how one work borrows directly from another and how they both participate in the practice of late medieval fixed-form poetry.

The Imperative of Filiation

In Christine de Pizan's lyric poetry, each poem's dialogue with the tradition to which it belongs is the most important aspect of its intertextuality. The direct borrowing illustrated by the English version of "Seulete suy" is uncommon in lyric. In her narrative poetry, Christine is more explicit about the interaction of her work with other named or identifiable authors and models. While imitating an acknowledged model ensured acceptability, so did reference to and imitation of recognized masters, the authors who conveyed respectability and worthiness on new works that demonstrate their influence.

Again, we need to see past the aesthetics of postmedieval literature. Whereas Harold Bloom described "anxiety of influence" as the desire of writers to "clear imaginative space for themselves" and avoid the influence of their precursors (5), the opposite was true for medieval poets. They needed not only to enter the imaginative space constructed by their forebears but also to make those forebears recognizable in their work and to claim a place beside them. What inspired medieval poets was not the anxiety of influence but rather an imperative of filiation. Their writing had to be a worthy contribution to the accumulation of received wisdom, and they themselves had to demonstrate their filial relationship to the esteemed who came before them.

Such acknowledgement can be explicit or implicit. One example of explicit naming is the exchange of letters Christine instigated concerning the *Roman de la rose*, in which she and her interlocutors argued vehemently about vocabulary, morality, and the ethics of writing, based on how each of them interpreted the long second part of the romance, written by Jean de Meun. The dossier of letters Christine collected on the subject and sent to aristocratic patrons showcases her own learning and intellectual acumen but also draws attention to a powerfully influential earlier text, the legacy of which she and her contemporaries were constantly rewriting.

Elsewhere in Christine's corpus we find examples of less explicit but equally important recognition of other texts and authors. The scholarly activities of reading and writing most often provide the pretext to the creation of a new work. In her *Livre de la cité des dames* (*The Book of the City of Ladies*), the most obvious reference Christine makes to other authors is her lament concerning the misogyny she discovers in the book by Matheolus that she picks up to read in her study in a moment of repose. Matheolus aside, many other literary works, titles, and authors underlie the conception of her *Cité*. The title alone would immediately evoke for the medieval reader Saint Augustine's fourth-century Latin work, *De civitate Dei* (*The City of God*). For the content of her *Cité*, which consists of a series of stories concerning noteworthy women from history, scripture, mythology, and her own society, Christine was clearly inspired by the fourteenth-century Italian writer Giovanni Boccaccio and his Latin work *De mulieribus claris* ("On Famous Women"), itself modeled on the contemporary Italian author Petrarch's *De viris illustribus* ("On Famous Men"), which in turn resembles works by the classical Greek author Polybius and the Roman Livy. Obviously, in her *City of Ladies* Christine used to great effect numerous forms and ideas that she and her readers knew from other, illustrious authors, a matrix that at once validated her enterprise and allowed for creative recombination to suit her own purposes.

So deeply engrained in medieval literature are the cultivation and awareness of literary filiation that the period bequeathed to us some striking images of what we now call intertextuality. One of the best known is John of Salisbury's notion of dwarfs standing on the shoulders of giants so they can see farther, an image from his *Metalogicon* (1159). While John's metaphor was originally intended to describe the process of scholastic education, it is equally applicable to the literary process; in both, each generation builds on the foundation laid by its predecessors.

This essay has examined prime examples of intertextuality—the naming of and alluding to other authors and works—in Christine's corpus. They demonstrate the author's impulse and imperative to inscribe herself into a lineage of authority. This obligatory gesture was all the more crucial for Christine, a singular figure in the collective enterprise that shaped medieval literature. For her even more than for most others, convention and filiation through intertextuality were key to acceptability, readership, and reward.

Neither singularity nor convention can be taught in a vacuum. In order to make the works of Christine meaningful, we need to consider them in the context of the larger literary culture that both produced her as a writer and was in turn shaped by her work.

NOTES

[1]The sonority of this poem has not gone unnoticed by composers. As an example, see Nicholas Fairbank's setting, which uses the first four lines plus short excerpts from Christine's *Livre de la cité des dames* (fairbankmusic.ca/musiccatalogue/seulete-suy).

[2]For discussions of the broader rhetorical impact of the *Cent balades* and of "Seulete suy," see Adams, *Christine de Pizan*; Morand-Métivier.

APPENDIX
Christine de Pizan, Ballade 11

Original from Roy, *Œuvres poétiques de Christine de Pisan*, vol. 1, p. 12. Translation by Barbara K. Altmann.

Seulete suy et seulete vueil estre,
Seulete m'a mon doulx ami laissiée;
Seulete suy, sanz compaignon ne maistre,
Seulete suy, dolente et courrouciée;
Seulete suy en languour mesaisiée;
Seulete suy plus que nulle esgarée;
Seulete suy sanz ami demourée.

Seulete suy a huis ou a fenestre,
Seulete suy en un anglet muciée,
Seulete suy pour moy de plours repaistre,
Seulete suy, dolente ou apaisiée,
Seulete suy, riens n'est qui tant me siée,
Seulete suy en ma chambre enserrée,
Seulete suy sanz ami demourée.

Seulete suy partout et en tout estre.
Seulete suy, ou je voise ou je siée,
Seulete suy plus qu'autre riens terrestre,
Seulete suy de chascun delaissiée,
Seulete suy durement abaissiée,
Seulete suy souvent toute esplouré,
Seulete suy sanz ami demourée.

Prince, or est ma doulour commenciée:
Seulete suy de tout dueil menaciée,
Seulete suy plus tainte que morée,
Seulete suy sanz ami demourée.

Alone am I and alone I wish to be,
Alone has my love\r left me;
Alone am I, without companion or master,
Alone am I, sorrowful and filled with anger;
Alone am I, miserable in languor;
Alone am I, more lost than any other;
Alone am I, left with no lover.

Alone am I, in a doorway or a window,
Alone am I in a hidden corner,
Alone am I to take my fill of tears,
Alone am I, sorrowful or tranquil,
Alone am I, nothing suits me as well,
Alone am I, enclosed in my room,
Alone am I, left with no lover.

Alone am I, all over and in every place.
Alone am I, whether I go or stay,
Alone am I, more than any earthly being,
Alone am I, abandoned by everyone,
Alone am I, harshly abased,
Alone am I, often bathed in tears,
Alone am I, left with no lover.

Prince, now has my sorrow begun:
Alone am I, susceptible to all sadness
Alone am I, stained blacker than a berry
Alone am I, left with no lover.

The Literary Geographies of Christine de Pizan

David Joseph Wrisley

Christine de Pizan's wide grasp of history and geography is apparent when one reads her oeuvre. Generally, scholars focus on her devotion to France or to Italy—for example, in her line to Minerva in *Les fais d'armes et de chevallerie* (*The Book of Deeds of Arms and of Chivalry*): "Je suis comme toy, femme ytalienne" ("I am like you an Italian woman")—but these geographic references are usually thought of as markers of identity. Scholars have sometimes argued, through close reading, for the importance of geography to an understanding of her sources in specific works. In *Le livre du chemin de lonc estude* (*The Book of the Path of Long Study*) Christine demonstrates a knowledge of contemporary travel narratives; among others, those of Jean Mandeville and Guillebert de Lannoy are inspiration for her imaginary voyage (Willard, "Source"). The importance of geography across her whole body of work has not, however, been a scholarly preoccupation. Perhaps the reason we have ignored the complexity of her knowledge and use of geography is that the setting of some of her best-known writing is not always a chronotope (Bakhtin) based on real places but rather imaginative, allegorical space such as in *Le livre de la cité des dames* (*The Book of the City of Ladies*). Other premodern French authors have benefited from being studied from the perspective of geography: for example, ReNom, a project developed by the Bibliothèques Virtuelles Humanistes, has studied the places and people in works of Pierre de Ronsard and François Rabelais. A larger corpus of medieval French literature has been examined from a distant perspective by Visualizing Medieval Places, a project developed by myself and others (vmp.djwrisley.com/). Given the diversity of genres and sources in Christine's corpus, it would be valuable to study the geographies she includes to gain an understanding of the world she knew and evoked in her writing. This essay suggests that researchers, teachers, and students do so by using digital mapping environments.

Mapping the Geographies of a Literary Corpus

Literary geography emerged at the intersection of two interdisciplinary trends, the spatial turn in literary studies and the cultural turn in human geography (Alexander 3–4). The former focuses on the importance of location, landscape, and other spatial notions in imaginative narrative. The latter opens up the creative space of narrative as inspiration for rethinking the descriptive, even scientific, world of human geography. The study of literary geography does not require the use of maps, yet an increasing body of research in the spatial humanities argues for bringing maps back, as a heuristic abstraction, in the humanities in general and in literary studies in particular. In the early twentieth century, maps constituted a fundamental part of the genre of the literary atlas (Ferré; Bartholomew). The limitations of such printed maps of literary phenomena were many, and in particular their print-bound, static nature opened them up to criticism that they were nationalistic and reduced elements of literature to touristic voyeurism. Maps are not, however, "a one-time thing," nor are they limited to representing the national space of a language; maps are both flexible research objects and platforms that help us portray graphical representations in an interactive and iterative way (Presner et al. 15). A literary geography is an open-ended inquiry into place in a literary corpus, free to be manipulated and remixed with other literary data.

The approach taken in this essay is that of humanities geographic information systems (GIS): it uses dynamic, Web-based environments to create map visualizations of the places mentioned in Christine's writing. The map of these places (www.djwrisley.com/maps/cdep/) does not attempt to think through medieval spatial conceptions, nor does it engage with medieval mapmaking practices (although these would be excellent follow-up projects that might reuse this article's companion dataset). It is worth acknowledging from the outset the gap, and the potential anachronism, created by pushing a distant past into the digital present.

Whereas traditional GIS projects in urban planning or social history might rely on precise spatial data and computational analysis, the mapping techniques suggested here are adjusted for the kind of representation we want to make—coarsely granular, oriented to visual exploration, and tolerant of spatial uncertainty (Wrisley, "Spatial Humanities" 107). The data are multivariate; that is, they contain different kinds of places (medieval and ancient, real and imaginary) as well as different scales (cities, regions, countries, and continents). Gathering the place-names found in Christine's works and creating faceted visualizations (more than one thousand places in a dozen or so works) attempts to draw critical attention to patterns in the geographic data and to allow us to study the use of historical places across her oeuvre.

Making literary geographies opens up new frames of analysis and suggests new readings of Christine based on place. The plural "geographies" in the title of this essay is intentional, asserting that place is not an unchanging object for her. She wrote in many genres and about many topics, and her geographies are, as such, diverse. Just as she uses many different toponymic strata, mapped literature is not to meant to relegate geography to a static technology but rather to open it up to new forms of reflection, using locational aspects of literature and frameworks of dynamic visualization. Maps are not simply flat mirrors of the world but tell multiple "deep" narratives about lived and historical space (Bodenhamer 13). Furthermore, visualizations created in digital environments are useful as companions to traditional prose arguments made about texts.

If mapping is a complex process of "picturing, narrating, symbolizing, contesting, re-picturing, re-narrating, re-symbolizing, erasing and re-inscribing a set of relations" (Presner et al. 15), the map objects we create must be thought of as "a conversation and not a statement; they are inherently unstable, continually unfolding and changing in response to new data, new perspectives, and new insights" (Bodenhamer et al. 3–4). We might think of mapping locational elements of Christine's writings as an open-ended inquiry, therefore, to be combined with other forms of curation and analysis.

The starting point of our inquiry is a human-curated dataset, a tabularly arranged collection of place-names in Christine's writings, which has been geotagged (associated with geographic coordinates). Geotagging involves certain challenges and assumptions. Coordinates were collected from *GeoNames*, a geographic database, and from *Wikipedia*. A first version of the dataset has been published concurrently with this essay, in the Zenodo research data repository (zenodo.org/record/35350), and readers are invited to reuse it.[1] An accompanying interactive map was created for the purpose of exploring Christine's geographies, but creative, active use of the data is recommended over planned, interactive use of a map. I encourage instructors teaching Christine and medieval literature to have students learn to make a map with the dataset and to reuse the dataset to explore geography and other notions of space in Christine. Digital humanities, after all, values learning through doing, as well as sharing and remixing data.

Christine de Pizan and the (Textual) Digital Humanities

There are other digital resources for exploring Christine (some of which are mentioned in Mark Aussems's essay in this volume). *Christine de Pizan: The Making of the Queen's Manuscript*, a digital project at the University of Edinburgh based on the British Library's Harley 4431 manuscript, is a rich resource for learning firsthand about scribal culture in Christine's day. The project facilitates discovery of the materiality of a medieval presentation manuscript, analysis of text and image in a manuscript context, and even learning how a markup language such as TEI-XML can be used to describe and transcribe a complex textual object. Any of these aspects of scribal culture could be examined in the classroom, even where students are not reading Christine in the original French. The *Christine de Pizan Digital Scriptorium* provides a comprehensive handlist of manuscripts containing Christine's work, access to manuscript images, and a database of proper names. The *Christine de Pizan Database*, an excellent entry point into Christine's language, is a set of lists and concordances of Harley 4431.

An open, digitized manuscript is a strong starting point for digital analysis of Christine's work. However, we are far from having her entire corpus in open, digital format, because Harley 4431 is missing key texts, texts that are some of the most geospecific. Students and researchers can find some of Christine's works digitized from older editions (those in the public domain) in open repositories such as *Internet Archive* and *Project Gutenberg*. Because her corpus was rediscovered and edited more fully after the 1920s (the current cutoff for copyrighted material to enter the public domain), it is not fully available for free, open, digital analysis. To address this gap, scholars could encourage their graduate students to create open-access digital editions of Christine's works as thesis topics and their undergraduates to contribute more basic plain text versions of editions in the public domain at the Open Medieval French Initiative (github.com/OpenMedFr).

Christine de Pizan and the Spatial Humanities

Place-name indexes, like proper-name indexes, are one of the important paratextual elements of traditional critical editions. Such indexes have facilitated the study of place in traditional literary criticism. How a literary text manipulates geographic space has piqued the interest of scholars across time. For example, the absence and presence of the city of Paris in medieval French literature has been shown to be both a locus and a topos (Planche). Furthermore, topography and monuments of medieval Paris served as a backdrop for localizing the chansons de geste (Olschki). With electronic texts and basic concordancing software, we are able to look for patterns in texts without relying on predigital technology such as the index. Take, for example, a search for "Auvergne" in *Le livre des fais et bonnes meurs du sage roy Charles V* (*The Book of the Deeds and Good Conduct of the* Wise *King Charles* V), which reveals a table of occurrences from chapter 14 about Charles's brother, Louis, the duke of Bourbon. Such software is designed to allow for different kinds of reading, as readers can move from the keyword in context (KWIC) view to the larger text with just one click.

A digital map can function as another kind of index of place. But the map of the places mentioned in Christine's work also allows for spatial recognition of patterns. Whereas a digital text search returns a set of occurrences of "Auvergne" in a table, on a map, place-names from the *Fais et bonnes meurs*—Aquitaine, Poitou, Picardy, Champagne—appear as clusters. A map does not explain the appearance of clusters of nearby places, but their proximity to one another suggests that a closer analysis and interpretation could be valuable. Clusters of places mentioned in the *Fais et bonnes meurs* covers major areas of Charles V's realm at a time when the English were claiming vast areas of France. Geographic mentions in Christine's work thus form part of her political argument as well.

Patterns beyond Continental France

Christine's geographic scope is large because the oeuvre includes many genres, such as personal and universal history. In fact, there is no better way to imagine a global Christine than to consider her through her various literary geographies.

The *Fais et bonnes meurs*, her text with the largest geographic imprint, populates Aquitaine, northern France, and the Charente area with multiple points. Other areas well represented in her corpus are the western Maghreb, central France, Italy, biblical Palestine, the Aegean coast of Asia Minor, the Peloponnese, Attica, and Boeotia. Since absence speaks just as loudly as presence on a map, we might compare Christine's geographies with a much larger set of medieval French literary geographies (djwrisley.com/maps/VMP). The absences in Christine's geography appear to be Spain, Britain, Scandinavia, the Holy Roman Empire, central Europe, central Asia, eastern Asia, India, the Balkans, the Caucauses, and Greece (Epirus, the Cyclades, and Crete). Christine mentions these places, but the number of such references is much smaller than the norm in medieval French literature. These geographic presences and absences generate many questions. Why does Christine turn a blind eye to the Crusader states? Why are the Punic Wars so interesting to her, while the rise of the Ottomans seems to have no spatial imprint on her work?

There are some problems with representing places on such a simple map. First, some places cannot be reduced to a single point (Africa, for example) but require vectors or even polygons. Other places are unknown—for example, Lake Allefabter, from *La cité des dames*, or even the mythical Magog or the mysterious Gouffre Perilleux. These unknown places cannot be represented on a contemporary map interface, but they should be taken into account when thinking about the aggregate of Christine's places. A list of Christine's unmappable places thus contains both abstractions and large-scale toponyms. Additionally, there are seemingly real places that are difficult to map—places that are unknown or cannot be disambiguated, because either they come from unidentified geography (often ancient or biblical) or their names are simply too generic and could correspond to many possible real places.

If we explore the places found in Christine's oeuvre, by manipulating the larger dataset in a Web-based mapping environment, some of her toponymic strata—Roman, Greek, biblical, French, and Italian—come into sharp focus. Geography, it seems, is quite closely linked to the argument of each work. For this reason, mapping different works together helps us compare the geographic focus and scope of each. If we compare the place-names found in two works, *La cité des dames* and *Le livre de la mutacion de Fortune* (*The Book of the Mutability of Fortune*), for example, the sweep of historical space is distinct, though the works share a common perspective of universal history. The *Mutacion* extends to India, Persia, and the British Isles and, compared with *La cité des dames*, which is more focused on France, has much denser coverage of the Hellenic world, Palestine, and Asia Minor. *L'epistre Othea* (*Othea's Letter to Hector*), however, highlights a simpler Mediterranean geography (Italy, Greece, the eastern Mediterranean, Mesopotamia, and Persia). The *Othea* is a mythological compendium that gave contemporary readers perhaps the most compact version of ancient mythology available at the time, an observation seemingly confirmed by its concise geography of antiquity.

Students might consider a map of two works in which Christine expounds her views on the moral conduct of princes and governments, *Fais et bonnes meurs* and *Le livre de paix* (*The Book of Peace*). Although the *Livre de paix* has fewer geographic mentions, the two texts display similar clusters in a kind of geographic echo. After all, in *Paix* Christine is appealing to warring factions to make peace according to a model provided by Charles V. Students could be asked if this is borne out by similar spatial morphologies.

Finally, looking at the corpus of all of Christine's writings while zeroing in on the eastern Mediterranean reveals a clear split: *Le livre du corps de policie* (*The Book of the Body Politic*) clusters in Attica, the Peloponnese, and the Italian peninsula, while *La mutacion de Fortune* clusters along the Aegean coast, in Asia Minor, and Palestine. These two works seem to cleave the Greco-Roman Mediterranean in two.

Putting Christine on the Map: Affordances and Limitations

The visual corpus analysis of Christine (djwrisley.com/maps/cdep) stems from a dataset that was built manually of the place-names found in Christine's writings (zenodo.org/record/35350). Advanced digital humanities projects build datasets by automatic extraction of names, which is an imperfect process. The orthographic variance of medieval language troubles accuracy further. The companion dataset for this essay was assembled with some semiautomatic extraction but began with the proper-name indexes of editions of Christine's works; the places mentioned were meticulously matched (that is, geotagged) with information contained in gazetteers. This method of building the database of place-names is admittedly not without its flaws. Place-names and personal names are often indistinguishable: "Bourgogne," whether used alone or in the name "duc de Bourgogne," appears as a glyph on the map of Burgundy. What is more, different editors apply different criteria in preparing indexes. The Middle French edition of *La mutacion de Fortune* edited by Suzanne Solente gives the following entry in its index of place-names: "[Bénévent] (Italie méridionale). *Pyrrhus y fut vaincu par les Romains* (275 av. J.-C.) 19312–19314" (4: 116). Yet the word *Benevento* never occurs in the text; Solente deduced this location from narrative cues. Something similar occurs in Maureen Churney Curnow's dissertation, an edition of *La cité des dames*. This phenomemon is less a shortcoming of an edition, however, and more an illustration of Christine's use of setting, which may be evoked through mythographic intertextuality rather than mentioned by name.

These caveats call for cautious interpretation of map visualizations and indeed of data extracted from literary sources. The real place-names mentioned in a work of literature have a multidimensional quality, and when they appear out of context or extracted in a tabular dataset, they lose that multidimensionality. Places evoked in literature can point to patronage, locality, source citation, and even political or social history (Wrisley, "Locating"). It is in visualizing the aggregate of data, noticing patterns, and then returning to the text that we are able to analyze more fully the importance of place. Distant views of literary phenomena eventually lead us back to close reading, but initially they step away from the linear (or semilinear) reading of traditional criticism.

Putting Christine on the digital map responds to many instructors' shared pedagogical values: for one, it inspires students to engage critically with significant cultural texts using innovative forms of technology. Engagement through extraction of data and abstraction might best be seen as a form of critical "deformance" (McGann and Samuels), in which students break apart texts in order to revisualize them along conceptual and technological lines. Such critical thinking is concept-based, iterative, hypothesis-driven, and bold. Close readings allow us to be as precise as we want to be—discussing material or political context, comparing a text with others in the same genre, engaging with theoretical perspectives. Distant readings take one aspect of the text and abstract it, collecting many examples across a large corpus. Such a practice may sacrifice detail for distance and some degree of accuracy for scale. Close and distant readings produce different kinds of conclusions.

Changing Notions of Student Work and Class Time

The methodology presented here of visualizing the companion dataset uses low-entry, interactive techniques common in the digital humanities, such as mapping; these can foster student-centered, exploratory learning in the literature classroom. Putting the means of creating abstract visualizations in the hands of instructors and learners leads to new ways of thinking about and seeing literature. Such exploration, using maps and layered toponymy from different periods of human history, has the salutary effect of reinforcing student knowledge of history and geography while affording the opportunity for hands-on work.

These pedagogical practices are inspired by larger-scale research in the digital humanities, but they do not require elaborate or expensive investments in technology. (The distant reading of place suggested here requires only simple spreadsheets and either free downloadable software or Web-based platforms.) They provide a chance for students to incorporate visual forms of argumentation into their course work. Not least, they encourage students to gain digital skills and literacies through the study of humanistic material, skills and literacies that, in tandem with close reading, are transferable to other contexts.

My strategy for finding time for such student-centered experimentation with digital tools in the literature classroom is to set up a portion of the class meeting time as a literary lab session, perhaps every second week. In lab sessions, students explore and play with texts, and the instructor and perhaps some more advanced students help them learn the tools. I encourage students to compose visual essays, in which they embed the exported visuals (screenshots or live, embedded maps in their blogs) of their map deformance into academic prose. Like citation from primary texts, such visuals enhance and drive forward the argument at hand. These new visual rhetorics are challenging and exciting yet demand new rubrics through which we can assess their use by students as evidence.

Although a literary dataset can always be improved by additions and corrections and attributions of place can be refined, we can begin to expand our experiments with the data, reusing and building on them. Some day the geographic dataset on Christine de Pizan might be combined with the linguistic data created by, for example, *The Making of the Queen's Manuscript*. Students could build a similar dataset for purposes of comparison with contemporary authors (Guillaume de Machaut, Eustache Deschamps, Jean Froissart, Jean Gerson, or writers from the Burgundian court) or with subsequent translations of Christine's works, such as that by the sixteenth-century author Brian Anslay, published by Henry Pepwell: the first approach would allow different authorial geographies to be compared; the second would show how rewriting and translation change such geographies. More advanced students could take the data gathered from critical editions to study the question of how (or if) geographies shift with manuscript variance. Using the model of the University of Virginia course On Haj with Ibn Jubayr: Reconstructing the Twelfth-Century Mediterranean, in which students remix the contents of the famous medieval Arabic travel narrative with historical materials in a multimodal environment, students could take the data of one or more of the Christine works provided in my dataset to do an in-depth visual and textual (or sonic, textural, emotional?) exploration of a subset of her literary places. Students could create digital literary exhibits on Holy Land places Christine mentions, the monuments of Paris she cites, her Mediterranean mythological sites, or even digital storytelling of the imaginary voyage in *Le chemin de lonc estude*. Given the preponderance of castles and strongholds in the dataset (all tagged as "landmark"), a larger project could map Christine's oeuvre against key places in the Hundred Years War.

Map visualizations are aesthetic and critical provocations for discussing literature; they place productive pressure on standard academic prose interpretations of literary work, generating new avenues of engagement and iterative discovery of texts along nonlinear trajectories, with a strong visual element. They also encourage both comparison and historicism, inviting creative weaving of text and interpretation in a larger frame of geographic reference.

NOTE

[1]The dataset carries a Creative Commons CC0 license that places it "as completely as possible in the public domain, so that others may freely build upon, enhance and reuse the works for any purposes without restriction under copyright or database law" ("About CC0"). It is easily downloadable and can be visualized in one of the numerous Web-based mapping environments available to the general public.

Christine and the Canon: Great Books and Worthy Women

Ellen M. Thorington

Christine de Pizan is among the most rewarding female canonical authors to teach, for students readily identify with her. This identification is due to the autobiographical nature of her writings: her own words tell the loss of her husband and her subsequent need to find work to support her family. To students, these are modern difficulties, and they feel a kinship toward Christine, seeing her as a real person with real problems for whom writing becomes both a comfort and a means to earn her living. I have taught Christine in French courses and in the honors humanities course that this essay focuses on. The humanities class, taught in English, is unusual in that the same professor teaches three courses to the same group of students over three semesters, covering literary, artistic, and cultural perspectives from antiquity to the present day. During the first semester, the readings come from the ancient world and include the *Epic of Gilgamesh*, the Old Testament, Greek plays, and works by Homer, Sappho, Plato, Catullus, and Virgil. The second course focuses on the Middle Ages, the Renaissance, and the Enlightenment. Selections are drawn from the Icelandic sagas, Abelard and Heloise, Dante, Chaucer, Marie de France, Boccaccio, Shakespeare, Voltaire, and, of course, Christine. For the first two semesters, I use the first volume of Brian Wilkie and James Hurt's anthology, *Literature of the Western World*. In the third semester, which focuses on the eighteenth century to the present, we read Jane Austen's *Pride and Prejudice*, Charles Dickens's *A Tale of Two Cities*, F. Scott Fitzgerald's *The Great Gatsby*, and selected poetry. I like to end with Azar Nafisi's *Reading* Lolita *in Tehran*. In all three semesters, I provide supplements on art, culture, music, architecture, and the like, from various sources. To guide students through such a variety of material and time periods, I choose overarching themes and questions related to human experience: What does it mean to be human? What is the human experience? How is this experience expressed in the works studied? How is the human experience framed by the place of the author, artist, or composer in society? By his or her gender?

As the first female writer to compose a defense of women, Christine provides a fascinating perspective on questions of gender and offers a thought-provoking counterpart to other works read in the course. The students encounter her about midway through the second semester, when they already have some familiarity with the Western humanities. Having read many of the authors that inform Christine's work, they are also beginning to pose some of the same questions she raises about women's voices and experiences.

In preparing to read Christine with students, I like to focus first on the notion of the book and textual transmission. During the first semester we look at examples of cuneiform preserved in clay tablets and at images of papyrus scrolls. In the second semester I focus on manuscripts and manuscript illumination. This is critical to understanding Christine's role as an editor and a bookmaker, for her work, like that of many medieval writers, uses links between image and text to create a contextual whole.

One of the best ways to highlight such links is to begin with the Book of Kells, available online from the digital collections of Trinity College Dublin. We examine specific pages, such as the Chi Rho (fol. 34r), which illustrates the link between image and text: the Christogram is the verbal expression of the incarnation and at the same time represents the cross of the Crucifixion. Inscribed in the manuscript on calfskin parchment, this is "the word made flesh" in the most literal of forms (Farber). The Christogram is also noteworthy as the manuscript abbreviation for Christ and because Christine uses it to sign her name: "Xpine" (Walters, "Signatures"). We also examine the illumination of the Madonna and Child (fol. 7v), which portrays the Virgin in the *sedes sapientia* ("throne of wisdom") position, illustrating her importance and her part in the Incarnation. The Virgin is a symbol, a female model, and a mother figure, and her significance to the medieval world—and particularly to medieval women like Christine—cannot be overstated.

In addition to looking at iconography and symbolism, we also focus on the book as an object. Such a lavishly decorated copy of the four Gospels would not have been used for private reading and devotion but as part of the liturgical service. We discuss the realities of bookmaking: the Book of Kells, like many medieval manuscripts, is made of vellum (polished calfskin): 185 calves were required to make enough vellum for the book (Meehan and Cains 184). I also show students a six-minute documentary, *Making Manuscripts*, from the J. Paul Getty Museum ("Making Manuscripts").

As a follow-up activity, the students create their own illuminated manuscript pages in class. They complete a design in pencil, then use calligraphy pens for the image and text. For the illumination, they experiment with techniques used in the Middle Ages: glair technique (pigment in whipped egg white) and egg tempera (pigment in egg yolk). The materials required are inexpensive: I provide calligraphy pens, powdered tempera paint, plain paper or artist's parchment, water, paintbrushes, raw eggs, plastic plates for mixing, paper towels for cleanup.[1] After the project, the students write a short reaction paper (1–2 paragraphs) about what they learned from the activity. Most have gained a real appreciation for the skill—and forbearance—of medieval artists and manuscript illuminators. This introduction to material culture and the interplay between text and image is applicable both to Christine's work and to that of her predecessors and contemporaries.

Christine, like all medieval authors, participates in a kind of conversation between authors and authorities, drawing on common iconography, like that seen in the Kells manuscript, and on a common textual tradition. While many works illustrate these connections, I find those by Abelard and Heloise, Marie de France, and Chaucer particularly relevant for introducing students to themes found in Christine. The *Letters of Abelard and Heloise* offer the example of a writing woman whose experience in many ways parallels Christine's. Like Christine, Heloise loses her beloved husband (although not to death) and finds consolation in writing. I ask students to read Abelard's *Historia Calamamitatum* ("The Story of My Misfortunes") and Heloise's first letter to him in either Betty Radice's or Henry Adams Bellows's translations (Abelard and Heloise, *Letters* 3–43, 47–55; Abelard, *Historia*).

These two letters are particularly good for dispelling students' preconceived notions about medieval women. At first, students want to see Heloise as Abelard's victim. Through class discussion, however, they come to view her as a forceful presence in the *Historia*, as someone who attracts attention for the strength of her opinions as well as for her part in a love story that champions ". . . the values of love and reason" (Mews, *Lost Love Letters* xiv). Her ability to argue so decisively against marriage to Abelard—while pregnant with their child—speaks both to her strong personality and to her familiarity with the methods of *disputatio*, or scholarly debate. Her arguments are based on her understanding of the dangers marriage represented if Abelard hoped to advance in the Church and of the incompatibility of marriage with scholarly life. In her own letter, she states her feelings on marriage and her love for Abelard even more bluntly: "[I]f Augustus, Emperor of the whole world, thought fit to honour me with marriage and conferred all the earth on me to possess for ever, it would be dearer and more honourable to me to be called not his Empress but your whore" (Abelard and Heloise, *Letters* 51). Heloise is clearly "a major figure in her own right" (Mews, *Lost Love Letters* xvi) who chose Abelard for herself and was not afraid to take him to task.

Heloise's absolute love for Abelard and her extraordinary learning would seem to make Heloise an example of a wise and pious woman. Yet Christine portrays her as a negative model: during the debate over the *Roman de la rose*, Christine reproaches Pierre Col for his love of the poem, arguing that he prostitutes himself like Heloise against the cause of reason (Hult 189). Her paraphrase of the passage from Heloise's first letter to Abelard, quoted above, is drawn directly from Jean de Meun's citation of it in the *Roman de la rose*; she does not cite the *Letters* elsewhere in her works. In *Le livre de la cité des dames* (*The Book of the City of Ladies*) she positively reinterprets many other negatively typed female figures, such as Circe (Schibanoff 98); her condemnation of Heloise is therefore surprising and furnishes an excellent point of departure for student essays or reaction papers.

The work of Marie de France also complements study of Christine. Like Christine, Marie composes works of a didactic nature, and her *Lais* and *Fables* often draw on visual-textual links. It is likely that Christine knew Marie's *Fables*, as a copy is listed in the inventory of the library of Philip the Bold (De Winter 50). I teach selections from the *Lais* (*Bisclavret* and *Yonec*) and from the *Fables*. The *lai* of *Yonec* offers a particularly good example of the visual-textual connection, for it employs Annunciation imagery as a means to portray greater truth. The tale tends to be problematic for students. While they sympathize with the unhappily married heroine, they do not know what to make of her fantastic leap from the tower when she follows her Hawk-Knight lover to his home. Because they miss the allusions to the Annunciation, they find the end of the story entirely unbelievable. When I teach *Yonec*, I begin by showing the students images of the Annunciation scene. Good examples include the sculptural representation of this scene at the cathedral of Amiens ("*Annunciation and Visitation*"), which dates to the end of the thirteenth century; a thirteenth-century embroidered bookbinding ("Embroidered Bookbinding"); and a fourteenth-century altarpiece by Simone Martini and Lippo Memmi ("*Annunciation with St. Margaret and St. Ansanus*"). Earlier examples may be found in Laura Saetveit Miles's article on the subject. In these scenes, Mary is often represented praying or reading in a closed space when Gabriel enters. The parallels with *Yonec* become immediately obvious: a winged figure (Gabriel; the Hawk-Knight) enters an enclosed space where a female figure (Mary; the wife in *Yonec*) has been occupied with devotional tasks—reading, praying, lamenting. The Annunciation scene from the embroidered bookbinding, in fact, could be taken as an illumination for the story of *Yonec*. This secular transposition of Annunciation imagery reveals the sense of the story (Verderber). The Hawk-Knight arrives in answer to the heroine's prayer and enters into an almost impenetrable space, in an echo of the Immaculate Conception. His willingness to say the credo testifies to his godliness. It is in this context of belief that the new narrative can grow, just as a new life and new truth form in the womb of the wife, who has become the echo of Mary. The Hawk-Knight's cruel death, brought about by the jealous husband's treachery and foretold by the Hawk-Knight himself, becomes a kind of crucifixion. Yet death brings revelation. Yonec, the knight born of this illicit union, later chooses to believe his mother's dying words and the signs she bears. This belief, which recalls the Hawk-Knight's credo, leads him to avenge his father's death and then assume his true place as lord in his father's kingdom.

Marie highlights the themes of metamorphosis and human transformation. This is most evident in the person of Yonec. Born to one father, the miracle of his mother's words transforms him into the son of another, better man and allows him to meet the needs of his father's people. It is possible to see parallels to Christine's work here, particularly in view of her claim that Fortune transformed her from a woman into a man so that she might meet the needs of her fatherless family ("*Book of Fortune's Transformation*" 106–07). Moreover, Marie's use of Annunciation imagery, which enables her to emphasize the miraculous nature of her story and the importance of women's truth and women's words, plays a similar role in Christine's work, notably in the beginning of *The City of Ladies*.

Chaucer's Wife of Bath is a figure who functions particularly well as a direct introduction to Christine's writings, as a wonderful foil and as a way to discuss the misogyny Christine encounters. My students read the selections from *The Canterbury Tales* in Wilkie and Hurt's textbook (1674–1761). The prologue to the Wife of Bath's Tale, in which Alysoun tells the story of her life, is essential for working with Christine (1708–26). As many scholars have noted, the Wife is a problematic character. She can be read as Chaucer's critique of women, as his defense of women, or as some mixture of the two. Parallels between the Wife and Christine are obvious: both are widows; both claim authority through experience, notably female experience; and both protest that male authors portray a biased view of women to suit their own ends (Rigby). Yet the Wife can also be seen as exactly the type of woman who elicited the misogyny of clerics: lusty and self-serving, she even twists biblical quotations and other written sources to gain sexual favors as well as her husbands' money and lands. This is in direct contrast with Christine, who, as a moralist and an exemplar, seeks not only to better the lot of women but also to ensure the future of the kingdom of France. For Christine, women must act in a moral and noble manner in order to influence the men around them for the greater good. As S. H. Rigby suggests, much of Christine's didactic writing appears intended to teach women to avoid the type of behavior exhibited by the Wife, behavior that can lead to the condemnation of women (151). Reading selections from *The City of Ladies* along with the prologue of the Wife of Bath's Tale provides a rich set of topics for discussion and essay writing: students can be asked how Christine might have reacted to the Wife, and vice versa. Heloise can be brought into the mix, in discussing the following questions: What does it mean to be a virtuous woman? What is a woman's role? What does marriage mean for women like Christine, the Wife of Bath, and Heloise?

Finally, in turning to Christine herself, I like to begin by emphasizing her biography. One way to introduce her to students is to have them watch the nine-minute film written and produced by Sarah Lotfi, *La mutacion de Fortune*, which provides, through animated stills, the essence of the biographical material from Christine's text. The film can be used on its own or supplemented with selections from *The Book of the Mutability of Fortune* and *The Vision of Christine* from Blumenfeld-Kosinski's anthology (88–109, 173–201). One of the points to emphasize is Christine's claim of metamorphosis: in order to care for her family after her husband's death, Fortune transformed her into a man. Students will want to see this point in terms of gender orientation; discussion of both the importance of metaphor and the realities for widows at this time will help avoid anachronism (Hanawalt, Introduction xi). The Wife of Bath makes an excellent reference at this point.

Because of the broad scope of the course, I limit the readings to the selections from *The City of Ladies* in Wilkie and Hurt (1765–83). My approach to Christine continues to be influenced in great part by manuscript tradition. I remind students of the Chi Rho page from the Book of Kells and show them that Christine uses the manuscript abbreviation for Christ to write her name. Following V. A. Kolve's lead, we examine her use of Annunciation imagery at the beginning of *The City of Ladies* and discuss the opening sequence as an Annunciation to Christine. Like the wife in Marie's *Yonec*, Christine reads and prays alone at the beginning of *The City of Ladies*. Driven to despair through her reading of Matheolus, she seeks divine intervention. Author portraits produced under her direction show her in just this way: for example, in Harley MS 4431 (London, British Library), she sits alone in a stone chamber, writing (fol. 4r).[2] Most often, she is portrayed wearing blue, the color of the Virgin. The textual imagery of *The City of Ladies* reinforces these subtle associations. As Kolve observes (179), the sudden appearance of the ray of light on Christine's lap (Wilkie and Hurt 1767; *Book of the City of Ladies* [Richards] 1.2.1) is a clear allusion to the Annunciation, and the three ladies, Reason, Rectitude, and Justice, appear as a female trinity. This scene is beautifully rendered in Harley MS 4431 (fol. 290r): Christine stands, with her books in front of her, across from the three crowned ladies (see Tarnowski in this volume). A later rendition of this same scene (BNF MS Français 1177, fol. 3v), produced after Christine's lifetime, shows the ray of light and can serve as a point of comparison.[3] As students are already familiar with the use of Annunciation imagery from Marie de France's *Yonec*, discussion of this scene and of the manuscript images usually leads to certain questions: Why do Marie and Christine, as female authors, employ Annunciation imagery? What does the imagery say about their work? How does Christine's use of it add to her defense of women in *The City of Ladies*? Students can begin to see that Christine is basing her own authority as a female author on the Marian model. Mary's role as the vessel for the incarnation of the Word thus becomes the foundation for Christine's own writing and for her defense of women. With this in mind, students can explore additional examples from *The City of Ladies*. I tend to give them authors or stories we have already seen, such as Sappho (Wilkie and Hurt 1775–76), or those, like the story of

Susannah (1777), that will come up again in readings later in the course, for example, in Marguerite de Navarre's *Heptameron*.

Christine's work remains a touchstone for much of the rest of the course. Depictions of women in Boccaccio's *Decameron* and themes of otherness in Shakespeare's *Tempest* can be brought out by reference to Christine. I like to emphasize in particular *The God of Love's Letters*, in which she asserts that "if women had written these books, I know for a fact that they would have been written differently" (23). This attention to perspective is something with which Caliban would no doubt agree, as would Montaigne's cannibals, or even Voltaire's Cunegonde. Yet Christine's efforts as one of the first writers to mount a defense of women are particularly relevant to discussions of even later works. *Pride and Prejudice*, for example, shares a kinship with Christine's work in its emphasis on codes of behavior and its exploration of the idea of the virtuous woman. Similar themes can be seen in *The Great Gatsby*, where Daisy's unthinking actions invite condemnation. Here again it is worth asking the question of perspective: Had the story been told more from Daisy's point of view or by a female author, how would our perceptions of Daisy change? Another work that challenges students to examine their own perspectives and biases is Azar Nafisi's autobiographical *Reading* Lolita *in Tehran*. Her group of female readers in postrevolutionary Tehran and my coeducational students in the Midwest read many of the same works of literature, but from the perspective of different cultural backgrounds. The members of Nafisi's reading group and Christine in many ways share a similar background: they live in a conservative culture where religious belief and practice rule the actions of both sexes but weigh most directly on women. They encounter discrimination as they go about their daily lives and must defend the cause of women. For my students, Nafisi offers another way of reading the works we have studied while at the same time proposing a public (Nafisi's group of women) that is surprisingly close to Christine.

Christine de Pizan and her work are central to the class I teach. As readers, students begin much in the same place Christine claims for herself. The canon, for all its good points, comprises predominantly male authors; by the time students reach Christine they are delighted to discover a female author whose defense of women resonates. Yet it would undervalue Christine's writings to see them as speaking only to women's issues. Christine's points on perspective, on moral duty, and on what it means to be virtuous and wise conjure themes expressed by authors from Aristotle, whose arguments Christine invokes, to Nafisi. Christine's biography as well as her literary and publishing career make her a particularly modern figure whose work has relevance and meaning for students.

NOTES

[1]Detailed instructions for both techniques are offered in Thompson (glair at 50–57; egg tempera at 62–65). Video demonstrations are available on *YouTube*: www.youtube

.com/watch?v=WIueunmWQjs, www.youtube.com/watch?v=SVlwnUJGrBo (egg tempera); www.youtube.com/watch?v=rYizTKA3fes (glair technique).

[2]This image is available in the gallery of the Web site *Christine de Pizan: The Making of the Queen's Manuscript* (www.pizan.lib.ed.ac.uk/gallery/index.html).

[3]BNF MS Français 1177 is available on *Gallica*, the digital library of the Bibliotèque Nationale de France (gallica.bnf.fr/ark:/12148/btv1b84497026/).

Reading *The Treasure of the City of Ladies* with Women's Studies Students

Karen Robertson and Christine Reno

We recently completed our fourth iteration of a team-taught course at Vassar College on medieval and Renaissance women, which is cross-listed in two multidisciplinary programs, medieval and Renaissance studies and women's studies. Over the years we have refined the structure of the course and modified a core set of texts.

The first two times we taught the course, we focused on exceptional lives and organized the course into two halves: the first exploring, against the backdrop of ordinary women's lives and work (Hanawalt, *Women*; Wiesner), problems of agency and voice through the lives of five extraordinary women: Heloise, adolescent prodigy turned abbess; Joan of Arc, a peasant turned military leader; Margery Kempe, mother and businesswoman turned mystic; Julian of Norwich, anchorite and mystic; and Queen Elizabeth I. In the second part of the course, we began by examining the problem of writing women's history when almost no models for doing so existed, and we read Christine de Pizan's *Book of the City of Ladies* in its entirety. We also read shorter works by other European authors: from the Continent, Marie de France, especially for her portrayal of wives, Vittoria Colonna, and Louise Labé (whose existence had not yet been seriously questioned [Huchon]); from England, Aemilia Lanyer and Isabella Whitney, for whom we foregrounded questions of genre and audience.

We later amplified the attention paid to ordinary women's lives and began the course with a close reading of Judith Bennett's biography of Cecilia Penifader of Brigstock, which allowed us to discuss the ways nonliterate women's lives are recoverable from the historical record. This iteration thus reshaped the course from the perspective of social hierarchy, proceeding to women in towns and convents and culminating with Elizabeth I, whose speeches and self-representations we studied in detail.

Our most recent version of the course is our favorite to date. This time we organized the readings according to two major matrices of women's power—religion, especially mysticism, and the court—and we did not follow a strict chronology. The mystically inspired Joan of Arc, who saved the French crown, served as a pivot between these two matrices. We began the course with biblical passages on Eve, then, in the broadly construed segment on religious figures, read Abelard and Heloise's letters (*Abelard and Heloise: The Letters*), Julian of Norwich's *Showings* or *Revelations of Divine Love* (both the short and long versions that Julian wrote), Willard Trask's *Joan of Arc in Her Own Words*, Marie Dentière's *Epistle to Marguerite de Navarre and Preface to a Sermon by John Calvin*, Arcangela Tarabotti's *Paternal Tyranny*, and excerpts from Teresa of Avila's *Autobiography*. The segment on women at court included two *lais* by Marie de France; Giovanni Boccaccio's tale of Griselda (*Decameron* 10.10); Christine de Pizan's *Treasure of the City of Ladies*; selected letters, poems, and speeches by Elizabeth I; and Aemilia Lanyer's *Salve Deus Rex Judaeorum*.

Christine's *Treasure* was central to our study of women at court, and we devoted three seventy-five-minute class periods to it. Most of the initial class was spent framing the work. We presented a brief biography of the author and a summary of *The City of Ladies*, to which Christine refers so prominently at the beginning of *The Treasure*. Images of the miniatures from the three parts of *The City of Ladies* from the British Library's Harley MS 4431 (fols. 290r, 323r, 361r) brought the work to life for students.[1] We also projected from a slide the single illumination of *The Treasure* from the Boston Public Library manuscript (Boston, PL, MS FR Med. 101) to highlight Christine's strategy of foregrounding herself as an exhausted but ever-diligent defender of women. The famous presentation miniature in Queen Isabeau's apartments, from Harley MS 4431 (fol. 3r), afforded images of the women Christine addresses in *The Treasure*. Additionally, the inscription from the Boston manuscript of Diane de Poitiers's father, Saint-Vallier, allowed us to present, in a nutshell, the high-status women known to have read this work—they are identified in the English translation edition of Charity Cannon Willard and Madeleine Pelner Cosman (Christine de Pizan, *Medieval Woman's Mirror* 43–44).

In this version of the course we did not choose the Willard-Cosman translation of *The Treasure*, the style of which we found somewhat ornate in places; we used Sarah Lawson's translation instead.[2] This translation is not, however, without drawbacks, as it contains an error that could have far-reaching consequences. In the chapter on the third teaching of Prudence (*Treasure* 68), Lawson mistranslates the phrase "mal condicionné" and has Christine cautioning against princesses having anyone of "low rank" in their entourage; however, the matter is not of rank but of women of questionable conduct, as both the Willard-Cosman translation (Christine de Pizan, *Medieval Woman's Mirror* 103) and Liliane Dulac's modern French translation indicate (*Livre des trois vertus* [ed. Régnier-Bohler] 594). While it is true that Christine devotes the greatest attention to highborn ladies, in this work she does not pass judgment based on class distinctions. Indeed, it is important for students to understand that her inclusion of women of all ranks, including prostitutes, is respectful of the potential of all women to conduct themselves honorably. This attitude, which dissolves divisions of rank, is a perspective remarkable for the period.

Our first class covered another important framing element of the work, the three Virtues. We drew students' attention to Christine's very curious theology, as announced in the prologue (*Treasure* 31), where the Virtues allude to the [council] of Virtues[3] with whom they have deliberated and who have decided that Christine's inspired work has to continue. We asked students to reflect on the effect of presenting a work as being sanctioned by a divinely connected council of Virtues as well as on possible origins of those Virtues. We were delighted when a student immediately brought up the female figure of Wisdom in the Old Testament. Bonnie Birk's study of the probable biblical origins of Christine's allegorical figures is a good source of information for this affiliation.

As a final framing element, we examined the puzzling image of the bird snares that Christine paints in the next paragraph and introduced the students to Dulac's suggestion (*Livre des trois vertus* [ed. Régnier-Bohler] 561n2) that the image is an ironic reference to Christine's bête noire, the *Roman de la rose*, in which bird snares are strewn around the fountain in Guillaume de Lorris's garden, thus making Christine's text a negative counterpart to the adventure of courtly love.

This first class concluded with an exercise in which students were asked to jot down a single word that summed up their initial impression of the work. They briefly explained their choices, among which the most apt were *strategic*, *discreet*, and *honor*. The initial discussion of their words raised more questions than could be adequately answered and left several issues in the air for the following classes.

We repeated our exercise on the second day, requesting a single, salient word. The most promising were *wise*, *forceful*, *rigorous*, *constrained*, *controlled*, *thoughtful*, *peacemaking*, and *strategic*. While these words did epitomize the precision of Christine's advice to a potentially arrogant princess, we found that *strategic*, repeated from the first day, offered the most useful way into the paradoxes of the text.

Christine describes a patriarchal hierarchy fraught with danger, in which a young woman must cautiously thread her way. Christine also presents the princess, lying voluptuously on her sheets, tempted to indulge in pride, gluttony, and lust, and an easy target of envy and slander. The circumstances of elite marriage, already opened up through the reading of Marie de France's "Laüstic" and discussion of different versions of the Griselda story, came into even clearer focus while reading *The Treasure*. Slowly the students came to see that the lady has no natural allies in the court. *Strategic* describes her necessary calm, peacemaking, and humility before her husband's relatives and allies. Her quiet demeanor and restraint before others is a strategic effort to preempt the malicious gossip and envy that are provoked simply by her position. *Strategic* also describes the rhetorical stance of the writer as she attempts to guide and bridle a young woman with little evident reason to behave with restraint. One student researching a paper on Agnes Sorel, the first official royal mistress at the French court, began to recognize that Sorel had no natural allies and was entirely dependent on the favor of Charles VII.

Books that prescribe the conduct of a person who is constrained in a rigidly hierarchical society encounter two types of resistance in the American classroom: American notions of individualism that suppress recognition of class structures and our society's valuation of emotional authenticity. As any experienced teacher can attest, the existence of a strictly defined social hierarchy is alien to most American students. Curiously, those students whose patience for the abstruse writings of medieval women mystics earned our respect lacked awareness of social hierarchies. The myth of American individualism promises that resistant social structures will yield to the confident heroine. That belief is intensified by Disney fairy tales, like *Cinderella* and *Sleeping Beauty*, that reward traditional feminine virtues of patience and submission. Moreover, the strategic discipline required of the princess in *The Treasure* challenges deeply embedded American notions of authenticity of feeling and expression. The students were reluctant to look favorably on practices that seemed to them hypocritical and manipulative. Despite these resistances, modern analogues did come to mind: a Southern student, for example, described the superficial sweetness of sorority life belied by the cruel judgments made in private. The behavior of high school "mean girls" and the dynamics of female adolescent friendships were brought up in an attempt to understand the cruel gossip that patrolled conduct in a late medieval court (Simmons; Wiseman). Students began to recognize that acting could allow the princess to shape the way she was perceived in an environment where she had little control.

The question of how Christine depicts men at court also met with resistance. Although the text provides numerous criticisms of male behavior—warnings about the false promises of the lover, the gossip of men, their violence—the students were reluctant even to point to these passages, while they had no trouble documenting women's faults.[4] Their reluctance provoked a diversionary question about who bought into a code of conduct that seemed to allow little leeway for women. We reminded the students of the number of surviving manuscripts of *The Treasure*, including one in Dutch, and explained that the existence of plain paper manuscripts as well as the early French and Portuguese printed editions of this conduct book indicates that many ordinary readers had access to it (Solente, *Christine de Pisan* 51–54).

The question of manuscript circulation usefully returned us to the historical context in which the book was written and read, France of the Hundred Years War. One student brought up Joan of Arc's remarkable transgression of feminine codes of behavior. Suddenly the students recognized the extraordinary restrictions placed on women at court and were reminded of the dangers the mystic had encountered. They were also prompted to compare Joan's saints, who encouraged leadership in war, with the allegorical figures of Christine's text.

We asked again about Christine's subtle depiction of men in the text. And again we met with reluctance to acknowledge her implied criticism of men, a reluctance we found characteristic of students in other women's studies classes at that time. This hesitation to voice criticism of men indicated that college-age students had shifted somewhat away from feminist attitudes and were more likely to defend a belief that full gender equality had been achieved. Despite their reticence to criticize any men whatsoever, even of the fifteenth century, students did find a contemporary analogue to the first part of the work, seeing in the media scrutiny of Michelle Obama's every act and comment during two presidential campaigns a parallel to the dangers that beset a medieval princess.

Attempting to shift the class from assessment of individual conduct to recognition of social hierarchies worked more successfully when we asked students whether they knew of or had experienced environments that demanded careful self-discipline. This time they admitted that high school had required caution, though not as extreme as that described in Christine's text, and mentioned again the effects of envy and slander on the behavior of adolescent girls they knew. At the close of the discussion, we asked them to come to the following class with a written response to the text and with a passage that they wanted to bring to their classmates' attention.

We organized the final class around their written responses to the text, a reading of Dame Sibyl's letter in the *Treasure*, and a discussion of whether they would characterize *The Treasure* as feminist or perhaps protofeminist. We began with their responses. For the most part, these seemed to struggle with the collision between ideals and social realities as presented in the text, whether the ideal was of social order or Christine's individual self-governance. A medieval and Renaissance studies major spoke about the importance of order in medieval society and found in Christine's insistence on practices of household order a model for the macrocosm of the state. Another student picked up his point, and used the words *consistency*, *constancy*, and *congruency* to describe how the individual woman had to align her inner feelings with the public persona taught in the text. Recognition of the difficulties of bringing about such an alignment was implicit in a history major's reminder of the social networks necessary for an individual woman's survival. Another student returned to the notion of the gap between the real and the ideal and questioned the effectiveness of conduct books, doubting that the behavior of privileged women was modified by such books: witness the lazy princess and the pretentious bourgeois new mother inscribed in the text. At this point, we brought up Roberta Krueger's observation that Dame Sibyl's decision to leave court as a last measure, as well as the tenor of her letter, seem to indicate that Christine was aware of the gap between the ideal conduct she was promoting and the behaviors that would probably continue in the real world (Krueger, "Christine's Anxious Lessons" 32–34). Our awareness of the real world of the court was amplified by a medieval and Renaissance studies major who had taken a course in the history of fashion and who shared with the class the remarkable development of clothing styles in the period. To our delight, this student referred back to the presentation miniature in the Harley manuscript (fol. 3r) and astutely drew attention to the difference between Christine's sober clothing, which reflected the writer's ideal self-portrayal and formed a striking contrast with the fashionable dresses of Queen Isabeau and her ladies-in-waiting, not to mention with the excessive luxury of the noble and bourgeois women criticized in the text.

Summing up the class discussions, a freshman registered her dismay over the social realities portrayed in the text, which she described as a "landscape of twisted social constructions." This student concluded that the best a woman could do was try to find a safe path through this perilous labyrinth. Her comment was echoed in somewhat more positive terms by a music major who found that the text provided a model for empowering women in a highly regulated social order that particularly limited the possibilities of noblewomen. This student did recognize that the baronesses operating on their own estates had the greatest possibility for action, as they took on traditional male roles in the absence of their husbands (who are in fact absent from the text).

We asked the class whether their (small, liberal arts) college campus bore any resemblance to the early-fifteenth-century French court, and we were surprised when the students insisted they saw no resemblance at all. For them, the lack of a single nexus of power seemed to negate the comparison.

Thwarted in what we expected to be an illuminating path of inquiry, we turned to our final question: whether students could identify this text as feminist or protofeminist. They rejected the term *feminist* outright but slowly refined their responses. One student remarked on his surprise at encountering such a modern self-assertiveness in the voice of the prideful and lazy princess. Other students saw that Christine presents women as capable and that her book celebrates a distinctly feminine path to virtue in a world that threatens virtue repeatedly. The ideal laid out in the text establishes a high standard for women and in fact demands a moral heroism on par with the exceptional behavior of individual women singled out in *The City of Ladies*. One student best summed up the consensus the class had reached, that although the text does not challenge the social order, it does provide guidelines for female empowerment within the constraints of a patriarchal societal structure. We suggested that the text, in doing so, tacitly points to the injustice of the patriarchal systems in which women are forced to live and thus lays the foundation required for any subsequent challenge to those systems.

We concluded the third class with a segue into the following week's readings and asked the students to apply the lessons of *The Treasure* to Elizabeth I's letters, speeches, and strategies as a Tudor princess. Our focus on the rhetoric of Elizabeth's careful letters to her father; to her stepmother, Katherine Parr; and to her half-sister, Queen Mary, registered the scrupulous attentiveness to hierarchy and status set out in *The Treasure* and suggested its continuing relevance for behavior at a different court, a century and a half later. Our reading of *The Treasure* also served, in subsequent weeks, to illuminate Aemilia Lanyer's attempts to use rhetoric to position herself, in her quest for patronage, among the influential ladies at the court of James I.

NOTES

[1]Images from Harley MS 4431 are available at the Web site *Christine de Pizan: The Making of the Queen's Manuscript* (www.pizan.lib.ed.ac.uk/).

[2]This essay cites the 1985 edition of Lawson's translation.

[3]We have corrected another error in Lawson's translation, which reads "with the counsel of virtues" (Lawson 31). The original text is "ou conseil des vertus" (*Le livre des trois vertus* [Willard and Hicks] 8). See *Medieval Woman's Mirror* (69) and Dulac's translation of *Le livre des trois vertus* (561), which give, respectively, "in the Council of Virtues" and "à l'assemblée des Vertus."

[4]Attitudes on campuses surrounding feminism have changed radically since this essay was written. Were we to teach this class again, we might expect students to react differently to these questions.

Teaching Christine de Pizan in a Department of English

Theresa Coletti

Christine de Pizan's literary fortunes were entwined with England and the English from the early days of her career. The writer herself details these connections in *Le livre de l'advision Cristine* (*The Vision of Christine*), where she reports how her acquaintance with fellow poet John Montagu, earl of Salisbury, in the late 1390s led to her son Jean's residence abroad in the Montagu household. By 1400, English aristocratic admiration for Christine's writing as well as affection for her son seem to have been well established. When Montagu's loyalty to Richard II led to Montagu's execution that year, the new king, Henry IV, stepped into the breach, welcoming Jean and inviting his mother to join him at the English court. But Christine was not about to nurture attachments to what she, in a ballade dedicated to Louis d'Orléans, called that "mal pais d'Angleterre" ("evil country, England"; *Œuvres poétiques* 1: 233; my trans.). Through a ruse involving a gift of some books to Henry, she engineered Jean's return to France; the prospect of a journey across the Channel is never again mentioned (*Livre de l'advision* 112–13).

It was probably Christine's courtly verse, her early endeavors with the lyric genre especially, that first garnered English aristocratic attention. Thomas Hoccleve's 1402 translation of her *L'epistre au dieu d'amours* as *The Letter of Cupid* further confirms awareness of her early literary work in late medieval England. In the first half of the fifteenth century, a taste for French literary culture was vibrant among members of the English aristocracy, who sought out French literary manuscripts that included works by Christine. In 1455, drawing on familiarity with such manuscripts, John Talbot, earl of Shrewsbury, presented Henry VI's French bride, Margaret of Anjou, with a magnificent compilation in which Christine's *Livre des fais d'armes et de chevallerie* (*The Book of Deeds of Arms and of Chivalry*) prominently figures (Bossy). Alice Chaucer, granddaughter of Geoffrey, owned a copy of *Le livre de la cité des dames* (*The Book of the City of Ladies*) (Meale 86–87). Fifteenth-century English taste for French books and texts doubtlessly benefited from opportunities for cultural appropriation—benign and aggressive, ideological and material—provided by English successes in the Hundred Years War. Surely one of the most dramatic acts of textual appropriation was the one that placed the celebrated manuscript of Christine's collected works into the hands of John, duke of Bedford, who acquired what is now the British Library's Harley MS 4431 when he purchased the royal libraries of Charles V and Charles VI in 1425. This acquisition crucially influenced Christine's English literary fortunes across the fifteenth century. Bedford's widow, Jacquette of Luxembourg, became the manuscript's next owner; she later bequeathed it to her son Anthony Woodville (Campbell 663), who would eventually translate Christine's *Proverbes moraulx* (*Moral Proverbs*) for William Caxton's press, a collaboration that in 1478 produced the first imprint of a work by Christine to appear in England and France (Brown 217).

Although contemporary literary canons have foregrounded works by Margery Kempe and Julian of Norwich, these acts of textual appropriation and production in fact made Christine the best-known woman writer of late medieval and early Tudor England. Reviewing the historical justifications for this claim, this essay addresses issues that accompany teaching the French works of a French writer in English language and English literary historical contexts. It suggests that the complexities generated by such circumstances offer teachers and students opportunities for a critically aware pedagogy from which English literary curricula and Christine de Pizan studies may also benefit.

Anyone who considers teaching Christine's texts in a department of English (or, for that matter, in any academic unit other than a department of French or Romance languages) must face the likelihood that those texts will be taught in modern English translation. This issue has many facets, beginning with the ostensibly simple prospect of teaching from available translations in courses where the fact of translation need not pose intellectual or methodological complications because the focus is otherwise directed—say, to literary types and traditions. Medieval Literature in Translation is one such course occasionally taught in my department (the legitimacy of such courses nonetheless may be adjudicated by curriculum oversight committees charged with addressing concerns raised by foreign language departments). Beyond this example's obvious truth in advertising, courses emphasizing a thematic or disciplinary focus, such as medieval women's history, women's biography and autobiography, rhetorical theory by women, the history of feminist theory, or even introductory courses in women's literature or Western world literature—all of which lend themselves to inclusion of Christine's texts—similarly may render working with translations relatively unproblematic. Fortunately, the increasing availability of Christine's works in modern English editions is creating new opportunities for studying her contributions to the broad range of intellectual and disciplinary conversations that her texts engage. But for teachers and advanced students of language and literature, readers for whom the text itself comes under heightened analytic scrutiny, the need to work with the words that Christine actually wrote exerts pressure on the design of syllabi and the selection of readings.

Recent scholarship on Christine's literary presence in late medieval and early Tudor England furnishes a framework for assessing this fundamental challenge and a meaningful context for reading Christine's texts in translation. Scholars have examined English circulation, translation, and emendation of her writings through the fifteenth and early sixteenth centuries.[1] Between 1402 and 1521, Christine's *L'epistre au dieu d'amours*, *Epistre Othea* (*Othea's Letter to Hector*), *Livre des fais d'armes et de chevallerie*, *Proverbes moraulx*, *Livre du corps de policie* (*Book of the Body Politic*), and *Livre de la cité des dames* were all translated into English. Of these, the *Epistre Othea* seems to have had the highest insular profile; English versions are extant in both manuscript and print, and the work was translated from the French three times between circa 1440 and 1540 (*Epistle of Othea* xi–xxi). Collectively, these English translations provide an important if not entirely representative sample of Christine's canon. With the exception of *L'epistre au dieu d'amours*, her courtly writings, lyrics, and narrative dits make no appearance; neither do her long allegorical poems or her most polemical textual performances—the letters she contributed to the *querelle de la Rose*. Still, the image of Christine conveyed by these English texts largely corresponds to the one she herself increasingly promoted in France, that of the sagacious, learned counselor to princes who is particularly attuned to feminine sources of wisdom and authority (Schieberle 139–91).

All the texts that represent the Englishing of Christine eventually appeared in print, though they were not consistently attributed to her. In fact, the early history of Christine in England is, in part, a story about the transformations wrought upon her texts and authorial identity by the male translators, patrons, and printers who introduced these works to English readers. Investigating how gender ideologies shaped these textual mediations, important critical assessments of this process have produced competing interpretations worthy of classroom debate. Whereas some find Christine's identity and authority as a woman writer suppressed and her accomplishments redirected to more masculine purposes (Chance, "Gender Subversion"; Mahoney; Summit, *Lost Property*), others associate the Englishing of her work with the recuperation of her feminine voice for rhetorical and political purposes (Downes, "Fashioning"; Schieberle). The migration of her French texts to English early print culture was also influenced by late medieval and early Tudor patterns of anthologizing in manuscript and print culture, by conventions for representing authorship, by translation practices, and by the economic exigencies of the printing business (Coldiron, "Taking Advice"; Coletti).

Christine's literary presence in fifteenth- and early-sixteenth-century England is therefore deeply implicated in bibliographical studies, material and cultural histories of the book, and gendered literacies. The circulation of her French texts and their English translations in manuscripts commissioned or owned by English readers and patrons further embeds her work in the social history of reading in late medieval England. The three manuscript witnesses of Stephen Scrope's mid-fifteenth-century translation of the *Epistre Othea* furnish a case in point; the dedication of each to a different patron calls attention to the social contacts that sustained the labor of translation as well as to the contexts for English reception of Christine's work (*Epistle of Othea* xviii–xx).

In addition to bridging national and linguistic borders, Christine's works in English translation, like their counterparts in French, also straddle the putative historical divide that separates the Middle Ages from the Renaissance. In the light of a bibliographic history that extends nearly to the mid–sixteenth century with Robert Wyer's 1549 publication of the *Othea* as *The .C. Hystoryes of Troye*, Christine's English presence has furnished scholars on both sides of this divide with compelling opportunities for cultural and literary interpretation (e.g., Ferguson 179–244). By crossing recognized borders of historical periodization, Christine's English texts further call attention to her affinity for the authorial self-definition and the values and rhetorical modes of a Continental humanism to which Christine legitimately laid claim by birth as well as by education. Although anchored in the political conflicts of late medieval France, her works participate in an international cultural dialogue about political counsel and vernacular letters that itself bears witness to crucial continuities among practitioners of an ethical-political rhetoric across the medieval and early modern divide.

There are thus compelling reasons to include texts by Christine in the matrix of late medieval English and early Tudor literary studies. Fortunately, widespread access to *Early English Books Online* (*EEBO*) now makes possible classroom use of her English texts in their early printed versions.[2] Up to now these have been available in out-of-print facsimiles, such as the late Diane Bornstein's forward-looking collection *Distaves and Dames*, or expensive scholarly editions such as those of the *Epistle of Othea* and Caxton's translation of *The Book of Fayttes of Armes and of Chyualrye*, both produced for the Early English Text Society (EETS). Although it is surely idealistic to expect students to devour several hundred gothic font pages of Brian Anslay's 1521 translation, *The Boke of the Cyte of Ladyes*, *EEBO* and digital projection equipment have created new opportunities for teachers and students to examine together crucial evidence of Christine's shifting identities in early print culture. Further, I would argue that the high profile of English translations of her texts among early English book owners and makers offers a rationale for classroom study of those works in one or more of the forms, even including modern translations, in which they are now readily available. Caxton's 1478 edition of *The Morale Prouerbes of Cristyne*, for example, presents a reasonably accessible entrée to Christine's self-fashioned image of feminine sagacity and the English attraction to it. Because the work is brief (five columns on three pages), students can tackle its early printed version from *EEBO*, which offers them the opportunity to decipher and transcribe the text's pithy couplets in the gothic font that early printers employed to imitate manuscript hands. Toggling between early print and modern editions and translations can have pedagogical value in its own right, making students aware of the material and social interventions by which a text becomes available to a reading public, whether of the fifteenth or the twenty-first century, and underscoring the many ways that late medieval texts could have been encountered.

Along similar lines, the introductory pages of Caxton's translation of Christine's *Le livre des fais d'armes et de chevallerie* as *The Book of Fayttes of Armes and of Chyualrye*, also available through *EEBO*, can be juxtaposed with both the EETS edition—which includes the glossary that the *EEBO* version lacks and partial collation with Christine's sources and early French printed editions—and with Sumner Willard's modern translation of the French text from manuscript sources, *The Book of Deeds of Arms and of Chivalry*. Most of our students will never encounter Christine's texts in their original manuscript context, but these exercises with *EEBO* can at least make the primary work available in the virtual form of its historical original. If, as teachers and students, we keep in view the historical and ideological circumstances under which her English texts were produced, we find many options for their study open to us. Such a perspective must also admit that sometimes cost and convenience are factors as influential in the selection of teaching texts as anticipation of students' interests and patience.

Since the early 1990s I have taught Christine's works in three graduate seminars and in an undergraduate course on medieval English women writers. In all these classes, I highlighted the early translation of Christine's texts and their notable presence in late medieval English literary-textual culture as a rationale for investigating her works in courses addressing English literary-historical issues, even if we were reading *La cité des dames* or *Le livre des fais d'armes* in modern English versions. In my graduate courses, though, I ventured beyond the works by Christine that have been deemed suitable for inclusion in an English department course by virtue of their late medieval and early Tudor English translations. The more one investigates Christine's English presence, the more one will be drawn to texts outside the early English Christine canon and the more one will confront her writing in French. I make clear to students that anyone with professional goals in mind who wants to study the body of her writing outside her English canon must be able to work with the texts in French. For the students thus motivated and equipped with the requisite language skills, the experience of Christine's writing in modern English can lead to more ambitious pursuit of her French texts. One student with an established interest in Christine reencountered in our seminar her contributions to the *querelle de la Rose* (Christine de Pizan, *Le débat* [Hicks]).[3] The student went on to write a seminar paper that later became the basis for a chapter on Christine's epistolary texts in a dissertation on the rhetoric of medieval and early modern women's letters (Sadlack). Another student was motivated to consult Andrea Tarnowski's edition of *Le livre du chemin de lonc estude* (*The Book of the Path of Long Study*) while developing a promising comparative analysis of that text and Margaret Cavendish's *Blazing World*; the student was first introduced to the *Chemin* through the long excerpts of it in Renate Blumenfeld-Kosinski's *Selected Writings of Christine de Pizan*.

My graduate teaching of Christine's texts may invoke the English presence of her work as a starting point, but it is just as engaged with exploring the possibilities for cultural and historical analysis that open up when her writings are juxtaposed with the late medieval English texts to which they bear so many generic, thematic, and ideological affinities. In seminars on Chaucer and Christine and on Chaucer and his immediate and near contemporaries (John Gower, John Lydgate, Thomas Hoccleve, and Christine), my students and I have investigated the shared preoccupations of this cohort of vernacular writers, including the problems and possibilities of courtliness and the gendered construction of literary authority. Indeed, it was the experience of teaching a semester-long course on Chaucer and Christine that convinced me that their provocative juxtaposition was worthy of serious literary investigation. As I have argued elsewhere, in texts, careers, and literary influences, the so-called father of English poetry and medieval Europe's first professional woman writer crisscross each other with dizzying complexity (Coletti). Analyzing those connections in the classroom requires a look beyond the canon of Christine's works in English translation, for example, to her courtly lyrics and dits, visionary writings such as *Le chemin de lonc estude*, and her letters about the *Roman de la rose*. Yet her presence as a writer known to English readers such as Hoccleve remains a key element in cross-channel comparison.

Aspects of this approach to Christine's works could be adapted for undergraduate instruction; up to now, however, my own undergraduate teaching of Christine has occurred in an upper-level course, mainly for English majors, on women's writing in medieval England. I frame the course broadly as an examination of women's contributions to and participation in literate culture, a framework that gives us the opportunity to consider issues of literacy and reading; the production, circulation, and ownership of texts; and translation practices that made available to English audiences the work of Continental women writers such as Marguerite Porete, Mechtild of Hackborn, Catherine of Siena, and Christine. The course emphasizes the genres of women's writing—romance, lyric, saints' lives, biography, visionary texts, and literary and cultural criticism—as well as the social and institutional contexts (church, home, and court) in which medieval women read and wrote. Texts by women writing in French, Marie de France's *Lais* at the beginning and Christine's *Cité des dames* at the end, bracket a syllabus of primary readings that includes Clemence of Barking's *Life of Saint Catherine*, Julian of Norwich's *Showings* (or *Revelations of Love*), the Paston Letters, English and Continental women's poetry, and *The Book of Margery Kempe*. Students read the French works (including women troubadours) in translation and the Middle English ones in various forms: modern editions of the Paston Letters (Davis) and Kempe's *Book*, a modern translation for Julian's *Revelations*, and Middle English for the religious and secular poetry.

In giving such prominence to French texts, the course comports with recent approaches to women's writing in England that have highlighted cultural and bibliographical reasons for embracing Marie de France, Clemence of Barking, and, of course, Christine. Alexandra Barratt's important anthology *Women's Writing in Middle English*, which provides our syllabus's selections of women's lyric poetry, represents an early marker of this trend. Barratt's collection is absolutely true to its title: Christine's work appears in excerpts from the Middle English translations of the *Othea* and *Le livre du corps de policie*; Marie de France is represented by the Middle English version of her *Lai le Fraisne*. The move to configure more broadly the field of medieval England's women's writing to include women writing in French is cogently articulated in Laurie

Finke's *Women's Writing in English: Medieval England*, a critical book that makes a useful companion to this course as required secondary reading. Giving the French texts a legitimate place in a course on women's writing in medieval England has the practical benefit of broadening the generic range of materials studied. Marie's *Lais* are a particularly welcome component because they enable discussion of a woman writer's approach to intriguing issues that circulate around romance—love, sex, marriage, chivalric masculinity, adultery, and power—issues that students consistently find engaging. Marie's *Lais* and the first two sections of Christine's *La cité des dames* also account for a significant portion of the readings having a secular focus, an advantage for a course aspiring to balance secular and religious primary texts.

But the inclusion of texts that are French in origin more importantly addresses a central intellectual question posed by the course: What categories best organize women's writing in medieval England when so much of that writing is not (linguistically) English in origin? Study of these texts can productively begin with the literary and cultural legacies of the Norman Conquest, the prominence of insular writing in French, and the multilingual society of medieval England. These issues all lend themselves to exploration in the classroom because they frame literary study of medieval texts in terms of analytic categories—for example, of dominant and subordinate cultures and languages, which students are likely to encounter in other literature courses and for which they can find meaningful reference points in contemporary culture. The literary and textual politics ushered in by the conquest remain relevant for the fifteenth century, when English ambivalence to all things French helps explain how Christine's work was valued and why her texts were so frequently translated into English (Williams).

With this historical and cultural background in mind, we approach *La cité des dames* as the course's final text. Reading that work in Earl Jeffrey Richards's translation, *The Book of the City of Ladies*, which must be credited with sparking interest in Christine beyond medieval French literary studies, we examine how it recapitulates the course's central themes. Its interest in exemplary female holiness harks back to Clemence of Barking, even reprising *The Life of Saint Catherine. La cité des dames*'s attention to women's contributions to many spheres of cultural activity provides a context for thinking about Julian of Norwich's work as a theologian (where might she be placed in the city of ladies?) and about Margaret Paston's courageous management of her family properties. Paston and even Margery Kempe might merit symbolic inclusion in *La cité des dames*'s company of faithful wives, as do the anonymous feminine voices of the Findern lyrics (McNamer) that lament the loss of lovers and mates. *La cité des dames*'s opening meditation on reading, female authorship, and authority implicitly resonates across virtually all the readings for the course, but it finds its most harmonious correspondence in Marie's preface to the *Lais* and Clemence's opening to *The Life of Saint Catherine*, both of which offer sophisticated, reasoned justifications for undertaking the textual work at hand. Significantly, these French witnesses to women's writing in medieval England provide the most extensive commentary on the ideological issues at stake for the woman writer.

La cité des dames furnishes an appealing culmination to this course on women's writing in medieval England. In fact, it provides so many perspectives from which to synthesize the issues of the course that I usually turn the teaching of it over to the students themselves, who work in groups to explore and present, by whatever creative means they choose, key concepts of the text: authorship and authority, women's creativity, feminine piety and virtue, female bodies, building a city. The products of this assignment are almost always illuminating and frequently highly entertaining; one male student dressed as an Amazon to perform ideas of feminine authority; others debated Christine's views on women in a legal trial; still other students pitched the idea of the city of ladies as a medieval time-share, complete with hierarchical tiers of investment depending on the proximity of the properties to the city's rich and famous inhabitants. The students' work attests that *La cité des dames* speaks to them probably more effectively than any other text in the course—because it offers such narrative variety with a polemical edge, I suspect. Christine thus stands out in the course's syllabus, as she does in the canons of medieval English and French literature, as a secular, female authorial voice with the broadest range of intellectual and social interests and commitments.

Teachers of medieval literature in departments of English therefore have good reason to lay pedagogical claim to medieval Europe's first professional woman writer. Their acknowledgment of a cultural, linguistic, and bibliographical history that meaningfully relocates Christine's French texts to medieval England also affords a timely opportunity to recognize recent scholarly attention to the large, and largely unstudied, corpus of French writing that survives from medieval England (Wogan-Browne). Ardis Butterfield's recent argument about the interdependent literary cultures of late medieval England and France underscores the importance of writing in French to textual and literary activity in late medieval England, thereby also highlighting the cultural forces that provide the crucial backdrop for Christine's rise to insular literary prominence. Perhaps now more than ever, the historical migration of her literary enterprise to the international, multilingual culture of late medieval England has reason to be embraced by teachers and students of English literary history, who can teach and study this phenomenon for the distinctive achievement that it is.

NOTES

[1] See Chance, "Gender Subversion"; Coldiron, "Taking Advice"; Collette; Critten; Downes, "Fashioning," "Reading," and "A 'French Booke'"; Finke, "Politics"; Knapp; Long; Mahoney; Schieberle; Summit, *Lost Property*.

[2]Christine's works appear in *EEBO* under the name "Christine de Pisan." Hope Johnson's edition of Ansley's *Boke of the Cyte of Ladyes* is costly for classroom use but still welcome.

[3]See also the Middle French edition and English translation of these texts in Christine McWebb's *Debating the* Roman de la Rose*: A Critical Anthology*.

Teaching the Early Modern English Translations of Christine de Pizan

A. E. B. Coldiron

The reception of Christine de Pizan in early modern England has been a topic of increasing scholarly interest, stimulated by the transnational turn in the humanities; it is also a richly promising classroom subject. The early printed English translations of Christine's work invite questions about particular textual transformations as well as general questions about cultural difference, literary history and historiography, periodization, and canon formation. From the time of William Caxton's press through the end of the Tudor period (and beyond), English translators and printers put Christine's works—and not just *Le livre de la cité des dames* (*The Book of the City of Ladies*)—into wider print circulation, reaching readerships well beyond a court elite. Known now primarily as the protofeminist author of *La cité des dames*, Christine was known in her own time not only as the originator of the *querelle des femmes* but also as a major author writing in many genres and on many subjects, including political theory, military history and theory, moral advice, and revisionary mythography (not to mention educational treatises, lyric poetry, and royal biography). Beginning in 1478, the record of early print shows that she was known and read in English as a serious, wide-ranging, authoritative writer.

That fact alone should give us (and our students) pause, on several counts. For one thing, it reveals the uneven contours of her reputation in the French versus the English canon, canons that differed over time in the degree of enthusiasm for her work and also in the reasons for that enthusiasm. The English reception may also point out gaps in our collective historical imagination; the *auctoritas* of a dead Frenchwoman would not seem likely, from today's commonest view, to have been eagerly welcomed, translated, printed, and promulgated in Tudor England, a culture so frequently at war with France and so infrequently prizing women's writing. Views of women's writing in England are changing, thanks to generations of feminist scholars, but canonical change is a slow, layered, long-term process. The five main early printed translations of Christine's works encourage us to advance that process on some new fronts, for they reveal her advisory authority to have had considerable reach through early modern English culture: *The Morale Prouerbes of Cristyne* (1478 [reprinted as *The Morall Prouerbes of Christyne*; 1526]), *The Fayttes of Armes and of Chyualrye* (1489), *The Booke [of] the Body of Polycye* (1521), *The Boke of the Cyte of Ladyes* (1521), and *The .C. [Hundred] Hystoryes of Troye* (before 1549; *The Epistle of Othea*). Provenance records and the printers' and translators' paratexts show that these works were not only read by Tudor royals and nobles but also intended for and available to "the universall people," as one of Christine's translators puts it.[1] So these translations bring about not only a cultural and linguistic repositioning of her work, but an *épanouissement* in terms of social class as well.

The reception of Christine's work in England has received some fine scholarly treatment,[2] yet the full potential of the topic does not always make it into English or French classrooms. Broad questions about literary reception, periodization, canon formation, the history of feminism, material textuality, genre, cross-cultural contact, and more—and the specific textual variations on which these matters hinge—have been topics in my graduate and undergraduate seminars, titled Christine de Pizan in Early Modern England, and variously dubbed by students and colleagues La Christine Anglaise, The English Christine, and The More-Than-Tudor Christine. In my seminars, students accustomed to medieval and Renaissance literature being taught separately were led to interrogate how the period boundary was established and maintained and if it has any meaning other than as a convenience. Likewise, French majors and students with backgrounds in French joined English majors without background in French; both concluded that literary histories in the two languages have intersected much more than their curricula reflect. In another vein, students who had encountered Christine in survey or medieval literature courses, where she is typically presented as the first feminist author, read beyond *The City of Ladies* into her military history, political theory, mythography, and more. This immediately raised questions: What does it mean to label an author a feminist? How was a woman author of nonfeminist material received in medieval French and Tudor English cultures, respectively? What are the limits of applying our own terms, such as *feminist*, to medieval and early modern authors and texts? Reading and discussing several essays from Renate Blumenfeld-Kosinski's *Selected Writings of Christine de Pizan* in the first week of class stimulated critical thinking about historiography and anachronism as well as feminism.[3]

Students also came to question the processes of canon formation by which Christine was first lauded in two nations; then largely ignored; and later slotted as "an early feminist," which obscured her status as a broadly engaged writer well outside her own nation and era. In examining directly the record of early English print, students learned that it conflicts with the conventional wisdom set forth by most eighteenth- and nineteenth-century English antiquarian canon founders. (In this, Christine is by no means exceptional; Charles d'Orléans, who wrote the first single-author lyric sequence in English literature, was until recently almost completely ignored in English literary canons.) Finally, through hands-on projects and exercises students learned about how editorial decisions may affect the reception and staying power of works and therefore their accessibility, readability, and impact. One student declared in a course evaluation, "I'll never again look at an edition or a translation without wondering what editors did to the words the author actually wrote, and I'll wonder what was there that was 'edited out' or never edited at all." Our semester-long courses allowed for a close, comparative encounter with the early modern English printed texts, but surveys and seminar courses could also incorporate some of this material as individual units or project topics. This essay offers a descriptive overview rather than a full explanation of their implications, aiming to suggest some of the pedagogical opportunities presented by the avid, active printing and translation of Christine's works in early modern England.

Students, Goals, Methods

The courses were conducted at Florida State University. Graduate and undergraduate versions of the course differed considerably in student backgrounds, class size, class duration, and curricular purpose.[4] I focus here on the undergraduate version, where I was most pleasantly surprised at the results. Both courses shared certain features:

- a radically scaffolded (that is, each activity building up to the subsequent one) semester project, with a critical edition of a short excerpt at its heart, culminating in presentations (PechaKuchas for undergraduates and conference-style talks for the graduates) and a term paper with annotated bibliography;
- close textual comparisons between or among versions, including considerations of both linguistic translation and acculturation, as well as variations of material textuality, mise-en-page, woodcuts, and typography;
- background lecture notes and weekly discussions of individual readings; in the second phase of the course, students presented their research findings and the background notes accompanying their edited, annotated excerpts.

Because the course was conducted in English, the reading assignments were in English translation, with French texts available. One of my tasks was to keep reminding students that what they were initially reading in weeks 2 through 6 were modern English translations of Christine's French works, intended as an orientation, to be carefully distinguished from the Tudor translations we would soon be working on in earnest. I taught different ways of reading for different purposes and emphasized that any translation is necessarily an interpretation that imagines a particular audience. Although I posted modern French and Middle French texts for each reading on our course site to stimulate interest in and awareness of the texts' original language and although I encouraged French students to do their work in French, the course was in practice much less bilingual than I had hoped.

Phase 1: Backgrounds and Demonstrations

My goal for the first phase of the course (about six weeks) was to have us quickly read through all five translated, or "Englished," printed works and to introduce the research tools that students would need to do their semester projects well. I also wanted to establish a textual vocabulary and some grounding for students in editorial theory and praxis, so that they could accurately discuss editions, issues, copies, quire construction (differing in manuscript and print), letterforms (both script and print), mise-en-page, incipits and explicits, colophons, and other relevant, signifying elements of the codex (Clanchy, "Parchment"; Hollinga; Shaw). We visited FSU's Special Collections for hands-on encounters with fourteenth- and fifteenth-century manuscripts and sixteenth-century printed books—though, alas, not books by Christine; instructors at institutions with larger collections will have better luck. The first phase of the undergraduate seminar began with an orientation to Christine's life and works and to the scholarship about it (Margolis, *Introduction*; Blumenfeld-Kosinski, *Selected Writings*), with ample notes and images in class or on our course site about the relevant medieval French backgrounds to the texts and the relevant Renaissance English backgrounds to the translations. These background materials—historical, biographical, textual, literary-historical—were keyed to each week's reading assignments.

For each work, I demonstrated in class the comparative editorial method I wanted students to use in their own projects, with close work on a passage where a difference between the fifteenth-century French manuscript text and the early modern English printed text mattered interpretively, biographically, historically, or culturally. For example, I first used four versions of Christine's *Proverbes moraulx* as a sampler for textual comparisons in class: images of Christine's French manuscript; my own translation of that into English, which they had read for homework; the early modern English version of 1478, printed by Caxton (Christine de Pizan, *Morale Prouerbes of Cristyne*); and the slightly revised version of 1526, *The Morall Prouerbes of Christyne*, printed by the king's printer to Henry VIII, Richard Pynson. The work is short, 202 lines, and the background readings were keyed to the general subject. In class I demonstrated first how to use the Web site *Christine de Pizan: The Making of the Queen's Manuscript* to find images of the British Library's Harley MS 4431and then how to use the printed *English Short Title Catalogue* (*ESTC*), the *Early English Books Online* (*EEBO*) database, and the *EEBO–Text Creation Partnership* (*EEBO-TCP*) database to find the early modern English versions. As questions came up, I digressed to other screens to show other tools we might need, such as the *Oxford English Dictionary* (*OED*) and the *Middle English Dictionary* (*MED*), the Bibliothèque Nationale de France Web site, the British Library site, *Gallica*, the *Archives de littérature du Moyen Âge*, among other online resources.

We began with a simple question: "What differences do you notice, and which ones seem to matter the most?" Students noted the tremendous visual differences in the pages and in presentational strategies. We discussed the way that lavish manuscript mise-en-page created spacing between Christine's couplets that, with supporting rubrication, emphasized them as such, while the English printers' more economical designs ignored the rhetoric of the couplet, despite attempts at preserving in English the couplet rhyming patterns. Meanwhile, students learned a lot of terms and processes involved in manuscript culture and talked about the poem as part of the wisdom literature tradition that spanned both cultures. They noticed Caxton's remarkable colophon poem praising Christine as the "mireur [and] maistresse" of "Intelligence" in the first printing of her work in England (*Morale Prouerbes*, fol. 4v; Coldiron, "Taking Advice" 134–41); I pointed out that the rhyme royal poem was not in the English copy available online, only in the Rylands Library copy, a facsimile page of which I had provided. This textual variation led us to several important points: the importance of paratext in constructing an author's reputation (Christine is visibly and highly praised rather than suppressed or ventriloquized in these printed English versions); the persistence of rhyme royal, normally considered a medieval form, in early modern England, often as an elevated or epideictic form; editions versus issues versus copies; the perils and promise of digitization. In the next English version, the *Morall Prouerbes* (1526), students saw that Pynson took Christine's poem, edited it, and recontextualized it in a Chaucerian collection called the *Boke of Fame*. This material-textual situation showed that Christine's authorship, while not in 1526 the subject of a praise poem like Caxton's, was implicitly validated for English readers by its position alongside the poetry of Chaucer and Lydgate. During this week, encounters with specific textual variants allowed students to use research tools to make wider interpretive sense of Christine's early modern reception in England. We moved from observations of evidence to research inquiry to analysis and discussion. The hands-on praxis was important, too, because most of the undergraduates had not used these resources in any extended way.

Likewise, for Christine's *Book of the Body Politic*, we read Kate Langdon Forhan's translation for an overview, and I provided background notes on medieval French versus Tudor English theories of monarchy and on the reigns of Charles and Henry, respectively, as well as excerpts from John of Salisbury and Plutarch to which Christine alludes or on which she draws. In class I demonstrated further how to find Christine's other manuscripts and works about them and how to find images and transcriptions of the early printed English versions. Once we had a key passage, I juxtaposed on screen an image of the French manuscript passage and an image of the passage as printed in English (from *EEBO*). At their desks, the students held their modern translation of the French (Forhan) and the *EEBO-TCP* transcription of the sometimes barely legible English version. I first used short passages on the limits of monarchy from book 1 of *Body Politic*, followed by the body-politic analogies from book 3. To examine each of these in the four versions, I selected a few sentences that were directly connected to the background readings. This allowed us to discuss textual variation in terms of its larger ideological and cultural contexts. I must admit that it was heavy lifting at first, but by the third week, students were excited to point out their own observations about the textual variations and were posing questions about material textuality as a factor in reception and interpretation.

Phase 2: Taking Up the Pioche d'Inquisition

The second, nine-week phase of the course, devoted to workshops on the students' projects and research, largely justified the hard labor of the first phase. Students chose one of the five English printed works as their focus and grouped themselves in class to brainstorm their next steps and to share resources and tips. Fortune, or perhaps Prudence, smiled on us, and the choices were evenly distributed: in the undergraduate course, four students chose *Morale Prouerbes*, five chose *Fayttes of Armes*, six chose *Cyte of Ladyes*, seven chose *Body of Polycye*, and seven chose *.C. Hystoryes of Troye* [*Othea*]. In groups focused on each text, students established on our course site working documents such as bibliographies, useful links, locations lists, page images, digitized texts, and other shared resources. We also set up a section for queries, where students could ask one another for help with snags in research. I checked in there about once a week in case all were stumped. Group work was general and related to backgrounds and to sharing resources and strategies; individuals edited and annotated specific passages of 700–750 words, providing critical and textual notes.

Having chosen a passage in one of the five English works where variations seemed salient and meaningful, each student presented in a class workshop the textual variants in their excerpts that they thought mattered most. I set up the workshops to follow the chronology of the English printings, beginning with workshops on *Morale Prouerbes* (1478) and ending the semester with the *Othea* (c. 1549) workshops. Students presented their chosen passages in order of appearance in the work; as a result, the whole class closely reread some important parts of what we had plowed through in phase 1. Before their presentations, students posted images and comparative transcriptions of their passages as reading assignments for the class, just as we had done in the demonstrations, and I continued to assign related secondary readings. In the workshops, students showed their page images in French and English and walked us through the most interesting moments in their passages, especially moments of variation, informing us of their research progress and seeking help as needed. These were lively sessions full of discussion, as students in a group became more expert and students outside the group could point out connections with what they had learned in their own inquiries. They addressed variations in these versions as we had done in phase 1, in terms of material production and historical contexts, some more successfully than others.

Students with background in French seemed dismayed at the Tudor translation of a key phrase in *La cité des dames* for the intellectual tool of thorough critique that will dig the foundations of the city, "la pioche d'inquisition" (literally, the pickaxe, mattock, or trowel of inquiry). The rendering by Bryan Anslay, a Tudor translator, in 1526 was "the pycoys of thyne vnderstandynge" (*Boke of the Cyte of Ladyes* [Pepwell] Ddi). As one student said, shaking her head, "It's just not the same thing." Although she couldn't explain her aesthetic response in terms of historical contexts or textual production, her impression registered the fact that the etymons *pioche* and *pycoys* were not being used the same way, a *pioche* of inquiry being a tool to break up hard ground in a preconstruction process but a *pycoys* of understanding suggesting something gained and held later. Such comparisons became *pioches* in themselves, enabling a workshop habit of aesthetic attention and lexical inquiry. It was an opportunity to practice tracing words like *pycoys* in the *MED* and the *OED* and in full-text databases containing fifteenth- and sixteenth-century uses of the word. We discussed the personalizing addition of "thyne" and the difference between French *inquisition* ("inquiry") and English *understanding*. More successful instances abounded in workshops on *Fais d'armes et de chevallerie* (in one modern translation titled *Deeds of Arms and of Chivalry*; in early modern England, the *Fayttes of Armes and of Chyualrye*, which we called the *Feats of Arms and Chivalry* or just *Feats*). Students working on that text brought images of medieval versus Tudor battle techniques and war gear to bear on specific passages they had chosen and showed interest in what Christine's translators did to the moral limits she imposed on soldiers. Also successful were the student workshops on *.C. Hystoryes of Troye*, in which students found visual variations between French and English page designs, which they linked not only to Tudor print-production values but also to various medieval and Renaissance rewritings of the classical intertexts (the Medea and Dido stories were especially fruitful). My samples in phase 1 of *Body Politic* had demonstrated how Christine's arguments about right kingship and the limits of monarchical power meant one thing in late medieval France at the unstable courts of Charles—during the chaotic years of the Hundred Years War, circulated among elite readers of manuscript—but something quite different during the strenuous Tudor consolidation of monarchical power, just before the dissolution of the monasteries and the divorce crisis. Students working on *Body Politic* projects applied this insight more broadly, considering how the English text was made public in both vellum and paper printed copies to wide readerships, not only to insiders. A critique of power, students found, looks different to those holding power and different still in times of falling versus rising power. They discovered this by delving into the details of textual variation.

The success of the hands-on research workshops and the queries board had a downside: nearly all the students created critical notes that had blossomed quite out of hand. I finally had to impose limits. We returned to some basic editorial theory (Greetham; Keleman; Greg; Bowers; McGann) and pondered our imagined readers' needs and the uses of apparatus. I pointed out that while a two-page or even a two-paragraph critical note is excessive in most situations, and certainly in ours, the pruned parts could be the basis of well-informed prewriting for their term essays. The prunings did not always add up to tightly made arguments, but every student practiced using primary observations combined with research to make a case about a literary text. The best students excelled in this. Likewise, the annotated bibliographies arose fairly naturally from their workshops and queries, with frequent reminders from me about keeping track of all the new resources they were using by annotating. Even weaker students benefited from the scaffolding and the comparative method of treating and researching variants.

In addition, teaching the works of Christine the Pizan invites and rewards interdisciplinary pedagogical collaborations. I had the good fortune to have a colleague in the Modern Languages Department, Lori Walters, an expert on the French corpus and manuscripts, who was willing to coordinate by teaching a graduate seminar on Christine's French works in the same semester but at different times. Thus, interested students could study both the French and English sides of the oeuvre in an intensive semester. From this followed several dissertation and thesis projects that contained chapters drawing on both sides of Christine's oeuvre. Even barring such semester-long coordination, shorter sessions that draw on different colleagues' expertise would be possible. Colleagues in history, political science, gender studies, or medieval studies might also collaborate pedagogically on this author's multifaceted works.

The early printed translations of Christine make possible a rich pedagogical praxis. Not just for French students, and not just for students of feminism, these works illuminate the periodization issues between medieval and Renaissance or early modern, and they illuminate the fraught and important French-English relations in the period. They offer great case studies in translation (especially in prose) and in the history of material texts, particularly the transformation of manuscripts to printed texts and how this material transformation is another form of reacculturation that animates the concomitant verbal and cultural translations. The English printed translations reveal that Christine was famous and greatly respected in the broadening readerships of early modern England, not only as a protofeminist but also as a serious adviser across genres, despite what her status as a Frenchwoman might lead us to predict. And they offer excellent praxis for students—in developing research skills and critical thinking skills, in gaining knowledge in cultural and literary history, and in editorial theory and practice. In French courses, this English reception history might form one module or unit or provide optional project topics. In English surveys, Christine should certainly figure beyond the *City of Ladies* and thereby might come to appear more vigorously in English curricula in general. Her work is relevant to both medieval and early modern studies courses. In all its variation, her work can help us give our students both a "pycoys of . . . vnderstandynge" and a "pioche d'inquisition."

NOTES

[1]The Tudor translator and printer John Skot titles book 3 of the *Body of Polycye* (1521) "To the Universall People."

[2]Among others, see Bornstein, "French Influence"; Campbell; Coletti; H. Johnston; Mahoney; Malcolmson; Summit, *Lost Property*; Walters, "Christine de Pizan as Translator" and "Woman Writer."

[3]Readings in Blumenfeld-Kosinski's *Selected Writings* include Delany, "Mothers"; Gottlieb, "Problem"; and Blumenfeld-Kosinski, "Christine de Pizan and the Misogynistic Tradition."

[4]The graduate course aimed to satisfy a pre-1800 requirement for MA and PhD students, a professional predissertation training for medievalists and early modernists in French and English, and a requirement for PhD students in the History of Text Technologies program. The undergraduate course was a capstone seminar for the undergraduate English major or upper-level literature elective.

Christine de Pizan and the Moral Education of Women: Teaching *Le livre des trois vertus*

Roberta L. Krueger

Christine de Pizan wrote *Le livre des trois vertus* (*The Book of the Three Virtues*) as a practical companion to *Le livre de la cité des dames* (*The Book of the City of Ladies*). Dedicated in 1405 to young Margaret of Burgundy, who was eleven when she married the dauphin, Louis of Guyenne, the previous year, *Trois vertus* offers instruction and advice to women of all social ranks, from princesses to prostitutes, about how to maintain and improve social and spiritual well-being. This work has been judged both more "personal" and "original" than *Le livre de la cité des dames* (Wisman, "Aspects socio-économiques" 27). It is one of Christine's most accessible works for undergraduates. It incorporates few literary or historical exempla and may be understood without extensive knowledge of late medieval society or politics. Its allegorical framework is straightforward and well organized. Reason, Rectitude, and Justice, the three Virtues who directed Christine to record the stories of famous women in *La cité des dames*, here command the author to compose an instructional treatise for all women. She obliges by penning a tome in three parts: for princesses (book 1), for ladies-in-waiting and ladies of the manor (book 2), and for middle-class women and commoners (book 3). Although the text's narrative voice is complex, her counsel is presented clearly. As she addresses women of different ages, conditions, and social rank, Christine offers precious insights into late medieval women's material, social, domestic, economic, moral, and spiritual lives. *Trois vertus* offers a rich source for courses in medieval history and culture; additionally, its carefully constructed, self-reflexive allegory and astute social analysis will stimulate critical inquiry in the literature classroom.

Christine wanted her book to circulate well beyond its royal dedicatee. In the epilogue, the narrator, who signs her name "Christine," says she hopes her "noble work" will "multiply" in "pluseurs copies" (225, "many copies") throughout the world, reaching not only princesses and ladies but also other women; she wants the book to be published "en tous païs" (225; "in all countries"). Judging from the work's twenty-one extant manuscripts, three printed editions (dated 1497, 1503, and 1536), and a Portuguese translation for Isabelle of Portugal extant in both manuscript and print (1518), we can conclude that Christine succeeded. The existence of paper manuscripts along with more deluxe vellum copies suggests that the book appealed to bourgeois as well as noble readers (Willard, "Manuscript Tradition" 436). Anne of France, sister and regent of Charles VIII, may have drawn inspiration from *Trois vertus* in her *Enseignements à sa fille* (*Lessons for My Daughter*), written in 1505 for her young daughter, Suzanne (Willard, "Anne de France" 62–68). After the mid–sixteenth century, *Trois vertus* appears to have dropped out of fashion, most likely because new treatises on conduct reflected contemporary mores and tastes. Fortunately, Charity Cannon Willard and Eric Hicks's 1989 edition made the book accessible to scholars and graduate students, and Liliane Dulac's 2006 modern French translation made the work accessible to French-speaking undergrads. Two English translations in affordable paperbacks are ideal choices for students in courses on medieval literature or culture.[1]

Christine's *Trois vertus* is a treasure trove for teachers. As Kenneth Varty has argued, the book provides a wonderful introduction to medieval notions of hierarchy and status, courtly love and marriage, dress and fashion, religious practice, and literary personification and allegory ("Autour"). I have taught the book in translation in courses on women writers of the Middle Ages and the Renaissance and in a course cotaught with my former English department colleague Edward Wheatley (now at Loyola University) entitled Education and Morality in Medieval and Renaissance Society. Advanced students pursuing research topics in women's social history, in late medieval didactic writings, and in other areas can benefit from a growing body of scholarship on the work.[2] Recent studies have laid a solid critical base and opened questions for further analysis.

Trois vertus is a transitional text: it circulated in both manuscript and early printed editions among aristocratic and bourgeois audiences and reflects both medieval hierarchies and emerging social realities. It can thus be positioned as a cornerstone, a bridge, or a capstone at the beginning, midpoint, or conclusion of a course. For its analysis of the social roles of noblewomen, wives, unmarried women, and widows and its inclusion of artisan and bourgeois women, the book could conclude a course on medieval women writers that begins with Héloïse's correspondence with Abelard and Marie of France's *Lais* and *Fables*. In a comparative context, Christine's advice to women could be set alongside other European didactic treatises for women such as the anonymous fourteenth-century English work *How the Good Wife Taught Her Daughter* or the French works discussed below.[3] *Trois vertus*, paired with Christine's romance-like *Livre du duc des vrais amans* (*The Book of the Duke of True Lovers*)—which first presents the chaperone's letter to the young married lady that Christine redeploys in her conduct book—could be read as the initial text in a course on pre-1800 teachings about love and marriage, which might include *La princesse de Clèves* and *Les liaisons dangereuses*. And, of course, Christine's mirror for the princess can be compared fruitfully with many other works by Christine, including not only *La cité des dames*, which is replete with exempla of valorous women from the past, but also her mirrors for princes, such as the *Epistre Othea* (*Othea's Letter to Hector*), *Le livre du corps de policie* (*The Book of the Body Politic*), and *Le livre de paix* (*The Book of Peace*).

Trois vertus provides an excellent example of an important genre that until recently has been little studied: the medieval conduct book. From the twelfth century onward and increasingly in the later Middle Ages, a spate of didactic treatises teaching young men and women proper behavior, social skills, and moral values circulated throughout European courts and bourgeois households in a variety of forms: books teaching table manners, service, and etiquette at court (sometimes known as courtesy books); *enseignements* of moral precepts; books of chivalry; mirrors for princes that incorporated political theory; and books offering counsel to young women on spiritual and practical duties ranging from prayer to household management.[4] Christine excelled in this genre, composing important instructional works for the families of King Charles VI and the dukes of Burgundy and for her own son (Willard, "Christine de Pizan as Teacher"). *Trois vertus* follows a tradition of works in French for women that begins with Saint Louis's letter of pious instructions for his daughter Isabelle and includes works as diverse as Robert de Blois's *Chastoiement des dames*, Geoffrey de la Tour Landry's *Livre du chevalier de la Tour Landry pour l'enseignement de ses filles*, *Le ménagier de Paris*, and Philippe de Mézières's *Livre de la vertu du sacrement de mariage* (see Bornstein, *Lady*; Hentsch). Christine appears also to have drawn inspiration from Durand de Champagne's *Speculum dominarum*, a Latin mirror addressed to Queen Jeanne de Navarre.[5] Christine's work is the only medieval French conduct book written by a woman and also the only one that explicitly addresses all ranks of women.

When I present *Trois vertus* in this context, I sometimes ask students to reflect on the self-help genre in contemporary American culture. In Christine's time, books on conduct in life were prominently featured in court and household libraries. Advice books of many stripes are no less popular today. I ask students to visit a local bookstore (not simply the Internet) with the following questions in mind: What can we learn about the importance of this genre by the placement and organization of the self-help section? What topics are treated? Who is the audience for these books? Students report on ten titles on various problems written for audiences differentiated by age, gender, and other demographics.

Trois vertus differs considerably from its twenty-first-century offspring. Many subjects that loom large on today's bookshelves—pregnancy and childbirth, sexuality and sexual orientation, wedding planning and divorce, for example—are absent from Christine's work. Her divisions by rank and her advice about many practical matters, from military defense to agriculture, no longer pertain to daily life. But *Trois vertus* broaches a surprising number of other topics treated in contemporary books: spiritual well-being, communication and the arts of speech, household finances, etiquette, dress, leisure, children's education, adolescence, marital difficulties, and widowhood, to name a few. Books today tend to focus on one problem and to address a specific demographic: an advice book for mothers will not be the same as one for teenage girls. By contrast, students may remark, Christine speaks to women of all ages and conditions of life. Her vision of society is organic; she stresses the interdependence of women's roles. Her holistic approach and her sympathetic engagement with a diverse audience of readers distinguishes her work among medieval moral treatises as well.

This advice book breaks new ground in comparison with two nearly contemporary treatises that Christine may have known: *Le livre du chevalier de la Tour Landry pour l'enseignement de ses filles* (1372) and *Le ménagier de Paris* (1385).[6] Her attitude toward her female readers differs strikingly from that of the male moralists. The knight of Tour Landry expresses fatherly concern for his daughters, who are young and lacking in understanding. But his examples, drawn largely from clerical sources, often mete out harsh punishments for transgressive women. Preoccupied with his daughters' chastity and marital obedience, he says little about their broader social roles. *Le ménagier*, whose fictional author is a prosperous bourgeois householder, offers his young bride, an aristocratic orphan, a hefty tome replete with lessons on marital obedience as well as practical instructions and recipes. Although this encyclopedia of household management implies that women were expected to play important roles in running the estate, the author's repeated insistence that wives should do exactly as their husbands say seems to show little regard for a woman's initiative or personal fulfillment. In both *Le livre du chevalier de la Tour Landry* and *Le ménagier de Paris*, a male narrator intrudes frequently to address his readers—"my lovely daughters" or "my dear sister"—thus reminding each of her place as dutiful child or wife in the family.

By contrast, Christine eschews punitive exempla and does not overwhelm her reader with tasks that must be done exactly as she says. In literature classes, where students have learned to analyze narrative voice, I ask them to observe Christine's narrative strategies throughout the work. How does Christine present herself as author in the prologue? How does her authorial voice shape the ensuing chapters? If we compare her rhetorical strategies to those of male didactic narrators, does she seem to present an alternative pedagogy? Does she invite her readers to participate more actively in their own moral education?

Reading the prologues of *Le livre du chevalier de la Tour Landry* and the *Le ménagier de Paris* alongside the opening of *Trois vertus*, we might characterize her approach as collaborative and interactive. As she struggles to set a good example and to better women's condition, she learns and improves along with her readers. The prologue depicts an exhausted author reclining in bed after having penned *La cité des dames*, chided by the Virtues for abandoning her task in midstream, like a recreant knight or a lazy chambermaid. (This scene is represented in an opening illumination in several manuscripts; Christine is pulled from bed by the Virtues on the left; on the right, Lady Prudence addresses a group of women in headdresses that indicate different social ranks.) The Virtues urge Christine to act like a wise bird catcher: to lay devices and nets to entrap the wild birds (women) so that they may be tamed and brought into the "glorious city of ladies" (7–9). If she implies by this image that moral instruction involves rigorous discipline, she also reminds us that wise women may expect rich earthly and heavenly rewards.

This distinctive autobiographical vignette dramatizes Christine not only as an accomplished author but also as a faithful servant who toils to improve the lot of all women, from princesses to commoner, by her pen. Students might compare this portrait with her authorial persona in *La cité des dames* or in *Le livre du chemin de lonc estude*. They might recall Marie of France's authorial presence in the prologue of her *Lais* and *Fables* and be asked to anticipate Louise Labé's appeal to women's intellectual capacities in the dedicatory letter to Clémence de Bourges in her book of poetry and prose. As Christine labors to produce a book to foster "l'accroissement du bien et honneur de toute femme" (*Trois vertus* 3; "the increased well-being and honor of every woman"), she enhances her own literary, moral, and social worth.

In the work, a narrator identifying herself as Christine does not carry on a conversation with Reason, Rectitude, and Justice, as she does in *La cité des dames*. Instead, the author transcribes the advice of commingled Virtues and other didactic voices (Temptation, Our Lord, Worldly Prudence, and Envy, among others) in a way that blends with her own voice (Tarnowski, "Autobiography"). The narrator adapts her discourse for women of different ranks (Lorcin 145–48). In book 1, the longest part of the text, the princess receives the sternest admonishments from another allegorical figure or from her own internal voice, perhaps because it would have been unseemly for Christine to chastise her directly (women offer advice to themselves at several points in *Trois vertus*; Christine depicts them reflecting on moral issues, as she might want her readers to do). In book 3, the shortest section, the narrator employs direct address in the second person most frequently (Lorcin 148). Here, rather than suggest or describe ideal behavior, as she often does for the ladies addressed in books 1 and 2, she tells lower-ranked women explicitly what to do. For example, at the end of the chapter entitled "Of the Wives of Merchants," Christine urges these women to share their wealth with the poor through charitable deeds and warns them to avoid hoarding, cheating, and fraud (book 3, ch. 3).

Christine appeals to her diverse spectrum of readers through prolific and various narrative voices. She sometimes presents her counsel not as a directive voiced in the imperative but in the form of a question that invites the reader's own response: "Mais que fera la bonne princepce quant ainsi temptee se sentira?" (14; "But what will the good princess do who feels herself tempted in this manner?"). At other times, she presents the reader's moral reflections in the form of an internal monologue or dialogue, as, for example, when the narrator explains the princess's thoughts throughout book 1, chapter 4, which begins: "Adviser te convient, ce dit a soi meismes la bonne princepce de Dieu inspiree, laquelle de ces susdictes voyes tu velux tenir" (25; "The good princess inspired by God says to herself, 'You must decide which of these paths you wish to follow'"). What other examples of interactive rhetorical strategies can students find, and how do these engage the reader? How does the narrator of *Trois vertus* invite the reader's participation in her moral education?

As they examine Christine's discourse, students can be asked to observe her remarks about women's language, which emphasize the importance of effective speech and praise "the art of persuasive language" (Dulac, "Representation" 21). How does each of the three books comment on women's abuse of the tongue or on their skillful manipulation of speech? How can women of different ranks use language to influence family members, direct members of the household, or enlist aid? How does Christine herself exemplify savvy speech, carefully crafted and deployed for the common good? Recent studies have emphasized her promotion of prudent duplicity, "virtuous artifice," and subtle dissimulation; these may be useful, even necessary, strategies for the princess who seeks to curate her social reputation and foster harmonious relations in household and court (Velissariou; Rouillard; Denery, "Christine"). Students can be asked to identify how and to analyze why Christine justifies such social hypocrisy.

One of the most fruitful approaches to *Trois vertus* is to trace a common thread throughout the text and to observe the way Christine's representation reflects differences in women's social condition. Working in pairs or small groups, students can examine one of her topics in each of the three books. If the same obligation to be pious and virtuous applies to women of all estates (as the narrator frequently reminds us), how does the moralist's advice on wealth and material possessions, costume and fashion, piety, diet, education, leisure, and work differ as she speaks to women of the nobility, to ladies of the manor, to merchants' wives, and to the poor? How do expectations, restrictions, and opportunities differ for women according to their position in the social hierarchy?

Such questions encourage students to read the text attentively and to avoid jumping to easy conclusions about the lot of medieval women. As groups report their findings, they may be surprised by the organic conception of society conveyed in *Trois vertus*. Although each social estate has its duties, women are interconnected by mutual obligations and service. The princess should speak charitably to poor women in her town; she should visit them when they are sick and send gifts to those in need (book 1, ch. 17). Ladies of the manor should work on their estates alongside other women, girls, and young women to make clothing that all will use (156; book 2, ch. 10). Prostitutes may find redemption doing laundry for those who live in the great houses or tending to those who are sick or with child (book 3, ch. 10).

Students should be wary of assuming that Christine's ideals for women always reflect historical realities. *Trois vertus* describes the lives that women ought to lead more often than it recounts the conduct in which actual women engaged (although there are several compelling realistic portraits, particularly in book 3). Yet Christine's representations of women's economic, domestic, moral, and religious life offer valuable insights into social practice and medieval mentalities (see Willard, "Fifteenth-Century View"; Wisman, "Aspects"; Laigle). For class presentations or research papers, students can consult recent work in social history that fleshes out and contextualizes Christine's writings about, for example, women's education, widowhood, medieval women's devotional texts, medieval dress and fashion, women and the family, the medieval household, and women's economic roles (helpful introductions to and recent bibliography for these and other topics appear in Schaus). For students of literature, one of the most fascinating aspects of *Trois vertus* is Christine's authorial persona and, in particular, her striking autocitation, mentioned above. The fictional letter penned by the governess Sibyl de la Tour in *Le livre du duc des vrais amans* (1403) appears verbatim in *Trois vertus*. In that romance-like narrative, which Christine says she recounts reluctantly in the first-person voice of the duke, the chaperone takes leave of her wayward charge, a young married lady engaged in an illicit love affair; the departed governess sends her former mistress a lengthy epistle warning of the dire consequences of her behavior. The letter reappears in *Trois vertus*, book 1, chapter 27, at the end of a chapter on foolish love, wherein Prudence advises the governess to leave the service of a princess who persists in her wicked behavior and to send such a letter after her departure. The author of *Trois vertus* prominently cites her previous work:

> Pour ce que l'epistre qui est contenue ou *Livre du duc des vrais amans*, ou il est mis que Sebile de la Tour l'envoia a la duchece, puet server au propos que ou chapitre cy aprés ensuit, sera de recheif recordee. (109; ch. 26)
>
> Because the letter that is included in the *Book of the Duke of True Lovers*—where it is explained that Sibyl de la Tour sent it to the duchess—applies to the subject of the following chapter, it will be presented again.

Christine suggests that those who already know the letter may skip over it, even as she reminds us that its teachings are good and profitable for all highborn ladies.

The letter encapsulates many of the precepts of virtuous behavior that Christine has expounded in *Trois vertus* and roundly denounces the ethos of courtly love, precepts that serve male desire at the expense of female honor. The insertion of Sibyl's letter into *Trois vertus* initiates a dialogue between an amorous fiction and a book of conduct. The complex embedding of contrasting narrators (Sibyl de la Tour in the duke's story; Sibyl in Prudence's advice) in Christine's autobiographical, extradiegetic frame creates a sophisticated mirror that invites critical analysis. Scholars have explored this rich literary nexus without exhausting the terrain (see, e.g., Brownlee "Rewriting Romance"; Tarnowski, "Autobiography"). How does Christine's letter respond to writings by previous (male) commentators about courtly love, including the chevalier de la Tour?[7] How might Sibyl's letter be read as a *mise en abyme* of Christine's own pedagogical enterprise? What does Christine convey about the teacher-pupil relationship in this twice-repeated scene of moral instruction?

Inevitably, *Trois vertus* raises the question of whether Christine was a protofeminist. In their initial encounter with the text, students sometimes express disappointment or frustration that she, evidently a strong woman herself, seems to acquiesce to conventional norms and to preach resignation—for women in unhappy marriages, for example—rather than liberation. Many critics have duly noted the treatise's support of traditional values. Willard observed in an early article that "a reading of the *Trois Vertus* might well prove disappointing to a militant feminist" ("Manuscript Tradition" 440). "There is no indication,"

Willard writes, "that Christine expected women to do more than accept their place in society; she merely wanted them to make better use of their opportunities" (442). Colette Winn has characterized the approach of women authors of ancien régime manuals of education, including that of Christine, as "timid, prudent, and very respectful of laws and social conventions" (24; my trans.). Winn suggests that the moralists' androgynous narrative voices blend with the teachings of masculine authorities who seek to transmit and preserve cultural norms (28).

Yet as students examine Christine's portrait of women's roles more closely and as they learn more about medieval society, they may gain appreciation of her representation of female agency throughout *Trois vertus*.[8] As we have seen, the female narrator writes at the behest of female Virtues and filters her voice through an array of mostly feminine figures. Although Christine urges women to fulfill the respective duties of their estates and expects each to maintain her honor and good reputation, she emphasizes that women bear responsibility for constructing their social identities; one critic refers to this emphasis as Christine's "politics of visibility" (Brown-Grant, *Christine* 200). Christine encourages women to move in and between their social domains as active agents. Never idle, the princess should act as a mediator for her husband and intercede to promote peace (book 1, ch. 9), oversee the education of her children and the behavior of her ladies-in-waiting (chs. 15 and 18), and manage finances (ch. 19), all the while cleverly navigating the shoals of interpersonal conflicts arising in the family and at court. Baronesses living in great castles should have a "cuer d'omme" (151; "man's heart"; book 2, ch. 9) in preparation for commanding the troops and governing the estate in their husbands' absence (book 2, ch. 9). Ladies living in manor houses should know all that they can about estate revenues and expenses, crop rotation and planting, animal care and sheep shearing, as well as household chores (ch. 10). Wives of artisans and field workers are expected to be prudent housekeepers, enhancing the household economy through their efforts (173–77; book 3, ch. 1).

Students who carefully analyze the narrator's counsel about particular matters (tracing individual themes through rank, as I've suggested) may reevaluate the author as an advocate for women's participation and influence in powerful social networks. Classroom debate about Christine's conservatism or feminism will be more nuanced as students delve further into the text.

Christine's advice for bourgeois women in book 3 might frame the students' concluding discussion of *Trois vertus*. Christine supports the traditional hierarchy and rails against social climbers who dress above their station. Yet as she describes the prosperity and vitality of certain *bourgeoises*, she seems to forecast their inevitable social ascension. What do students make of her remarkable portrait of the textile merchant's wife in book 3, chapter 3, whose extravagant lying-in arrangements constitute the work's longest, most detailed material description (184–88)? She reports that the expectant mother, who had been recently observed in fancy attire reclining on a richly decorated bed in an elegantly appointed chamber, has become the talk of the town; word of her room has even reached the queen's chamber (186). Should readers consider the merchant's wife merely as a negative example of ostentatious display, a vulgar woman reaching too high above her station? Or might we see her—despite the author's dismay at her extravagance—as a wife who has increased her well-being through shrewd domestic management and savvy social skills, the very qualities that Christine praises elsewhere?

As Christine's narrator offers counsel on a host of issues, she invites women's active construction of their social identities and, perhaps unwittingly, promotes the advancement of bourgeois women, who would read later copies of her book in paper manuscripts and early printed editions. Instructional texts and advice books for women continued to proliferate among widening circles of readers in early modern Europe. The basic precepts expressed in Christine's book would be adapted and refashioned for new venues in changing social spheres. As their transmission moved from royal and aristocratic courts to bourgeois households, conduct books played a major role in furthering female literacy and in contributing to women's moral education and social welfare. Christine's *Trois vertus* helped foster a vogue for women's instructional literature, whose distant, variegated legacy remains visible in hundreds of self-help books for women on prominent display in stores today. New editions, translations, and critical studies have enabled instructors to bring medieval conduct books and other didactic and devotional treatises into sharper focus in the classroom alongside the perennial classics of lyric poetry and courtly romance. *Trois vertus* should be welcomed as an accessible and intriguing work whose narrative framework and social analysis raise compelling questions for students and their professors alike.

NOTES

In this essay citations in Middle French are from *Le livre des trois vertus*, edited by Willard and Hicks, and translations are my own.

[1]For the Middle French edition, see Christine's *Le livre des trois vertus*, edited by Willard and Hicks. For English translations, see *The Treasure of the City of Ladies*, translated by Lawson, and *A Medieval Woman's Mirror*, translated by Willard and edited by Cosman. Willard and Cosman's edition includes an introductory essay, a glossary, and twenty illustrations drawn from medieval and Renaissance manuscripts and books. Lawson's edition, which I have used in teaching, contains an introduction and a very serviceable translation.

[2]See Fresco, "Gendered Household Spaces"; Krueger, "Christine's Treasure" and "*Nouvelles choses*"; Tarnowski, "Autobiography"; Brown-Grant, *Christine* 175–214. For an early comprehensive overview that remains a fine introduction, see Willard, "Fifteenth-Century View." See also Laigle, *Le livre des trois vertus*.

[3]See Mustanoja's edition of *How the Good Wife Taught Her Daughter*. Other European works for women include *Enseignements*, written by Louis IX, king of France, for his daughter Isabelle; Amanieu de Sescás's *Essenhamen de la donzela*; Francesco

da Barberino's *Reggimento et costumi di donna*; and the anonymous fifteenth-century Castilian *Castigos y doctrinas que un savio dava a sus hijas*. For full or partial translations of these texts, see M. Johnston, *Medieval Conduct Literature*.

[4]Recent critical approaches to conduct literature are presented by Ashley and Clark. Translations of and commentary on representative European didactic texts for youth are included in M. Johnston, *Medieval Conduct Literature*. For an overview of the genre, see my introduction in that volume.

[5]Karen Green notes that Christine's conception of female virtue is considerably more focused on charitable activity and "worldly prudence" than that advanced by Durand de Champagne ("From *Le miroir*" 103).

[6]Geoffrey de la Tour Landry's *Livre*, edited by Montaiglon, has no modern French translation. A Middle English translation and early printed edition by Caxton makes the work accessible for English readers. A fine bilingual edition (Middle French and modern French) of *Le ménagier de Paris* brings this work to undergraduate students in French; see *Mesnagier de Paris*, edited by Brereton and Ferrier and translated by Ueltschi. For an English translation, see *Good Wife's Guide*.

[7]De Gendt has noted similarities between the arguments made by Sibyl de la Tour and the wife of the chevalier de la Tour in ch. 124 of his book.

[8]For an overview of Christine's promotion of women's agency throughout her literary career and an assessment of her contributions to evolving feminist thought, see Krueger, "Towards Feminism."

Christine's Prologue: An Approach to the Queen's Manuscript

Lori J. Walters

Digital Resources for Studying the Queen's Manuscript

Christine de Pizan's *Livre de la cité des dames* (*Book of the City of Ladies*) and *Livre des trois vertus* (*Book of the Three Virtues*) are widely used in literature and women's and gender studies courses. But we are now discovering that Christine's influence was even greater than previously thought. If we have acknowledged her importance as a writer, we have not understood the significance of her role as director of her own scriptorium. Christine not only wrote some forty texts, she also personally produced over fifty of the surviving manuscripts of those texts, and she began, and inspired others to continue, the dissemination of her books to England and throughout the Continent. We are just beginning to understand the extent of the authority of this author and bookmaker, who held a prominent place at the early-fifteenth-century court of King Charles VI and Queen Isabeau de Bavière.[1]

I regularly offer seminars that combine graduate and advanced undergraduate students and feature digital surrogates of medieval manuscripts. I have developed these courses in conjunction with Florida State University's History of Text Technologies Program, which studies the multiple technologies "designed to supplement the fragile human mind by providing a more durable artificial memory system" (hott.fsu.edu/). All these courses call upon the many resources of the Web site devoted to Christine's masterpiece, her so-called Queen's Manuscript, the British Library's Harley MS 4431 (www.pizan.lib.ed.ac.uk/). It is the most extensive and luxuriously illuminated of the four extant collections that Christine assembled for patrons at the French royal court (other large collections that she produced survive in fragmentary form [Ouy et al. 6]). The making of the Queen's Manuscript represented an amazing effort on Christine's part. With 398 folios, each with a recto and a verso, the manuscript is the equivalent of an eight-hundred-page book. Christine not only wrote the manuscript's thirty texts but also oversaw the execution of its extensive iconographic cycle and acted as scribe, textual editor, and planner of its mise-en-page. She likely offered the book to Queen Isabeau as a New Year's Day gift in 1414.

For the Queen's Manuscript Christine composed a ninety-six-verse prologue addressed to the queen to serve as its introduction. The prologue is a simultaneous announcement and distillation of key themes treated by Christine, both a culminating summary and a new beginning. As such, it resembles other well-known prologues in orienting the interpretation of the text to follow.

The *Christine de Pizan Digital Scriptorium* (pizanmanuscripts.org) houses digital versions of all manuscripts of the author's works held at the Bibliothèque

Nationale de France, including detailed codicological information and other metadata. Currently the project is being expanded, with two objectives: to make available all Christine's extant presentation copies (those produced by Christine in her own scriptorium) as well as all manuscripts of her texts produced by others and to link these manuscripts both to the Roman de la Rose *Digital Library*, maintained by Johns Hopkins University's Sheridan Libraries (romandelarose .org), and to Web sites devoted to other texts and authors.

The Prologue as a Guide to the Queen's Manuscript

An important document for understanding the Queen's Manuscript is my transcription of the Middle French prologue and its translation into English and modern French (www.pizan.lib.ed.ac.uk/Translations of Prologue.rtf), which I cite in this essay. The translations make the prologue available for study in a variety of classroom situations. This essay's focus is on using the translations in an advanced seminar centered on Christine and the Queen's Manuscript. But there are ways to integrate such study into courses with a broader range. For example, the English translation makes feasible a comparative study of the dissemination of Christine's text in Tudor England (see Coldiron's essay in this volume). The prologue could be read in a women's and gender studies course in conjunction with David Hult's translation of the letters from the debate on the *Roman de la rose* (49–194).

The following remarks present some of the many ways that the prologue can provide a basis for class discussion of Christine's role as supervisor of the making of the Queen's Manuscript.

Ordonnance

Christine speaks of her *ordonnance*, the ordering or structuring of the texts in the Queen's Manuscript. True to her frequent reference to herself as a compiler, she transforms twenty-nine of her previously composed texts by their placement and layout in the manuscript and adds a table of contents as well as the prologue. The "Table des dictiez en general" ("Table of the Poems in General") occupies two columns and lists thirty entries. Christine's desire to order her collection becomes clear in the prologue's fifth stanza:

> Si l'ay fait, ma dame, ordener
> Depuis que je sceus que assener
> Le devoye à vous, si que ay sceu
> Tout au mieulx, et le parfiner
> D'escripre et bien enluminer
> Dès que vo command en receu

> Selons qu'en mon cuer j'ay conceu
> Qu'il faloit des choses finer
> Pour bien richement l'affiner
> Affin que fust apperceü
> Que je mets povoir, force et sceu
> Pour vo bon vueil enteriner. (lines 49–60)

> I therefore had it prepared, Madame, as soon as I knew I had to present it to you, so that I could completely finish the writing and illuminate it well, as soon as I received the order to do so from you. [I did so] after having understood in my heart that I had to bring things to a good end by finishing them so richly, so that it be noted that I put my power, force, and knowledge into the full accomplishment of your good wishes.

In this stanza Christine plays on the resonances of the Old and Middle French term *ordonnance*, which can refer to an order or commission from a patron. She suggests this meaning when she says to the queen, "Dès que vo command en receu ("as soon as I received the order to do so from you"). A related verb, *ordener*, means "to prepare by ordering." The queen's *ordonnance*, or command, to Christine to produce a collection for her, called forth an *ordonnance*, or ordering, of its constituent texts by her. With this play on a cognate of *ordonnance*, Christine implies to the queen that she has placed the texts in a certain order to give the collection a higher meaning.

Christine has given the Queen's Manuscript clearly marked beginning, middle, and end sections. The beginning is made up of the dedication miniature, the prologue, Christine's author portrait, and the *Cent balades* (*One Hundred Ballades*). The middle comprises the forty-folio *Livre du chemin de lonc estude* (*Book of the Path of Long Study*). The end consists of the *Cent balades d'amant et de dame* (*One Hundred Ballads of a Lover and Lady*); this series of ballades finishes with the "Lai de dame," or "Lai mortel" ("Lady's Lai"; "Mortal Lai"),[2] which also concludes the collection as a whole.

A good class exercise on the ordering of the Queen's Manuscript is to compare it with the organization of the earlier collection that Christine prepared for Queen Isabeau between 1399 and 1405, Chantilly, Musée Condé 492–493 (Ouy et al. 186–212). The Chantilly manuscript lacks a prologue and thus has no informing statement. Also, because Christine designed the Chantilly manuscript in two discrete stages, each of its two sections includes an author portrait: at the *Cent balades*, just as in the Queen's Manuscript, and at the *Livre de la mutacion de Fortune* (*Book of the Mutability of Fortune*), which is absent from the Queen's Manuscript. Authors of the time typically asserted their authority by means of the author portrait. Instructors might guide students to consider some of the following questions: How does Christine have herself portrayed in the author portrait? Besides her manner of dress, how else does she declare her authority in the Chantilly manuscript? What can we suppose the queen to have known and thought about Christine when the author offered her the Queen's Manuscript about a decade after presenting her with the Chantilly manuscript?

Patroness and Author

In the prologue, Christine defines her relationship with her patroness Isabeau. She punctuates the prologue's twelve stanzas with flowery address, beginning in stanza 1, lines 1–3: "Très excellent de grant haultesse / Couronnée, poissant princesse, / Tresnoble roÿne de France" ("Very excellent princess, / crowned, powerful, and of high majesty, / very noble queen of France"). She follows this in stanza 2, lines 13–14, with "Haulte dame, en qui sont tous biens, / Et ma tressouvrainne" ("My lofty and very sovereign lady, / in whom is everything that is good"). She picks up her address to the queen again in stanza 6, line 61, by calling her "très haulte et digne" ("very high and worthy [lady]"). In stanza 8, lines 85–86, she gives the queen a final compliment, calling her "Haulte dame d'atractïon / D'empereurs de digne memoire" ("lofty lady of the line / of emperors of worthy memory"). She concludes by asking for Isabeau's "benigne devocïon" ("benevolent devotion"):

> Qu'en benigne devocïon
> Vous plaise mon entencïon
> Prendre en gré, qui loyale et voire
> Est et sera. (lines 88–91)

> Please accept in benevolent devotion my intention, which is and will be loyal and true.

With the phrase "benigne devocïon," Christine couches her appeal to the queen in the language of religious devotion. When in stanza 2, line 15, she calls herself the queen's "créature," she means that her obligations toward Isabeau are similar to those that, as a Christian, she owes to God (Hult 99n130). She analogically places the queen in the position of her creator. The address of the loyal, adoring subject to the French queen is like that of the pious soul praying to God. Students can be asked to find other examples in the manuscript of analogies between religious devotion to God and the saints and devotion to earthly rulers; the latter were considered God's representatives on earth.

Because authors typically depended on patrons for their livelihood, it is not surprising to find mention of earthly concerns in the manuscript. In the prologue's final stanza, Christine diplomatically expresses her hope of gaining benefits from this transaction with the queen. She refers to the position that she holds at the queen's court in the final verses of stanza 8:

> Et si notoire
> Ceste mienne posicïon
> Vous soit qu'à tousjours mencïon
> Soit de moy en vostre memoire,
> Si que vostre grace m'avoire
> Qu'ayés a moy affectïon . . . (lines 91–96)

> May my position with you be so noteworthy that mention of me is forever present in your memory, so that your favor shows me conclusively that you hold me in your affection.

Through the gift of her book, Christine trusts that she will retain the queen's good graces, and indeed, strengthen her position. I ask my classes to look at the prologue and the dedication miniature placed above it (fol. 3r) to assess both Christine's position and her duties and responsibilities.

To encourage further thinking about patronage and Christine's position with regard to the queen, the class can analyze Christine's representation of her persona—in the prologue, in the dedication miniature, and in the whole volume's 132 miniatures. *Persona* originally signified a mask worn by a performer; it is a constructed image within a highly codified tradition of self-depiction. To analyze her self-representation as author, we can consult the detailed chart "Christine de Pizan mise en scène" in the *Album Christine de Pizan* (Ouy et al. 749). The prologue's capacious three-quarter-page dedication miniature seems to subsume all other dedication miniatures. Students can explore what Christine may imply about the importance of Isabeau's court and the prominent role that she ascribes to herself by placing her portrait and the image of her book dead center in this picture.

I have compiled a summary of the depictions of books and parchment sheets in the Queen's Manuscript (www.pizan.lib.ed.ac.uk/waltersbooksandletters.rtf). The manuscript contains only two other book presentation scenes, the ones heading the *Epistre Othea* (*Othea's Letter to Hector*), dedicated to Louis d'Orléans, and *Le livre du chemin de lonc estude* (*The Book of the Path of Long Study*), dedicated to King Charles VI. Charles VI and Louis were the two most important older men in the queen's life: Charles was her husband, while Louis, her brother-in-law, took over with her the upbringing of the dauphin during the king's frequent bouts of mental illness. Here instructors can prompt students to explore the following questions: What do the Queen's Manuscript's three book presentation scenes imply about the efforts of Isabeau and Christine on behalf of the dauphin? How are those efforts apparent elsewhere in the manuscript?

The notion of judgment is another important consideration. It appears in three judgment poems in the manuscript: *Le livre du debat de deux amans* (*The Book of the Debate of Two Lovers*), *Le livre des trois jugemens* ("The Book of Three Judgments"), and *Le dit de Poissy* (*The Tale of Poissy*). But it is also fundamental to the *Chemin de lonc estude*, where the text's protagonist, also named Christine, brings a debate about the qualities incumbent on a leader to the attention of the king and the dukes. In positioning the *Chemin* at the very center of her collection, does Christine not imply that the *Chemin* should be central to the queen's preoccupations?

The only other text that Christine addressed to a queen or princess was *Le livre des trois vertus*. She dedicated it around 1405 to Marguerite de Guyenne, the wife of Isabeau's son, the dauphin, Louis de Guyenne. When Christine composed her dedication, she could reasonably assume that Marguerite would in due course become the next queen of France. This dedication is preserved in only three manuscripts, none of which was produced by Christine (*Livre des trois vertus* [Willard and Hicks], pp. 3–4). It provides interesting parallels with Christine's dedication to Queen Isabeau in the Queen's Manuscript. Students can compare and contrast how Christine addresses Isabeau and Isabeau's daughter-in-law, Marguerite.

The Epistre Othea, *Illuminated Heart of the Queen's Manuscript*

The *Epistre Othea*, which contains 101 of the collection's 132 miniatures, can be considered to be the manuscript's illuminated heart. As a manual of moral instruction supposedly composed for the Trojan prince Hector, the *Epistre Othea* spotlights the queen's relationship with her son, the dauphin and the heir to the throne. With a beautifully executed miniature heading each of the text's exempla, the *Epistre Othea* was meant to bring the queen's attention to her responsibility for the dauphin's education. In January 1414, when Christine presented the manuscript to the queen, the fifteen-year-old dauphin was likely to soon mount the throne (though these hopes were dashed when he died unexpectedly about two years later). The *Epistre Othea* remained in the manuscript as a permanent reminder to the queen, and to those who would succeed her, of the solicitude owed by queens to heirs to the throne. The luxuriously illuminated *Epistre Othea* fixed the queen's gaze on the need for continued vigilance over Louis, who was known for his riotous living and extravagant habits.

Christine skillfully frames her *Epistre Othea* with miniatures foregrounding her authorial persona as teacher and book producer. In the dedication miniature she offers the finished book to her patron, Louis d'Orléans. In the next miniature Christine likens herself to Othea, the goddess of wisdom, who presents her letter to her son Hector, dressed suggestively as a miniature version of the duke of Orléans, the dauphin's Valois namesake. In the *Othea*'s final miniature (fol. 141r) Christine associates herself with the sibyl, who has Augustus Caesar express his devotion to the Virgin and Child. The sibyl was the prophetess whose books were consulted by Roman emperors. Both Othea and the sibyl are examples of wise women. Teachers might ask students how Christine's use of these two figures suggests her ideas about the Queen's Manuscript as a whole. Students can be directed to her references to herself as a sibyl in other texts, such as *Le livre du duc des vrais amans* (*The Book of the Duke of True Lovers*) and the *Chemin de lonc estude*. Seven of the *Chemin*'s eight miniatures represent Christine as the sibyl's apprentice. As the text occupies the focal middle of the manuscript, this gestures toward Christine's prophetic authority (Tarnowski, "Le geste"; Walters, "Magnifying").

Studying the *Epistre Othea* further opens up the issue of relations between text and image in the Queen's Manuscript. Christine supervised the placement and character of its 132 images, as she notes in two spots in the prologue (lines 18, 52–53). Although Christine was not one of the manuscript's artists, she implies that she supervised the execution of its iconographic cycle.

Students can explore her use of color symbolism, especially the range of meaning of the color blue. In the miniatures in the Queen's Manuscript, blue is worn by Christine herself, by some of her patrons, and by the Virgin Mary.[3] The blue dress Christine typically wears (Ouy et al. 749), compared with that of the Virgin in another miniature (fol. 265r), should incite discussion on how she legitimizes her authority by associating herself with sacred figures. This practice can be likened to her habit of writing her name as a form of the Chi Rho (www.pizan.lib.ed.ac.uk/waltersanagrams.html).

Debating the Roman de la rose

The prologue can be seen as a letter from Christine to the queen. Yet the letter lacks the name of the addressee and the signature of the letter writer. The end of stanza 8 of the prologue implies that Christine was trying to ensure herself a stable position at the queen's court or secure better financial recompense. The term *posicïon* can also be understood to mean that the position, or line of argument, that she took would lead to a position with increased security and financial rewards at court.

Christine's tactics in the prologue become clearer when we consider that this form of unaddressed and unsigned epistle has its positive counterpart in the manuscript's twenty-first text: the letter that heads the *Livre des epistres du debat sus le* Rommant de la rose (*Letters on the debate of the* Romance of the Rose). That dedication (fol. 237a) has a clearly marked addressee and authorial signature: its heading is "la premiere epistre a la royne de France" ("the first epistle to the queen of France"). Christine's name follows, transcribed as a form of Christogram; the first two letters of Christ's name in Greek, *chi* (x) and *rho* (p), are used to write her own name: "Xpine." She closes the letter to Isabeau by signing "La toute tres humble Xpine de Pizan" ("Your most humble and totally devoted servant Xpine de Pizan"). The sacred abbreviation thus authorizes her right to act as a mouthpiece for the divinely sanctioned French monarchy.[4] Christine stakes the claim that in coming to the defense of the feminine sex she is doing God's work, and she portrays this defense as part of her humble and devoted service to the queen.

A look at the prologue to the *Rose* debate letters brings up the issue of mise-en-page. Christine stresses the importance of the letter by situating it beautifully on the page: it is framed by her opening address to the queen and her signature at its end. Students may compare the prologue of the *Rose* debate letters with the prologue of the Queen's Manuscript and discuss how they complement each other and add to our understanding of the collection. The *Rose* debate letters form a compilation within a compilation, which Christine has arranged to make a statement. If students are asked to look at the epistles in David Hult's English translation, *Debate of the* Romance of the Rose, they can determine the significance of her ordering of the letters she has chosen to include and the significance of those she has left out.

Prologue as Prayer

From the prologue's first stanza, Christine indicates that the collection as a whole is a prayer for the queen and for France. She ends the stanza thus:

> Pry Dieu qu'il vous tiengne en souffrance
> Lonc temps vive, et après l'oultrance
> De la mort vous doint la richece
> De Paradis, qui point ne cesse,
> Et au monde sanz decevrance
> Paix, joye et toute recouvrance
> De quanqu'il affiert à léece. (fol. 3a, lines 6–12)
>
> I pray God to give you a long, peaceful life, and that after the last extremity of death He grant you the riches of paradise, which never cease, and [that He grant you] without end, peace, joy, and the recovery of everything that belongs to your happiness in the world.

Christine closes the manuscript with the "Lai de dame," or "Lai mortel" ("Lady's Lai"; "Mortal Lai"), whose narrator and protagonist (the lady) laments the end of a love affair and of her life. Christine describes the lady as hearing "le message / De mort qui corps & visage / Me fera tourner en cendre"/ ("the message / of death, which will turn my body and face / to ashes"). More than anything else, the despairing lady needs a prayer.

In another text in the collection, the *Oroyson Nostre Dame* (fols. 265b–266d; *Prayer to Our Lady*), Christine prays in her own voice. The miniature that accompanies this work shows the author reading a petition to the seated Virgin and Child. Christine prays for the queen in stanza 5:

> Pour nostre roÿne de France
> Te pry qu'elle n'ait ja souffrance
> De peine infernal, et lui donnes
> Joye et paix et tiens en souffrance
> Lonc temps au monde. Après l'oultrance
> De la mort, de son ame ordonnes. (fol. 265d, lines 6–11)
>
> For our queen of France, I pray [to you] that she not suffer the pains of hell. Give her joy and peace and a long life in the world. After death's last extremity call her soul to you. (my trans.)

These verses constitute a prayer for France's queen as she faces death and final judgment; as such, they link the despondent lady of the "Lai de dame" and Queen Isabeau. The use of many of the same terms in the *Oroyson Nostre Dame* and in the prologue's opening stanza suggests that Christine consciously planned for the queen to view the collection as a prayer for the queen's betterment in life and after death.

The Queen's Manuscript as the City of Ladies *Writ Large*

A final feature of the Queen's Manuscript to introduce to students is the presentation of *Le livre de la cité des dames*. By far the longest text in the manuscript (fols. 288c–374a), it is the only one to have an independent table of contents and thus can be regarded as a microcosm of the whole collection.[5] At its end Christine addresses the ladies of her city:

> Et moy vostre servante vous
> soit recommandée en priant dieu, qui par
> sa grace en cestui monde me doint vivre
> et perseverer en son saint service. Et a la
> fin soit piteable a mes grans deffaulx
> et m'ottroit la joye qui a tous jours dure.
> La quelle ainsi par sa grace vous face.
> Amen. (fol. 374a, lines 12–19)
>
> I, your servant, commend myself to you. I pray God to shed his grace on me and allow me to live and persevere in his holy service in this world. May he pardon my great failings and grant me everlasting peace when I die, and may he do likewise unto you. Amen. (my trans.)

As in the Queen's Manuscript as a whole, at the close of the *Cité des dames* Christine prays to God that the queen and other ladies take her advice and avoid the pains of hell; we might thus say that the manuscript is the *City of*

Ladies writ large. The prologue's three-quarter-page dedication miniature visually represents the concept of the city of ladies, those constituted by the queen and her entourage: they grow in wisdom, virtue, and eloquence by reading and discussing books such as Christine's. By means of the order she imposes on the Queen's Manuscript, Christine implicitly asks the queen to heed her message, so that Isabeau can occupy the city's highest turrets of virtue.

If the *Cité des dames* is a condensed version of the Queen's Manuscript, we should compare the illustration of the *Cité* within the collection with that of the collection as a whole. For example, students can reflect on the implications of the final image in the *Cité* text in the manuscript, which shows the Virgin and her circle of female saints entering the city of ladies. This is in some respects similar to the dedication miniature of Christine and other ladies grouped in Isabeau's chamber. Christine associates both the queen and herself with sacred models; I mention to students that Christine calls the Virgin the "chief du sexe femenin" ("head of the female sex") at the beginning of book 3 of the *Cité* (fol. 361d, line 5).

In the class discussion that follows, connections can be made to the interpretation of the Queen's Manuscript as a prayer for the country's betterment. The *Oroyson*'s fourth stanza contains a prayer for the sick king and his ailing kingdom:

> Pour le roy de France te pry
> Qu'en pitié tu oyes le cry
> De ses bons et loyaulx amis,
> Paix et vraye santé descry
> A lui et ou livre l'escry
> Ou Dieu a tous ses esleus mis. (fol. 265c, lines 28–33)

> For the king of France I pray you
> That in compassion you hear the cry
> Of his good and loyal friends,
> Proclaim for him peace and true health
> And write it down in the book
> Where God has placed all his elect. (my trans.)

Christine places this stanza here to remind Isabeau that she still has work to do, because the king is ill and the dauphin has a reputation as a wastrel. At the beginning of 1414, though the queen might have suspected that her husband would never recover his mental faculties, she could not have known that he would remain largely incapacitated until his death in 1422. In addition, she could not have known that the dauphin would soon die, as would his younger brother and successor, Jean de Touraine. Isabeau would have to direct prayers for the survival and success of her sixth and youngest son, Charles. After the disastrous 1415 defeat of the French at the Battle of Agincourt and the later English appropriation of the crown, it seemed unlikely that Charles was destined to reign over France. He ultimately secured the throne with what was believed to be divine help in the person of Joan of Arc, the subject of Christine's final poem, *Le ditié de Jeanne d'Arc* (*The Song of Joan of Arc*). King Charles VII would go on to rule for almost four decades, from 1422 to 1461, by the end of which time France would largely rout the English from its territories.

NOTES

[1]The queen is referred to as "Isabeau" throughout this essay, in keeping with the standard historical form of the name and for the sake of continuity vis-à-vis other contributions in the volume. But Christine writes the name as "Ysabel" both in the Queen's Manuscript and in all other presentation copies. The queen herself always signed her name "Ysabel," and this was the way her name was written on her official seal (Verdon 21, 213). See my "The Queen's Manuscript (London, British Library, Harley 4431) as a Monument to Peace" (87, 106–09) for the significance of the queen's name.

[2]The title means that it is the *lai* of each and every human being.

[3]For the historic and symbolic uses of the color blue, see Pastoureau.

[4]For a study of the three ways that Christine writes her name in the Queen's Manuscript, see my "Signatures and Anagrams in the Queen's Manuscript (London, British Library, Harley MS 4431)" (www.pizan.lib.ed.ac.uk/waltersanagrams.html).

[5]A separate table introduces each of the text's three sections: see Ouy et al. 334–35.

The *Ditié de Jehanne d'Arc* and the Poet's Passion

Nadia Margolis

Christine de Pizan's *Ditié de Jehanne d'Arc* (31 July 1429; *The Tale of Joan of Arc*) is the author's last known and crowning work—crowning at least ideologically.[1] While overtly public and political in its aims, the poem is also intensely personal: Joan is the answer to the aging poet's prayers—ending her previous work, the sober *Heures de contemplacion sur la passion de Nostre Seigneur* (*Hours of Contemplation on the Passion of Our Lord*) of a decade earlier, composed when France's situation, and Christine's life, despite much professional renown, seemed at their bleakest. The newfound light and joy permeating the *Ditié* and works by such contemporaries as Alain Chartier welcome the arrival of France's savior (Dulac, "Un écrit militant" 118, 130). Joan also fulfills Christine's long-frustrated conviction that her adopted country would be redeemed, and by a woman, thereby redressing the stigma of Eve and the Fall cultivated by the Church. The *Ditié* is the only nonanonymous work to celebrate Joan in French during the heroine's lifetime. Addressed to a multiplicity of readers or listeners, ranging from nobles to soldiers, on both sides of the Hundred Years War, its use of voice and register varies considerably from stanza to stanza, sometimes deliberately to shock its audience though primarily to reassure the French about Joan's miraculous victories. This miracle and its legitimacy, along with its corresponding legitimation of Charles VII, form the story line and main message of the poem.

The poem's stylistic disparateness and nonlinear development of themes, together with its many historical and literary-folkloric allusions and textual echoes, pose multiple pedagogical challenges for students of all levels, in classes conducted either in French or English. And yet the *Ditié*'s complexity can be rendered accessible and universal; students need not understand every detail to appreciate its significance and verve. It can be taught in courses in several disciplines: medieval history (as an eyewitness document), religion (as visionary or prophetic literature), political science (the rise of nationalism and patriotism), rhetoric, besides the more predictable women's literature survey, French medieval civilization courses, and courses—increasingly common—devoted entirely to Joan's literary, historical, and visual iconography through the ages.

Introducing the Historical Background

Regardless of the type of course in which the *Ditié* figures, certain background information, must be presented and intertwined with the poem's exposition (e.g., *Ditié* [Kennedy and Varty] 60–73; Wood 125–50). I introduce the poem by first outlining the signal events of the Hundred Years War and their impact.

I also draw connections between France's history and Christine's life, particularly because, at least from her *Livre de la mutacion de Fortune* (*Book of the Mutability of Fortune*), completed in 1403, the poet often portrays her feelings and fortunes as microcosmic mirrors of current events. To accompany this background information, I attempt a lively, panoramic recreation of Christine's and Joan's milieus through a dozen images from contemporary chronicle manuscripts and through extracts of historical and literary writings of the early fifteenth century in France and England.

My rapid, simplified tableau defines the Hundred Years War as a multiphase war of dynastic succession between France and England. Because Christine alludes to it repeatedly in the *Ditié*, in the summary that follows I have inserted relevant stanza numbers. The war began in 1337, when Philip VI, first of the Valois line, after assuming the French throne and thus thwarting Edward III of England's claim to it, continued aggressive policies toward Edward, particularly the confiscation of Aquitaine (the southwestern French region brought under English rule by another consequential woman, Eleanor of Aquitaine, on her marriage to Henry II Plantagenet in 1152). Although this long conflict began as a military stalemate between Edward and Philip, several crucial battles ensued—Crécy (1346), Poitiers (1356), and Agincourt (1415)—each increasingly disastrous for France territorially and, more profoundly, for its existence as a sovereign kingdom with its own dynastic purity, as symbolized by the fleur-de-lis (*Ditié*, stanza 12, line 96). The fact that almost every military victory of England over France was quasi-miraculous—especially Henry V's at Agincourt, since France had the larger, better-equipped army—strengthened England's claim to rule France by divine right and, with a bit of Plantagenet-Valois lineage tweaking, by royal blood (here I show a slide of the pro-English Laurent Calot's ingeniously subverted fleur-de-lis diagram from c. 1423 to justify Henry V's legitimacy over Charles VI's son, the dauphin [Hinkle 66–75]). The dauphin's path to becoming King Charles VII was menaced by several factors. Most consequential among these was his true paternity, doubted even by his own mother, Queen Isabeau: was he the son of Charles VI and thus rightful heir or was he actually sired by Charles VI's brother and the queen's supposed lover, the ambitious, brilliant, but headstrong Louis, duke of Orléans? Louis's smoldering conflict with cousin John the Fearless, duke of Burgundy, would reach a full blaze during the ensuing decade (resulting in the death of both) and deeply divide the kingdom between Armagnacs and Burgundians as to who should rule France. Based on her experience in composing the *Livre des fais et bonnes meurs du sage roy Charles V* (1404; *Book of Deeds and Good Practices of the Wise King Charles V*), memorializing the dauphin's grandfather, Christine was well versed in kingship theory and practice, along with civil and personal turmoil, as the contexts for the dauphin's problems (*Ditié*, stanzas 5, 13, 16).

Thus, by the time of Joan's birth (c. 1413; *Ditié*, stanza 35), France was suffering unrest from within: divided between the Burgundians—led by John the Fearless—and the Armagnacs, first led by Louis, duke of Orléans, then the dauphin Charles. This discord would soon benefit the English takeover of the kingdom. After John had Louis assassinated in Paris in 1407, Armagnacs and Burgundians engaged in all-out civil war. In 1418, the Burgundians took over Paris, massacring many Armagnacs, which forced the dauphin to flee southwestward, eventually to Château de Chinon. The Armagnacs avenged Burgundian misdeeds, including the assassination of the duke of Orléans, by murdering John of Burgundy in 1419, at Montereau Bridge, where he and the dauphin were supposed to meet to negotiate peace. Charles's involvement in this crime not only heightened suspicions that he was Louis's son but also so infuriated John's son, Duke Philip the Good, that this new duke of Burgundy allied with Henry V against Charles. Since by this time Philip's Burgundian duchy extended throughout modern-day Netherlands, Belgium, Luxembourg, and much of northeastern France and Henry controlled much of western France, Charles's holdings had diminished severely. Yet in these Anglo-Burgundian occupied territories, Joan's village of Domremy and nearby Vaucouleurs, on the northeastern frontier, remained one of the few holdouts against the occupation. Fiercely loyal to Charles as the rightful king, Christine would liken the French to the Israelites and the English to Pharoah and the Egyptians (stanza 23), associating Joan with Moses (23), then Joshua (25).

Christine too had to flee Paris to avoid being slaughtered with other prominent Parisian literati in 1418. The situation was so perilous that she could not count on protection from her previous Burgundian patronage or from her son Jean's official connections. She probably retreated to the Royal Dominican abbey of Poissy, where her daughter was a nun and where Christine is thought to have remained for the rest of her life (though there is recent scholarly doubt about this [Green, "Was Christine at Poissy?"]). By this time she had abandoned all lyric poetry and even polemical prose and verse in favor of more spiritual prose, namely the *Epistre de la prison de vie humaine* (*Letter Concerning the Prison of Human Life*), dedicated to Duchess Marie of Berry and intended to console other widows of Agincourt. A few years later Christine penned the *Heures de contemplacion*, probably between 1420 and 1425, perhaps to console herself for the death of her son Jean (Margolis, *Introduction* 123). Such misfortune contributed to her weeping and the cold, dark winter referred to in *Ditié* stanzas 1–4, which Joan's arrival would transform into laughter and sunny springtime, although Paris remains uncertain even as she writes the *Ditié* (stanza 53), inveighing against the fallen capital, other "rebel cities" ("villes rebelles"; stanza 57, line 449) and their Burgundian occupiers (54–57) in a manner reminiscent of Dante's judgments against Florence and Pisa (*Inferno*, canto 26, lines 1–12; canto 33, lines 79–84).

Also in 1420, France's sovereignty received its worst blow: the Treaty of Troyes, in which the dauphin's father, the mentally ill King Charles VI, in the wake of Henry's conquest of all of Normandy and the new Anglo-Burgundian alliance, signed away his son's inheritance to Henry V of England, who would marry the dauphin's sister, Catherine, and then, on Charles VI's death, assume the French throne, stripping the dauphin of all claims. However, Charles VI and Henry V died in the same year, 1422, leaving the latter's infant son to become Henry VI, with the duke of Bedford acting as regent. Charles, meanwhile, exiled at Chinon, assumed the title of Charles VII and presided dejectedly over a court whose treasury was fast being depleted by several unsuccessful wars to regain his territories.

Another historical angle important for understanding the poem is the aftermath of the Great Schism (1378–1417). Involving two adversarial popes—one in Avignon, France, and one in Rome—the schism's effect, like its cause, was more political than theological. The Council of Constance's resolution of it in 1416–18 by returning the legitimate papacy to Rome signaled France's defeat by its other major rival, Italy. The resultant dissolution of the Avignon papacy eroded France's self-image as a kingdom chosen by God in a supramilitary way—just after the loss at Agincourt. To the theologians of the University of Paris, it meant a considerable loss of prestige: they could no longer consider themselves God's brain trust and exclusive messengers. Their smarting resentment, together with the Burgundian takeover of Paris, would account for the University of Paris's circumspect reception of Joan's claim to direct ties to God during her trial in 1429 and, later, its participation in her martyrdom at Rouen. However, for now, at least one Armagnac noble asked Joan to advise him of her papal preference (Wood 126). Christine also evokes Joan as healer of the wounds left by the schism (*Ditié*, stanza 42), a crisis she had lamented in the *Mutacion* (lines 4294–302).

Joan's upbringing, among relatively comfortable peasants in the village of Domremy, near the German border, imbued Joan with not only a simple, steadfast piety (stanza 32) but also a profound patriotism, cultivated at a safe distance from corrupt centers of church and state powers (Wood 130)—her patriotism is somewhat analogous to Christine's zeal as an adoptive citizen. Interestingly enough, the saints who became Joan's guiding voices and filled her visions from about midsummer 1424—Michael, Margaret, and Catherine—are consolidated by Christine into one anonymous "angel of the Lord" ("l'ange de Dieu"; stanza 29, line 227). While these saints and the Virgin Mary were revered in church, the villagers also held pre-Christian folk festivals at supposedly enchanted fountains and trees in the neighboring oak forest in spring, at harvest, and at other seasonal rituals uniting lord and peasant. Joan and her apologists would exploit her oak-forest origins to help validate her as the fulfillment of the so-called Merlin prophecy attributed to the twelfth-century historian Geoffrey of Monmouth—"From out of the oak forest a maiden shall come to give care to healing" ("Ex nemore canuto puella eliminabitur ut medelae curam adhibeat"; qtd. in *Ditié* 68)—and alluded to by Christine (*Ditié*, stanza 31), while anti-Joan propagandists would attempt to use Joan's worship of forest deities as evidence of witchcraft and thereby discredit her victories (Jeay).

But it would prove difficult for even the most waspish detractor to harm Joan's general charisma (in the true sense of the word). Her charisma was evident in her glowing self-assurance as savior of France, divinely appointed by her saints and symbolized by her wearing of male attire and by correctly announcing the dauphin's defeat at the Battle of the Herrings, before any messenger could have reached her. Baudricourt, the local constable, after her persistent visits, provided her with armor and a horse for her journey to interview the dauphin at Chinon, whom she recognized even though he disguised himself for their first meeting at his court. Joan confided to him a secret that restored his self-confidence even before the Siege of Orléans. At this time, in March 1429, she mysteriously knew of a special sword—supposedly once wielded by the earlier French savior, Charles Martel, and possibly even by Alexander the Great—buried at the monastery of Saint-Catherine-de-Fierbois. There circulated several prophecies—credited variously to Merlin, the Sibyl, and the Venerable Bede (*Ditié*, stanza 31)—among them, in addition to the Merlin prophecy, that France would be lost by a woman (Queen Isabeau's alleged profligacy fits here) and saved by a maiden (Joan, whose virginity was confirmed by none less than Yolanda of Aragon, the dauphin's powerful, strongly supportive mother-in-law). In addition, there was the cult of the Nine Worthies (Les Neuf Preux), commemorating heroes from classical antiquity, the Old Testament, and medieval legend, alongside which was developing a pantheon of female counterparts, the Nine Worthy Ladies (Les Neuf Preuses), to which Christine adds Joan, first to the feminine register, then boldly to the masculine (*Ditié*, stanzas 25, 28, 36). Furthermore, the theologians interrogating Joan at the royally mandated pre-Orléans examination at Poitiers (March 1429) found precedents in Old Testament heroines: Judith, Esther, and Deborah, as does Christine (stanza 28)—resuscitating part of her pantheon from the *Roman de la rose* debate from 1401–02 (*Le débat* [ed. Hicks] 19). The Poitiers theologians thus concluded that Joan's clothing, visions and voices, and professed mission—to crown the dauphin at Reims and to drive out the English—were not satanically inspired and could well be from God (*Ditié*, stanzas 29–30). In late April 1429, Joan sent her famous letter to the English commanders at Orléans, warning Henry and Bedford to leave Orléans and the rest of France or be forced to do so by extreme violence and "hahay" ("uproar"; "Lettre"; my trans.) so that Charles VII might rightly rule. The bold diction of this and some of Joan's other letters occasionally resembles that of Christine's polemical prose and verse.

The most spectacular proof of all was Joan's victory at Orléans on 8 May 1429, lifting the seven-month siege and driving the English from the city (*Ditié*, stanza 33). Other triumphs followed, most notably at Patay, considered the mirror opposite of Agincourt and thus perfect vengeance for the French. In reality, conquering the towns along the Loire was the only way Joan could convince the timid (or calculating) Charles to go to Reims for his coronation on 17 July, which Christine represents only favorably (stanzas 48–52) with confident, if incorrect, predictions of Joan's takeover of Paris (stanzas 54–56). Christine would have known of the battles and even the gist of the Poitiers examination from her various contacts, particularly her onetime ally in the *Roman de la rose* debate and eminent theologian, Jean Gerson. As one of the Poitiers interrogators, and former chancellor of the University of Paris, Gerson had written the most positive and decisive opinion on Joan.

Introducing the Poem's Literary Aspects

As a work of poetic art, the *Ditié*'s greatness and weakness derive from its overwhelming sense of political and personal urgency: the aged Christine, emerging from sorrowful retirement as a venerable sibyl, thanks divine Providence for France's good fortune, of which Joan is demonstrably a major part. In turn, Christine reaffirms Charles's kingship and France's victory over England as acts of God. Likewise, Joan incarnates Christine's lifelong contention that women can lead to redemption where men have failed. Stanza 34 begins with almost defiant glee: "Hee! quel honneur au femenin/ sexe!" ("Hey! What honor for the feminine sex!"; lines 265–66). These verses nearly echo the formula celebrating Charles's legitimacy in stanza 12, lines 87–89: "O quel honneur à la couronne / de France par divine preuve!" (Oh, what honor for the French / crown by divine proof!"). Yet, unlike Christine's truly didactic works, the *Ditié* is slow to specify its true message and goal as it moves among its various discursive levels, inserting, abandoning, then returning to key themes. This spontaneous, scattershot effect is gradually revealed to be deliberate, because Christine is less concerned to contribute yet another treatise or classically structured paean than she is to capture and manipulate positively the "crucial feeling of the moment" (Dulac, "Un écrit militant" 18–19).

Hence Christine's choice of genre: a poem steeped in orality—sound bites to capture the popular ear and heart, not another play-it-safe prose treatise for the clerkly elite—that conveys how this elite might defend Joan (*Ditié*, stanza 7). Its title, bestowed not by her but by later editors, is striking for being labeled a *ditié* and for identifying its subject as "Jehanne d'Arc," Middle French for Joan of Arc, instead of "la Pucelle d'Orléans" ("the Maid of Orléans"), the latter used by Christine, her contemporaries, and Joan herself, stressing the power of the saint's virginity. The term *ditié*, which Christine herself used to characterize her poem (stanza 61, line 482), indicates any verse piece or, generally, any literary composition, similar to the narrative dit ("tale"). Such genres evolved because they were mostly free of formalistic constraints, compared with ballades, rondeaux, and virelays. Christine's *Ditié* comprises 488 verses in sixty-one quatrains in (more or less) octosyllabic verse, each quatrain following the rhyme scheme *ababbcbc*; it is otherwise quite unfettered. This freedom allowed for a fresher expression of feeling while Christine treated serious ideas and narratives in the manner of a récit. So the *Ditié* contains attributes of both hymn and tale (Dulac, "Un écrit militant" 118). Despite her past prolific accomplishments in even the most restrictive poetic genres—only once, in the *Mutacion*, was she forced to resort briefly to prose, claiming illness and deadline pressure—

Christine required special license for this poem. The verse rhythms are sometimes painfully—or provocatively—uneven, sometimes clumsy, as are some rhymes and verse structures, replete with anacoluthon (*Ditié* 16–20). The work was likely composed quickly: only two complete fifteenth-century manuscripts are known and there are no known lavish presentation copies such as the ones Christine made for her major works during the prime of her career. It is possible that the poem was read aloud on some special, public occasion that required easy legibility, as exhibited in the extant copies. To illustrate this legibility for students, I often show a richly illuminated title page from a presentation copy of one of Christine's earlier works alongside a page from a *Ditié* manuscript and then have students comment on the contrasting manuscript types and speculate about their role in developing the author's relation to her public.

Why such urgency, beyond elation, in the wake of miraculous victory? Why the recurrent need to prove Joan's truth? Such mass doubt arose, paradoxically, when her shocking triumphs at Orléans and elsewhere caused the pro-English propagandists to redouble their calumnies of her as a witch, a harlot of the Armagnacs, and so forth. Christine astutely senses that Joan was always on trial in one way or another because of her extraordinary presence and achievements. In stanzas 3 through 15 alone, Christine's lexicon of doubt and proof—words denoting belief, doubt, verification, legitimacy, reassurance: for example, "veü de droit oil" (line 20), "legitime" (34), "voirement" (81), "evident" (83), "voire" (87), "divine preuve" (90), "si croy fermement" (113)—asserts itself at least fifteen times, all to confirm Joan as a miracle of divine Providence. This semantic frequency appears to continue throughout the *Ditié*, right to the end.

With my most advanced students I attempt to reconstruct the kinds of doubts Christine tries to assuage for her fellow French citizens, rather in the way scholars reconstructed from her rebuttal Jean de Montreuil's lost first letter praising Jean de Meun in the *Roman de la rose* debate:

What is the poet's standing to make such a proclamation, through her self-presentationin the *Ditié*? (stanzas 1–4, 7)

Was Joan, a woman who dressed as a knight, sent by God or Satan? (22, 29, 32)

Was her Orléans victory more than a fluke? (14, 33, 43)

Is she truly the virgin savior of the ancient prophecies and precursors? (28, 31)

Is Charles the rightful king, despite convincing English claims, as guaranteed by Joan? (5–6, 13, 48–50, 59–60)

Are the French thus chosen by God, to whom they must give thanks? (7–12, 17–20)

Are the "Englecherie" (the English and their Burgundian allies) really cursed by God? (The answer Christine provides to this question also applies to doubters of the previous assertions: yes, as the infidel, rebels, misguided and blind people, doubters.) (39–41, 45–47, 51–58, 61)

Interestingly, and poignantly, for all her patriotic, visionary élan, Christine concludes on a wary note; she does not expect to have convinced her whole audience. She knows that some malcontents will remain who "cannot look at the light" ("[n]e puet regarder la lumiere"; stanza 61, line 488).

Such an exercise not only encourages students to engage more actively with the poem's message but also initiates them into how scholars think. Furthermore, while the *Rose* debate involved the defamation of women and an author's moral responsibility to his or her public, Christine's *Ditié* incorporates these questions in a far broader scope, one encompassing nationalism and natural versus supernatural or divine forces. For if in the debate the younger Christine is the daring verbal activist countering the "inflammatory words" ("mots actisans") of Jean de Meun's character, Genius, against women (*Le débat* [ed. Hicks] 16),[2] in the *Ditié* she has honed her passion into more effective verbal agency ("parole agissante") to attain the broader goal of actually steering history, not just discourse, onto the right path (Dulac, "Un écrit militant" 120).

Angus Kennedy and Kenneth Varty delineate the *Ditié*'s major themes in the commentary of their edition. However, one primary theme I like to supplement—and this is but one example of what can be accomplished in class—is that of Joan's role as healer of France's ailing (male) body politic (from Charles VI's mental illness and beyond) through her pure, virginal (female) body; she also heals as a nourishing mother (stanzas 24, 35, 52), by her men's bodily sacrifice of "blood, body, and life exposed [to danger]" ("sanc, corps, et vie exposez"; stanza 38, line 297), and through the blood of slain Englishmen (41, 58). In this depiction, Christine's poem amplifies Joan's capacity as a woman beyond the Christian ideal of virginity (Lee Dow 239–43) and enriches the pagan image of a militant Amazon, though without actually using the term (whereas she did copiously in the *Mutacion*), preferring the equivalent *preux/preuse*. Most concisely, stanza 24 trenchantly intermingles the contradictory aspects of Joan's womanliness by rhyming *pucelle* ("maiden"; line 186) with *mamelle* ("breast"; line 189) around lines invoking Joan's God-given powers as France's "champion" (lines 187–88) who suckles France on the milk of peace, and then returns to Joan's prowess at defeating the *gent rebelle* ("rebellious people" [i.e., the refractory English]). When Christine dares to mimic others' incertitude or dismay about this as "oultre nature" ("beyond nature"; stanza 24, line 192), she certifies, as she does repeatedly throughout her poem, that it is from God's power and not Satan's (line 187).

Relative to the body-politic theme are Christine's frequent allusions to hierarchy, from paradise to hell (stanza 52), from God to mortal serf (46–47)—beyond those of social class and the body politic. One example is the hierarchy of Joan's mission, which Christine envisions as transcending the well-known expulsion of the English and continuing to national war and then holy war, in which Joan and Charles will reunify the Church while destroying the Saracens and other heretics (stanza 42). And yet Christine finally promises forgiveness and peace, by Charles and God, to all who follow king and God (stanzas 59–60).

The *Ditié* thus acts also as a sequel, not only to the *Heures de contemplacion* but also to the *Chemin de lonc estude* (1402–03; *The Path of Long Study*), to resolve the unanswered question driving the *Chemin*'s debate on who would be the ideal prince. After about three more decades of war, Christine—the allegorically appointed messenger-scribe in the *Chemin*—is ready to provide the answer in the *Ditié*. The ideal monarch is Charles VII, to whom Joan is God's messenger, comparable to Gideon (stanza 27, lines 209–13) as part of the preexisting second Charlemagne prophecy augmented by the poet's repeated linking of Charles VII with the ninth-century Frankish emperor (stanzas 6, 16, 42–43).

Christine's *Ditié*, a humbly clad summa of her oeuvre, makes its finest contribution by merging the cult of Joan and the cult of woman with the cult of the nation of France, well before the time when most nonmedievalists mark the birth of this last concept.[3] Such civic-minded intelligence, arguably harking back to Christine's roots in Italian humanism, fused with subjective, yet universal, emotion and lyricism, characterizes her cult of the poet. Daisy Delogu (*Allegorical Bodies* 167–78) discerns in these themes the paradox (hypocrisy?) of how France—traditionally proud to self-allegorize as spiritually and even bodily feminine yet, per Salic law, ruled only by male monarchs—inscribes itself, first gloriously in Joan's bigendered charisma, as celebrated by Christine and later contemporaries, and then tragically, after the *Ditié* (and, we hope, after Christine's death), in the cruelty of Joan's trial, execution, and postmortem treatment.

Students may also benefit from some knowledge of the poem's modern reception history. Critical opinion was rather negative among its first critics, in part because of the faulty early-nineteenth-century editions (*Ditié* 6–8). Nineteenth-century admirers of Christine's work were disappointed by the *Ditié*'s inferiority compared with her elegant lyric poetry. Thanks especially to better editions and translations, reaction is more favorable and sometimes highly enthusiastic (16–20). The *Ditié*'s political message also resonated through the modern era into World War II, through the works of some French Resistance authors and, outside France, exemplified by none less than the German Marxist playwright Bertolt Brecht (*Die heilige Johanna der Schlachthöfe* ["Saint Joan of the Stockyards"]) and Japanese antiwar novelist Jun Ishikawa (*The Bodhisattva*).

Essential Criticism

For further background information, Deborah Fraioli's *Joan of Arc: The Early Debate* analyzes the *Ditié* in context for medievalists. Charles T. Wood's *Joan of Arc and Richard III* (125–50) covers a great deal of background of Joan's story, while my chapter "Joan of Arc" for the *Cambridge Companion to Medieval Women's Writing* (256–66) and my *Introduction to Christine de Pizan* (26–27, 80–83, 155) simplify Wood's, Fraioli's, and others' arguments while contextualizing Joan's letters and Christine's *Ditié*. Kevin Brownlee's "Structures of Authority" and Christine McWebb's "Joan of Arc and Christine de Pizan" both incorporate literary theory. Liliane Dulac's classic essay "Un écrit militant" endures as an indispensable analysis for advanced francophone readers. Delogu's recent political-literary analysis, *Allegorical Bodies: Power and Gender in Late Medieval France*, will inspire the more sophisticated students. Craig Taylor's *Joan of Arc: La Pucelle* remains the most complete and reliable source for original texts and English translations of Joan's letters and other pertinent documents.

NOTES

[1] This essay cites the critical edition and translation of the *Ditié* by Kennedy and Varty.

[2] See also Solterer, "'Flaming Words.'"

[3] See D. A. Bell on the development of the cult of the nation in France, which Bell assigns to the period 1600–1800.

NOTES ON CONTRIBUTORS

Barbara K. Altmann is provost and professor of French at Bucknell University. She is the editor of *The Debate Poems of Christine de Pizan* (1998) and coeditor, with Deborah McGrady, of *Christine de Pizan: A Casebook* (2003). She is also the author of essays on late medieval French literature from Guillaume de Machaut to Alain Chartier, with a particular focus on lyric and debate poetry, epic, manuscript transmission, and the reception of medieval literature by later periods.

Mark Aussems holds master's degrees in medieval studies (Utrecht University) and book and manuscript studies (University of Amsterdam). In 2014, he received his PhD from the University of Edinburgh with a thesis on digital palaeography and Christine de Pizan's original manuscripts.

Patricia E. Black is professor of French at California State University, Chico. She is the author of essays on the medieval French epic, Rumi and the allegory, and the *Roman de la rose*, among others. Currently she is preparing an essay on the *Prise d'Orange*.

Renate Blumenfeld-Kosinski is distinguished professor of French at the University of Pittsburgh. She is the coeditor, with Kevin Brownlee, of *The Selected Writings of Christine de Pizan* (1997) and the author of *Poets, Saints, and Visionaries of the Great Schism, 1378–1417* (2006); *Two Women of the Great Schism* (Constance de Rabastens and Ursulina of Parma), with Bruce Venarde (2010); and *The Strange Case of Ermine de Reims: A Medieval Woman between Demons and Saints* (2015).

A. E. B. Coldiron, Berry Chair in English Literature at the University of St. Andrews (UK), is the author of *Printers without Borders: Translation and Textuality in the Renaissance* (2015); *English Printing, Verse Translation, and the Battle of the Sexes, 1476–1557* (2009); *Canon, Period, and the Poetry of Charles of Orleans: Found in Translation* (2000); and essays on Renaissance and late medieval literature, translation, poetics, and textuality.

Theresa Coletti is professor of English and distinguished scholar-teacher at the University of Maryland. Her scholarship focuses on medieval drama, medieval women writers, late medieval religion and spirituality, medievalism, and the historical novel. She is the author of *Naming the Rose: Eco, Medieval Signs, and Modern* (1988) and *Mary Magdalene and the Drama of Saints: Theater, Gender and Religion in Late Medieval England* (2004).

Daisy Delogu is professor of French at the University of Chicago. She is the author of *Theorizing the Ideal Sovereign: The Rise of the French Vernacular Royal Biography* (2008), of *Allegorical Bodies: Power and Gender in Late Medieval France* (2015), and coeditor, with Joan E. McRae and Emma Cayley, of *A Companion to Alain Chartier, c. 1385–1430: Father of French Eloquence* (2015). Her interests include practices of allegorical reading and writing, medieval debating literature and culture, and questions of identity and performance.

Susan J. Dudash is assistant director of the Arizona Center for Medieval and Renaissance Studies (ACMRS), assistant director of ACMRS Publications, and managing editor of *Early Modern Women: An Interdisciplinary Journal*. She is a recipient of awards from the Mellon Foundation, Medieval Institute at the University of Notre Dame, Pontifical Institute of Mediaeval Studies, and National Endowment for the Humanities. Her research and publications explore the intersection of late medieval French literature and politics, with a focus on social-class conflict, genre theory, and the art of war in the works of Christine de Pizan and her contemporaries.

Julia Simms Holderness has taught at Johns Hopkins, Michigan State, Wellesley, and most recently Boston University, where she led seminars on memory and national identity in medieval France. She has written widely on Christine de Pizan and other early women writers and in 2010 coedited, with Catherine Montfort and Laurence M. Porter, a special issue of *Women in French* entitled *Cooperation and Competition in Communities of Women*.

David F. Hult is professor of French at the University of California, Berkeley. He has published widely on medieval fiction, extending from the romances of Chrétien de Troyes to the courtly works of Alain Chartier and including meditations on editorial theory and practice. He is the translator of the *Debate of the* Romance of the Rose (2010).

Roberta L. Krueger is Burgess Professor of French at Hamilton College. She is the author of *Women Readers and the Ideology of Gender in Old French Verse Romance*, the editor of *The Cambridge Companion to Medieval Romance*, and essays on late medieval conduct literature. She is the translator, with Jane H. M. Taylor, of Antoine de la Sale's didactic romance *Jean de Saintré*.

Mary Gibbons Landor was an art historian and independent scholar. She taught courses on Italian Renaissance art at Vassar and Baruch Colleges and published *Giambologna: Narrator of the Catholic Reformation* (1998). She presented papers on Christine de Pizan at the Medieval Institute, the University of Western Michigan, Kalamazoo, and at conferences of the International Christine de Pizan Society. Her interest focused on the relation between image and text in Christine's oeuvre. She died in 2017.

Nadia Margolis retired from the French and Medieval Studies programs at Mount Holyoke College in 2014 but remains an active medieval scholar and teacher after relocating to Rockland, Maine. She has published studies, translations, and coedited volumes primarily on Christine de Pizan and Joan of Arc. She is the author of *An Introduction to Christine de Pizan*.

Deborah McGrady is associate professor of French at the University of Virginia. She is the coeditor of *Christine de Pizan: A Casebook* (2003) and the author of essays on late medieval francophone literature with particular attention given to the topics of readership, manuscript studies, patronage dynamics, visual culture, and poets as political agents. Her forthcoming book, *The Writer's Gift or the Patron's Pleasure? The Literary Economy in Late Medieval France*, explores literary exchange dynamics during the reigns of Charles V and Charles VI.

Cary J. Nederman is professor of political science at Texas A&M University. He is the coeditor, with Karen Bollermann and Thomas Izbicki, of *Religion, Power, and Re-*

sistance from the Eleventh to the Sixteenth Centuries: Playing the Heresy Card (2014) among his twenty-three books. He has published over one hundred articles and book chapters in political science, history, philosophy, and medieval studies.

Christine Reno is professor emerita of French and francophone studies at Vassar College. She is the coauthor, with Gilbert Ouy and Inès Villela-Petit, of the *Album Christine de Pizan* (2012), a study of the surviving original manuscripts of Christine de Pizan's works; the coeditor, with Liliane Dulac, of *Le Livre de l'advision Cristine* (2001); and the coeditor, with Bernard Ribémont, of a new edition of Christine's *Sept psaumes allegorisés* (2017).

Jeff Rider is professor of Romance languages and literatures and medieval studies at Wesleyan University. He is the coeditor of *The Inner Life of Women in Medieval Romance Literature: Grief, Guilt and Hypocrisy* (2011) and *Obscurity in Medieval Texts* (2013); the editor and translator of the thirteenth-century *Lai du conseil* (2013), and the translator of Galbert of Bruges's *The Murder, Betrayal, and Slaughter of the Glorious Charles, Count of Flanders* (2013).

Karen Robertson is senior lecturer of English and women's studies at Vassar College. She is the coeditor, with Susan Frye, of *Maids and Mistresses, Cousins and Queens: Women's Alliances in Early Modern England*. She writes on early modern drama and is completing a monograph entitled "Pocahontas at the Masque."

Benjamin M. Semple is professor of modern languages at Gonzaga University, where he directs the French program. His interests include medieval literature, language pedagogy, and cinema. He is the author of essays on Christine de Pizan and has served as the president of the North American Branch of the International Christine de Pizan Society.

Andrea Tarnowski is associate professor and chair of the Department of French and Italian at Dartmouth College. She is the editor and translator (into modern French) of Christine de Pizan's *Le chemin de longue étude* and coeditor of *Meaning and Its Objects: Material Culture in Medieval and Renaissance France*. She is translating *Le chemin* into English for The Other Voice in Early Modern Europe series, and working on a book conparing the allegorical and political writings of Christine de Pizan, Philippe de Mézières, and Alain Chartier.

Ellen M. Thorington is associate professor of French at Ball State University. Her research interests lie in medieval French poetry and poetics as well as gender studies and digital humanities. She is the author of essays on Christine de Pizan, Marie de France, and Chrétien de Troyes and the coeditor of *Dame Philology's Charrette: Approaching Medieval Textuality through Chrétien's* Lancelot. Her current book project considers women as figures of Wisdom in Old and Middle French literature.

Lori J. Walters is Harry F. Williams Professor of French at Florida State University. She divides her time between Tallahassee and Toronto, where she is a visiting scholar at the university's Center for Medieval Studies. A specialist of the manuscript context of medieval literature, she is working on a book on Christine de Pizan as author and scriptorium head.

David Joseph Wrisley is associate professor of digital humanties at New York University Abu Dhabi. His primary research interests are medieval French literature, Mediterranean studies, and the digital humanities (in particular, mapping and the spatial humanities).

SURVEY PARTICIPANTS

Tracy Adams, *University of Auckland*
Suzanne Akbari, *University of Toronto*
Barbara K. Altmann, *Bucknell University*
Patricia E. Black, *California State University, Chico*
Renate Blumenfeld-Kosinski, *University of Pittsburgh*
Rosalind Brown-Grant, *University of Leeds*
Tom Conley, *Harvard University*
Raymond Cormier, *Longwood University*
Daisy Delogu, *University of Chicago*
Susan J. Dudash, *Arizona Center for Medieval and Renaissance Studies*
Olga Anna Duhl, *Lafayette College*
Karen Fresco, *University of Illinois, Urbana-Champaign*
Kirsten Fudeman, *University of Pittsburgh*
Virginie Greene, *Harvard Unversity*
Kathryn Hall, *Mount San Antonio State*
Dominique Hoche, *Northern State University, Aberdeen*
Sylvia Huot, *Cambridge University*
Jean-Marie Kauth, *Benedictine University*
Christine McWebb, *University of Waterloo*
Leslie Zarker Morgan, *Loyola College, Maryland*
Cary J. Nederman, *Texas A&M University*
Amy Victoria Ogden, *University of Virginia*
Ana Pairet, *Rutgers University*
Lynn Ramey, *Vanderbilt University*
Jeff Rider, *Wesleyan University*
Paul Rockwell, *Amherst College*
Christopher Roman, *Kent State University*
Carolyn Snipes-Hoyt, *Pacific Union College*
Margaret Switten, *Mount Holyoke College*
Fiona Tolhurst, *Alfred University*
Sylvia Tomasch, *Hunter College*
Peter Travis, *Dartmouth College*

WORKS CITED AND CONSULTED

Works by Christine de Pizan

Autres balades. Roy, *Œuvres poétiques*, vol. 1, pp. 207–70.

Balades d'estrange façon. Roy, *Œuvres poétiques*, vol. 1, pp. 119–24.

The Boke of the Cyte of Ladyes. Translated by Brian Anslay, Henry Pepwell, 1521.

The Boke of the Cyte of Ladyes. Translated by Brian Anslay, edited by Hope Johnston, vol. 457, Arizona Center for Medieval and Renaissance Studies, 2014. Medieval and Renaissance Texts and Studies.

The Booke of the Body of Polycye. Translated by John Skot, 1521.

The Book of Deeds of Arms and of Chivalry. Edited by Charity Cannon Willard, translated by Sumner Willard, Pennsylvania State UP, 1999.

The Book of Fayttes of Armes and of Chyualrye. Translated by William Caxton, 1489.

The Book of Fayttes of Armes and of Chyualrye Translated and Printed by William Caxton from the French Original by Christine de Pisan. Edited by A. T. P. Byles, Kraus Reprint, 1988. Originally published by the Early English Text Society, original series 189, 1937.

"*The Book of Fortune's Transformation*." Blumenfeld-Kosinski, *Selected Writings*, pp. 88–109.

"*The Book of Peace*." Blumenfeld-Kosinski, *Selected Writings*, pp. 229–48.

"*The Book of Peace*." Willard, *Writings*, pp. 310–17.

The Book of Peace *by Christine de Pizan*. Edited and translated by Karen Green et al. Pennsylvania State UP, 2008.

"*The Book of the Body Politic*." Blumenfeld-Kosinski, *Selected Writings*, pp. 201–16.

The Book of the Body Politic. Edited and translated by Kate Langdon Forhan, Cambridge UP, 1994.

"*The Book of the Body Politic*." Translated by Diane Bornstein. Willard, *Writings*, pp. 275–91.

"*The Book of the City of Ladies*." Blumenfeld-Kosinski, *Selected Writings*, pp. 116–55.

The Book of the City of Ladies. Translated by Rosalind Brown-Grant, Penguin, 1999.

The Book of the City of Ladies. Translated by Earl Jeffrey Richards, Persea, 1998.

"*The Book of the City of Ladies*." Translated by Earl Jeffrey Richards. Willard, *Writings*, pp. 171–212.

"*The Book of the Deeds and Good Conduct of the Wise King Charles*." Blumenfeld-Kosinski, *Selected Writings*, pp. 113–15.

"*The Book of the Duke of True Lovers*." Translated by Thelma S. Fenster and Nadia Margolis. Willard, *Writings*, pp. 70–81.

"*The Book of the Long Road to Learning*." Translated by Thelma S. Fenster. Willard, *Writings*, pp. 104–08.

The Book of the Mutability of Fortune. Edited and translated by Geri L. Smith, Arizona Center for Medieval and Renaissance Studies, 2017. The Other Voice in Early Modern Europe.

"*The Book of the Three Virtues*." Blumenfeld-Kosinski, *Selected Writings*, pp. 155–73.

Cent balades. Roy, *Œuvres poétiques*, vol. 1, pp. 1–100.

Cent balades d'amant et de dame. Roy, *Œuvres poétiques*, vol. 3, pp. 209–317.

Cent ballades d'amant et de dame. Edited by Jacqueline Cerquiglini, Union Générale d'Editions, 1982.

Le chemin de longue étude. Edited and translated into modern French by Andrea Tarnowski, Librairie Générale Française, 2000. Lettres Gothiques.

Christine de Pizan: Othea's Letter to Hector. Edited and translated by Renate Blumenfeld-Kosinski and Earl Jeffrey Richards, Arizona Center for Medieval and Renaissance Studies, 2017. The Other Voice in Early Modern Europe.

"*Christine de Pizan's* Book of the Deeds and Good Character of King Charles V, the Wise." Translated by Judith Laird, 1996. University of Colorado, PhD dissertation.

"Christine de Pizan's *Epistre à la reine* (1405)." Edited by Angus J. Kennedy, *Revue des langues romanes*, vol. 92, 1988, pp. 253–64.

Christine de Pizan's Letter of Othea to Hector. Translated by Jane Chance, Focus Information Group, 1990.

"Christine de Pizan: *The XV Joys of Our Lady*." Translated by Glenda Wall. *Vox Benedictina*, vol. 2, 1985, pp. 134–47.

"*Christine's Teachings for Her Son, Jean du Castel*." Willard, *Writings*, pp. 59–60.

"*Christine's Vision*." Blumenfeld-Kosinski, *Selected Writings*, pp. 173–201.

The .C. Hystoryes of Troye. Robert Wyer, 1549.

La città delle dame. Edited by Earl Jeffrey Richards, translated into Italian by Patrizia Caraffi, Luni, 1997.

Complaintes amoureuses. Roy, *Œuvres poétiques*, vol. 1, pp. 281–95.

"A *Critical Edition of Christine de Pizan's* Dit de la pastoure." Edited by Mary Virginia Reese, 1992. University of Alabama, PhD dissertation.

Le débat de deux amans. Roy, *Œuvres poétiques*, vol. 2, pp. 49–110.

The Debate Epistles (1401–1402). McWebb, *Debating*, pp. 107–97.

Debate of the Romance of the Rose. Edited and translated by David F. Hult, U of Chicago P, 2010.

The Debate of Two Lovers. *An Anthology of Medieval Love Debate Poetry*, edited and translated by Barbara K. Altmann and R. Barton Palmer, U of Florida P, 2006, pp. 257–306.

"*The Debate of Two Lovers*." McWebb, *Debating*, pp. 94–105.

Le débat sur le Roman de la rose. Translated by Virginie Greene, Champion, 2006.

Le débat sur Le roman de la rose. Edited by Eric Hicks, Champion, 1977. Bibliothèque XVe siècle 43.

"*Le débat sur* Le roman de la rose." Translated into modern French by Thérèse Moreau and Eric Hicks. Polet and Pichois, pp. 138–39.

Le dit de la pastoure. Roy, *Œuvres poétiques*, vol. 2, pp. 223–94.

Le dit de la rose. Fenster and Erler, pp. 91–155.

Le dit de la rose. McWebb, *Debating*, pp. 219–53.

Le dit de la rose. Roy, *Œuvres poétiques*, vol. 2, pp. 29–48.

Ditié de Jehanne d'Arc. Edited and translated by Angus J. Kennedy and Kenneth Varty, Society for the Study of Medieval Languages and Literature, 1977. Medium Aevum Monographs 9.

Le ditié de Jehanne d'Arc. Translated by Margaret Switten. Régnier-Bohler, *Voix de femmes*, pp. 699–723.

Encore aultres balades. Roy, *Œuvres poétiques*, vol. 1, pp. 271–80.

Les enseignemens moraux. Roy, *Œuvres poétiques*, vol. 3, pp. 27–44.

The Epistle of Othea. Edited by Curt F. Bühler, translated by Stephen Scrope, Oxford UP, 1970. Early English Texts Series, original series 264.

The Epistle of the Prison of Human Life. Wisman, Epistle, pp. 2–69.

An Epistle to the Queen of France. Wisman, Epistle, pp. 70–83.

Une epistre a Eustace Morel. Roy, *Œuvres poétiques*, vol. 2, pp. 295–302.

*L'*Epistre a Eustace Morel *de Christine de Pisan*. Edited by Jean-François Kosta-Théfaine, *Le moyen français*, vol. 38, 1996, pp. 79–91.

"*L'epistre à la reine* de Christine de Pizan (1405)." Translated by Thérèse Moreau and Eric Hicks. *Clio*, vol. 5, 1997, clio.revues.org/417.

L'epistre au dieu d'amours. Fenster and Erler, pp. 34–89.

L'epistre au dieu d'amours. McWebb, *Debating*, pp. 50–91.

L'epistre au dieu d'amours. Roy, *Œuvres poétiques*, vol. 2, pp. 1–28.

Epistre de la prison de vie humaine. Edited by Angus J. Kennedy, Grant and Cutler, 1984.

Epistre Othea. Edited by Gabriella Parussa, Droz, 1999.

Épître d'Othéa. Translated by Hélène Basso, PUF, 2008.

"Français 1177." *Gallica*, Bibliothèque Nationale de France, gallica.bnf.fr/ark:/12148/btv1b84497026/.

"*The God of Love's Letters*." Translated by Kevin Brownlee. Blumenfeld-Kosinski, *Selected Writings*, pp. 15–29.

Heures de contemplacion sur la Passion de Nostre Seigneur Jhesucrist. Edited and translated by Liliane Dulac and René Stuip, Champion, 2017.

Jeux a vendre. Roy, *Œuvres poétiques* [1886], vol. 1, pp. 187–206.

"Lai leonine." Edited and translated by Liliane Dulac et al. *Desir n'a repos, hommage à Danielle Bohler*, edited by Florence Bouchet and Danièle James-Raoul, PU de Bordeaux, 2015, pp. 25–55.

"*La lamentacion sur les maux de la France* de Christine de Pisan." *Mélanges de langue et littérature françaises du Moyen Âge et de la Renaissance: Offerts à Charles Foulon*, edited by Angus J. Kennedy, Institut de Français, Université de Haute-Bretagne, 1980, pp. 177–81.

"*The Lamentation on the Evils That Have Befallen France*." Blumenfeld-Kosinski, *Selected Writings*, pp. 224–29.

"*Lamentation on the Woes of France*." Willard, *Writings*, pp. 304–09.

Lament on the Evils of the Civil War. Wisman, Epistle, pp. 84–95.

Lays. Roy, *Œuvres poétiques*, vol. 1, pp. 125–48.

Lesser Treatise on the Romance of the Rose, June-July, 1401. Translated by Eric Hicks. Willard, *Writings*, pp. 151–61.

"*The Letter from Othea.*" Translated by Renate Blumenfeld-Kosinski. Blumenfeld-Kosinski, *Selected Writings*, pp. 29–41.

"*The Letter of Othea to Hector.*" Translated by Earl Jeffrey Richards. Willard, *Writings*, pp. 96–103.

"*The Letter on the Prison of Human Life.*" Translated by Renate Blumenfeld-Kosinski. Blumenfeld-Kosinski, *Selected Writings*, pp. 248–52.

A Letter to Eustache Morel (February 10, 1404). Translated by Renate Blumenfeld-Kosinski. Blumenfeld-Kosinski, *Selected Writings*, pp. 109–12.

Letter to the Queen of France, Isabel of Bavaria. Willard, *Writings*, pp. 269–74.

Le livre de la cité des dames. Translated into modern French by Thérèse Moreau and Eric Hicks, Stock, 1986.

"The *Livre de la cité des dames* of Christine de Pisan: A Critical Edition." Edited by Maureen Cheney Curnow, 1975. Vanderbilt U, PhD dissertation.

Le livre de l'advision Cristine. Edited by Christine Reno and Liliane Dulac, Champion, 2001.

Le livre de la mutacion de Fortune. Edited by Suzanne Solente, Picard, 1959–66. 4 vols.

The Livre de la paix *of Christine de Pisan.* Edited by Charity Cannon Willard, Mouton, 1958.

Le livre des epistres du debat sus le Rommant de la rose. Edited by Andrea Valentini, Classiques Garnier, 2014.

Le livre des fais d'armes et de chevallerie. Edited by Christine Moneera Laennec. *Christine Antygrafe: Auhority and Self in the Prose Works of Christine de Pizan: With an Edition of BN MS 603,* University Microfilms, 1988. 2 vols.

Le livre des fais et bonnes meurs du sage roy Charles V. Edited by Suzanne Solente, Champion, 1936–40. 2 vols.

Le livre des faits et bonnes mœurs du roi Charles V le Sage. Translated into modern French by Eric Hicks and Thérèse Moreau, Stock, 1997.

Livre des faits et bonnes mœurs du sage roi Charles V. Translated into modern French by Joël Blanchard and Michel Quereuil, Pocket/Agora, 2013.

Le livre des trois jugemens. Altmann, *Love Debate Poems*, pp. 153–202.

Le livre des trois jugemens. Roy, *Œuvres poétiques*, vol. 2, pp. 111–58.

Le livre des trois vertus. Boston Public Library, MS FR Med. 101.

Le livre des trois vertus. Translated into modern French by Liliane Dulac. Régnier-Bohler, pp. 543–698.

Le livre des trois vertus. Edited by Charity Cannon Willard and Eric Hicks, Champion, 1989.

Le livre du chemin de long estude. Edited by Robert Püschel, R. Damköhler, 1887.

Le livre du corps de policie. Edited by Angus J. Kennedy, Champion, 1998.

Le livre du corps de policie. Edited by Robert H. Lucas, Librairie Droz, 1967.

Le livre du debat de deux amans. Altmann, *Love Debate Poems*, pp. 81–152.

Le livre du dit de Poissy. Altmann, *Love Debate Poems*, pp. 203–74.

Le livre du duc des vrais amans. Edited by Thelma S. Fenster, Arizona Center for Medieval and Renaissance Studies, 1995. Medieval and Renaissance Texts and Studies.

Le livre du duc des vrais amans. Roy, *Œuvres poétiques*, vol. 3, pp. 59–208.

Le livre du duc des vrais amants. Edited and translated into modern French by Dominique Demartini and Didier Lechat, Champion, 2013.

A Medieval Woman's Mirror of Honor: *The Treasury of the City of Ladies*. Translated by Charity Cannon Willard, edited by Madeleine Pelner Cosman, Bard Hall Press / Persea, 1989.

The Morale Prouerbes of Cristyne. Translated by Anthony Woodville, William Caxton, 1478.

Morall Prouerbes of Christyne. Translated by William Caxton, edited by Richard Pynson. Pynson, *The Boke of Fame*, 1526, sigs. [E4]–[E5].

More Ballades. Translated by June McCash and James Wilhelm. Willard, *Writings*, pp. 49–56.

"La mutation de Christine." Translated into modern French by Thérèse Moreau and Eric Hicks. Polet and Pichois, pp. 135–37. From *Le livre de la mutacion de Fortune*.

One Hundred Ballades. Translated by Regina De Cormier. Willard, *Writings*, pp. 41–48.

"*One Hundred Ballads and Other Ballads*." Blumenfeld-Kosinski, *Selected Writings*, pp. 5–15.

"*One Hundred Ballads of a Lover and a Lady*." Blumenfeld-Kosinski, *Selected Writings*, pp. 216–24.

"*One Hundred Ballades of a Lover and His Lady*." Translated by Nadia Margolis et al. Willard, *Writings*, pp. 82–88.

L'oroyson Nostre Dame. Roy, *Œuvres poétiques*, vol. 3, pp. 1–10.

Une oroyson de Nostre Seigneur. Roy, *Œuvres poétiques*, vol. 3, pp. 15–26.

"*The Path of Long Study*." Blumenfeld-Kosinski, *Selected Writings*, pp. 59–87.

Prologue to Harley 4431. Roy, *Œuvres poétiques*, vol. 1, pp. xiv–xvii.

Proverbes moraux. Roy, *Œuvres poétiques*, vol. 3, pp. 45–58.

"Les *Proverbes moraulx* de Christine de Pizan." Edited by Jean-François Kosta-Théfaine. *Le moyen français*, vol. 38, 1996, pp. 61–77.

"Les *Proverbes moraux* de Christine de Pizan: Une nouvelle édition critique et quelques problèmes." Translated by Gilbert Ouy and Christine M. Reno. *"Pour acquerir honneur et pris": Mélanges de moyen français offerts à Giuseppe Di Stefano*, edited by Maria Colombo Timelli and Claudio Galderisi, CERES, 2004, pp. 557–72.

La querelle de la rose: Letters and Documents. Translated by Joseph L. Baird and John R. Kane, U of North Carolina P, 1978.

Les XV joyes Nostre Dame. Edited by Jean-François Kosta-Théfaine, *Cahiers de recherches médiévales*, vol. 16, 2008, pp. 255–77.

Les XV joyes Nostre Dame. Roy, *Œuvres poétiques*, vol. 3, pp. 11–14.
The Republic. Translated by N. Rudd and J. G. F. Powell, Oxford UP, 1998.
"*Rondeaux*." Moulin, *Christine de Pisan*, pp. 69–86.
Rondeaux. Roy, *Œuvres poétiques*, vol. 1, pp. 147–86.
"*Rondeaux*." Varty, *Christine de Pisan's Ballades*, pp. 2–124, 128–64.
Rondeaux. Translated by James Wilhelm. Willard, *Writings*, pp. 52–55.
"Savantes femmes." Translated into modern French by Thérèse Moreau and Eric Hicks. Polet and Pichois, pp. 139–41. From *Le livre de la cité des dames*.
Sept psaumes allegorisés. Edited by Bernard Ribémont and Christine Reno, Champion, 2017.
Les sept psaumes allégorisés of Christine de Pisan. Edited by Ruth Ringland Rains, Catholic U of America P, 1965.
"The Song of Joan of Arc." *Maid of Heaven*, translated by Ben D. Kennedy, www.maidofheaven.com/joanofarc_song_pisan_contents.asp. Accessed 23 Aug. 2015.
"*The Tale of Joan of Arc*." Blumenfeld-Kosinski, *Selected Writings*, pp. 252–62.
The Tale of Poissy. Translated by Barbara K. Altmann. Willard, *Writings* pp. 61–69.
The Tale of the Rose. Fenster and Erler, pp. 93–131.
The Tale of the Rose. Translated by Thelma S. Fenster. Willard, *Writings*, pp. 162–70.
"*The Tale of the Shepherdess*." Blumenfeld-Kosinski, *Selected Writings*, pp. 45–59.
The Treasure of the City of Ladies; or, The Book of the Three Virtues. 1985. Translated by Sarah Lawson, Penguin Books, 2003.
"*The Treasury of the City of Ladies*." Willard, *Writings*, pp. 213–28.
"*Virelais*." Moulin, *Christine de Pisan*, pp. 103–12.
Virelays. Roy, *Œuvres poétiques*, vol. 1, pp. 101–18.
"*Virelays*." Varty, *Christine de Pisan's Ballades*, pp. 2–124, 128–64.
"*Virelays*." Willard, *Writings*, pp. 55–56.
La vision de Christine. Translated into modern French by Anne Paupert. Régnier-Bohler, *Voix de femmes*, pp. 407–502.
The Vision of Christine de Pizan. Translated by Glenda McLeod and Charity Cannon Willard, D. S. Brewer, 2005.

Primary and Critical Works

Abelard, Peter. *Historia Calamitatum: The Story of My Misfortunes, an Autobiography*. Edited and translated by Henry Adams Bellows, 1922. *Internet History Sourcebooks Project*, Fordham U, sourcebooks.fordham.edu/basis/abelard-histcal.asp.
Abelard, Peter, and Heloise. *Abelard and Heloise: The Letters and Other Writings*. Translated by William Levitan, Hackett Publishing, 2007.
———. *The Letters of Abelard and Heloise*. Edited and translated by Betty Radice. 1974. 2nd ed., Penguin Books, 2003.
The Aberdeen Bestiary. *The Aberdeen Bestiary Project*, U of Aberdeen Library, 2010, www.abdn.ac.uk/bestiary/index.hti.

"About CC0: No Rights Reserved." *Creative Commons*, creativecommons.org/share-your-work/public-domain/cc0/.

Adams, Tracy. "Christine de Pizan." *French Studies*, vol. 71, no. 3, 2017, pp. 388–400.

———. *Christine de Pizan and the Fight for France.* Pennsylvania State UP, 2014.

———. "Christine de Pizan, Isabeau of Bavaria, and Female Regency." *French Historical Studies*, vol. 32, no. 1, 2009, pp. 1–32.

———. *The Life and Afterlife of Isabeau of Bavaria.* Johns Hopkins UP, 2010.

———. "Love as Metaphor in Christine de Pizan's Ballade Cycles." Altmann and McGrady, pp. 149–64.

Alexander, Neal. "On Literary Geography." *Literary Geographies*, vol. 1, no. 1, 2015, pp. 3–6. *Literary Geographies*, literarygeographies.net/index.php/LitGeogs/article/view/1-2/pdf_8.

Allen, Graham. *Intertextuality.* Routledge, 2000.

Altmann, Barbara K., editor. *The Love Debate Poems of Christine de Pizan:* Le livre du debat de deux amans, Le livre des trois jugemens, Le livre du dit de Poissy. UP of Florida, 1998.

———. "Les poèmes de veuvage de Christine de Pisan." *Scintilla*, vol. 1, 1984, pp. 24–47.

Altmann, Barbara K., and Deborah L. McGrady, editors. *Christine de Pizan: A Casebook.* Routledge, 2003.

Anne de France. *Enseignements à sa fille: Histoire du siège de Brest.* Edited by Tatiana Clavier and Eliane Viennot, PU de Saint-Etienne, 2006.

———. *Lessons for My Daughter.* Translated by Sharon L. Jansen, Boydell and Brewer, 2012.

"*Annunciation and Visitation.*" *Jean and Alexander Heard Library*, 2007, Vanderbilt Library, diglib.library.vanderbilt.edu/act-imagelink.pl?RC=29442.

"*Annunciation with St. Margaret and St. Ansanus.*" *Wikipedia*, 2017, en.wikipedia.org/wiki/Annunciation_with_St._Margaret_and_St._Ansanus.

Aquinas, Thomas. "*Commentary* on Aristotle, *On Memory and Recollection.*" Translated by John Burchill, edited by Mary Carruthers and Jan Ziolkowski. *The Medieval Craft of Memory: An Anthology of Texts and Pictures*, U of Pennsylvania P, 2002, pp. 153–88.

———. *Summa theologiae.* Edited and translated by the Dominican Order, vol. 43, Blackfriars, 1964–81. 61 vols.

Ariès, Philippe, and Georges Duby. *A History of Private Life: Revelations of the Medieval World.* Vol. 2, Harvard UP, 1987.

Aristotle. *On Memory and Recollection. On the Soul, Parva Naturalia, On Breath.* Translated by W. S. Hett, Harvard UP, 1957, pp. 285–313. Loeb Classical Library.

———. *On the Soul.* Translated by W. S. Hett, Cambridge UP, 1964.

Ashley, Kathleen, and Robert L. A. Clark, editors. *Medieval Conduct.* U of Minnesota P, 2001.

Atkinson, Clarissa W. *The Oldest Vocation: Christian Motherhood in the Middle Ages.* Cornell UP, 1991.

Attwood, Catherine. *Dynamic Dichotomy: The Poetic "I" in Fourteenth- and Fifteenth-Century French Lyric Poetry.* Rodopi, 1998.

Augustine. *Confessions.* Translated by R. S. Pine-Coffin, Penguin Books, 1961.

Austen, Jane. *Pride and Prejudice.* Penguin Books, 1972.

Autrand, Françoise. *Charles V le Sage.* Fayard, 1994.

———. *Charles VI: La folie du roi.* Fayard, 1986.

———. *Christine de Pizan: Une femme en politique.* Fayard, 2009.

———. *Jean de Berry: L'art et le pouvoir.* Fayard, 2000.

Badel, Pierre-Yves. Le roman de la rose *au XIV*[e] *siècle: Étude de la réception de l'œuvre.* Droz, 1980. Publications Romanes et Françaises 153.

Bakhtin, Mikhail. "Forms of Time and of the Chronotope in the Novel." *The Dialogic Imagination: Four Essays*, edited by Michael Holquist, translated by Caryl Emerson and Holquist, U of Texas P, 1981, pp. 84–258.

Bailey, Andrew, et al., editors. *Broadview Anthology of Social and Political Thought: From Plato to Nietzsche.* Broadview Press, 2008.

Barratt, Alexandra, editor. *Women's Writing in Middle English.* Longman, 1992.

Barthes, Roland. "L'ancienne rhétorique: Aide-mémoire." *Communications*, vol. 6, 1970, pp. 172–230.

Bartholomew, John George. *A Literary and Historical Atlas of America.* Dent, 1911.

Beaune, Colette. *The Birth of an Ideology: Myths and Symbols of Nation in Late-Medieval France.* Translated by Susan Ross Huston, U of California P, 1991.

Beauvoir, Simone de. *Tout compte fait.* Gallimard, 1972.

Beck, Jonathan. "Formalism and Virtuosity: Franco-Burgundian Poetry, Music, and Visual Art, 1470–1520." *Critical Inquiry*, vol. 10, no. 4, 1984, pp. 644–67.

Bell, David A. *The Cult of the Nation in France: Inventing Nationalism, 1680–1800.* Harvard UP, 2001.

Bell, Dora M. *L'idéal éthique de la royauté en France au Moyen Âge.* Droz, 1962.

Bennett, Judith M. *A Medieval Life: Cecilia Penifader of Brigstock, c. 1295–1344.* McGraw-Hill, 1998.

Berges, Wilhelm. *Die Fürstenspiegel des hohen und späten Mittelalters.* Hiersemann, 1938.

Bevir, Mark, editor. *Encyclopedia of Political Theory.* Sage, 2010. 3 vols.

Birk, Bonnie. *Christine de Pizan and Biblical Wisdom: A Feminist-Theological Point of View.* Marquette UP, 2005.

Black, Antony. *Political Thought in Europe, 1250–1450.* Cambridge UP, 1992.

Blamires, Alcuin. *The Case for Women in Medieval Culture.* Oxford UP, 1997.

———, editor. *Woman Defamed and Woman Defended: An Anthology of Medical Texts.* With Karen Pratt and C. W. Marx. Clarendon Press, 1992.

Blanchard, Joël. "Christine de Pizan: Tradition, Expérience et Traduction." *Romania*, vol. 11, 1990, pp. 200–35.

———. "Compilation et légitimation au XVe siècle." *Poétique*, no. 74, 1988, pp. 139–57.

Blanchard, Joël, and Jean-Claude Mühlethaler. *Ecriture et pouvoir à l'aube des temps modernes.* PUF, 2002.

Bloom, Harold. *The Anxiety of Influence: A Theory of Poetry.* 2nd ed., Oxford UP, 1997.

Blumenfeld-Kosinski, Renate. "Christine de Pizan and the Misogynistic Tradition." Blumenfeld-Kosinski, *Selected Writings*, pp. 297–311.

———. "Christine de Pizan and the Political Life in Late Medieval France." Altmann and McGrady, pp. 9–24.

———. "Enemies Within / Enemies Without: Threats to the Body Politic in Christine de Pizan." *Medievalia et humanistica*, no. 26, 1999, pp. 1–15.

———. "Jean Gerson and the Debate on the *Romance of the Rose*." McGuire, *Companion*, pp. 317–56.

———. *Poets, Saints, and Visionaries of the Great Schism, 1378–1417*. Pennsylvania State UP, 2006.

———. *Reading Myth: Classical Mythology and Its Interpretations in Medieval French Literature*. Stanford UP, 1997. Figurae Series.

———, editor. *The Selected Writings of Christine de Pizan*. Translated by Blumenfeld-Kosinski and Kevin Brownlee, W. W. Norton, 1997. Norton Critical Edition.

Boccaccio, Giovanni. *De Mulieribus Claris*. Edited and translated by Virginia Brown, Harvard UP, 2001. I Tatti Renaissance Library 1.

———. *Des cleres et nobles femmes*. Edited by Jeanne Baroin and Josiane Haffen, Les Belles Lettres, 1993.

———. *Famous Women*. Edited and translated by Virginia Brown, Harvard UP, 2001. I Tatti Renaissance Library 1.

Bodenhamer, David J. "Narrating Space and Place." Bodenhamer et al., pp. 5–15.

Bodenhamer, David J., et al., editors. *Deep Maps and Spatial Narratives*. Indiana UP, 2015.

Boethius. *The Consolation of Philosophy*. Translated by Victor Watts, Penguin Books, 1999.

———. *De Consolatione philosophiae*. C. Winter, 1947.

———. *Tractates; Consolation of Philosophy*. Translated by H. F. Stewart et al., Harvard UP, 1973, pp. 130–435. Loeb Classical Library.

Boivin le Cadet. "Vie de Christine de Pisan, et de Thomas de Pisan son père." *Mémoires de littérature, tirez des registres de l'Académie Royale des Inscriptions et Belles Lettres*. Imprimerie Royale, 1736, pp. 704–14.

Book of Kells. *Trinity College Dublin*, digitalcollections.tcd.ie/home/index.php?DRIS_ID=MS58_003v.

Born, Lester K. "The Perfect Prince: A Study in Thirteenth- and Fourteenth-Century Ideals." *Speculum*, vol. 3, 1928, pp. 470–504.

Bornstein, Diane. "Anti-feminism in Thomas Hoccleve's Translation of Christine de Pizan's *Epistre au dieu d'amours*." *English Language Notes*, vol. 19, no. 1, 1981, pp. 7–14.

———. "French Influence on Fifteenth-Century English Prose As Exemplified by the Translation of Christine de Pisan's *Livre du corps de Policie*." *Mediaeval Studies*, vol. 39, 1977, pp. 369–86.

———. *The Lady in the Tower: Medieval Courtesy Literature for Women*. Archon Books, 1983.

———. *Mirrors of Courtesy*. Archon Books, 1975.

Bose, Mishtooni. "Jean Gerson, Poet." Dixon and Sinclair, pp. 56–68.

Bossy, Michel-André. "Arms and the Bride: Christine de Pizan's Military Treatise as a Wedding Gift for Margaret of Anjou." Desmond, *Christine*, pp. 236–56.

Boucher, David, and Paul Kelly, editors. *Political Thinkers from Socrates to the Present*. 3rd ed., Oxford UP, 2017.

Bovet, Honorat. *L'apparicion Maistre Jehan de Meun* et le *Somnium super materia scismatis*. Edited by Ivor Arnold, Les Belles Lettres, 1926.

Bowers, Fredson. "Greg's 'Rationale of Copytext' Revisited." *Studies in Bibliography*, vol. 31, 1978, pp. 90–161.

Brabant, Margaret, editor. *Politics, Gender, and Genre: The Political Thought of Christine de Pizan*. Westview, 1992.

Brecht, Bertolt. *Saint Joan of the Stockyards*. Edited by John Willett and R. Manheim, translated by Ralph Manheim, Arcade, 1998. Translation of *Die Heilige Johanna der Schlachthöfe*.

Bridenthal, Renate, et al., editors. *Becoming Visible: Women in European History*. Houghton Mifflin, 1987.

Briggs, Charles F. *The Body Broken: Medieval Europe, 1300–1520*. Routledge, 2010.

Brown, Cynthia J. "The Reconstruction of an Author in Print: Christine de Pizan in the Fifteenth and Sixteenth Centuries." Desmond, *Christine*, pp. 215–35.

Brown-Grant, Rosalind. "*L'avision-Christine*: Autobiographical Narrative or Mirror for the Prince?" Brabant, pp. 95–112.

———. *Christine de Pizan and the Moral Defence of Women: Reading beyond Gender*. Cambridge UP, 1999.

———. "Christine de Pizan as a Defender of Women." Altmann and McGrady, pp. 81–100.

Brownlee, Kevin. "The Image of History in Christine de Pizan's *Livre de la Mutacion de Fortune*." *Contexts: Style and Values in Medieval Art and Literature*, special issue of *Yale French* Studies, edited by Daniel Poirion and Nancy F. Regalado, Yale UP, 1991, pp. 44–56.

———. "Literary Genealogy and the Problem of the Father: Christine de Pizan and Dante." *Dante Now: Current Trends in Dante Studies*. Edited by Theodore J. Cachey, U of Notre Dame P, 1995, pp. 205–35.

———. "Martyrdom and the Female Voice: Saint Christine in the *Cité des dames*." *Images of Sainthood in Medieval Europe*, edited by Renate Blumenfeld-Kosinski and Timea Szell, Cornell UP, 1991, pp. 115–35.

———. "Ovide et le Moi poétique 'moderne' à la fin du Moyen Âge: Jean Froissart et Christine de Pizan." *Modernité au Moyen Âge: Le défi du passé*, edited by Brigitte Cazelles and Charles Méla, Droz, 1990, pp. 153–73.

———. "Le projet 'autobiographique' de Christine de Pizan: Histoires et fables du moi." Hicks, *Au champ*, pp. 5–23.

———. "Rewriting Romance: Courtly Discourse and Auto-citation in Christine de Pizan." Chance, *Gender*, pp. 172–94.

———. "Structures of Authority in Christine de Pizan's *Ditié de Jehanne d'Arc*." *Discourses of Authority in Medieval and Renaissance Literature*, edited by K. Brownlee and Walter Stephens, UP of New England, 1989, pp. 131–50.

Brownlee, Kevin, and Sylvia Huot, editors. *Rethinking the* Romance of the Rose: *Text, Image, Reception*. U of Pennsylvania P, 1992.

Brumble, H. David. *Classical Myths and Legends in the Middle Ages and Renaissance: A Dictionary of Allegorical Meanings*. Greenwood Press, 1988.

Buettner, Brigitte. *Boccaccio's "Des cleres et nobles femmes": Systems of Signification in an Illuminated Manuscript*. U of Washington P, 1996.

Bullfinch, Thomas. *Bullfinch's Mythology*. Edited by Richard Martin, HarperCollins, 1991.

Bullough, Vern L. *Universities, Medicine, and Science in the Medieval West*. Ashgate, 2004.

Burns, J. H., editor. *The Cambridge History of Medieval Political Thought, c.350–c.1450*. Cambridge UP, 1988.

Butterfield, Ardis. *The Familiar Enemy: Chaucer, Language and Nation in the Hundred Years War*. Oxford UP, 2009.

Bynum, Caroline Walker. *Christian Materiality: An Essay on Religion in Late Medieval Europe*. MIT P, 2015.

———. *Holy Feast and Holy Fast: The Religious Significance of Food to Medieval Women*. U of California P, 1988.

Campbell, John, and Nadia Margolis, editors. *Christine de Pizan 2000: Studies on Christine de Pizan in Honour of Angus J. Kennedy*. Rodopi, 2000.

Campbell, P. G. C. "Christine de Pizan en Angleterre." *Revue de littérature comparée*, no. 5, 1924, pp. 659–70.

Canning, Joseph. *A History of Medieval Political Thought, 300–1450*. Routledge, 1996.

———. *Ideas of Power in the Late Middle Ages, 1296–1417*. Cambridge UP, 2011.

Caraffi, Patrizia, editor. *Christine de Pizan: La scrittrice e la città*. Alinea, 2013.

Carruthers, Mary. *The Book of Memory: A Study of Memory in Medieval Culture*. Cambridge UP, 1992.

Carson, Cindy L., and Angela Jane Weisl, editors. *Constructions of Widowhood and Virginity in the Middle Ages*. Macmillan, 1999.

Cavendish, Margaret. The Blazing World *and Other Writings*. Edited by Kate Lilley, Penguin Books, 1992.

Cerquiglini, Jacqueline. "Christine de Pizan and the Book: Programs and Modes of Reading, Strategies for Publication." *Journal of the Early Book Society for the Study of Manuscripts and Printing History*, vol. 4, 2001, pp. 112–26.

———. "Christine de Pizan et le scandale: Naissance de la femme écrivain." *Les lettres romanes*, vol. 57, 2004, 45–56.

———. "L'étrangère." *Revue des langues romanes*, no. 92, 1988, pp. 239–51.

———. "1401." Hollier, pp. 114–18.

———. "The Stranger." Blumenfeld-Kosinski, *Selected Writings*, pp. 265–74.

Cerquiglini-Toulet, Jacqueline. *La couleur de la mélancolie: La fréquentation des livres au XIVe siècle, 1300–1415*. Hatier, 1993.

———. "Le goût de l'étude: Saveur et savoir chez Christine de Pizan." Hicks, *Au champ*, pp. 597–608.

Chance, Jane, editor. *Gender and Text in the Later Middle Ages.* UP of Florida, 2006.

———. "Gender Subversion and Linguistic Castration in Fifteenth-Century English Translations of Christine de Pizan." *Violence against Women in Medieval Texts*, edited by Anna Roberts, UP of Florida, 1998, pp. 161–94.

———. *Medieval Mythography: The Emergence of Italian Humanism, 1321–1475.* UP of Florida, 2015.

Charles d'Orléans. *The English Poems of Charles of Orleans.* Edited by Robert Steele and Mabel Day, Early English Text Society, 1970.

Chartier, Alain. *Le quadrilogue invectif.* Translated by Florence Bouchet, Champion, 2002.

Chaucer, Geoffrey. *Boece.* Edited by Ralph Hanna and Traugott Lawler. *The Riverside Chaucer*, general editor, Larry D. Benson, Houghton Mifflin, 1987, pp. 395–469.

———. *The Wife of Bath's Prologue. Literature of the Western World: The Ancient World through the Renaissance*, edited by Brian Wilkie and James Hurt, 5th ed., vol. 1, Prentice Hall, 2001, pp. 1708–26.

Christine de Pizan: The Making of the Queen's Manuscript (London, British Library, Harley Ms 4431). Edited by James Laidlaw, Edinburgh U Library, 2010, www.pizan.lib.ed.ac.uk/.

Cicero, Marcus Tullus. *Cicero on the Ideal Orator (De oratore).* Edited by James M. May and Jakob Wisse, Oxford UP, 2001.

———. *The Republic and the Laws.* Translated by N. Rudd and J. G. F. Powell, Oxford UP, 1998.

Clanchy, M. T. *From Memory to Written Record: England, 1066–1377.* 2nd ed., Blackwell, 1993.

———. "Parchment and Paper: Manuscript Culture, 1100–1500." Eliot and Rose, pp. 194–206.

Clarke, Danielle, editor. *Isabella Whitney, Mary Sidney, and Aemelia Lanyer: Renaissance Women Poets.* Penguin Books, 2000.

Clemence of Barking. *The Life of Saint Catherine. Virgin Lives and Holy Deaths: Two Exemplary Biographies*, edited and translated by Jocelyn Wogan-Browne and Glyn S. Burgess, J. M. Dent, 1996, pp. 3–43

Cohen, Mitchell, and Nicole Fermon, editors. *Princeton Readings in Political Thought: Essential Texts since Plato.* Princeton UP, 1996.

Coldiron, A. E. B. *Christine de Pizan in English Print, 1478–1549.* Modern Humanities Research Association, forthcoming.

———. *English Printing, Verse Translation, and the Battle of the Sexes, 1476–1557.* Ashgate, 2009.

———. "Taking Advice from a Frenchwoman: Caxton, Pynson, and Christine de Pizan's *Moral Proverbs.*" *Caxton's Trace: Studies in the History of English Printing*, edited by William Kuskin, U of Notre Dame P, 2005, pp. 127–66.

Coleman, Janet. *A History of Political Thought from the Middle Ages to the Renaissance.* Blackwell, 2000.

Coletti, Theresa. "'Paths of Long Study': Reading Chaucer and Christine de Pizan in Tandem." *Studies in the Age of Chaucer*, vol. 28, 2006, pp. 1–40.

Collette, Carolyn P. "Heeding the Counsel of Prudence: A Context for the *Melibee*." *Chaucer Review*, vol. 29, 1995, pp. 416–33.

Constable, Giles. *Three Studies in Medieval Religious and Social Thought*. Cambridge UP, 1995.

Copeland, Rita. "Lydgate, Hawes, and the Science of Rhetoric in the Late Middle Ages." *Modern Languages Quarterly*, vol. 53, 1992, pp. 57–82.

Courcelle, Pierre. *La consolation de philosophie dans la tradition littéraire*. Études Augustiniennes, 1967.

Critten, Rory G. "Imagining the Author in Late Medieval France and England: The Transmission and Reception of Christine de Pizan's *Epistre au dieu d'Amours* and Thomas Hoccleve's *Letter of Cupid*." *Studies in Philology*, vol. 112, no. 4, 2015, pp. 680–97.

Crombie, Alistair C. *Medieval and Early Modern Science*. Doubleday, 1959.

Cropp, Glynnis. "Boèce et Christine de Pizan." *Le moyen âge*, vol. 87, 1981, pp. 387–417.

———, editor. *Le livre de Boèce de consolacion*. Droz, 2006.

Cuvelier. La chanson de Bertrand du Guesclin *de Cuvelier*. Edited by Jean-Claude Faucon, Éditions universitaires du Sud, 1990–91. 3 vols.

Dante Alighieri. *The Banquet*. Translated by Christopher Ryan, ANMA Libri, 1989.

———. *Il convivio*. Edited by Maria Simonelli, Patron, 1975. Vanderbilt U, PhD dissertation.

Davis, Norman, editor. *The Paston Letters: A Selection in Modern Spelling*. Oxford UP, 1983.

De Gendt, Anne-Marie. "'Plusieurs manières d'amours': Le débat dans *Le livre du Chevalier de la Tour Landry* et ses échos dans l'œuvre de Christine de Pizan." *Fifteenth-Century Studies*, vol. 23, 1990, pp. 121–35.

Delany, Sheila. "History, Politics, and Christine Studies: A Polemical Reply." Brabant, pp. 193–206.

———. "Mothers to Think Back Through: Who Are They? The Ambiguous Example of Christine de Pizan." Finke and Shichtman, pp. 177–97.

Delisle, Léopold. *Recherches sur la librairie de Charles V, roi de France, 1337–1380*. 1907. Gérard Th. Van Heusden, 1967. 2 vols.

Delogu, Daisy. *Allegorical Bodies: Power and Gender in Late Medieval France*. U of Toronto P, 2015.

———. "Christine de Pizan as *Architecteur*: Literary Compilation and Political Philosophy in the *Livre des fais et bonnes meurs du sage roy Charles V*." Dor and Henneau, pp. 147–57.

———. *Theorizing the Ideal Sovereign: The Rise of the French Vernacular Royal Biography*. U of Toronto P, 2008.

Delsaux, Olivier. *Manuscrits et pratiques autographes chez les écrivains français de la fin du Moyen Âge: L'exemple de Christine de Pizan.* Droz, 2013. Publications Romanes et Françaises 258.

Delsaux, Olivier, and Tania van Hemelryck, editors. *Le moyen français.* Vols. 75 (2014), 78–79, (2016).

Denery, Dallas G. "Christine de Pizan against the Theologians: The Viritue of Lies in *The Book of the Three Virtues.*" *Viator*, vol. 39, 2008, pp. 229–47.

———. *The Devil Wins: A History of Lying from the Garden of Eden to the Enlightenment.* Princeton UP, 2015.

Dentière, Marie. *Epistle to Marguerite de Navarre and Preface to a Sermon by John Calvin.* Edited and translated by Mary B. McKinley, U of Chicago P, 2004.

Deschamps, Eustache. "L'art de dictier." *Œuvres complètes d'Eustache Deschamps.* Edited by Le Marquis de Queux de Saint-Hilaire and Gaston Raynaud, vol. 7, 1878–1903, pp. 266–92. Société des Anciens Textes Français.

———. *Art de dictier.* Edited by Deborah Sinnreich-Levi, Colleagues Press, 1994.

Desmond, Marilynn. "Christine de Pizan." Gaunt and Kay, pp. 123–36.

———, editor. *Christine de Pizan and the Categories of Difference.* U of Minnesota P, 1998.

———. "The *Querelle de la Rose* and the Ethics of Reading." Altmann and McGrady, pp. 167–80.

Desmond, Marilynn, and Pamela Sheingorn. *Myth, Montage, and Visuality in Late Medieval Manuscript Culture: Christine de Pizan's* Othea. U of Michigan P, 2003.

De Winter, Patrick M. *La bibliothèque de Philippe le Hardi, duc de Bourgogne (1364–1404 : Étude sur les manuscrits à peintures d'une collection princière à l'époque du "style gothique international."* CNRS, 1985. Documents, études et répertoires.

Dinshaw, Carolyn, and David Wallace, editors. *The Cambridge Companion to Medieval Women's Writing.* Cambridge UP, 2003.

Dixon, Rebecca, and Finn Sinclair, editors. *Poetry, Knowledge, and Community in Late Medieval France.* D. S. Brewer, 2008.

Dor, Juliette, and Marie-Élisabeth Henneau, editors. *Christine de Pizan: Une femme de science, une femme de lettres.* Champion, 2008.

Dosher, Harry Randall. *The Concept of the Ideal Prince in French Political Thought, 800–1760.* 1969. U of North Carolina, PhD dissertation.

Downes, Stephanie. "Fashioning Christine de Pizan in Tudor Defences of Women." *Parergon*, vol. 23, 2006, pp. 71–92.

———. "A 'Frenche Booke Called the Pistill of Othea': Christine de Pizan's French in England." Wogan-Browne, pp. 457–68.

———. "Reading Christine de Pizan in England, 1400–1900." 2009. U of Sydney, PhD dissertation.

Duby, Georges, and Philippe Braunstein. "The Emergence of the Individual." Ariès and Duby, pp. 507–630.

Dudash, Susan J. "Christine de Pizan and the 'Menu Peuple.'" *Speculum*, vol. 78, 2003, pp. 788–831.

Dulac, Liliane. "Authority in the Prose Treatises of Christine de Pizan: The Writer's Discourse and the Prince's Word." Brabant, pp. 129–40.

———. "Le chevalier Hercule de l'*Ovide moralisé* au *Livre de la mutacion de fortune* de Christine de Pizan." *Cahiers de recherches médiévales [En ligne]*, no. 9, 2002, crm.revues.org/68?lang=en.

———. "De l'art de la digression dans *Le livre des fais et bonnes meurs du sage roy Charles V.*" Zimmermann and De Rentiis, pp. 148–57.

———. "Un écrit militant de Christine de Pizan: *Le ditié de Jehanne d'Arc.*" *Aspects of Female Existence: Proceedings from the St. Gertrud Symposium "Women in the Middle Ages," Copenhagen, September 1978*, edited by Birte Carlé et al., Gyldendal, 1980, pp. 115–34.

———. "Etat présent des travaux consacrés à Christine de Pizan." *Trente ans de recherche en langues et en littératures médiévales. Perspectives médievales*, 2005, pp. 167–90.

———. "La gestuelle chez Christine de Pizan: quelques aperçus." Hicks, *Au champ*, pp. 609–26.

———. "The Representation and Functions of Feminine Speech in Christine de Pizan's *Livre des trois vertus.*" Translated by Christine Reno. Richards, *Reinterpreting*, pp. 14–22.

———. "Thèmes et variations du *Chemin de long estude* à l'*Advision-Christine*: Remarques sur un itinéraire." *Sur le chemin de longue étude . . . Actes du colloque d'Orléans, Juillet 1995*, edited by Bernard Ribémont, Champion, 1998, pp. 77–86.

Dulac, Liliane, et al., editors. *"Desireuse de plus avant enquerre . . .": Actes du VIe colloque international sur Christine de Pizan (Paris, 20–24 juillet 2006): Volume en hommage à James Laidlaw*. Honoré Champion, 2008. Études Christiniennes.

Dulac, Liliane, and Bernard Ribémont, editors. *Une femme de lettres au Moyen Âge: Études autour de Christine de Pizan*. Paradigme, 1995.

Ehrhart, Margaret J. *The Judgment of the Trojan Prince Paris in Medieval Literature*. U of Pennsylvania P, 1987.

Eliot, Simon, and Jonathan Rose, editors. *A Companion to the History of the Book*. Blackwell, 2009.

Elizabeth I. *Collected Works*. Edited by Leah S. Marcus et al., U of Chicago P, 2000.

"Embroidered Bookbinding, Thirteenth-Century Annunciation." *Wikimedia Commons*, 2017, commons.wikimedia.org/wiki/File:Embroidered_bookbinding_13th_century_Annunciation.jpg.

Enders, Jody. "The Feminist Mnemonics of Christine de Pizan." *Modern Language Quarterly*, vol. 55, no. 3, September 1994, pp. 231–49.

Farber, Allen S. *The Chi-Rho Page from the Book of Kells: "The Word Made Flesh."* State U of New York, Oneonta, 2012, www.oneonta.edu/faculty/farberas/arth/arth212/book_of_kells.html.

Fenster, Thelma, and Mary Carpenter Erler, editors. *Poems of Cupid, God of Love: Christine de Pizan's* Epistre au dieu d'amours *and* Dit de la rose, *Thomas Hoccleve's* The Letter of Cupid, *with George Sewell's* The Proclamation of Cupid. E. J. Brill, 1990.

Fenster, Thelma S., and Claire A. Lees, editors. *Gender and Debate from the Early Middle Ages to the Renaissance.* Palgrave, 2002.

Ferguson, Margaret W. *Dido's Daughters: Literacy, Gender, and Empire in Early Modern England and France.* U of Chicago P, 2003.

Ferré, André. *Géographie littéraire.* Editions du Sagittaire, 1946.

Finke, Laurie A. "The Politics of the Canon: Christine de Pizan and the Fifteenth-Century Chaucerians." *Exemplaria*, vol. 19, 2007, pp. 16–38.

———. *Women's Writing in English: Medieval England.* Longman, 1999.

Finke, Laurie A., and Martin B. Shichtman. *Medieval Texts and Contemporary Readers.* Cornell UP, 1987.

Fitzgerald, F. Scott. *The Great Gatsby.* Scribner, 2013.

Fiumi, Lionello. "La fortune de Dante en France de Christine de Pisan à Saint-John Perse." *Bulletin de la Société d'Études Dantesques du Centre Universitaire Méditerranéen*, vol. 16, 1967, pp. 33–45.

Forhan, Kate Langdon. *The Political Theory of Christine de Pizan.* Ashgate, 2002.

———. "Polycracy, Obligation, and Revolt: The Body Politic in John of Salisbury and Christine de Pizan." Brabant, pp. 33–52.

———. "Reflecting Heroes: Christine de Pizan and the Mirror Tradition." Zimmerman and De Rentiis, pp. 189–205.

Fraioli, Deborah A. *Joan of Arc and the Hundred Years War.* Greenwood Press, 2005.

———. *Joan of Arc: The Early Debate.* Boydell Press, 2000.

Fresco, Karen. "Gendered Household Spaces in Christine de Pizan's *Livre des trois vertus.*" *The Medieval Household in Christian Europe, c. 850–c. 1550: Managing Power, Wealth, and the Body*, edited by Cordelia Beattie et al., Brepols, 2003, pp. 187–98.

Friedman, Lionel J. "La mesnie faux semblant: Homo interior / homo exterior." *French Forum*, vol. 14, supplement 1, 1989, pp. 435–45.

Froissart, Jean. *Chronicles.* Edited and translated by Geoffrey Brereton. Penguin Books, 1978.

Garnier, François. *Le langage de l'image au Moyen Âge II: Grammaire des gestes.* Léopard d'Or, 1989.

Gaunt, Simon, and Sarah Key, editors. *The Cambridge Companion to Medieval French Literature.* Cambridge UP, 2009.

Gaus, Gerald, and Fred D'Agostino, editors. *The Routledge Companion to Social and Political Philosophy.* Routledge, 2013.

Gauvard, Claude. "Christine de Pisan a-t-elle eu une pensée politique? À propos d'ouvrages récents." *Revue historique*, vol. 250, Oct.-Dec. 1973, pp. 417–29.

———. *La France au Moyen Âge du Ve au XVe siècle.* PUF, 2014.

Geary, Patrick. *Phantoms of Remembrance: Memory and Oblivion at the End of the First Millennium.* Princeton UP, 1994.

Genette, Gérard. *Palimpsests: Literature in the Second Degree.* Translated by Channa Newman and Claude Doubinsky, U of Nebraska P, 1997.

Geoffrey de la Tour Landry. *The Book of the Knight of the Tower.* Translated by William Caxton, edited by M. Y. Offord, Oxford UP, 1971.

———. *Le livre du chevalier de la Tour Landry pour l'enseignement de ses filles.* 1854. Edited by Anatole de Montaiglon, Kraus, 1982.

Geoffroi de Charny. *The Book of Chivalry of Geoffroi de Charny.* Edited and translated by Richard W. Kaeuper and Elspeth Kennedy, U of Pennsylvania P, 1996.

Gerson, Jean. *A.B.C. des simples gens. Œuvres complètes,* edited by Palémon Glorieux, vol. 7, Desclée, 1966, pp. 154–57.

———. "Considerate lilia." Hult, 2010, pp. 84–92.

———. *De consolatione theologiae. Œuvres complètes,* edited by Palémon Glorieux, vol. 9, Desclée, 1973.

———. "Jean Gerson to Pierre Col (Winter 1402–03)." Hult, pp. 222–31.

———. "Treatise against the *Romance of the Rose.*" Hult, pp. 106–30.

Gibbons, Mary Weitzel. "The *Bath of the Muses* and Visual Allegory in the *Chemin de long estude.*" Desmond, *Christine,* pp. 128–45.

Gilchrist, Roberta. "Medieval Bodies in the Material World: Gender Stigma and the Body." Kay and Rubin, pp. 43–61.

The Good Wife's Guide (Le Ménagier de Paris): A Medieval Household Book. Translated by Gina L. Greco and Christine M. Rose, Cornell UP, 2008.

The Good Wife Taught Her Daughter; The Good Wyfe Wold a Pylgremage; The Thewis of Gud Women. Edited by Tauno Mustanoja, Suomalaisen Kirjallisuuden Scuran, 1948.

Gottlieb, Beatrice. "The Problem of Feminism in the Fifteenth Century." Blumenfeld-Kosinski, *Selected Writings,* pp. 274–97.

Grabes, Herbert. *The Mutable Glass: Mirror-Imagery in Titles and Texts of the Middle Ages and English Renaissance.* Translated by G. Collier, Cambridge UP, 1982.

Grandes chroniques de France. Edited by Jules Viard, Société de l'Histoire de France, 1920–1953. 10 vols.

Grant, Edward. *The Foundations of Modern Science in the Middle Ages: Their Religious, Institutional and Intellectual Contexts.* Cambridge UP, 1996.

———. *Physical Science in the Middle Ages.* Wiley, 1971.

Gray, Douglas. "'A Fulle Wyse Gentyl-Woman of Fraunce': The *Epistle of Othea* and Later Medieval English Literary Culture." Wogan-Browne, pp. 237–49.

Green, Karen. "From *Le miroir des dames* to *Le livre des trois vertus.*" *Virtue Ethics for Women 1250–1500,* edited by Karen Green and C. J. Mews, Springer, 2011, pp. 99–113.

———. "On Translating Christine de Pizan as a Philosopher." Green and Mews, pp. 117–38.

———. "Was Christine de Pizan at Poissy 1418–1429?" *Medium Ævum,* vol. 83, no.1, 2014, pp. 91–105.

Green, Karen, and Constant Mews, editors. *Healing the Body Politic: The Political Thought of Christine de Pizan.* Brepols, 2005.

Greetham, D. C., editor. *Scholarly Editing: A Guide to Research.* Modern Language Association of America, 1995.

Greg, W. W. "The Rationale of Copy-Text." *Studies in Bibliography,* vol. 3, 1950–51, pp. 19–36.

Guenée, Bernard. *Un meurtre, une société: L'assassinat du Duc d'Orléans, 23 novembre 1407.* Gallimard, 1982.

———. *States and Rulers in Later Medieval Europe*. Translated by Juliet Vale, Blackwell, 1982.

Gueullette, Jean-Marie. "Virtue." *Encylopedia of the Middle Ages*, edited by André Vauchez, translated by Adrian Walford, vol. 2, Fitzroy Dearborn, 2000, p. 1524. 2 vols.

Guibert, abbot of Nogent. *The Autobiography of Guibert, Abbot of Nogent-sous-Coucy*. Translated by C. C. Swinton Bland, Routledge, 1926.

Guillaume de Lorris, and Jean de Meun. *The Romance of the Rose*. Translated by Charles Dahlberg, Princeton UP, 1995.

———. *The Romance of the Rose*. Edited by Charles W. Dunn, translated by Harry W. Robbins, Syracuse UP, 2002.

———. *The Romance of the Rose*. Edited and translated by Frances Horgan, Oxford UP, 1999. Oxford World's Classics.

———. *Le roman de la rose*. Edited by Félix Lecoy, Champion, 1965–70. 3 vols. Classiques Français du Moyen Âge 92, 95, 98.

———. *Le roman de la rose*. Edited and translated by Armand Strubel, Livre de Poche, 1992. Lettres Gothiques.

Guillaume de Machaut. *Le livre de la fontaine amoureuse*. Edited and translated into modern French by Jacqueline Cerquiglini-Toulet, Stock, 1993.

———. *Motets and Music from the Ivrea Codex*. Performance by The Clerks' Group, directed by Edward Wickham, Signum Classics, 1998.

Hadot, Pierre. *Philosophy as a Way of Life*. Edited by Arnold I. Davidson, translated by Michael Chase, Blackwell, 1995. Translation of *Exercices spirituels et philosophie antique*.

Hanawalt, Barbara A. Introduction. *Women and Work in Preindustrial Europe*, edited by Hanawalt, Indiana UP, 1986, pp. vii–xviii.

———. "Widows." Dinshaw and Wallace, pp. 58–69.

———, editor. *Women and Work in Preindustrial Europe*. Indiana UP, 1986.

Hasenohr, Geneviève, and Michel Zink, editors. *Dictionnaire des lettres françaises: Le Moyen Âge*. Le livre de poche, 1992.

Hedeman, Anne D. *The Royal Image: Illustrations of the 'Grandes Chroniques de France,' 1274–1422*. UP of California, 1991.

Hellinga, Lotte. "The Gutenberg Revolutions." Eliot and Rose, pp. 207–19.

Henninger, Daniel. "F***, S***, and Other Typos." *Wall Street Journal*, 14 June 2007. *Jews on First!*, www.jewsonfirst.org/07b/cul029.html.

Hentsch, Alice. *De la littérature didactique au Moyen Âge s'adressant spécialement aux femmes*. 1903. Slatkine, 1975.

Hicks, Eric, editor. *Au champ des escriptures: IIIe colloque international sur Christine de Pizan (Lausanne, 18–22 juillet 1998)*. Champion, 2000.

———, editor and translator. *Christine de Pisan, Jean Gerson, Jean de Montreuil, Gontier and Pierre Col, "Le débat sur le* Roman de la rose." Champion, 1977. Bibliothèque du XVe siècle 43.

———. "Excerpts and Originality: Authorial Purpose in the *Fais et bonnes meurs*." Campbell and Margolis, pp. 221–31.

Hicks, Eric, and Ezio Ornato. "Jean de Montreuil et le débat sur le *Roman de la Rose*." *Romania*, vol. 98, 1977, pp. 34–64, 186–219.

Hill, Jillian M. L. *The Medieval Debate on Jean de Meung's* Roman de la Rose*: Morality versus Art*. Edwin Mellen Press, 1991.

Hindman, Sandra. *Christine de Pizan's* Epistre Othéa*: Painting and Politics at the Court of Charles VI*. Pontifical Institute of Mediaeval Studies Press, 1986.

———. "The Iconography of Queen Isabeau de Bavière (1410–1415): An Essay in Method." *Gazette des beaux-arts*, vol. 102, 1983, pp. 102–10.

———. "With Ink and Mortar: Christine de Pizan's *Cité des dames*." *Feminist Studies*, vol. 10, no. 3, Autumn 1984, pp. 457–83.

Hinkle, William M. *The Fleurs de Lis of the Kings of France, 1285–1488*. Southern Illinois UP, 1991.

Histoire ancienne jusqu'à César. Partial edition. Edited by Marijke de Visser-van Terswiga, Paradigme, 1995 and 1999. 2 vols.

Hobbins, Daniel. *Authorship and Publicity before Print: Jean Gerson and the Transformation of Late Medieval Learning*. U of Pennsylvania P, 2009.

———. "The Schoolman as Public Intellectual: Jean Gerson and the Late Medieval Tract." *The American Historical Review*, vol. 108, no. 5, 2003, pp. 1308–46.

Hoccleve, Thomas. *The Letter of Cupid*. Fenster and Erler, pp. 175–218.

Holderness, Julia Simms. "Christine, Boèce et saint Augustin: La consolation de la mémoire." Dulac et al., pp. 279–89.

———. "Christine et ses 'bévues': Sens et portée de quelques assimilations abusives." Hicks, *Au champ*, pp. 149–60.

Hollier, Denis, editor. *A New History of French Literature*. Harvard UP, 1989.

Huchet, Jean-Charles. *Le roman médiéval*. PUF, 1984. Littératures Modernes.

Huchon, Mireille. *Louise Labé: Une créature de papier*. Droz, 2006.

Huizinga, Johann. *The Autumn of the Middle Ages*. Translated by Rodney J. Payton. U of Chicago P, 1997.

Hult, David F., editor and translator. *Debate of the* Romance of the Rose. U of Chicago P, 2010. The Other Voice in Early Modern Europe.

———. "The *Roman de la rose*, Christine de Pizan, and the *querelle des femmes*." Dinshaw and Wallace, pp. 184–94.

Huot, Sylvia. "Seduction and Sublimation: Christine de Pizan, Jean de Meun, and Dante." *Romance Notes*, vol. 25, 1985, pp. 361–73.

Illuminations: Treasures of the Middle Ages BBC. *YouTube*, uploaded by Livros Arte, 28 Oct. 2013, www.youtube.com/watch?v=LGLD_Bv43vw&list=PLS12qnwBb76cyPSanbORu4Kod8aRrUD72&index=2.

Ishikawa, Jun. *The Bodhisattva*. Edited and translated by William J. Tyler, Columbia UP, 1991.

Jacobus de Voragine. *The Golden Legend: Readings on the Saints*. Translated by William Granger Ryan, Princeton UP, 1993. 2 vols.

Jager, Eric. *The Book of the Heart*. U of Chicago P, 2000.

Jean de Meun. "Boethius' *De Consolatione* by Jean de Meun." Edited by V. L. Dédeck-Héry. *Mediaeval Studies*, vol. 14, 1952, pp. 166–275.

Jeay, Madeleine. "Clercs et paysans au XVe siècle: Une relecture de l'épisode de l'arbre aux fées dans le procès de Jeanne d'Arc." *Normes et pouvoir à la fin du Moyen Âge*, edited by M. C. Déprez-Masson, CERES, 1989, pp. 145–63.

Jehan Le Fèvre. *Lamentations of Matheolus*. Blamires, pp. 177–97.

Jerome. "The Commentaries of Eusebius Jerome the Presbyter on the Epistle of the Apostle Paul to the Ephesians." *The Commentaries of Origen and Jerome on St. Paul's Epistle to the Ephesians*, edited and translated by Ronald E. Heine, Oxford UP, 2002, pp. 75–272.

John of Salisbury. *Joannis Saresberiensis episcopi Carnotensis Policratici sive De nugis curialium et vestigiis philosophorum librui VIII*. Edited by Clemens Webb, Frankfurt, 1965.

Johnston, Hope. "How the *Livre de la Cité des dames* First Came to Be Printed in England." Dulac et al., pp. 385–96.

Johnston, Mark D., editor. *Medieval Conduct Literature: An Anthology of Vernacular Guides to Behaviour for Youths, with English Translations*. U of Toronto P / Medieval Academy of America, 2009.

Julian of Norwich. *Revelations of Divine Love*. Translated by Elizabeth Spearing, Penguin Books, 1998.

Kaminsky, Amy Katz, and Elaine Dorough Johnson. "To Restore Honor and Fortune: 'The Autobiography of Leonor López de Córdoba.'" *The Female Autograph: Theory and Practice of Autobiography from the Twelfth to the Twentieth Century*, edited by Domna C. Stanton, U of Chicago P, 1987, pp. 70–80.

Kantorowicz, Ernst H. *The King's Two Bodies: A Study in Mediaeval Political Theology*. Princeton UP, 1998.

Katzenellenbogen, Adolf. *Allegories of the Virtues and Vices in Medieval Art: From Early Christian Times to the Thirteenth Century*. W. W. Norton, 1964.

Kay, Sarah. *The Place of Thought: The Complexity of One in Late Medieval French Didactic Poetry*. U of Pennsylvania P, 2007.

Kay, Sarah, and Miri Rubin. *Framing Medieval Bodies*. St. Martin's Press, 1994.

Kelemen, Erick. *Textual Editing and Criticism: An Introduction*. W. W. Norton, 2008.

Kelly, Douglas. *Christine de Pizan's Changing Opinion: A Quest for Certainty in the Midst of Chaos*. Boydell and Brewer, 2007.

Kelly, Joan. "Did Women Have a Renaissance?" Bridenthal et al., pp. 137–64.

Kemp, Walter. "'Dueil Angoisseus' and 'Dulongesux.'" *Early Music*, vol. 7, no. 4, 1979, pp. 520–21. Keyboard Issue 1.

Kempe, Margery. *The Book of Margery Kempe*. Edited by Lynn Staley, W. W. Norton, 2001.

———. *The Book of Margery Kempe*. Translated by B. A. Windeatt, Penguin Books, 1994.

Kennedy, Angus J. *Christine de Pizan: A Bibliographical Guide*. Grant and Cutler, 1984.

———. *Christine de Pizan: A Bibliographical Guide, Supplement 1.* Grant and Cutler, 1994.

———. *Christine de Pizan: A Bibliographical Guide, Supplement 2.* Tamesis, 2004.

Kennedy, Angus J., et al., editors. *Contexts and Continuities: Proceedings of the Fourth International Colloquium on Christine de Pizan (Glasgow 21–27 July 2000) Published in Honour of Liliane Dulac.* U of Glasgow P, 2002. 3 vols.

Kirkman, Andrew, and Philip Weller. Review of *The Sacred Music of Gilles Binchois,* by Philip Kaye. *Music and Letters,* vol. 77, no. 4, 1996, pp. 566–96.

Klapisch-Zuber, Christiane, editor. *A History of Women in the West: Silences of the Middle Ages. A History of Women in the West,* vol. 2, Georges Duby and Michlle Perrot, general editors. Harvard UP, 1992.

Klibansky, Raymond, et al. *Saturn and Melancholy: Studies in the History of Natural Philosophy, Religion, and Art.* Nelson, 1964.

Knapp, Ethan. *The Bureaucratic Muse: Thomas Hoccleve and the Literature of Late Medieval England.* Pennsylvania State UP, 2001.

Kolve, V. A. "The Annunciation to Christine: Authorial Empowerment in *The Book of the City of Ladies.*" *Iconography at the Crossroads,* edited by Brendan Cassidy, Index of Christian Art, 1993, pp. 171–93.

Kosta-Théfaine, Jean-François. "La ballade XI ('Seulete suy et seulete vueil estre') de Christine de Pizan et la ballade 59 ('Alone am y and wille to be alone') des *Poésies anglaises* de Charles d'Orléans: Adaptation, traduction ou simple coïncidence?" *Disputatio,* vol. 3, 1998, pp. 51–63.

Krueger, Roberta L. "Christine's Anxious Lessons: Gender, Morality, and the Social Order from the *Enseignemens* to the *Avision.*" Desmond, *Christine,* pp. 16–40.

———. "Christine's Treasure: Women's Honor and Household Economies in the *Livre des trois vertus.*" Altmann and McGrady, pp. 101–14.

———. "'*Nouvelles choses*': Social Instability and the Problem of Fashion in the *Livre du chevalier de la Tour Landry,* the *Ménagier de Paris,* and Christine de Pizan's *Livre des trois vertus.*" *Medieval Conduct,* edited by Kathleen Ashley and Robert L. A. Clark, U of Minnesota P, 2001, pp. 49–85.

———. "Towards Feminism: Christine de Pizan, Female Advocacy, and Women's Textual Communities in the Late Middle Ages and Beyond." *The Oxford Handbook of Women and Gender in Medieval Europe,* edited by Judith Bennett and Ruth Karras, Oxford UP, 2013, pp. 590–606.

Krynen, Jacques. *L'empire du roi: Idées et croyances politiques en France, XIIIe–XVe siècle.* Éditions Gallimard, 1993.

———. *Idéal du prince et pouvoir royal en France à la fin du Moyen Âge, 1380–1440: Etude de la littérature politique du temps.* Picard, 1981.

Kuhn, Thomas S. *The Structure of Scientific Revolutions.* U of Chicago P, 1970.

Laidlaw, James C. "Christine and the Manuscript Tradition." Altmann and McGrady, pp. 231–49.

———. "Christine de Pizan—An Author's Progress." *The Modern Language Review,* vol. 78, July 1983, pp. 532–50.

———. "Christine de Pizan—A Publisher's Progress." *The Modern Language Review*, vol. 82, 1987, pp. 35–75.

———. "Christine de Pizan, the Earl of Salisbury, and Henry IV." *French Studies*, vol. 36, 1982, pp. 129–43.

———. "Christine's Lays—Does Practice Make Perfect?" Kennedy et al., vol. 2, pp. 467–81.

———. "The Date of the Queen's Manuscript (London, British Library, Harley MS 4431)." 2005, www.pizan.lib.ed.ac.uk/harley4431date.pdf.

———. "La production du manuscrit de la reine Isabeau (Londres, British Library, Harley 4431): Questions et réponses initiales." Christine de Pizan, une femme de science, une femme de lettres, 11–15 Jan. 2005, colloquium in Liège, Belgium.

Laigle, Mathilde. *Le livre des trois vertus de Christine de Pisan*. Champion, 1912.

Lanson, Gustave. *Histoire de la littérature française*. Hachette, 1926–27.

Lanyer, Aemilia. *The Poems of Aemilia Lanyer: Salve Deux Rex Judaerum*. Edited by Susanne Woods, Oxford UP, 1993.

Latini, Brunetto. *The Book of the Treasure*. Translated by Paul Barrette and Spurgeon Baldwin, Garland Library of Medieval Literature, 1993.

———. *Li livres dou tresor*. Edited by Francis J. Carmody, Slatkine Reprints, 1975.

Laurie, I. S. "Deschamps and the Lyric as Natural Music." *The Modern Language Review*, vol. 59, no. 4, 1964, pp. 561–70.

Lechat, Didier. "Histoire collective et histoire individuelle dans l'*Advision Cristine*."*L'individu au Moyen Âge: Individuation et individualisation avant la modernité*, Aubier, 2005, pp. 211–27.

Lee Dow, Tsae Lan. "Christine de Pizan and the Body Politic." Green and Mews, pp. 227–43.

Lefèvre, Sylvie. "Christine de Pizan." Hasenohr and Zink, pp. 280–87.

———. "Christine de Pizan et l'Aristote Oresmien." Hicks, *Au champ*, pp. 231–50.

Le Ninan, Claire. *Le sage roi et la clergesse: L'écriture du politique dans l'œuvre de Christine de Pizan*. Champion, 2013.

"Lettre de Jeanne d'Arc aux Anglais." *Des lettres*, www.deslettres.fr/lettre-de-jeanne-d-arc-aux-anglais/.

La librairie des frères captifs: Les manuscrits de Charles d'Orléans et Jean d'Angoulême. Brepols, 2007.

Lindberg, David. *The Beginnings of Western Science: The European Scientific Tradition in Philosophical, Religious, and Institutional Context, 600 B.C. to A.D. 1450*. U of Chicago P, 1992.

Loba, Anna, editor. *Ton nom sera reluisant apres toy par longue memoire*. Poznań, Wydawnictwo Naukowe UAM, 2016.

Long, Mary Beth. "A Medieval French Book in an Early Modern English World: Christine de Pizan's *Livre de la cité des dames* and Women Readers in the Age of Print." *Literature Compass*, vol. 9, no. 8, 2012, pp. 521–37.

Lorcin, Marie-Thérèse. "*Le livre des trois vertus* et le sermo ad status." Dulac and Ribémont, pp. 139–49.

Losco, Joseph, and Leonard Williams. *Political Theory: Classic and Contemporary Readings*. 2nd ed., Roxbury Publishing, 2003.

Lotfi, Sarah R., director. *La Mutacion de* Fortune. White Cloud Productions, 2010. *Vimeo*, uploaded by Sarah R. Lotfi, 8 Mar. 2012, vimeo.com/38158445.

Mahoney, Dhira B. "Middle English Regenderings of Christine de Pizan." *The Medieval Opus: Imitation, Rewriting, and Transmission in the French Tradition*, edited by Douglas Kelly, Rodopi, 1996, pp. 405–27. Faux Titre: Études de Langue et Littérature Françaises.

"Making Manuscripts." *The J. Paul Getty Museum*, www.getty.edu/art/collection/video/142876/making-manuscripts/.

Malcolmson, Cristina. "Christine de Pizan's *City of Ladies* in Early Modern England." *Debating Gender in Early Modern England, 1500–1700*, edited by Cristina Malcolmson and Mihoko Suzuki, Palgrave Macmillan, 2002, pp. 15–35.

Mâle, Émile. *L'art religieux du XIIIe siècle en France*. Armand Colin, 1925.

Mann, Jill. "Allegorical Buildings in Mediaeval Literature." *Medium Ævum*, vol. 63, 1994, pp. 191–210.

Margolis, Nadia. "Clerkliness and Courtliness in the Complaintes of Christine de Pizan." Richards, *Christine de Pizan and Medieval French Lyric*, pp. 135–54.

———. "Elegant Closures: The Use of the Diminutive in Christine de Pizan and Jean de Meun." Richards, *Reinterpreting*, pp. 111–23.

———. *An Introduction to Christine de Pizan*. UP of Florida, 2011.

———. "Joan of Arc." Dinshaw and Wallace, pp. 256–66.

———. "The Poetess as Historian." *Journal of the History of Ideas*, vol. 47, 1980, pp. 361–75.

Marie de France. *Fables*. Edited and translated by Harriet Spiegel, U of Toronto P, 1987.

———. *Lai of Yonec*. *Literature of the Western World: The Ancient World through the Renaissance*, edited by Brian Wilkie and James Hurt, 5th ed., vol. 1, Prentice Hall, 2001, pp. 1341–53.

———. *Lais of Marie de France*. Translated by Glyn S. Burgess and Keith Busby, Penguin Books, 1999.

Marsilius of Padua. *The Defender of Peace*. Translated by Alan Gewirth, Columbia UP, 1956.

Martin, Henry Marie Radegonde. *La miniature française du XIIIe siècle*. G. van Oestr, 1923.

Mauss, Marcel. *The Gift: Forms and Functions of Exchange in Archaic Societies*. Translated by Ian Cunnison, W. W. Norton, 1967.

McCormick, Betsy. "Building the Ideal City: Female Memorial Praxis in Christine de Pizan's *Cité des dames*." *Studies in the Literary Imagination*, vol. 36, no. 1, 2003, pp. 149–71.

McGann, Jerome. "The Rationale of Hyper Text." *Text*, vol. 9, 1996, pp. 11–32.

McGann, Jerome, and Lisa Samuels. "Deformance and Interpretation." *New Literary History*, vol. 30, 1999, pp. 25–56.

McGrady, Deborah. "Authorship and Audience in the Prologues to Christine de Pizan's Commissioned Poetry." Hicks, *Au champ*, pp. 25–40.

———. "De 'l'onneur et louenge des femmes': Les dédicaces épistolaire du *Débat sur le* Roman de la rose et la réconfiguration du champ littéraire." *Publics et publications dans les éloges collectifs de femmes à la fin du Moyen Âge et sous l'Ancien Régime*, special issue of *Études françaises*, edited by Renée-Claude Breitenstein, vol. 47, no. 3, 2011, pp. 11–28.

———. "What Is a Patron? Benefactors and Authorship in MS Harley 4431, Christine de Pizan's Collected Works." Desmond, *Christine*, pp. 195–214.

McGuire, Brian Patrick. *A Companion to Jean Gerson.* Brill, 2006.

———. *Jean Gerson and the Last Medieval Reformation.* Penn State UP, 2005.

McKinley, Mary B. "The *Essays* as Intertext." *Approaches to Teaching Montaigne's* Essays, edited by Patrick Henry, Modern Language Association of America, 1994, pp. 116–22.

McNamer, Sarah. "Female Authors, Provincial Setting: The Re-versing of Courtly Love in the Findern Manuscript." *Viator*, vol. 22, 1991, pp. 279–310.

McWebb, Christine, editor. *Debating the* Roman de la Rose*: A Critical Anthology.* Routledge, 2007.

———. "Joan of Arc and Christine de Pizan: The Symbiosis of Two Warriors in the *Ditié de Jehanne d'Arc.*" *Fresh Verdicts on Joan of Arc*, edited by Bonnie Wheeler and Charles T. Wood, Garland, 1996, pp. 133–44. The New Middle Ages 2.

Meale, Carole. "Reading Women's Culture in Fifteenth-Century England: The Case of Alice Chaucer." *Mediaevalitas: Reading the Middle Ages*, edited by Piero Boitani and Anna Torti, D. S. Brewer, 1996, pp. 81–101.

Méchoulan, Eric. "From Music to Literature." *Literary History*, special issue of *SubStance*, issue 88, 1999, pp. 42–56.

Meehan, Bernard, and Anthony Cains. "Direction of the Spine of the Calf." *The Book of Kells, MS 58, Trinity College Library Dublin: Commentary*, edited by Peter Fox, Faksimile Verlag Luzern, 1990, pp. 183–84.

Le mesnagier de Paris. Edited by Georgina E. Brereton and Janet M. Ferrier, translated by Karin Ueltschi, Librairie Générale Française, 1994. Lettres Gothiques.

Mews, Constant J. "Latin Learning in Christine de Pizan's *Livre de Paix.*" Green and Mews, pp. 61–80.

———. *The Lost Love Letters of Héloïse and Abelard: Perceptions of Dialogue in Twelfth-Century France.* 2nd ed., Palgrave Macmillan, 2008.

Mézières, Philippe de. *Le livre de la vertu du sacrement de mariage.* Edited by Joan B. Williamson, Catholic U of America P, 1993.

———. *Songe du viel pelerin.* Edited by Joël Blanchard, Droz, 2015. 2 vols.

———. *Songe du vieux pèlerin.* Translated by Joël Blanchard, Pocket / Agora, 2008.

Miles, Laura Saetveit. "The Origins and Development of the Virgin Mary's Book at the Annunciation." *Speculum*, vol. 89, no. 3, 2014, pp. 632–69.

Minnis, Alastair. *Magister amoris: The* Roman de la Rose *and Vernacular Hermeneutics.* Oxford UP, 2001.

Mombello, Gianni. "Quelques aspects de la pensée politique de Christine de Pisan d'après ses œuvres publiées." *Culture et politique en France à l'époque de l'humanisme et de la Renaissance*, edited by Franco Simone, Accademia delle Scienze, 1974, pp. 43–153.

Morand-Métivier, Charles Louis. "'Seulette suis': Christine de Pizan's Rhetoric of Power through Loneliness and Poverty." MLA Annual Convention, 9–12 Jan. 2014, Chicago.

Morel, Octave. *La grande chancellerie royale et l'expédition des lettres royaux de l'avènement de Philippe de Valois à la fin du XIV siècle (1328–1400)*. A. Picard, 1900.

Moulin, Jeanine, translator. *Christine de Pisan*. Seghers, 1962.

Munrow, David. "The Art of Courtly Love." *Early Music*, vol. 1, no. 4, Oct. 1973, pp. 194–99.

Nabert, Nathalie. "Christine de Pizan, Jean Gerson, et le gouvernement des âmes." Hicks, *Au champ*, pp. 250–68.

Nafisi, Azar. *Reading* Lolita *in Tehran: A Memoir in Books*. Random House, 2004.

Nederman, Cary J. "Body Politics: The Diversification of Organic Metaphors in the Later Middle Ages." *Pensiero Politico Medievale*, vol. 2, 2004, pp. 59–87.

———. "Christine de Pizan and Jean Gerson on the Body Politic: Inclusion, Hierarchy, and the Limits of Intellectual Influence." *Storia del pensiero politico*, vol. 3, 2013, pp. 465–79.

———. "The Living Body Politic: The Diversification of Organic Metaphors in Nicole Oresme and Christine de Pizan." Green and Mews, pp. 19–33.

———. "The Mirror Crack'd: The Speculum Principum as Political and Social Criticism in the Late Middle Ages." *The European Legacy: Toward New Paradigms*, vol. 3, June 1998, pp. 18–38.

Nederman, Cary J., and Tsae Lan Lee Dow. "The Road to Heaven Is Paved with Pious Deceptions: Medieval Speech Ethics and Deliberative Democracy." *Talking Democracy: Historical Approaches to Rhetoric and Democratic Theory*, edited by Benedetto Fontana, Nederman, and Gary Remer, Pennsylvania State UP, 2004, pp. 187–211.

Nederman, Cary J., and Kate Langdon Forhan, editors. *Readings in Medieval Political Theory*, Hackett, 2000.

Nowacka, Keiko. "Reflections on Christine de Pizan's Feminism." *Australian Feminist Studies*, vol. 17, no. 37, 2002, pp. 81–97.

Oakley, Francis. *The Watershed of Modern Politics: Law, Virtue, Kingship and Consent (1300–1650)*. Yale UP, 2015.

Olschki, Leonardo. *Paris nach den altfranzösischen nationalen Epen: Topographie, Stadtgeschichte und lokale Sagen*. Winter Verlag, 1913.

Olsson, Elmer. "The French Chanson between 1400 and 1450." *Bulletin of the American Musicological Society*, no. 11–13, Sept. 1948, pp. 36–37.

Ouy, Gilbert, et al. *Album Christine de Pizan*. Brepols, 2012.

Ouy, Gilbert, and Christine Reno. "Manuscrits copiés en série: Les quatre témoins contemporains du *Livre des fais et bonnes meurs du sage roy Charles Ve d'icelluy nom*." *Cahiers de recherches médiévales (XIIIe–XVe siècles)*, vol. 16, 2008, pp. 239–52.

Paden, William D. "Christine de Pizan and the Transformation of Late Medieval Lyrical Genres." *Christine de Pizan and Medieval French Lyric*, edited by Earl Jeffrey Richards, UP of Florida, 1998, pp. 27–52.

Page, Christopher. "Mauchaut's 'Pupil' Deschamps on the Performance of Music: Voices or Instruments in the Fourteenth-Century Chanson." *Early Music*, vol. 5, no. 4, October 1977, pp. 484–91.

Parkes, Malcolm B. "The Influence of the Concepts of *Ordinatio* and *Compilatio* on the Development of the Book." *Medieval Learning and Literature (Festschrift R. W. Hunt)*, edited by J. J. G. Alexander and M. T. Gibson, Clarendon, 1976, pp. 115–41.

Parsons, John Carmi, and Bonnie Wheeler, editors. *Medieval Mothering*. Garland, 1996.

Pastoureau, Michel. *Blue: The History of a Color*. Translated by Markus Cruse, Princeton UP, 2001.

Paupert, Anne. "Christine et Boèce: De la lecture à l'écriture, de la réécriture à l'écriture du moi." Kennedy et al., vol. 3, pp. 645–62.

Phillippy, Patricia A. "Establishing Authority: Boccaccio's *De Claris Mulieribus* and Christine de Pizan's *Le livre de la cité des dames*." Blumenfeld-Kosinski, *Selected Writings*, pp. 329–61.

Picot, Guillaume, editor. *La poésie lyrique au Moyen Âge. Nouveaux Classiques Larousse*, vol. 2, Larousse, 1975.

Pintoin, Michel. *Chronique du religieux de Saint-Denys*. 1842. Edited and translated by M. L. Bellaguet. Editions du Comité des travaux historiques et scientifiques, 1994. 6 vols.

Planche, Alice. "Présence et absence de Paris dans la littérature jusqu'au milieu du XIIIe siècle." *L'image de la ville dans la littérature et l'histoire médiévales*, Centre d'études médiévales de Nice, 1979, pp. 60–69.

Poirion, Daniel. *Littérature française: Le Moyen Âge, 1300–1480*. Arthaud, 1971.

———. *Le poète et le prince: L'evolution du lyrisme courtois de Guillaume de Machaut à Charles d'Orléans*. Slatkine, 1978.

Polet, Jean-Claude, and Claude Pichois, editors. *Patrimoine littéraire européen, Vol. 6: Prémices de l'humanisme, 1400–1515*. De Boeck U, 1995.

Presner, Todd, et al. *Hypercities: Thick Mapping and the Digital Humanities*. Harvard UP, 2014.

Quilligan, Maureen. *The Allegory of Female Authority: Christine de Pizan's* Cité des dames. Cornell UP, 1992.

Quintilian. *Institutio oratoria*. Translated by H. E. Butler, vol. 4, Harvard UP, 1961. Loeb Classical Library.

Randel, M. "Emerging Triadic Tonality in the Fifteenth Century." *The Musical Quarterly*, vol. 57, no. 1, 1971, pp. 73–86.

Régnier-Bohler, Danielle. "Imagining the Self." Ariès and Duby, pp. 311–94.

———, editor. *Voix de femmes au Moyen Âge: Savoir, mystique, poésie, amour, sorcellerie, XIIe–XVe siècle*. Robert Laffont, 2006.

Rehm, Wolfgang. *Die Chanson von Gilles Binchois (1400–1460)*. B. Schott and Sons, 1957. Kommission für Musikwissenschaft Musikalische Denkmäler 2.

Reno, Christine. "Christine de Pizan: At Best a Contradictory Figure?" Brabant, pp. 171–91.

Richards, Earl Jeffrey. "Christine de Pizan and Dante: A Reexamination." *Archiv für das Studium der Neueren Sprachen und Literaturen*, vol. 222, 1985, pp. 100–11.

———. "Christine de Pizan and Jean Gerson: An Intellectual Friendship." Campbell and Margolis, pp. 197–208.

———, editor. *Christine de Pizan and Medieval French Lyric*. UP of Florida, 1998.

———. "Christine de Pizan and Sacred History." Zimmermann and De Rentiis, pp. 15–30.

———. "Christine de Pizan and the Freedom of Medieval French Lyric: Authority, Experience, and Women in the Republic of Letters." *Christine de Pizan and Medieval French Lyric*, edited by Richards, UP of Florida, 1998, pp. 1–26.

———, editor. *Reinterpreting Christine de Pizan*. U of Georgia P, 1992.

Richarz, Michael. "Prudence and Wisdom in Christine de Pizan's *Le livre des fais et bonnes meurs du sage roy Charles V*." Green and Mews, pp. 99–116.

Rigby, S. H. "The Wife of Bath, Christine de Pizan, and the Medieval Case for Women." *The Chaucer Review*, vol. 35, no. 2, 2000, pp. 133–65.

Rose, Mary Beth, editor. *Women in the Middle Ages and the Renaissance: Literary and Historical Perspectives*. Syracuse UP, 1986.

Rouillard, Linda. "'Faux semblant ou faire semblant?' Christine de Pizan and Virtuous Artifice." *Forum for Modern Language Studies*, vol. 46, 2010, pp. 16–28.

Rouse, Richard H., and Mary A. Rouse. *"Illiterati et uxorati" Manuscripts and Their Makers: Commercial Book Producers in Medieval Paris, 1200–1500*. Harvey Miller, 2000. 2 vols.

Roux, Simone. *Christine de Pizan: Femme de tête, dame de cœur*. Payot, 2006.

Roy, Maurice, editor. *Œuvres poétiques de Christine de Pisan*. Firmin Didot, 1886–96. 3 vols.

———, editor. *Œuvres poétiques de Christine de Pisan*. 1886–96. Johnson Reprint, 1965. 3 vols.

Sadlack, Erin. *"In Writing It May Be Spoke": The Politics of Women's Letter Writing, 1377–1603*. 2005. U of Maryland, PhD dissertation.

Samaran, Charles. "Notes sur Jean Castel, chroniqueur de France." *Mélanges de philologie et d'histoire offerts à Antoine Thomas*, Champion, 1927, pp. 395–404.

Schaus, Margaret, editor. *Women and Gender in Medieval Europe: An Encyclopedia*. Routledge, 2006.

Schibanoff, Susan. "Taking the Gold out of Egypt: The Art of Reading as a Woman." *Gender and Reading: Essays on Readers, Texts, and Contexts*, edited by Elizabeth A. Flynn and Patrocinio P. Schweickart, Johns Hopkins UP, 1986, pp. 83–106.

Schieberle, Misty. *Feminized Counsel and the Literature of Advice in England, 1380–1500*. Brepols, 2014.

Schulenberg, Jane Tibbetts. "Heroics of Virginity: Brides of Christ and Sacrificial Mutilation." Rose, pp. 29–72.

"Seulete suy." Text by Christine de Pizan, music by Nicholas Fairbank, fairbankmusic.ca/wp-content/uploads/2015/03/SeuleteSuy-sample.pdf.

Shaw, David J. "The Book Trade Comes of Age: The Sixteenth Century." Eliot and Rose, pp. 220–31.

Sherman, Claire Richter. *Imaging Aristotle: Verbal and Visual Representation in Fourteenth-Century France*. U of California P, 1995.

———. "Representations of Charles V (1338–1380) as a Wise Ruler." *Medievalia et Humanistica*, vol. 2, 1971, pp. 83–96.

Simmons, Rachel. *Odd Girl Out: The Hidden Culture of Aggression in Girls*. Harcourt, 2002.

Skemp, Mary L. "Autobiography as Authority in *Lavision-Christine*." *Le moyen français*, vol. 35–36, 1994, pp. 17–31.

Slavin, Dennis. "In Support of 'Heresy': Manuscript Evidence for the 'A Cappella' Performance of Early Fifteenth-Century Songs." *Early Music*, vol. 19, no. 2, 1991, pp. 178–86, 189–90.

———. "Questions of Authority in Some Songs by Binchois." *Journal of the Royal Musical Association*, vol. 117, no. 1, 1992, pp. 22–61.

Solente, Suzanne. *Christine de Pisan*. Imprimerie Nationale-Klincksieck, 1969. Histoire littéraire de la France 40.

———. Introduction. *Le livre des fais et bonnes meurs du sage roy Charles V*, by Christine de Pizan, edited by Solente, Slatkine Reprints, 1977, pp. i–civ.

———, editor. *Le livre de la mutacion de Fortune par Christine de Pisan*. Picard, 1959–66. SATF. 4 vols.

———, editor. "Un traité inédit de Christine de Pisan: *L'epistre de la prison de vie humaine*." *Bibliothèque de l'école des Chartes*, vol. 85, 1924, pp. 263–301.

Solterer, Helen. "'Flaming Words': Verbal Violence and Gender in Premodern Paris." *Romanic Review*, vol. 86, 1995, pp. 355–78.

———. *The Master and Minerva: Disputing Women in French Medieval Culture*. U of California P, 1995.

Strubel, Armand, editor. *Guillaume de Lorris and Jean de Meun*, Le roman de la rose. LGF, 1992.

Struve, Tilman. *Die Entwicklung der organologischen Staatsauffassung im Mittelalter*. Hiersemann, 1978.

Summit, Jennifer. *Lost Property: The Woman Writer and English Literary History, 1380–1589*. U of Chicago P, 2000.

———. "Women and Authorship." Dinshaw and Wallace, pp. 91–108.

Syse, Henrik, and Gregory M. Reichberg, editors. *Ethics, Nationalism and Just War: Medieval and Contemporary Perspectives*. Catholic U of America P, 2007.

Tarabotti, Arcangela. *Paternal Tyranny*. Edited and translated by Letizia Panizza, U of Chicago P, 2004.

Tarnowski, Andrea. "Autobiography and Advice in *Le livre des trois vertus*." *Une femme de lettres au Moyen Âge*, Paradigme, 1995, pp. 151–60.

———, editor and translator. *Le chemin de longue étude*. Librairie Générale Française, 2000. Lettres Gothiques.

———. "Christine's Selves." Dulac et al., pp. 181–88.

———. "Le geste prophétique chez Christine de Pizan." *Apogée et déclin: Actes du colloque de l'URA 411, Provins, 1991*, edited by Claude Thomasset and Michel Zink, PU de Paris-Sorbonne, 1993, pp. 225–36.

———. "The Lessons of Experience and the *Chemin de long estude*." Altmann and McGrady, pp. 181–97.

———. "Pallas Athena, la science et la chevalerie." *Sur le chemin de longue etude . . . : Actes du colloque d'Orléans, juillet 1995*, edited by Bernard Ribémont, Champion, 1998, pp. 149–58.

Taylor, Craig, editor and translator. *Joan of Arc: La Pucelle*. Manchester UP, 2006.

Taylor, Jane H. M. "Lyric Poetry of the Later Middle Ages." Gaunt and Kay, pp. 153–66.

———. *The Making of Poetry: Late-Medieval French Poetic Anthologies*. Turnhout, 2007.

Teresa of Avila. *The Life of Teresa of Jesus: The Autobiography of Teresa of Avila*. Translated and edited by E. All., Doubleday, 1991.

Thompson, Daniel V. *The Materials and Techniques of Medieval Painting*. Dover Publications, 1956.

Thorington, Ellen. "Sympathetic Serpents and Distrustful Dragons: Fantastic Reptiles in the *Fables* of Marie De France." *Pur Remembrance: Mélanges en souvenir de Wolfgang Spiewok*, edited by Anne Berthelot, Reineke Verlag, 2001, pp. 298–310.

Thorndike, Lynn. *A History of Magic and Experimental Science*. Columbia UP, 1923–58. 8 vols.

Trask, Willard. *Joan of Arc in Her Own Words*. Turtle Point, 1996.

Trowbridge, Lynn M. "Style Change in the Fifteenth-Century Chanson: A Comparative Study of Compositional Detail." *The Journal of Musicology*, vol. 4, no. 2, Spring 1985–Spring 1986, pp. 146–70.

Ullmann, Walter. *A Short History of the Papacy in the Middle Ages*. Routledge, 2003.

Van den Borren, Charles. "Considérations générales sur la conjonction de la polyphonie italienne et de la polyphonie du Nord pendant la première moitié du XVe siècle." *Revue belge de Musicologie / Belgisch Tijdschrif voor Muziekwetenschap*, vol. 21, nos. 1–4, 1967, pp. 45–55.

Varty, Kenneth. "Autour du *Livre des trois vertus* ou si Rayson, Droicture et Justice faisaient des cours d'introduction à la civilisation française du Moyen Âge?" Dulac and Ribémont, pp. 161–71.

———. *Christine de Pisan's Ballades, Rondeaux, and Virelais: An Anthology*. Leicester UP, 1965.

Velissariou, Alexandra. "Discrete dissimulacion et prudent cautele: Les stratégies comportementales de la princesse dans le *Livre des Trois Vertus* de Christine de Pizan." *Le Moyen Âge*, vol. 116, 2010, pp. 577–90.

Verderber, Suzanne M. "Refiguring the Veil: The Transvaluation of Human History in Marie de France's *Yonec*." *New Medieval Literatures*, edited by Rita Copeland et al., Oxford UP, 2004, pp. 79–106.

Verdon, Jean. *Isabeau de Bauvière, la mal aimée.* Taillandier, 2001.

Vincent-Cassy, Mireille. "Vices and Virtues." *Encyclopedia of the Middle Ages*, edited by André Vauchez, translated by Adrian Walford, vol. 2, Fitzroy Dearborn, 2000. 2 vols.

Walters, Lori J. "Christine de Pizan as Translator and Voice of the Body Politic." Altmann and McGrady, pp. 25–41.

———. "Christine de Pizan comme biographe royal." Translated by Laurence Costa. *L'Écriture du passé au Moyen Âge et la Renaissance: Entre autorité et invention*, edited by Pierre Chastang and Michel Zimmermann, PU de Paris-Sorbonne, 2007, pp. 223–36.

———. "Christine de Pizan, France's Memorialist: Persona, Performance, Memory." *Journal of European Studies*, Apr. 2005, pp. 191–207.

———. "Constructing Reputations: *Fama* and Memory in Christine de Pizan's *Charles V* and *L'advision Cristine.*" *Fama: The Politics of Talk and Reputation in Medieval Europe*, edited by Thelma Fenster and Daniel Lord Smail, Cornell UP, 2003, pp. 118–42.

———. "The Figure of the *Seulette* in the Works of Christine de Pizan and Jean Gerson." Dulac et al., *"Desireuse de plus en avant enquerre . . . ,"* pp. 119–39.

———. "Gerson and Christine, Poets." Dixon and Sinclair, pp. 69–81.

———. "Magnifying the Lord: Prophetic Voice in *La cité des dames.*" *Cahiers de recherches médiévales*, vol. 13, 2006, pp. 239–53.

———. "Performing the Nation: The Play Performed at the Great Feast in Christine de Pizan's Biography of Charles V." *Cultural Performances in Medieval France: Essays in Honor of Nancy Freeman Regalado*, edited by Eglal Doss-Quinby et al. Brewer, 2007, pp. 219–32.

———. "The Queen's Manuscript as a Gift of Wisdom." *Digital Philology: A Revue of Medieval Cultures*, vol. 5, no. 2, Fall 2016, pp. 228–46.

———. "The Queen's Manuscript (London, British Library, Harley 4431) as a Monument to Peace." *Le moyen français*, vol. 75, 2014, pp. 85–120.

———. "La réécriture de Saint Augustin par Christine de Pizan: De la *Cité de Dieu* à la *Cité des dames.*" Hicks, *Au champ*, pp. 195–215.

———. "Signatures and Anagrams in the Queen's Manuscript (London, British Library, Harley Ms 4431)." *The Making of the Queen's Manuscript*, Edinburgh U Library, 2012, www.pizan.lib.ed.ac.uk/waltersanagrams.html.

———. "'Translating' Petrarch: *Cité des dames* II.7.1, Jean Daudin, and Vernacular Authority." Campbell and Margolis, pp. 283–97.

———. "The Woman Writer and Literary History: Christine de Pizan's Redefinition of the Poetic *Translatio* in the *Epistre au dieu d'amours.*" *French Literature Series*, vol. 16, 1989, pp. 1–16.

Wandruszka, Nikolai. "Familial Traditions of the *de Piçano* at Bologna." Kennedy et al., vol. 3, pp. 889–907.

Warren, Nancy Bradley. "French Women and English Men: Joan of Arc, Margaret of Anjou, and Christine de Pizan in England, 1445–1540." *Exemplaria: A Journal of Theory in Medieval and Renaissance Studies*, vol. 16, no. 2, 2004, pp. 405–36.

Weisl, Angela Jane. "The Widow as Virgin: Desexualized Narrative in Christine de Pizan's *Livre de la cité des dames*." Carson and Weisl, pp. 49–62.

Wheeler, Bonnie, and Charles T. Wood, editors. *Fresh Verdicts on Joan of Arc*. Garland, 1996.

Wiesner, Merry E. *Women and Gender in Early Modern Europe*. Cambridge UP, 2000.

Wilkie, Brian, and James Hurt, editors. *Literature of the Western World: The Ancient World through the Renaissance*. 5th ed., vol. 1, Prentice Hall, 2001.

Willard, Charity Cannon. "Anne de France: Reader of Christine de Pizan." *Literary Reception of Christine de Pizan from the Fifteenth to the Nineteenth Centuries: Visitors to the City*, edited by Glenda McLeod, Edwin Mellen Press, 1992, pp. 59–70.

———. "Christine de Pizan as Teacher." *Romance Languages Annual*, vol. 2, 1992, pp. 132–36.

———. "Christine de Pizan: From Poet to Political Commentator." Brabant, pp. 17–32.

———. *Christine de Pizan: Her Life and Works: A Biography*. Persea, 1984.

———. "The Dominican Abbey of Poissy in 1400." Campbell and Margolis, pp. 209–18.

———. "A Fifteenth-Century View of Women's Role in Medieval Society: Christine de Pizan's *Livre des trois vertus*." *The Role of Women in the Middle Ages*, edited by Rosemarie T. Morewedge, State U of New York P, 1975, pp. 90–120.

———. "The Manuscript Tradition of the *Livre des trois vertus* and Christine de Pizan's Audience." *Journal of the History of Ideas*, vol. 27, 1966, pp. 433–44.

———. "Une source oubliée du voyage imaginaire de Christine de Pizan." *"Et c'est la fin pour quoy sommes ensemble": Hommage à Jean Dufournet, professeur à la Sorbonne: Littérature, histoire et langue du Moyen Âge*, edited by Jean-Claude Aubailly, vol. 1, Champion, 1993, pp. 321–36.

———, editor. *The Writings of Christine de Pizan*. Persea, 1993.

Williams, Deanne. *The French Fetish from Chaucer to Shakespeare*. Cambridge UP, 2004.

Wilson, Katharina M., and Nadia Margolis. *Women in the Middle Ages: An Encyclopedia*. Greenwood Press, 2004.

Winn, Colette H. "'De mères en filles': Les manuels d'éducation sous l'Ancien Régime." *Atlantis*, vol. 19, 1993, pp. 23–29.

Wiseman, Rosalind. *Queen Bees and Wannabes: Helping Your Daughter Survive Cliques, Gossip, Boyfriends, and Other Realities of Adolescence*. Three Rivers Press, 2002.

Wisman, Josette A. "Aspects socio-économiques du *Livre des trois vertus* de Christine de Pizan." *Le moyen français*, vol. 30, 1992, pp. 27–43.

———, editor and translator. The Epistle of the Prison of Human Life *with* An Epistle to the Queen of France *and* Lament on the Evils of the Civil War *by Christine de Pizan*. Garland, 1984.

Wogan-Browne, Jocelyn, editor. *Language and Culture in Medieval Britain: The French of England, c. 1100–c. 1500*. York Medieval, 2009.

Wogan-Browne, Jocelyn, et al., editors. *Medieval Women: Text and Contexts in Late Medieval Britain: Essays for Felicity Riddy*. Brepols, 2000.

Wood, Charles T. *Joan of Arc and Richard III: Sex, Saints, and Government in the Middle Ages*. Oxford UP, 1988.

Wrisley, David Joseph. "Locating Medieval French, or Why We Collect and Visualize the Geographic Information of Texts." *Speculum*, vol. 92, no. S1, 2017, pp. S145–S169.

———. "Spatial Humanities: An Agenda for Pre-Modern Humanities Research." *Porphyra*, vol. 22, 2014, pp. 96–107.

Yates, Frances. *The Art of Memory*. U of Chicago P, 1966.

Zimmermann, Margarete. "Christine de Pizan: Memory's Architect." Translated by Gesa Stedman. Altmann and McGrady, pp. 57–77.

———. "Mémoire, tradition, historiographie: Christine de Pizan et son *Livre des fais et bonnes meurs du sage roy Charles V*." Zimmerman and De Rentiis, pp. 158–73.

Zimmermann, Margarete, and Dina De Rentiis, editors. *The City of Scholars: New Approaches to Christine de Pizan*. Walter de Gruyter, 1994.

Zink, Michel. "Des poètes courtois aux premiers humanistes." *La France et les arts en 1400: Les princes des fleurs de lis*, edited by Thierry Crépin-Leblond et al., Réunion des Musées Nationaux, 2004, pp. 35–52.

———. *Introduction à la littérature du Moyen Âge*. Le livre de poche réferences, 1993.

———. *Littérature française du Moyen Âge*. PU de France, 1992.

Zumthor, Paul. *Le masque et la lumière: La poétique des grands rhétoriqueurs*. Éditions du Seuil, 1978.

INDEX